Religious Freedom
and Evangelization
in Latin America

Religion and Human Rights Series

Series Editors
John Witte Jr.
Abdullahi Ahmed An-Na'im
Emory University

Board of Advisors
Azizah al-Hibri, University of Richmond
Donna Arzt, Syracuse University
Irwin Cotler, McGill University
Frances Deng, The Brookings Institution
Jean Bethke Elshtain, University of Chicago
David Little, United States Institute of Peace
Ann Elizabeth Mayer, University of Pennsylvania
José Míguez Bonino, Facultad Evangélica, ISEDET, Buenos Aires
Chandra Muzzafar, University of Malaysia
John T. Noonan Jr., U.S. Court of Appeals
Kusumita Pedersen, St. Francis College
Lamin Sanneh, Yale University
Max Stackhouse, Princeton Theological Seminary
M. Thomas Thangaraj, Emory University

Other Books Published in the Series

Proselytization and Communal Self-Determination in Africa
  Abdullahi Ahmed An-Na'im, editor
Proselytism and Orthodoxy in Russia: The New War for Souls
  John Witte Jr. and Michael Bordeaux, editors

RELIGION & HUMAN RIGHTS SERIES

Religious Freedom and Evangelization in Latin America

The Challenge of Religious Pluralism

Paul E. Sigmund
Editor

ORBIS BOOKS

Maryknoll, New York 10545

The Catholic Foreign Mission Society of America (Maryknoll) recruits and trains people for overseas missionary service. Through Orbis Books, Maryknoll aims to foster the international dialogue that is essential to mission. The books published, however, reflect the opinions of their authors and are not meant to represent the official position of the Society. To obtain more information about Maryknoll and Orbis Books, please visit our website at www.maryknoll.org.

Manufactured in the United States of America.
Copy editing and typesetting by Joan Weber Laflamme.

Library of Congress Cataloging-in-Publication Data

Religious freedom and evangelization in Latin America : the challenge
    of religious pluralism / Paul E. Sigmund, editor.
        p.   cm.   —   (Religion & human rights series)
    Includes bibliographical references and index.
    ISBN 1-57075-263-X (pbk.)
    1. Religious pluralism—Latin America.   2. Religious pluralism—
Christianity.   3. Evangelicalism—Latin America.   4. Freedom of
religion—Latin America.   I. Sigmund, Paul E.   II. Series.
BR600.R395   1999
278'.0829—dc21   99-20498
                                                                       CIP

CONTENTS

THE RELIGION AND HUMAN RIGHTS
SERIES PREFACE

The relationship between religion and human rights is both problematic and unavoidable in all parts of the world. Religion, broadly defined to include various traditional, cultural, and customary institutions and practices, is unquestionably a formidable force for violence, repression, and chauvinism of untold dimensions. But religion is also a natural and necessary ally in the global struggle for human rights. For human rights norms are inherently abstract ideals—universal statements of the good life and the good society. They depend upon the visions and values of human communities to give them content, coherence, and concrete manifestation. Religion is an inherent condition of human lives and human communities. Religion invariably provides the sources and scales of dignity and responsibility, shame and respect, restitution and reconciliation that a human rights regime needs to survive and to flourish.

This book series explores the interaction of religious ideas and institutions with human rights principles and practices. It seeks to discover the religious sources of human rights—both their cultivation and their corruption in the discourse of sacred texts, the activism of religious organizations, and the practices of religious polities. It seeks to uncover the legal sources of human rights—both their protection and their abridgment in international human rights instruments and in domestic constitutions, statutes, and cases. It seeks to address some of the cutting edge issues of religion and human rights in theory and practice.

This series is made possible, in part, by the generous funding of The Pew Charitable Trusts, Inc. and the Ford Foundation. Pew's support came through its funding of a three year project on "Soul Wars: The Problem and Promise of Proselytism in the New World Order." Ford's support came through its funding of a three year project on "Cultural Transformation in Africa: Legal, Religious, and Human Rights Perspectives." Several of the early volumes in this Series are parts and products of these two projects. They provide pilots and prototypes for the type of rigorous interdisciplinary and interreligious analysis that the subject of religion and human rights requires.

We wish to express our gratitude to our friends at the two foundations for their generous support of this effort. We also wish to thank the Maryknoll Fathers and Brothers and Bill Burrows and Bernadette Price of Orbis for their sage stewardship of this Series.

— JOHN WITTE JR.
ABDULLAHI AHMED AN-NA'IM
EMORY UNIVERSITY, ATLANTA

INTRODUCTION

◆

Paul E. Sigmund

It should not have come as a surprise—although it did—that Latin America, after two decades of military domination, moved so unanimously in the 1980s and 1990s to adopt constitutional democracy as its system of government. That move was part of a worldwide "third wave" of democratic governments, described by Samuel Huntington (Huntington 1991). However, unlike the other "new" democracies, Latin America had participated—fitfully and usually unsuccessfully—in both of the earlier waves of democratization, in the nineteenth and early twentieth centuries and after World War II. This time, however, it seems to be for real. And one reason for this is that societal and cultural patterns now seem much more favorable to the persistence of liberal democracy in Latin America than at any earlier time.

One of those social patterns is a much greater degree of religious pluralism than in the past. In addition, in the political culture there is now much more widespread support for meaningful legal and constitutional guarantees of freedom of worship and expression. While the predominant Roman Catholic Church has long been disestablished in most countries of Latin America, in practice—and sometimes in law—until recently Catholicism has had a privileged position in many parts of the continent. (In this respect, Mexico, with—until the early 1990s—strong constitutional and legal limitations on Catholicism, would be a significant exception.) Now in one Latin American country after another, the religious playing field is being leveled.

New constitutions have been adopted or old ones substantially amended in almost every Latin American country, in the process extending the guarantee of religious freedom. Only three countries, Argentina, Bolivia, and Costa Rica, while guaranteeing religious freedom, distinguish in their constitutions between Catholicism and other religions, and in the first two, strong arguments for repeal of those clauses have been made. (For the constitutional debate in Argentina on the subject, see the Míguez Bonino chapter in this volume.) In two other countries, Chile and Colombia, there is discussion of modifying or generalizing the special legal status of Catholicism resulting from earlier agreements with the Vatican.

There are two principal reasons why Latin America has finally modernized and liberalized its religious regime. One is that, with the end of the Cold War, the political and economic failures of the authoritarian regimes that dominated Latin America for twenty-five years, and the worldwide triumph of market-oriented democracy, the norms of liberal democracy are no longer contested by extremists of the left and the right who favor more authoritarian models of church-state relations. In addition, the earlier hostility of leftists and nationalists to missionaries as agents of foreign powers or alien cultures has lessened in a globalized world, and the conservative alliance with Catholicism has been abandoned by both conservatives, many of whom are now enthusiasts of laissez-faire in culture as well as economics, and by Catholics since the adoption of the Second Vatican Council's *Decree on Religious Freedom* (*Dignitatis Humanae*, 1965).

A second, and equally important element, is the dramatic expansion of evangelical Protestantism, which constitutes a new and increasingly visible presence in the social and political life of Latin America. While the estimates of the increase in the numbers of Protestants, especially of Pentecostals, can be exaggerated and often tend to ignore the fact that a significant number of converts to Protestantism (surveys in Brazil and in Chile put the figure around 50 percent) later return to Catholicism or move back and forth between the two, most writers place the number of Protestants in Latin America at between 12 and 15 percent of the population—a dramatic increase from an estimated 1 percent in 1930 and 4 percent in 1960. The largest percentages are in Guatemala, Brazil, Chile, El Salvador, and Nicaragua, but the expansion is continent-wide. The Catholic bishops talk of eight thousand conversions to Protestantism every day, some writers estimate that Guatemala will be one-third Protestant by the year 2000, and Brazilians claim that a new evangelical church is opened each week in Rio de Janeiro. Brazil's home-grown Universal Church of the Kingdom of God has half a million members, operates its own television network and many radio stations, and sends missionaries to evangelize Hispanic populations in the United States and other countries. Meanwhile, Catholic bishops denounce the "sects," the pope warns of "ravening wolves" seeking to convert the Catholic faithful, and Catholicism seeks more grassroots influence by reorganizing its worship and decentralizing its structure through Ecclesial Base Communities. (See the chapter by Anthony Gill in this volume, and Gill 1998, on the effects of competition in "the religious market," as well as evaluations of the Base Communities in Hewitt 1991, and Burdick 1993.)

In evaluating this phenomenon, it is important to distinguish between two types of Protestantism in Latin America—a distinction that is reflected in the two separate chapters on Latin American Protestantism in this book. On the one hand, there are the mainstream, mainline, or historic Protestant churches such as the Anglicans, Presbyterians, Methodists, and Lutherans, which were originally established as a result of foreign immigration or early missionary activity by American Protestant churches. Some of these churches are affiliated with the World Council of Churches and have good relations with Catholicism. Their membership is more middle class; they are often liberal in their politics; and they do not engage to the same degree in the active proselytism carried out by their evangelical co-religionists.[1] A second group of Protestant churches are those usually described in English as *evangelical*—a confusing term for this study, since in Latin America *all* Protestants are known as *evangélicos*. As the name implies, the members of these churches are specifically committed to the spreading of the gospel (*evangelio*), and to making the Bible central to their religious life as the source of personal transformation (the "born-again" experience).

The Pentecostals—with a religious focus on the action of the Holy Spirit similar to that of the Holy Spirit upon the apostles at Pentecost, fifty days after Christ's resurrection—are the most visible and dynamic form of evangelical Protestantism in contemporary Latin America. We know most about them because of the numerous studies of Latin American Pentecostalism published in recent years. (See Smith 1998, for a review and evaluation of those studies. Ireland 1991 has in-depth studies of individual Brazilian Pentecostals and there are useful studies of Pentecostal growth by Mariz [1994], Chesnut [1997], and Bowen [1996].) There have been Pentecostals in Latin America since shortly after the movement was initiated in the United States early in this century. However the principal growth of Pentecostalism has taken place during the last twenty-five years. Pentecostals distinguish themselves from the Charismatics, a more recent development, but share with them an emphasis on the gifts (*charismata*) of the Holy Spirit such as healing, speaking in tongues, and personal transformation through the experience of being born again. While decentralized in organization, they are now linked nationally and internationally through the radio and television, and sometimes through a single leader or preacher such as Edir Macedo, the leader of the Universal Church of the Kingdom of God in Brazil.

Why have the Pentecostals grown so rapidly in recent decades? Initial theories that emphasized foreign—mainly U.S.—money and influence have been abandoned in the face of overwhelming evidence that Pentecostal growth is promoted and financed by the Latin American Pentecostals themselves. There is now widespread agreement that the appeal of local support groups that promote physical healing and the moral and personal transformation of the rural and urban poor that comprise the bulk of their membership, as well as the energy with which Evangelicals spread their message, are more satisfactory explanations. There is still disagreement on the relation of evangelicalism to modernization, development, and democracy. (See the chapter by Pedro Moreno in this volume, as well as Smith 1998 and Martin 1990).

There is also agreement that relations between Catholicism and Pentecostalism are not characterized by the same cordiality and mutual respect that are typical of Catholic relations with the historic Protestant churches. The rise of militant evangelicalism has provided a political and social base for pressures for greater religious freedom and the equal treatment of all religions that is characteristic of liberal constitutional democracy. Yet because their preaching often literally demonizes Catholicism, evangelical growth has also led to criticism by the Catholics who view the Evangelicals as threats to Latin American culture (see chapters by Cleary and Smilde in this volume), and to demands for legislative regulation of religion in ways that seem to represent a continuation, in a different context, of the long history of state influence and control of religion in Latin America.

That history began, as many chapters in this book indicate, with the institution of the *patronato real*—royal patronage—a term that sounds strange in English, until we recall that in American politics the term *patronage,* has long been used to describe the exchange of jobs for political support. As a church institution it goes back to the Middle Ages when wealthy patrons who subsidized the building of churches or monasteries secured the right to name the pastor or abbot. However, the Spanish crown secured far more from the papacy in the way of influence over the church in its colonial empire. In return for promoting the conversion of the Indians, sometimes by force, it received the right to nominate bishops, to collect and distribute the tithe (*diezmo*) or 10 percent church tax, and to control the entrance of new religious orders, the activity of missionaries, and the creation of new dioceses (Shiels 1961). While the church authorities retained some autonomy, and bishops like Bartolomé de Las Casas and Antonio Valdivieso were highly critical of the treatment of the Indians by colonial authorities, the cross and the sword were closely associated, and the Inquisition was active at various times and places in Latin America to assure orthodoxy.

The close link with the Spanish monarchy created problems at the time of independence when most bishops supported Spain, but as explained in various chapters below, the papacy was able to reassert control several decades after independence, and to contest with more or less success the claims of the Latin American republics to continue the *patronato*—although elements of that relationship have survived down to recent decades. (See the chapters on Venezuela, Peru, and Argentina. In the last case, the requirement that the president of Argentina be a Catholic, only abolished in 1994, was linked to the religious rights and duties related to the *patronato nacional* in the 1853 constitution.) In many countries, the classic nineteenth-century party split between Liberals and Conservatives was associated in varying degrees of intensity with the division between Conservatives who wished to maintain the privileges of the Catholic church, and the sometimes militantly anticlerical Liberals who wished to abolish them. By the end of the century Liberal predominance in many countries had led to the abolition of church control over cemeteries, marriage, education, and the registry of births and deaths. It also led to constitutional provisions extending toleration to other faiths, and by the early twentieth century, to the disestablishment of Catholicism (Mecham 1966).

In the twentieth century, a new relationship with the state was forged by the Catholic church—dubbed by some, neo-Christendom. The Vatican negotiated and signed concordats or treaties with Latin American states, outlining its rights in areas like education, marriage, and exemption from taxation. The church also attempted to influence the state through more indirect means—the establishment of Catholic Action, organizing students, workers, and intellectuals committed to extending the influence of Catholicism, and the creation of Catholic universities, and sometimes religious instruction in public schools. Founded by lay people and open to non-Catholics, but influenced by Catholic social teachings, Christian Democratic Parties also emerged after World War II with strong influence in Chile, Venezuela, and Central America. From the time of the Second Vatican Council, the church generally ceased to insist on special privileges, preferring regimes of religious liberty. However, later, when efforts were made to remove references to "support" for Catholicism in the Bolivian and Argentine constitutions, the church resisted, possibly because bishops in Argentina and Bolivia receive a salary from the government and in Argentina the church receives a small subsidy to pay for the cost of priests in the former Indian missions. (See the Míguez Bonino chapter in this volume on the link between the subsidies and the silence of the hierarchy concerning the human rights violations during "the dirty war" in Argentina in the late 1970s.)

Today the preaching and practice of religion in Latin America is freer than it has ever been. This should be clear from the overview chapters on Catholicism and mainline and evangelical Protestantism. (A planned chapter on Judaism could not be written by its projected author for personal reasons.) The individual case studies provide new material on the changing religious patterns in the various countries. The chapters on Mexico describe the striking alteration in that country's church-state relations during the 1990s, involving constitutional amendments and new laws repealing most, but not all, of the earlier limits on church activities. The Mexico chapters also explain the relative lack of success of liberation theology in that country, except in the Indian areas of Chiapas in the South. The Cuban chapter traces the numerous shifts in Castro's policy toward Catholicism up to and including the visit by Pope John Paul II in January 1998. It suggests the possibility of a remarkable religious revival in a country that was not particularly religious before Castro's victory in 1959. The chapter on Guatemala helps to explain why two of its recent presidents have been Evangelicals, and disputes the argument that Evangelicals tend to be authoritarian and apolitical. The chapters on Nicaragua and El Salvador provide contrasting views of the relation of the Catholic hierarchy to the civil wars in the two countries, since, in the first case, it took a strongly partisan position, and in the second, acted as mediator and defender of human rights. The chapter on Colombia is principally devoted to a description of the persecution of Protestants in the 1950s, but it also explains why the Colombian church has been a bastion of conservatism in Latin America. The Venezuelan chapter discusses the issue of government regulation of missionary activity and of preaching in public places. In Peru, we find a brief and not notably successful foray of Evangelicals into the political arena in 1990, countered by an even more unsuccessful effort by the Catholic hierarchy to work against them. The Chilean chapter examines the work of the churches against the repression carried out by the Pinochet regime in the 1970s and

1980s, as well as the current refocussing of Chilean Catholicism on issues of sexual and personal morality. The chapter on Argentina attempts to explain why the Catholic hierarchy, in contrast to those in Chile and Brazil, did not take a public position against the human rights violations under the military regime in the late 1970s, and gives a personal view by José Míguez Bonino, the distinguished Protestant theologian, of the 1994 debates on the proposed amendment of the clauses of the Argentine constitution that give special privileges to the Catholic church. Finally, the chapter on Brazil explains the growth of evangelical and spiritist religions in that country, and describes the political activism of the Catholic hierarchy during the military regime, and the recent Vatican-promoted emergence of more conservative elements. Overall, the chapters should call into question common stereotyped views of the monolithic character of Latin American Catholicism or of the passivity and authoritarianism of evangelical Protestantism. The religious scene in Latin America is a varied one, within and between religious groups. It is becoming more varied, as other groups not discussed in this volume expand their membership, such as the Jehovah's Witnesses, the Seventh-day Adventists, and especially the Mormons—who, it is estimated, now have more members in Latin America than in the United States (*Time*, August 4, 1997).

While one can say that with the exception of Cuba, religious freedom prevails in Latin America, many problems remain.

First, there are issues such as contraception, divorce, and abortion that involve the relation of religious doctrine and public policy. So far, no Latin American country has legalized abortion although the number of illegal abortions is very high. While the Catholic church has largely abandoned its earlier efforts to prevent the distribution of contraceptive information and materials, it remains very strongly opposed to abortion, and unlike its position on contraception and divorce, its position on abortion is shared by evangelical Protestants. Divorce is now permitted in every Latin American country except Chile, which today is the only country in the world in which it is illegal, a situation which is partially explicable because a convenient but fraudulent annulment procedure is available. However, as Christian Democratic members of the Chilean Congress discovered when they attempted a limited legalization, the opposition of the Catholic hierarchy is also an important explanation for the continuation of the ban.

Second, there remain some direct state subsidies to the Catholic church in countries such as Argentina, Bolivia, Colombia, and Venezuela. They are under attack by Protestant and lay groups. Similar criticisms are made of instruction in Catholicism in public schools in some countries, and in Colombia since 1993 parents may opt for instruction in other religions. Catholic universities also receive state funds in a number of countries, but since this permits tuitions to be lower, and the universities are open to all without discrimination, there is no significant pressure to end the subsidy. Catholic hospitals and other charitable institutions also receive state money, and church property used for religious purposes is tax-exempt.

Third, there are issues connected with government issuance or revocation of permits for religious activities. In some countries the assignment of areas for missionary activity has caused serious evangelical-Catholic controversies. David Smilde's chapter on Venezuela contains a detailed analysis of a recent controversy on the subject. The same chapter also highlights evangelical resistance to government efforts to regulate preaching in public places. Several of the case studies also describe efforts to register—and perhaps to control—religious bodies, with Departments of Religious Affairs which are located in different ministries in different countries. In Mexico, for example, it is part of the Interior Ministry (*Gobernación*); in Venezuela, it is located in the Ministry of Justice; and in Argentina and Bolivia, the foreign ministry is officially entitled the Ministry of Foreign Affairs and Worship. In Central America efforts have also been made to revoke the visas of members of the Unification Church of Reverend Moon, and in Venezuela the government has withdrawn its permission for it to operate in that country.

Fourth, Evangelicals are beginning to press for Protestant chaplaincies in the armed forces and in hospitals which heretofore have been exclusively Catholic. (Only in Argentina is there a significant Jewish community, and few or no Jews are in the military.) In 1993 Colombia adopted a Religious Liberty Law which authorized Protestant chaplaincies in the armed forces, the police, and state-run hospitals as well as parental choice on religious instruction in public schools (Moreno 1996, 228).

Fifth, there are cases of religious discrimination in the military, education, and the civil service, and such cases were much more numerous in the past, as Edward Cleary's chapter reports. The Cuban government has frankly admitted that at least until the 1990s believers could not secure positions in fields such as education or psychology, or advancement in government. The Communist Party was closed to believers as well, although that prohibition was removed in 1991. As Margaret Crahan's chapter demonstrates, church-state relations are better in Cuba today, but there continue to be serious tensions.

Sixth, there remain occasional instances of outright religious conflict and persecution in Colombia, Guatemala, and southern Mexico, often involving Indian villages. The Rutherford Institute in Charlottesville, Virginia, tracks other examples of religious discrimination and persecution in Latin America and elsewhere (Moreno 1996). As Elizabeth Brusco's chapter documents, much more serious cases of persecution of Protestants took place in Colombia in the 1950s, while the persecutions of the Catholic clergy in Argentina in the mid-1950s and in Mexico in the 1920s are well known.

As for the future, the movement toward greater religious freedom in Latin America seems irreversible. Instant communication via satellite and the Internet as well as the increased vigilance of the global human rights movement give worldwide publicity to instances of religious persecution. Anomalous situations or survivals from an earlier regime will gradually be harmonized with the legal and political requirements of liberal constitutional democracy. Tensions will continue, and support for freedom of worship will be subjected to strains from competing pressures to use the instruments of the law and the state in favor of one or another religious group. Yet, as the human rights movement becomes stronger in the Americas and the world, the right to preach and to practice one's religion is likely to receive increasing support throughout the hemisphere.

Part One

PERSPECTIVES ON THE CHURCHES AND EVANGELIZATION TODAY

———◆———

1.

THE CATHOLIC CHURCH

——————◆——————

Edward L. Cleary

As Americans are becoming more aware of the issue of religious liberty in the world,[1] Latin America will be one of the highlighted regions. Although today religious persecution is a problem only in Cuba, Guatemala, and some frontier sections of Mexico, Latin America furnishes a central stage for Catholic–non-Catholic debates and for viewing the church as a public actor fostering freedom for citizens.

Latin America is the largest Catholic region in the world. It is also the scene of dramatic growth of the second largest Christian body, the Pentecostals. Further, Latin America is the largest Christian region undergoing the travails of establishing stable democracies. The church has been crucial in this task.

What follows are a policy study[2] and a study of culture, as well. The following three sections take up the turbulent history of church-state relations, Vatican policy in tension with Latin American culture, and political demands non-Catholics are making.

TURBULENT HISTORY OF RELIGIOUS FREEDOM AND CHURCH-STATE ISSUES

The insurrections that brought independence from Spain (and were called revolutions) brought revolutionary change in neither theory nor practice. Nor did they bring change for religious institutions, as did the insurrection against Great Britain in the United States. For three centuries the Catholic church had operated in a strong church-state bond with the Spanish and Portuguese states. From a governmental viewpoint, the church was a mechanism of state administration.[3]

11

Fourteen years of war (1810-24) for independence in Spanish colonies brought great uncertainty for members of the church.[4] As Latourette remarks: "The domination of the crown in Portuguese and especially in Spanish America made for a passive Christianity."[5] That kind of dependency engendered fear of the unknown in church leaders. However, revolutionary leaders were not irreligious.[6] They manifested an allegiance to the Catholic church.[7]

The fate of the church during this crucial period of forming new nations was largely in the hands of Latin Americans. Spain blocked communication from Latin American governments to Rome for a crucial period. Spanish navies dominated the sea lanes to Europe. Further, the Spanish king still exercised control over the Spanish American church. The *patronato real* agreement provided that all communication to Rome had to pass through the king's hands.[8] He impeded communication with Rome, making it futile to try. Bishoprics fell vacant; many parishes had no priests; war impoverished the clergy in resources and in spirit. By 1829 not one bishop was left in Mexico.[9] The Spanish embassy acted in Rome as the chief obstacle to the establishment of relations with the Vatican.[10] This "great incommunication" continued from 1810 until 1831.[11] Then Pope Gregory XVI announced the appointment of new Latin American bishops.

Nineteenth-century liberalism infused, to a greater or lesser degree, both liberal and conservative thinking. Conservatives tended to group together, sharing class interests but without a consistent doctrine. John Lynch believes liberals had a coherent policy: "They stood for constitutional government, the basic human freedoms, economic *laissez-faire*, and opposition to military and ecclesiastical privilege."[12]

National elites showed many contradictions between policy and practice. They maintained structures of profound inequality between elites and masses, the *gente decente* and the *gente humilde*. Regarding religion, W. Eugen Shiels remarks: "They unwittingly fell into the trap of keeping the very institution that was most undemocratic of all the emblems of royal control."[13] They simply substituted national control (patronage) over the church for royal patronage. This policy continued subjection of the church to the political arm of society, although Rome had not consented.

Rome was anxious to cast off the outmoded royal control. Scholars had argued for centuries that patronage of the church was of the essence of national sovereignty. By contrast, Rome argued that the *patronato* was a concession to Spain and Portugal and that national sovereignty did not legally or logically imply control of the church.[14] The church and national governments disputed issues of appointing bishops and other church officers, creating new dioceses, and controlling monasteries and communication with the Holy See. In a letter to the bishops of Latin America, Pope Gregory XVI ordered the bishops to refuse to recognize patronage. A generation later Pius IX continued to deny that national patronage was a right inherited from the Spanish kings.[15] Most clerics, Shiels believes, "were unwilling victims" of the arrangement of national patronage.[16]

When Latin American countries established communications with Rome, the new nations attempted to assure Rome that their governments would safeguard the church. Rome and the Latin American nations established diplomatic relations, beginning in 1835. Internunciatures were founded in Nueva Granada[17] and Brazil.[18] Rome had weak influence over the new churches. *Patronato* structures obstructed reforms. Rome could neither create new dioceses nor appoint many bishops for a rapidly increasing population, especially of European immigrants in the Southern Cone. The Vatican itself was in profound danger, under threat of loss of the Papal States and of its own political autonomy.

NINETEENTH-CENTURY LIBERAL GOVERNMENTS

The nineteenth century brought many conflicts with liberal states for the church in Europe and Latin America.[19] As the century progressed, observers pointed to beneficial arrangements in Holland and Germany. Greater separation of church and state there brought more benefits to sizeable Catholic minorities than in countries where the states protected Catholicism.[20]

In Latin America, by the mid-nineteenth century, anticlericalism and secular philosophies, especially Comtean positivism, were making a strong impact. These ideologies led political leaders and intellectuals to reduce the influence of the church in politics and in education and to loosen the ties between church and state. The Catholic church was persecuted periodically in nineteenth-century Latin America, discriminated against in law and practice, stripped of possessions, suffered exile of bishops and mass expulsion of religious orders, and lost the right to own property or to participate in public life. Mecham believes that these measures were typically "acts of vengeance wreaked upon the clergy by their political opponents."[21]

While some anticlerical campaigns were episodic, other campaigns were systematic and effective. Anticlerical measures greatly reduced the clergy of Central America in the nineteenth and twentieth centuries. More than any other national church in Latin America the church in Guatemala suffered prolonged debilitation at the hands of anticlerical liberals. The anticlerical laws persisted well into the twentieth century.[22]

Even after the defeat of the *Cristero* rebellion (1926-29), the Mexican governments of the 1930s engaged in horrendous "defanaticization" campaigns, desecrating churches and engaging in massive anti-God and anti-church indoctrination campaigns.[23] These campaigns mostly failed, but other legal measures reduced the Mexican church for a long time to a largely mute presence. Finally in 1992 the Mexican government recognized the right of churches to own property in their own names.

In sum, one could characterize religious liberty in the first 140 years of the national period in the following way: the Catholic church enjoyed a privileged position in all countries at the beginning. Through the nineteenth century it continued to enjoy privileged status in most countries but suffered periodic repression, as in Guatemala and Mexico. In some countries it was fully established. In others, Latourette says, "Separation of church and state was accomplished, but usually the Roman Catholic church, since it represented the faith of the majority and because of its historic position, was able to exert a special influence and to obtain aid, direct or indirect, from the government."[24]

The heritage of the Iberian church thus continued in the relatively passive condition of the church. Ivan Vallier has written that the church at this stage was weak in influence, maintaining itself through informal ties of churchmen with governing elite members.[25]

While separation of church and state was considered a major step by modernization advocates, some Catholic leaders opposed the measure. They wanted the protection (but not the dominance) of the state. Two noteworthy cases of church-state separation occurred in Brazil and Chile.[26] Separation of church and state took place in Brazil as the country gained sovereignty peacefully from Portugal. Marshall Deodoro da Fonseca decreed separation of church and state on January 7, 1890. Brazilian bishops enthusiastically agreed to the measure. E. Bradford Burns believes that the Brazilian hierarchy "sought a freedom for the Roman Catholic church similar to that insured it in the United States."[27] The church had not been persecuted; it had only been tolerated by the state.[28] In 1996, looking back on separation of church and state, the Brazilian Bishops' Conference wrote: "The separation created the conditions for the fortifying and the renovation of Catholicism."[29]

Chile began in the early twentieth century to offer a welcome to other religions. Mecham believes: "Separation of church and state was a cherished political ideal of advanced thinkers in Chile."[30] Chilean historian Luis Galdames described Chileans as ready for the separation of church and state because of "simple tolerance and religious indifference."[31] Much more was involved. Leaders within church and civilian sectors strongly opposed separation. Only the leadership of Archbishop Crescente Errázuriz, President Arturo Alessandri, and Vatican Secretary of State Pietro Gasparri secured acceptance of the terms of separation in 1925.[32] Most Chilean bishops and priests were willing to accept this as the lesser of potential evils.[33]

Lack of space precludes lengthy analysis of the contexts and consequences of these church-state arrangements beyond three key observations. Once the *patronato* was set aside, the two churches were strengthened structurally. Rome created new dioceses, named many more bishops, recruited missionaries, and improved the church's presence in remote territories. Both Chilean and Brazilian churches became leaders of Catholic church renewal in Latin America. Both countries have also witnessed indigenous Pentecostal and other non-Catholic growth of unusual proportions.

CHURCH-STATE RELATIONS AND DEMOCRACY

In the 1920s and 1930s European and North American democratic influences began reaching clerical and lay leaders in Brazil and Chile. Refined by 150 years of debate, French Catholic thought especially influenced Latin Americans. Jacques Maritain and Emmanuel Mounier offered alternative Christian-based views of liberty to counter Latin American populism or bureaucratic authoritarianism. Christian liberation theology would be born in Latin America partially from these influences.[34] These ideas also affected church grassroots groups called Christian base communities. The communities provided strong motivation for many members to act as citizens within democracies.[35]

By the 1960s the church stood on the threshold of a profound church-state crisis. During the 1960s and 1970s the military's takeover of civilian governments affected the church in most Latin American countries. Military governments denied or constrained civil liberties, as thousands, including many church professionals, were killed, disappeared, or imprisoned, death threats made, and censorship imposed. Both Catholic and some Protestant churches were affected.[36]

In many countries under military rule, the Catholic church became the only institution left with a measure of autonomy. The church became a voice of the voiceless in the public forum. Important sectors had moved the church from passivity and dependency on government to becoming a systematic defender of human rights.

More was involved than opposing the military. The foremost achievement of the church for government has been its substantial contribution to the establishment of democracy. Pope John XXIII gave a mandate for this in 1963 when he called for "democratic and participatory" forms of government in *Pacem in Terris*.[37] Samuel Huntington assesses the church's influence as second only to socioeconomic development as the strongest force in Latin America moving toward democracy in the 1980s.[38]

In the 1990s important church sectors continue building the basis for democracy by strengthening civil society,[39] through working for new laws and the enforcement of law. Human-rights organizations have grown rapidly in Latin America.[40] They have moved beyond monitoring torture to safeguarding women, children, Indians, laborers, and the environment.

The Brazilian church has taken the lead among Latin American churches in pointing the way toward a new church-state model. Under Portuguese control, the church in Brazil participated in a Christendom model, a Christian state and society. Then, after some years of national independence and liberal domination, in the 1920s and 1930s the church moved toward a "New Christendom" model which allowed the church, under the populist state, to hold large public congresses and to teach Catholic faith in public schools, something forbidden the church by the liberals.[41]

The New Christendom model dissolved in Brazil with Vatican II. New theologies questioned what they saw as its implicit assumption of two worlds, two histories, secular and religious. Under military rule the Brazilian church became the voice of the voiceless. What role was it to take in democratizing society? After fostering free elections, political parties, and social movements, the Brazilian church has found a role in building up civil society through human rights protection.[42] The Brazilian church's national plan (1997-99) calls explicitly for education in, and advocacy of human rights.[43] Church policy in the Latin American church and the Vatican has thus been establishing democracy and cooperating with the state in promoting human rights and the rule of law.[44] In many ways, the church has gone from an institution passively enjoying a large measure of religious freedom to one that is actively seeking freedom for citizens.

POLICY AND CULTURE OF RELIGIOUS LIBERTY

Viewed across the universe of regions and nation-states, the Catholic church shows marked contrasts. In Rome the Vatican interacts on a daily basis with 160 governments and many church bodies. In Latin America the ponderous weight of Latin culture holds the church fast. While there are occasional bright spots of inter-church cooperation, there is little evidence of the contemporary world of religious pluralism.

Both arenas of church policy should be kept in mind regarding religious liberty and relations to non-Catholic groups in Latin America. Only a multilevel approach will yield a satisfactory view. More than ideologies are involved. Cultural explanations are also necessary.

MAJOR SHIFTS IN APPROACH

Religious liberty became a great question of nineteenth-century continental Europe.[45] Did persons have to profess the same faith as the king? Did they have to believe at all to be citizens? Did they have the right to hold "erroneous beliefs"? Western civilization based on religious belief seemed to be breaking apart. Secularism was thrusting the church from its central role in society.

One current of Catholic thought followed the lead of Thomas Aquinas, who believed that it was wrong to use coercion in the area of faith.[46] To deal with a variety of national situations theorists had emphasized a "thesis-hypothesis" theory. To paraphrase Eric D'Arcy slightly: The "thesis" asserted that the state has the obligation to acknowledge the Catholic church as the only religious society with a God-given right to public existence and action, and to recognize this by law. In principle, other religions should have no legal right to public existence and action, and ought to be repressed by the state. Error and evil are counter to the rational and moral nature of man, to the common good of society, and to the right of people to be protected from occasions of defecting from the truth. On the "hypothesis," however, that such a constitutional arrangement was unworkable, the church might forego her right to establishment as the one true religion of the state, and accept the legal toleration of other religions.[47]

A common interpretation held that the "thesis" applied where most of the citizens in a country were Catholic; in other cases, the "hypothesis" could be accepted. The temper of the times in Europe explains what to contemporary ears sounds odd. Countries had long identified themselves as Catholic or Protestant, with little or no ground for religious outsiders. Two outposts, Scandinavia and Latin America, exemplify the lack of religious liberty. Sweden completely forbade the presence of Catholics until the late eighteenth century. Until 1873 Swedes did not have the legal right to leave the Lutheran church and to join another Christian community. Persons born in Sweden were automatically considered members of the state-sponsored Lutheran church unless they gave official notification to the contrary. This was difficult to do until 1952.

In Latin America national independence brought a degree of religious liberty for non-Catholics. As in Mexico and many other countries, public opinion shifted from intolerance to greater tolerance for Protestants. In public affairs this fluctuation depended on whether anticlerical and pro-Protestant political leaders were in power. On the street and in schools, individual Catholics periodically expressed their hostility to Protestants. Protestants over forty years old whom I have interviewed can recount numerous stories of harassment and discrimination.[48]

Basic changes in religious liberty in Latin America have been made. Latin American countries, on their own or with cooperation from Rome, have legally established freedom of conscience and freedom of religion.[49] These basic rights enjoy full support of the Catholic church according to principles that were elaborated at Vatican Council II (1962-65). Debate on religious liberty began at the end of the 1963 session, occupied a large segment of the 1964 session, and a final document on the subject received almost unanimous consent in 1965.[50]

The Catholic church recognized at Vatican II that God cannot be worshiped under constraint. This is evident in a landmark statement on religious liberty, *Dignitatis Humanae*.[51] The document views religious liberty as an inherent right of the human person. This marked a shift from defending *libertas ecclesiae* to *libertas personae*.[52] But the Council fathers did not fully integrate religious liberty into a comprehensive view of Christian freedom.[53] Vatican II provided an impulse, a beginning.[54] Postconciliar debates added substance to Vatican II's useful initiative. Guided by theologians within and without the Vatican, the church has shifted from emphasis on the "rights of truth" to the "rights of persons."

NEW ERA OF RELIGIOUS LIBERTY

The larger world of global politics and international agreements has also shifted. After World War II, governments signed international documents on religious freedom.[55] These agreements established the dignity of the human person as the foundation of religious liberty, affirmed the right to profess religion or not, and delineated state obligations to respect religious practice. National legislation in some countries has also attempted to define a more pluralist world.

Before 1945 the nations of the world had not attempted to deal with religious freedom through international agreements. The recognition of the Holocaust and the emphasis on prisoners of conscience through Amnesty International campaigns expressed a growing human rights sensitivity missing in previous historical periods. In response to efforts to promote religious rights many countries adjusted their national legislation about religion. Some countries unconditionally granted religious freedom. Other nations, such as Sweden or Greece, modified restrictions on religious practice.

However, other countries, especially fundamentalist Islamic or communist ones, allowed very limited religious freedoms. The difference between historical eras was a changed global climate. Nations had to play out their actions on an international stage. Modern religious and secular journalism publicized abuses. International regimes of religious liberty began to take hold.

Often national constitutions avoid mentioning God. Thus God cannot be invoked as the ultimate foundation of all human rights. Some constitutions, such as that of France, consider religion as a private opinion. For the Vatican these disparities with its policies did not matter as much as the practical freedom that persons and communities enjoy. This was especially true in an era when national Catholic churches barely functioned in large portions of the Islamic world or in China.

The day-to-day world of the Vatican thus differs vastly from that of the Latin American church. The Vatican has had to play on a world stage. Especially after the collapse of the Soviet Union, major sectors of the political and religious environment have changed drastically in the last ten years. Instead of the Vatican denouncing persecution in eastern Europe and the Soviet Union, the Holy See now hears complaints about Catholics and Pentecostals invading the Orthodox domain in the countries of the former Soviet Union.

GLOBAL ISSUES

Two issues of religious freedom have surfaced globally as issues of negotiation between nations and the Catholic church and between Catholics and non-Catholics. These are national legislation about church-state relations and acceptable rules of engagement between religious competitors.

The Catholic church's general principles may clash with national church-state relations inherited from the past and firmly held by cultural preferences. Many churches show the deep imprint of time on the way churches and states and individual believers relate to one another. A 1996 meeting showed the different church-state arrangements among nations. Christian world communions (Lutherans, Methodists, and other groups) are major players in the global dynamics of religion. When secretaries of these world communions met, Professor Roland Minnerath of Strasbourg represented the Catholic view on church-state relations and religious liberty issues. He pointed out four legal patterns: 1) established churches; 2) legally protected churches; 3) separation without legal recognition or cooperation between church and state; and 4) separation between church and state, with mutual cooperation.[56]

The Church of England and the Lutheran churches of Sweden, Denmark, and Norway exemplify the nationally established church. The Catholic church has rejected past trends toward establishing by secular law separate national churches. (The church's conflict with Henry VIII partially centered on this issue.) While the *patronato* system for Latin America came closest to this model, neither Spain nor Portugal succeeded in establishing a separate national church.

The second church-state system bestows special legal status and protection for a particular church. In Latin America some national constitutions grant special recognition to the Catholic church. However, in recent years this has not been the preference of the Holy See. Since Vatican II, new conventions signed by Rome with Argentina, Colombia, Peru, and other countries have removed any reference to Catholicism as a state religion.

Not since the Second Vatican Council has the Vatican granted governments the right to appoint church officials.[57] The Holy See has signed approximately thirty concordats or conventions since Vatican II. It elaborated church-state relations within a framework of the common right to religious freedom.[58] These agreements do not imply any privileged legal position for the Catholic church in relation to other churches.

If non-Catholics in Latin America have felt aggrieved at times under this system, Roman Catholics in Greece have been strongly assertive in addressing their minority position. As the "dominant church" the Greek Orthodox church has the right to limit the rights of the other, so-called free churches. Greek Catholics have reacted to these measures, bringing many cases of violations of religious rights to the European Court of Human Rights at Strasbourg.

Where total separation exists without church-state cooperation, the Catholic church has prospered in the United States and suffered greatly in eastern Europe before 1989. Different arrangements, such as those of France or the Netherlands, have been developed under this model.

The Catholic church has considered closer to ideal another model of separation of church and state, one with cooperation. Here church and state are said to be "distinct" but not "separate," leaving room for institutional cooperation, as in Italy, Austria, and Germany. Both parties recognize church and state as independent and sovereign in their own spheres. Cooperation between institutions can be permitted or encouraged and established by national law or international concordat. Cooperative areas include religious education in public schools; legal validation of religious weddings; religious assistance to persons in prisons, hospitals, or barracks; and access to nationally controlled television or radio.

The second global issue has been acceptable rules of engagement between religious competitors. Here one needs an understanding of the greater complexities of global religions. The Vatican has two agencies that relate to other religious bodies. One deals with unity among Christians and the other with dialogue among world religions. The first works to promote the ecumenical spirit within the Catholic church and with ecclesial partners to overcome divisions among Christians.[59] The second agency acts as only one part of the Christian church dealing with Islam, Buddhism, and other world religions. A third agency deals with evangelization (increasing biblical and traditional understandings of God, Christ, and the church) among Catholics.[60]

In Latin America, North America, and Western Europe, the dominant religions are Christian. As a basic principle guiding policy, the Catholic church understands that it shares deep bonds of relationship with other churches and ecclesial communities, even a real, though imperfect communion.[61] Catholic church policy for interaction among Christians is, on one hand, respect among family members, and, on the other, opposition to proselytism among Christians. Besides the key question of freedom under civil law, another crucial factor is respect for the local church. For example, the Catholic church believes that Lutherans in Sweden have witnessed to the Gospel for centuries.

Monsignor John Rodano of the Pontifical Council for Christian Unity calls attention to a related issue, the "unchurched." He points to the joint statement of Roman Catholics and the World Council of Churches: "Different theological and pastoral understandings of the meaning of certain ideas can also contribute to tension in relationships. . . . Some [churches] aim at the re-evangelization of baptized but non-practicing members of other churches. But there are different interpretations of who is 'unchurched' or a 'true' Christian believer. Efforts to understand the perspectives of other Christian communities on these matters are therefore necessary."[62]

For Latin America, the language of some Protestant mission leaders has intensified this contentious issue. They have used the term *"campos blancos"* (target areas). By this they mean millions of Catholics needing the Pentecostal or evangelical plows to till the fertile soil of Catholics needing their pastoral care. Given that some thirty million of the forty million *evangélicos* in Latin America are Pentecostal Christians, a major area of Catholic–non-Catholic relations is Catholicism-Pentecostalism.

CENTRAL QUESTION

A difficult question for the Catholic church in Latin America, and elsewhere, as well, is proselytism. This is not only an issue for the global Catholic church but for mainline Protestant churches, as well.[63] In 1991, the World Council of Christian Churches (WCC) and the Catholic church prepared a joint statement defining and describing proselytism.[64] This statement grew from many hours of reflection on experiences worldwide and years of attempts by WCC and Vatican officials to refine the statement. For one key Vatican official, proselytism is always negative. In his view, it leads to religious conflict. When proselytizers take advantage of religious freedom, they express attitudes contrary to ecumenism.

What is this negative proselytism? Cardinal Edward Cassidy, president of the Pontifical Council for Promoting Christian Unity, explains: "I mean the use of unworthy means to attract members of other churches or even unchurched persons to their fold. Misrepresentation of the other, or of one's own community, is a common source of tension. Some of the tension between churches comes from the way in which new converts to one community denigrate their former ecclesial home."[65]

When John Paul II opened the Santo Domingo Conference of Latin American Bishops (1992), he delivered his most important address in Latin America in over a decade. In one part of his address, the pope said the sects were like "ravenous wolves" devouring Latin American Catholics and "causing division and discord in our communities."[66] Who were these ravenous wolves? Pentecostals immediately came to mind since the term *sects* often is used by Catholic leaders to refer to the religious groups growing fastest in Latin America[67] and the greatest growth has been among Pentecostals.[68]

Santo Domingo's final document affirmed "ecumenism as a priority for the church."[69] However, the conference organizers had invited neither the Latin American Council of Churches nor Pentecostals as observers. Faced with serious understaffing and dwindling resources, the Latin American church has focused on meeting the pastoral demands of its own members. By 1996 the president of the Latin American Bishops' Conference (CELAM), Archbishop Oscar Rodríguez, had to consider closing CELAM's section on ecumenism due to lack of results.[70]

Criticism of the pope's indiscriminate characterization followed the Santo Domingo meeting.[71] Several months later Cardinal Cassidy addressed ecumenical officers of bishops' conferences from around the world, saying: "We must be careful . . . not to confuse the issue by lumping under the term 'sect' groups that do not deserve that title. I am not speaking here, for instance, about Pentecostals."[72]

Such Roman ability to amend and to move forward with dialogue does not generally mark the Latin American church, angry over anti-Catholic attacks and lacking historical knowledge of other Christian religions. Latin American Catholics have become increasingly sensitive to groups with anti-Catholic biases. Brazilian Catholics awoke one October day in 1995 to find TV replays of a Neo-Pentecostal bishop beating and kicking a statue of Mary, the Mother of Jesus.[73] Hyperkinetic newspapers and journals wondered about holy wars. The statue-kicking bishop came from The Universal Church (*A Igreja Universal*), a prominent Brazilian church with more than three million members. *Veja*, a *Time*-like weekly, said: "A common practice of The Universal Church is deprecating other religions and attacking its symbols."[74]

When Cecil Robeck entered the discussion,[75] he was quick to point out that the majority of Pentecostals oppose stealing sheep of another church. Robeck, a major Pentecostal scholar teaching at Fuller Theological Seminary, also warns his own: "Pentecostals on the whole are not engaged in the discussions of proselytism. . . . They are not condemning the activity. . . . As the world becomes smaller, members of other world religions are looking to such groups for help in putting a stop to evangelism/proselytism. . . . This is a very dangerous state of affairs."[76]

The proselytism issue directly affects millions of Hispanic Catholics in the United States. Robeck presented his views on proselytism to Catholic ecumenical officers from various U.S. dioceses. Robeck reviewed many recent studies and found that many charges of proselytism had been made, including the use of force, unjust stereotypes, and unhealthy competition. He said: "Within the Americas, one or more of these charges is raised against almost any non-Roman Catholic group. . . . A great many of them have been raised against Pentecostals."[77]

In Rome, the Vatican watched the global spread of Pentecostalism and its Charismatic cousin within Catholic and mainline Protestant churches. Since Vatican II, Rome has sponsored profound dialogues with other Christian churches, leading toward greater understanding. The Catholic church had only carried on these formal theological exchanges with established churches. However, the Vatican has also engaged a sector of Pentecostalism open to dialogue, one that the Vatican called "classical Pentecostals." In a crucial move, the Vatican invited Pentecostal pastor David Duplessis to act as an observer at Vatican Council II. Almost twenty years later, the Catholic-Pentecostal dialogue took shape. The partners have carried on the exchange with enthusiasm.[78] Though it has received high marks from its participants, Guillermo Cook believes the dialogue goes unnoticed in Latin America.[79] For one staff person in the Vatican, the issue has become lack of Pentecostal interlocutors in Latin America: "With whom can we talk?"[80]

In Mexico, Paul E. Sigmund asked the archbishop of Guadalajara, Cardinal Juan Sandoval Iñíguez, at the 1997 meeting of the Latin American Studies Association to comment on *evangélicos* in Latin America. Cardinal Sandoval observed that there are some cooperative Protestants, such as the Anglicans in Guadalajara. However, he maintained, the majority are aggressive and some are abusive, "daily condemning me in front of my cathedral. They are here on the initiative of the United States, as we know from the Rockefeller Plan." Mexico's other cardinal, Norberto Rivera Carrera, has expressed similar views. One of Mexico's principal sociologists of religion believes that neither churchman has basic knowledge of the history of other religions in Mexico and Latin America.[81]

POLITICAL ISSUES IN CATHOLIC-PENTECOSTAL RELATIONS

Given this cultural lag, non-Catholics have begun to organize politically. While non-Catholic church groups enjoy fundamental legal freedoms in Latin American states, they have contested related issues. The major target of non-Catholics has been the privileged position that the Catholic church still holds in many Latin American countries. As Brian Smith notes, both Pentecostals and the religiously nonaffiliated are exerting pressure on lawmakers. They want, Smith notes, "to complete the separation of church and state and thus remove some of the vestiges of Catholic privilege that still exist in law, special mention of Catholicism in national constitutions, and the teaching of Catholic doctrine and morals in public schools."[82]

Globally, religious liberty has not meant religious equality. A prominent watchdog of religious liberty, Paul Marshall, points out: "While a state church necessarily infringes on religious equality, it need not be much of a problem depending on how many privileges it has. Such churches exist in Western Europe, including the United Kingdom, and have not produced any major outcry, since they are combined with effective guarantees of freedom for other religious groups. This is one reason why international human rights documents do not condemn state churches *per se* as violations of religious freedom."[83]

Political action by Protestants, especially Pentecostals, has been a recent phenomenon. From the mid-1980s, journalists, leftists, and Catholic observers noted with some amazement the growing activism of Pentecostals, entering the public arena in Central America, Peru, Colombia, and Brazil, and using existing parties or forming their own. By 1996 they had created many evangelical parties, twenty-four in eleven countries.[84]

Researchers have not carried out extensive studies on these Protestant parties. However, Paul Freston's 1993 study of newly elected Brazilian Pentecostal officials showed that their agenda included removing legal privileges for the Catholic church and promotion of material benefits for their churches.[85] (However, Leandro Piquet Carneiro has shown that claims about a Protestant vote and a Protestant congressional bloc in Brazil have been exaggerated.[86]) Nicaraguan Pentecostal political leaders also sought an end to government subsidies to Catholic schools and to the requirement that Catholic doctrine be taught in public schools.[87] Catholic bishops in some countries have attempted to use their influence to block such initiatives.

Why now? Why have Pentecostals taken so long to enter politics? They have had for some time a critical mass sufficient for political action in, say, Chile. Earlier scholars offered several reasons for Pentecostal apolitical attitudes.[88] They said that Pentecostals were authoritarian followers, fatalistic in politics, and supinely obedient. Pentecostals were compliant because the Bible told them to be obedient or because of their theological belief in the evil of human enterprises, especially politics. Most such explanations do not hold up. Pentecostals are not otherworldly; they are in politics for pragmatic reasons.[89]

Strong implications for Latin American democracies are now surfacing. Pentecostals face the active opposition of Catholic bishops and Latin American inertia in their efforts to change the pattern of the church-state relations. Their political activism represents an appropriate response in a democratic context. Brian Smith, in an incisive view of Catholics and Pentecostals, warns: "Until this thorny constitutional issue of unequal treatment of denominations before the law is settled, there is little hope of any strategic alliance between

Catholics and Pentecostals. . . . There is growing evidence that each side sees the demands of the other as morally unacceptable and politically nonnegotiable."[90]

Contentious Issues

Several issues merit special attention. Protestants have been citizens of several Latin American countries for generations. They do not understand why they should be treated in some countries as second-class citizens. In Argentina the Catholic church has enjoyed a special legal status and the government has treated other religious groups as associations, equivalent in legal status to charities. As Marshall explains: "Their houses of worship have the same legal status as shops or dance halls. The government requires information about pastors and leaders, times of services, and numbers in attendance."[91] Argentine Protestants have worked politically to address the situation (see the chapter in this volume by José Míguez Bonino).

Chilean Pentecostals also want equal status for their churches. They seek not only a share of material benefits but also have symbolic reasons. Over a period of almost ninety years Pentecostals have transformed Chile from a traditionally Catholic country to one that is also Pentecostal. Recognition in law and in practice of the social and political importance of the Protestant world in Chile is long overdue.[92]

Historical Protestants began ministering to immigrant groups in Latin America in the 1800s. Pentecostals formed their first communities in the 1910s. Then in the 1960s wildly dissimilar cults, sects, and New Age groups spread widely through Latin America. These groups quadrupled the number of non-Catholic religions in Bolivia from 1960 to 1995.[93] Other countries in the Southern Cone region reported hundreds of non-Catholic religious groups. The non-Catholic religious spectrum in Latin America thus embraces many churches, exotic cults, beliefs, and personalities.

Polite listening to foreign religionists gave way to bewilderment for many Catholics. Late-night and daytime radio, print, and television programs recounted histories and doctrines of Mormons, Jehovah's Witnesses, New Age, and health-and-wealth religions. Shirley MacLaine, reincarnation, *Watchtower,* and the Book of Mormon increased Latin Americans' consciousness of religious diversity. In the center of Buenos Aires in 1992 the Claretian Bookstore prominently offered four books to Catholics offering them guidance to the menace of these "sects." The Catholic books were polemical and global, lumping all but historical Protestants into the same category of sect, or worse, cult.

To keep a measure of control over the welter of religious ideologies in the 1970s, military governments, such as Bolivia's and Argentina's, relied heavily on registration of non-Catholic groups. Bolivia created in 1971 an undersecretariat for worship within the ministry of foreign relations. This provided a government channel for groups seeking legal recognition. Civilian gov-

ernments, succeeding military ones, found this registration-and-control structure useful. They had the power to deny permission to remain in the country
to groups accused of brainwashing. Bureaucrats also slow the registration process to inertial pace to oppose Mormon and other groups.[94]

Bolivia has been more open than Argentina in its treatment of non-Catholic
groups. Many groups entering Bolivia could only obtain legal recognition as
educational or health organizations. Subsequently Bolivia's undersecretariat
of worship has begun registering groups as religious organizations.

Bolivia illustrates the debate and the learning process taking place in some
governments. The Bolivian constitution "recognizes and supports the apostolic Roman Catholic religion." ANDEB (the National Association of
Evangelicals) in 1992 collected twenty-four thousand signatures supporting a
proposed constitutional amendment recognizing all denominations equally.
Latinamerica Press in 1992 reported that the proposal was stuck in legislative
committee and would probably be tabled for several years.[95]

Nonetheless, in 1996 Bolivia's undersecretariat for public worship acknowledged that Bolivia had created its constitution in an outdated historical context. It argued: "Legislation should be brought into line with a pluralist religious spirit, one that respects diversity. New models of church-state relations
need to be developed."[96] Bolivia's ambassador to the Holy See, Armando Loaiza
Mariaca, confirmed in 1997 that Bolivia's policy position concerning non-
Catholic religious groups would increasingly be in the direction of religious
pluralism.[97]

Bolivia also illustrates an aspect of Rome's tutoring of a national church.
Ambassador Loaiza, a Catholic, recalled that Bolivian bishops complained to
the pope on a Bolivian trip about aggressive non-Catholics. According to Loaiza,
the pope told the bishops that these other religious groups were nourishing the
people. Further, the pope said that if Pentecostals are gaining adherents, it is
because the bishops and Bolivian Catholics are not doing their job. The pope
also pointed to Pentecostal use of contemporary methods, especially television.[98]

Rather than continuing to create evangelical parties, Bolivia's politically
active Protestants ran as candidates for national elections within established
secular parties. Not only are political parties actively recruiting them, but the
Bolivian people grant them an approval previously lacking. A polling firm in
1997 found that 80 percent of Bolivians believe that political action by various religious groups was appropriate.[99]

CONCLUSION

Why do diocesan officers in the United States invite a Pentecostal scholar to
explain his views on proselytism and Mexican cardinals persist in non-histori-
cal views of Pentecostalism? Dr. Jeffrey Gros, a Christian Brother formerly at

the National Council of Churches and now an ecumenical officer at the National Catholic Conference, explains this as a cultural difference. In a word, the reception of *Dignitatis Humanae*, Vatican II's *Declaration on Religious Liberty,* "differs according to the culture into which it was received. . . . The debates arising from those not understanding or not convinced by the arguments of the Council, as well as the dialectic of those who did not wish its theology and policy to be successful, are part of the 'reception' or 'nonreception' process."[100]

His view of Latin America: "It may be impossible for the ecumenical project of the Council to be realized in cultures where the Roman Catholic church predominates, at least until there is an understanding of religious liberty, religious pluralism, and the difference between religious liberty and tolerance. . . . This is a particularly sensitive problem in the Western Hemisphere."[101]

Segundo Galilea, a major pastoral theologian with wide experience of the Spanish-speaking world, summed up in 1987 the reception of Vatican II: "Except [for historical Protestant churches], ecumenism . . . has not followed a creative and productive path in Latin America."[102] In 1997, the president of the Latin American Bishops' Conference (CELAM), Archbishop Oscar Rodríguez, admitted: "Ecumenism and interreligious dialogue have not been a priority in Latin America." Rodríguez was taking a more active approach than his CELAM predecessors. Following the lead of Richard John Neuhaus, Rodríguez met with leaders of evangelical churches in New York, seeking cooperation rather than competition.[103]

Rodríguez's initiative took place on the eve of the Synod for America in Rome. This special three-week meeting brought bishops together from North and South America in November-December 1997. Latin American bishops expressed their anger over the "fanaticism" of their religious competitors. Cardinal Cassidy, as head of the Council for Promoting Christian Unity, spoke to the assembly. He courageously reminded Latin Americans that Catholics have a duty to take the lead in ecumenism where Catholics are in the majority. He made a plea not to use the word *sects* indiscriminately.[104] The final five-thousand word "Message to the World" from the Synod reaffirmed Cassidy's message.[105] Rome was making a strong step toward Pentecostals. Would the Latin Americans, the largest bloc in the church, follow?

The Latin American church has almost no intellectual resources to enter into a dialogue with indigenous Pentecostalism. A few, almost unknown, Catholic theologians and bishops in Latin America have made progress in thinking about religious liberty.[106] Catholics, Protestants, and Jews routinely collaborate in many projects, say, in São Paulo or Buenos Aires. They risked their lives together for human rights protection during military repression. But facing death has been a more welcome task for Catholics than studying Pentecostal history or understanding major facets of Pentecostalism, such as speaking in tongues or non-practice of baptism. Most Latin American Catholic theologians and bishops seldom address Pentecostalism, appear oblivious of its Latin American origins, and prefer to take up other themes.

Whatever the condition of high-level dialogue between world communions of Christians or the classical Pentecostal movement with the Vatican, the day-by-day realities of Catholic and non-Catholic relations will be determined in politics. Religion and national politics offer a lively set of issues. It will affect parties, churches, and governments for many years to come.

2.

HISTORICAL PROTESTANTISM

———————◆———————

John H. Sinclair

The Protestant movement in Latin America must be set in the broader context of the Reformation of the sixteenth century. Even though that movement did not reform the whole church, much less European society, the Protestant Reformation brought about significant social and political change. While that movement influenced the balance of political power, both locally and internationally, it was not a political revolution in the accepted sense of the term. However, the transformations brought about on the religious landscape had a profound, if not definitive, cultural and political impact.

In much the same way, the arrival of Protestant Christianity in Latin America in the nineteenth century sowed seeds of individual rights, political freedom, and social justice which have flourished in Latin soil. Despite the shortcomings of the Reformation, the Protestant Reformers attempted to fashion a religion more in accord with human nature as well as with divine decree. In like manner amid all the changes in Latin America in this century, in no area has change been more dramatic than in the realm of religion.

As we examine the role of the churches in Latin America which are rooted directly or indirectly in the Protestant Reformation of the sixteenth century, we witness the same struggle for human dignity, individual choice, and freedom to worship according to the dictates of one's conscience. The understanding of religious freedom has changed forever in the Southern Hemisphere because of the advent of Protestant Christianity.

HISTORICAL PERSPECTIVES

In our consideration of *historic* or *traditional* churches we focus mainly on Lutheran, Presbyterian, Reformed, Episcopal, and Baptist denominations which have roots in the Reformation of the sixteenth century. We also include the denominations which grew out of the Post Reformation of the seventeenth and eighteenth centuries, such as the Methodist, Mennonite, Moravian, Quaker, and Congregational.

By referring to these churches as historic, we do not imply that churches formed later are not also historic, since they, too, are a part of the history of the Christian church. In fact, some historians now refer to the "historicization" of the Pentecostal denominations as they take their rightful place in Christian history. A basic tenet of the Protestant Reformation is that God does not have "stepchildren"—only sons and daughters! Therefore, all Christian churches belong to the wider family and each has a history.[1]

FROM RELIGIOUS TOLERATION TO LIMITED RELIGIOUS FREEDOM: 1528-1884

The present issues of evangelization and religious freedom in Latin America must be understood within the context of progress from religious toleration to religious freedom. During the eighteenth and nineteenth centuries the majority of Protestant nations (Great Britain, Holland, Germany, and the United States) established their first permanent contacts with governments in Latin America. These contacts triggered conflict about religious freedom from the beginning. Were foreign merchants, sailors, diplomats, and immigrants to be guaranteed the free exercise of their religious beliefs, and permission to erect places of worship and to establish their own cemeteries? Could these foreigners bring into Roman Catholic countries books and periodicals which were forbidden by the Church? And what rights did the children of Protestant parents have who chose to settle permanently and marry native-born citizens in their adopted countries? It soon became clear that mere religious toleration was never to be a final solution.

EARLY ATTEMPTS OF PROTESTANT COLONIZATION

Much has been written about the failed attempts of the Lutheran Welsers in Venezuela (1528-46), the French Huguenots in Rio de Janeiro (1555-60), the Dutch Reformed in Bahia de San Salvador (1630-61) and the Scottish Presbyterians in the Isthmus of Panama (1698-1700).[2] The purpose of those colonies was largely commercial and not religious. However, some of the colonists took their religious faith seriously and were strongly opposed by Catholic authorities. The failure of all those early attempts at colonization was certainly not due primarily to religious persecution, but the Catholic Church was pleased to see the first Protestant colonies fade away.

LA SANTA INQUISICION

Baez Camargo has documented the actual cases of "pirates, privateers, and Protestants" who were condemned by the Holy Inquisition in the sixteenth and seventeenth centuries.[3] His research confirmed that probably not more than 310 cases were actually brought to trial and only 27 resulted in executions. The campaign against "the Lutheran heretics" continued in New Spain as attempts were made to smuggle forbidden books in boxes of merchandise and trunks. The distribution of the Bible was kept tightly under the control of the church authorities. The works of Erasmus, Luther, Eck, and Calvin were among the prohibited books.[4]

PROTESTANTISM AND THE ENLIGHTENMENT

The spirit of tolerance and freedom of conscience was foreign to the mentality of both the Roman Catholic kings and the Church. Even though the reformers in the New World were intrigued with many ideas of the Enlightenment, they did not incorporate the idea of religious freedom into their call for independence. Even the Mexican patriot-priests Miguel Hidalgo and José María Morelos were conservatives in relation to religious freedom for those of different religious opinions. Notwithstanding, Hidalgo was accused by the Inquisition of "sedition, formal heretical schism, Lutheranism, and Calvinism." The Mexican patriots did not foresee religious pluralism. The mindset of the liberators from Spain was essentially conservative and Catholic. Some Protestant ideas might have been useful to them in the independence process, but the patriots did not envision full religious freedom as it was understood in Europe and the United States.[5]

Perhaps the most revealing statement was made by Simón Bolívar when he explained why the Constitution of Angostura in 1821 contained no article on religion:

> When the Constitution of Colombia was drawn up, knowing that tolerance of any religion other than the Catholic would not be permitted, I was careful that nothing should be said in the constitution about religion. . . . The people of Colombia were not yet prepared for any change in the matters of religion.[6]

IMMIGRATION FROM PROTESTANT COUNTRIES[7]

The leaders of the new nations wished to broaden education to include the masses so that they could be incorporated into the new society. They also saw that contacts with wealthy Protestant nations would increase their trade and at the same time introduce liberal ideas to support their aims. In this context the first Bible society agents were permitted to distribute their books and the first popular educators were invited in from Great Britain and the United States. James Thomson, a Scottish colporteur, traveled through nine countries (1818-25), organizing Bible societies in six countries. He was encouraged in the distribution of Bibles by the Liberators San Martin, O'Higgins, and Bolivar. Joseph Lancaster, an English lay preacher and educator, was invited to establish primary schools in Chile, Colombia, Venezuela, Peru, and Ecuador using the Bible as a basic text and older students trained as tutors for younger children. Later in the century Domingo Sarmiento (1868-74) invited eighty-five teachers from the United States to organize a modern school system for Argentina.

Italian Waldensians settled in Uruguay (1856), German Lutherans in Chile (1852) and Venezuela (1845), Scottish Presbyterians (1825) and Welsh Baptists in Argentina (1890). These commercial and agricultural colonies demanded full religious freedom and brought their own clergy.[8]

COMMERCIAL TREATIES AND THE IMMIGRANT/ETHNIC CHURCHES

As early as 1810 an Anglo-Portuguese treaty permitted British subjects in Rio de Janeiro to build a chapel and later to establish their cemetery in 1819. Permission was given for the construction of a Protestant chapel in Maracaibo with an adjoining cemetery in 1834. However, permission was given for a church building in Valparaiso for the English-speaking colony in 1855 "only if the building was behind a high board fence and without a steeple or bell."[9]

Initial steps of religious toleration were taken, but religious freedom did not exist. The full exercise of religious freedom was to come to the children born to the first Protestant settlers. Their children were baptized, married, and many became citizens of the land of their birth. Decisions had to be made regarding their education since education was then the exclusive domain of the Catholic Church. Religious pluralism had to be addressed in public debate. With the arrival of more immigrants and the birth of another generation, both expatriates and nationalized foreigners had to join the struggle for full religious freedom.[10]

DAVID TRUMBULL AND ESSENTIAL GUARANTEES FOR RELIGIOUS FREEDOM[11]

Rev. David Trumbull, a Congregationalist/Presbyterian, became the champion of full religious freedom in Chile. He organized a Bible society in Valparaiso in 1861. In 1865 the Chilean legislature changed the article in the constitution that prohibited non-Catholic worship services. The next victory came in 1883 when the law of civil cemeteries was promulgated, followed by the law to establish civil registries for births and marriages. Finally legislation which granted *personeria juridica* (legal standing) to non-Catholic religious institutions was approved. The reaction of David Trumbull to these constitutional reforms was unique in the history of intercultural relations. He made a vow that if these laws were passed by the congress he would become a Chilean citizen, which he and his family did in 1884.

Then came the struggle for the right to evangelize in the Spanish language outside the walls of the church building. Since Trumbull had already quietly been doing this, he only continued and expanded his activities. Now it was legal for him as a Protestant who had become a Chilean citizen. However, since the early Protestants had lived for nearly four decades in a religious ghetto, the community was ill equipped to be transformed into an evangelizing church. For that and other reasons, Presbyterians have had slow growth in Chile even to the present.

The explosion of indigenous Protestantism in Chile did not happen within the Presbyterian Church but rather within the Methodist Church in 1909 with the birth of the Pentecostal movement. That first dramatic growth in Chilean Protestantism took place in the liberal port city of Valparaiso among the Methodists-turned-Pentecostals, in the same city where Trumbull spent his life struggling for religious freedom.

Religious Freedom in Other Parts of Latin America

Most countries took only small steps toward religious freedom for many decades: Venezuela established religious toleration by congressional decree in 1834, apparently only to encourage European immigration. Colombia decreed the separation of church and state in 1850, opening the way for the arrival of the first Protestant missionary, Rev. Henry B. Pratt, in 1856. Not until the liberal Constitution of 1857 was Protestant worship legal in Mexico. Freedom of worship was decreed by Justo Rufino Barrios in Guatemala in 1873 and by President Eloy Alfaro in Ecuador in 1895. Bolivia permitted the establishment of non-Catholic cemeteries as early as 1846, but delayed until 1905 the promulgation of the decree of freedom of worship. In most of Latin America the issues of full religious freedom were delayed until well into the twentieth century.

The Struggle Continues Today in a Different Context

In the 1990s religious freedom issues have again come to the fore in the light of the rapid growth of Evangelical Christianity in a culture which still has to grapple with fundamental rights of the coexistence of religious bodies in a democratic and pluralistic society. The question continues: Can a democratic society survive unless it offers all religions equal right to protection under the law, the guarantees of full exercise of public worship, and the right to propagate openly their religious beliefs?

THE PROTESTANT MISSIONARY MOVEMENT IN LATIN AMERICA

The Missionary Societies of North America and Europe

The first Protestant pastors and teachers were sent from North America, Great Britain, and Europe in response to the requests of foreign residents. The Methodist Episcopal Church, North, sent a pastor to Buenos Aires in 1833 and to

Rio de Janeiro in 1836. The Anglicans provided a chaplain for English colonists in Buenos Aires in 1831.

Some of the first consular officials of the United States, such as William Wheelwright in Chile, were active in the distribution of Scriptures from their homes by the 1830s. Merchants and sea captains who were active Evangelical Christians aided in the introduction of Bibles, Scripture portions, and Protestant literature.

Clergy were also sent in response to requests from spontaneous reform movements led by dissident Catholic clergy. Two examples are the Iglesia Evangelica Brasileira (1879) to which the Presbyterians responded and the Iglesia de Jesus in Mexico in the same year, for which the American Episcopalians provided clergy. However, these independent religious societies were a minority who sought foreign support more to bolster up their activities against powerful clerical opposition than to establish authentic Protestant churches. Both movements faded away.[12]

THE BEGINNINGS OF PERMANENT MISSIONARY WORK[13]

The pioneer missionary society in the United States was the American Board of Commissioners for Foreign Missions, founded in Boston in 1810. This agency was supported by Presbyterians and Congregationalists but did not become involved in Latin America until the late nineteenth century. This society was followed in 1817 by the United Foreign Missionary Society, a joint effort of the three Reformed church bodies in the United States. The South American Missionary Society, the first British society to enter South America, was founded as the result of the missionary work and martyrdom of Alan Gardiner in Patagonia in 1851.

The inauguration of work by the Presbyterian Church (1856, Colombia), the Methodist Episcopal Church, North (1839, Argentina), and the Methodist Episcopal Church, South (1845) marked the arrival of the major mission boards. Several mission boards were at work in Mexico by the early 1860s. The Northern Presbyterians sent their first missionary to Guatemala in 1883. The Central America Mission arrived in Costa Rica in 1891, the Regions Beyond Missionary Society in Peru in 1893; the Gospel Missionary Union began work in Ecuador in 1896, and the Scandinavian Missionary Alliance in Venezuela and Colombia in 1899. These mission societies founded the first permanent Protestant churches and schools from the banks of the Rio Grande in Mexico to the Straits of Magellan between 1845 and 1900.

Plymouth Brethren lay missionaries arrived in several South American countries from Canada and Great Britain in the 1880s and 1890s. An example of these self-supporting missionaries was the Bryant family from England. Mr. Bryant was employed as the manager of the Caracas-La Guaira railroad. They settled in Caracas in 1883.

The twentieth century witnessed the arrival of the Assemblies of God in Venezuela in 1900, the Church of the Nazarene in 1901, and the California

Friends Yearly Meeting in 1902 in Guatemala, the Evangelical Free Church in Venezuela in 1917, the Orinoco River Mission in 1921, the Oregon Friends Yearly Meeting in Bolivia in 1924, the Wycliffe Bible Translators in the 1940s, the New Tribes Mission to Venezuela in 1945, and the Interamerican Mission to Colombia in the same year. These are only a few of the dozens of American missionary societies which entered Latin America in the early years. Many of these societies were small and prone to splinter.

A Typical Statement of Purpose of a Mission Board

The constitutive act of the Methodist Episcopal Missionary Society stated its purpose as follows:

> The purpose is both charitable and religious and conceived in order to shed abroad the blessings of education and Christianity; to promote and support missionary schools and Christian missions through the United States, the American continent and foreign countries; to promote the use of the Bible, to seek the improvement of the moral and material conditions of the people and the education of the masses, giving to them all useful and practical knowledge, both human and divine.[14]

The society's declared purpose was to both civilize and evangelize, that is, to preach for conversion, to promote the living of holiness in the world, and to modernize society. In reality the Gospel which was presented had a high cultural content, equating, as has frequently happened in history, a particular cultural, economic, and political system with the message itself. The cultural core of the missionary societies was to be found largely in "the American way of life" of the developing middle classes of North America.

The Missionary

The first American missionaries were largely educated in universities and seminaries such as Harvard, Yale, Princeton, Vanderbilt, and Richmond. Later the societies recruited personnel who came from the farms, ranches, and villages of the expanding American frontier. These missionaries saw themselves as crusaders and "pioneers for Christ" such as those who had won the Far West. They felt they were being sent out to civilize and bring moral uplift by organizing churches and schools. Thus they would bring about in Latin America the same transformation as had been witnessed in the taming of the Western frontier of North America.

Generally the missionaries were recruited from the middle and upper classes of society and carried with them to Latin America many bourgeois attitudes. Many came from the South and Northeast of the United States. Some held racist attitudes toward blacks, Indians, and Mexicans. They reflected in their attitudes a cross-section of the class and racial biases present in American society. Most mission boards instructed their personnel to refrain from political involvement in the host country. This position may have served inadvertently as a model of political abstinence for national church leadership. A generation of young missionaries in the latter half of the twentieth century challenged these limitations and sometimes found themselves deeply into political issues! The prophetic dimension of most foreign missionaries was varied. A notable example of concern for international justice is seen in the work of certain missionaries of the Latin American Mission in Costa Rica in the 1920s.[15]

The missionary of the nineteenth century was usually convinced that with moral regeneration, economic benefits would soon follow. R. S. Storr's statement in 1889 to the American Board of Commissioners for Foreign Missions reflects the spirit of the period:

> Commerce and Gospel are in harmony on this at least, that the goal of each is cosmic. . . . It is not that our missionaries go out with this purpose, but wherever their teachings are accepted, there the road is open for expanding commerce.[16]

However, the American missionaries sent out in the 1960s were caught up in the controversies over the United States government's involvement in Vietnam and Cuba, and many questioned openly its policies, thus producing a new model of political concern for national church leadership. Gone were the days when missionaries could turn their focus away from blatant economic, social, and ideological challenges to Christian ideals.

THE CONGREGATION

The early missionaries gathered their converts into worshiping groups which had to survive in an inhospitable environment. In a certain sense these new congregations of believers were like the frontier communities of the West of the United States. They were seen as being in conflict with their neighbors ("indigenous people") as they struggled for space to create a new community, much like the settlers in the West.

The local congregation became the center of the life of its members. These first congregations quickly formed networks of mutual support, both economic and social. They also became seed beds of liberal political thought. For many individuals, membership in a Protestant congregation was their first experience with any sort of voluntary organization. There they learned leadership and organizational skills. Because of the emphasis on Bible study, most of the members were literate or became literate soon after their conversion. This was very impressive in majority-illiterate populations. Members were thus motivated and equipped to embrace new ideas about agriculture, health, and democratic institutions. Protestant congregations became laboratories for democracy in a society which had been built on authoritarian and patrimonial assumptions.

However, over the years, things have changed. According to Guillermo Cook: "As Evangelicals moved up in society through sobriety and hard work, they became more protective of their new status and thus more politically conservative. Thrust into the mainstream of Latin American life, Protestants are becoming afflicted by the same social malaise as their non-Protestant neighbors."[17]

THE PROTESTANT SCHOOL AND BOOKSTORE

One of the early contributions to Latin society by Protestants was the network of schools established by mission boards in large cities and provincial centers. The missionaries brought pedagogical innovations that challenged the nearly medieval educational system.

There was a conscious effort to build the school adjacent to the church building. This method was based on the popular Sunday School movement in Great Britain and the United States which was designed to use the facilities and personnel of the school for religious education on Sundays and weekday evenings. The Protestant educational enterprise was also designed to gain greater acceptance among the liberal sectors in society and recognition by governments of the contribution of missionary societies to the public welfare and cultural improvement. Many a Protestant school was named Colegio Americano to promote the United States as a cultural and political model. This also reflected the spirit of the times, which declared "the unity of the Americas," which was understood by North Americans in the terms of the Monroe Doctrine: "the Americas for the United States."

Schools often carried the names of persons who espoused liberal and anti-Catholic causes: Benito Juarez and Miguel Hidalgo in Mexico; David Trumbull in Chile; and Domingo Sarmiento in Argentina. Between 1880 and 1920 a network of dozens of Protestant schools was founded in most countries. Even persons like Pablo Neruda and Moises Saenz recognized the imprint of Protestant schools on their own character and ideas.

Closely related to the establishment of Protestant schools was the opening of publishing houses and bookstores in Mexico City, Santiago, Buenos Aires, São Paulo, La Habana, San Juan, Santo Domingo, San José, and Lima. In 1920 a journal of liberal Protestant thought, *La Nueva Democracia,* began a forty-year publication history which offered editorial space to emerging liberal voices of the continent such as Luis Alberto Sanchez, Gabriela Mistral, and their contemporaries. Protestant periodicals appeared—*El Evangelista Colombiano, La Estrella de la Mañana, Estandarte,* and *El Mensajero Cristiano*—as well as a few local newspapers published by Protestants.

COUNCILS OF CHURCHES AND INTERDENOMINATIONAL SEMINARIES

Missionary societies were involved in promoting and funding the first national councils of Protestant churches. These councils sponsored united programs of Christian education and youth, student, and women's work. United seminaries were organized in Mexico City, Santiago, Buenos Aires, San Juan, and São Paulo in the 1920s and 1930s which served to establish "a liberal face" of Protestantism in the preparation of pastors and lay leaders. The YMCA and the YWCA were established early in the twentieth century in major cities in Latin America and served as a cultural bridge between North American and Latin American cultures and between Protestants and Roman Catholics. However, the numerical growth and cultural penetration of Protestantism was not significant until the last four decades of the twentieth century.

PROTESTANT IDENTITY: BOTH LIBERAL AND EVANGELICAL

Most of the early Protestants were both liberal and Evangelical; that is to say, they supported causes of liberty, equality, civilian government, rights of women, popular education, and public welfare. Despite their confessional diversity, Methodists, Presbyterians, Baptists, Episcopalians, and Lutherans shared much of the same theology. They professed complete confidence in the Bible and full salvation through the atoning death of Christ. They affirmed salvation by grace, and good works were evidence of true belief, not the justification for salvation. In summary, "sola fe, sola escritura, solo Cristo" (only faith, only Scripture, only Christ) were their common ground for evangelization. They were interested in social betterment, but not always willing to deal with the root causes of poverty and corruption in society. They reflected largely an individual, Christ-centered religion based on "the Gospel" (*El Evangelio*).

However, they were at the same time conscious of the absolute need for the full exercise of religious freedom. They were not always willing to tackle the deeper problems of structural injustice, but positioned themselves in society so that they were seen as friends of social change. They appeared to shy away from encouraging political involvement in the early years. They acted as most minorities which were seeking a safe place to exist in society. Alberto Rembao referred to the liberal/Evangelical Protestant movement in the 1950s as "an Evangelical nation." This was to be understood as an emerging subculture which presented fresh options for human transformation and social change. Rembao referred to "la transculturación religiosa" which was taking place in Latin America through Protestant ideas and practices.[18]

THE CONTRIBUTIONS OF PENTECOSTALISM

The advent of Pentecostalism, less than a century ago, offered a new dimension of Protestant identity. Pentecostalism offered a revolutionary alternative to traditional Catholicism and Protestantism by virtually eliminating the distinction between qualified agents of religious discourse (the clergy) and the public which consumes "religious goods." In this sense, it offers common people "a religious experience of which they can be subjects and not mere objects."[19] Pentecostals developed pastoral strategies which take into account the deep problems of Latin American society and they believe that God can intervene to create a society of justice, health, and love.[20] Pentecostalism promotes an independent religious syncretism and a world view (*cosmovisión*) opposed to that held by the dominant culture. Levine views Protestantism, not as an expression of anomie or a retreat from the world, but as a creative response to changing social conditions that adjusts the religious message to fit the varying conditions of life.[21] Cook further affirms that Pentecostals see themselves as engaged in a holy war; they are buoyed up by a hope of "a final struggle" that will re-create the social order.[22]

Pentecostalism has definitely presented "a new face" of Protestantism in Latin America. The historic churches clearly have lost their monopoly over the religious life of Latin American society. This is true for both historic Catholicism and Protestantism. As Dennis Smith has stated, "Each day there are fewer spaces left in society where Catholics, Protestants, and indigenous religions can form common sociopolitical and cultural projects. The ecumenical movement is in crisis."[23] Much of this has come about because of the advent and dramatic growth of Pentecostalism.

Pentecostals present a challenge to both historic Protestantism and Catholicism in relation to evangelization. A significant Catholic-Pentecostal dialogue has continued over the past two decades, both at a theological and a practical level. "Pentecostals are better at new evangelization—ultimate challenges, decisions, and conversions—than we are" comments Killian McDonnell, the Catholic co-chair of the Vatican-sponsored dialogue with Pentecostals. Edward Cleary sees a Christian Church "united in purpose and spirit even if not in ecclesiastical structure, working together to evangelize the world."[24]

Sociologists and historians will now refer to "the Protestantisms" of Latin America. As was true after the Protestant Reformation of the sixteenth century, time is required to sort out the impact of these new ideas in the dominant culture. Latin American culture will continue to struggle to grant to the Protestant religious phenomenon its proper identity. Perhaps we must settle on recognizing "the many faces of Protestantism," as we have now come to identify the several expressions of Roman Catholicism.

ECUMENICAL COOPERATION BETWEEN THE CHURCHES

The new ecumenical crisis leads us to examine again the origin of this movement in the twentieth century and the situation it faces today.

The use of *ecumenical* in modern religious terminology came out of the geopolitical writings of the late nineteenth century. Count Keyserling wrote about forces in the modern world which had erased old boundaries and thus brought about new political configurations. Mission leaders such as John A. Mackay pioneered the use of the term *ecumenical* in religious circles. The term soon became identified with the movement toward Christian unity. Mackay wrote about "ecumenics as the science of the Church Universal." He referred also to "the ecumenical quadrilateral" which includes relationships between

Christianity and non-Christian religions, between the churches which make up Christianity, between non-Christian ideologies and Christian thought, and relationships within the historic missionary movement itself.[25]

Two aspects of the many-faceted expressions of ecumenism in Latin America have become increasingly important to the historic churches: relationships between Roman Catholics and Protestant Christians, and relationships among the Protestant churches themselves.

ROMAN CATHOLIC–PROTESTANT RELATIONSHIPS

There is ample record of the bitter persecution of Protestants by the Roman Catholic hierarchy over the last five hundred years. The record is one of mutual vituperation and condemnation. The bitter legacy of religious strife in Europe, Great Britain, and North America became the patrimony of both Roman Catholics and Protestants in Latin America.

However, even when the war became a "cold war" in the earlier part of the twentieth century, the issues of ecumenical understanding were not really faced until the advent of the Bible studies movement in the 1920s, the rediscovery of Latin America as a "mission field" by religious orders like Maryknoll in the 1940s, and the prophetic vision of leaders like Pope John XXIII in the late 1950s. By the mid-1950s the Chimbote (Peru) Catholic Action Congress sounded a call "to evangelize a dechristianized continent . . . where people live in actual neopaganism."[26] Before the Second Vatican Council had completed its work in 1965, it was clear that a new day in ecumenism had dawned.

The large number of Protestant observers invited to attend the Second Vatican Council was evidence of the intention of Rome to improve ecumenical relationships. However, it should be noted that those observers did not include many conservative theologians. Evangelical Protestants were wary of "getting too close to Rome."[27] The Secretariat on Christian Unity, formed after the Second Vatican Council, and ably led by Cardinal Willebrand of Holland, initiated a series of inter-church and inter-confessional dialogues which are still continuing three decades later.

In Latin America significant conferences of Latin American bishops were held in Medellín in 1968 and Puebla in 1979 in which the recommendations of the Second Vatican Council were considered for implementation. Protestant observers were invited to Medellín, but not to Puebla. Sharp differences emerged among the Latin American hierarchy over the meaning of *aggiornamento* in the church in today's world.

Separated brothers and sisters has been until recently the proper term to describe Protestant-Catholic relations. However, the present pope seems to be reconsidering this term. Guidelines for ecumenical dialogue were established in the 1960s, and interfaith marriages are looked upon with more tolerance. Until the death of John XXIII, there was significant progress in ecumenical relations. However, during the reign of Paul VI and John Paul II, the present pope, there has been a marked slowdown of grassroots ecumenism in Latin

America. Some of the serious issues of religious freedom in Latin America today are related to the near stagnation of ecumenical dialogue and related activities.

We should not overlook the progress made in cooperation in the translation and distribution of the Bible, in theological education, and in missionary studies. Perhaps the emergence of the Catholic charismatic movement, in which personal religious experience and testimony are considered essential to a vital Christian faith, may provide a bridge for fresh dialogue.[28] Edward Cleary is encouraged by the signs of renewed interest in ecumenical dialogue. He argues that the appeal of Protestantism offers a challenge to Catholic theologians and that non-Catholic religious growth is "a sign of the times and to be taken as part of the condition of God's people." He even goes so far as to suggest that Protestants and Catholics are "either rivals or siblings."[29] There are increasing signs of practical ecumenism in seminary education and collaboration in the writing of church history.

Some breakthrough has taken place in ecumenical relations in other parts of Christendom despite the lack of Vatican support. One example is the study commission in the Czech Republic formed by Catholics and Reformed Churches to study the period of history in which both non-Catholics and Catholics committed atrocities in the name of the Christian religion.[30]

The opinion of the aged Benedictine Godfrey Diekmann, a prominent figure of the Second Vatican Council, is stated clearly:

> Vatican II is by far the most radical, the most productive document and the most challenging document in the whole history of the Church, and we weren't ready for it. . . . I think we are suffering now as Roman Catholics with a collective stomach ache. We swallowed too much![31]

In the spirit of the Second Vatican Council, both Catholics and Protestants seem to be inclined to continue to take initiatives to right the wrongs of past intolerance and to ask probing questions as to future relationships.

Relationships among Protestants

In reality the past fifty years have witnessed parallel movements of Protestant cooperation. One stream began in the Congress on Christian Work in Latin America held in the Canal Zone, Panama, in 1916. Six subsequent continental conferences have been held in which most of the historic Protestant churches participated. Out of this movement came the Committee on Cooperation in Latin America (1913-63), which then merged to form the Latin America and Caribbean Department of the National Council of Churches, U.S.A. By 1983, from this movement within the historic churches, joined by several indigenous Pentecostal and independent churches, emerged the Latin American Council of Churches (CLAI).

The other stream of Protestant cooperation traces its origins to a meeting in San Jose in 1948. This movement represents largely "the non-conciliar" mission boards and churches which have chosen not to relate to ecumenical bodies and agencies such as the World Council of Churches. They trace their origins to the Holiness, Keswick, and Pentecostal movements during the first part of the twentieth century. Out of this movement emerged CONELA, an evangelistic association of Evangelical radio stations, media outlets, radio preachers, and joint publications.

Denominational Continent-wide Organizations of Churches

As cooperation was developing between denominations, Methodists, Presbyterians, Lutherans, and Episcopalians set up cooperative bodies among their member churches. However, there often appeared greater diversity within denominations than between denominations. Presbyterians organized as the Association of Presbyterian and Reformed Churches in Latin America (AIPRAL), which is now a section of the World Alliance of Presbyterian and Reformed Churches. The Methodists have organized along a similar pattern which relates to worldwide Methodism.

CLAI—The Latin American Council of Churches[32]

It became clear in the early 1960s that the time had come for an indigenous Protestant body to come into being in Latin America which was not controlled by North Americans. The historic churches took the initiative, supported by the World Council of Churches, to bring into being a Provisional Commission on Ecumenical Unity in 1964. The secretary chosen was an Uruguayan Methodist, Emilio Castro, who later became the general secretary of the World Council of Churches. This body would not have come into being without the support of many Evangelical and Pentecostal churches who were seeking a continental organization for Protestant identity and joint mission activities.

The steps toward the organization of CLAI were completed in 1983 and had taken two decades. The organization had been forged slowly and firmly as an authentic "Latin American organism for Protestant cooperation." However, even now, after four continental meetings (1983, 1988, 1992, and 1996), CLAI is far from mature. In 1997 a continental conference in San Jose (celebrating the eightieth anniversary of the historic Panama conference) was called by the Latin America and Caribbean Department of the National Council of Churches, U.S.A., to explore further the most effective form of ecumenical work for the coming millennium.

Two noted absences at the 1997 meeting in San Jose were Pentecostal and Roman Catholic delegations. Such an omission does not bode well for expanded ecumenical cooperation in the next decade. Ecumenical cooperation in Latin America is still far from complete after eighty years of cooperative endeavors.

MATURING HISTORIC PROTESTANTISM

A dynamic movement is always in the process of change. This is not always understood in relation to religious institutions, since there is a subtle implication that those institutions are by nature unchangeable. A unique aspect of Protestantism is "the reforming principle" implicit in the slogan *ecclesia reformata, semper reformando* (a reformed church is always a reforming church). Because of the principle of private interpretation of Holy Scripture, varieties of church government, and differing doctrinal standards, Protestantism will always find itself changing, yet changing within the parameters of this principle.

Rapid Social and Political Change

Latin America is today a more egalitarian and open society. The possibility for significant social and political change for the masses is greater today despite all the factors which have conspired to delay the coming new day. The enhanced role of women in society has also been a key factor in change despite major cultural attitudes which resist change. Latin America in the 1990s offers a more propitious atmosphere for the growth of Protestantism than the 1950s. This changing situation has encouraged the historic churches to understand more clearly their role in a changing society.

Changes in the Strategies of Mission Boards

Most mission boards awakened to the need for changes in strategies in the 1960s. Those changes brought about two significant results: changes in priorities in the use of personnel and funds; and changed attitudes within church leadership, both on the part of the "sending" and "receiving" churches. This has brought about today's "partnership in mission" concepts to replace old mission strategies.

The term *missionary* was softened in its cultural implications by the introduction of the name *fraternal worker* or *co-worker* by some boards in the 1960s. Foreign personnel were sent out by mission boards to serve for specific terms of service, not "for life." *Missions* and *mission stations* language was dropped in favor of *cooperating churches* and *work locations*. Fewer fraternal workers were assigned to pioneer evangelism and new church development, which became a major task of the national churches. Fraternal workers were now assigned more frequently to supporting ministries and ecumenical programs. In a few instances after the Second Vatican Council, assignments were made to work with Roman Catholics in joint mission programs.

After three decades of deliberate changes in mission strategies and in the use of mission personnel and funds, certain definite trends can be noted: a new openness to social involvement by some congregations, less suspicion of political involvement by individual members, and a growing awareness of the negative effects of maintaining sectarian attitudes toward other Christians. These changes came about at a high cost for some national churches. There were major divisions in Presbyterian denominations in Brazil, Chile, Venezuela, Colombia, and most recently in Guatemala which resulted largely from changing positions on social issues and the involvement by the churches in political issues. Other historic denominations have had the same experience.

GREATER INVOLVEMENT IN SOCIAL ISSUES

Even though a conservative theological position was maintained by most of the historic Protestant churches, there has been a growing awareness since the 1960s that the churches had to reevaluate their traditional aloofness toward society. Their leadership is now coming to realize that if they fail to respond to these challenges, their churches will not grow numerically and will betray their Protestant heritage of serving as a prophetic voice. (It should be noted that the situation in Central America was unique in that the fundamentalists and dispensationalists had set the agenda for this debate rather than the historic churches, as in South American countries. In Central America, historic Protestantism really did not play a prophetic role until the 1970s and 1980s.[33])

The Church and Society Movement (ISAL)

La Iglesia y Sociedad Movement, organized in Peru in 1961, was based on clearly stated theological premises:

- All Christian action grows from the conviction that God is present both in all of history and in concrete historic situations;
- Christians should recognize Jesus Christ as the Lord of history and therefore present in the here and now, not just in some abstract sense; and
- this assurance does not simplify the task of the Church but rather reminds us constantly of the need to discover Christ's presence in the events of history [from the statement of the purpose of ISAL].[34]

A second ISAL consultation was held in Rio de Janeiro in 1963 with a focus on "The Church and Social Service and Action." This meeting served to sharpen the focus on social service as one of the means of the proclamation of the Gospel, but not limiting social action only to social service.

Dissension within the Churches over Involvement

By taking this position, ISAL became actively involved in social-justice activities. Many church leaders and members were uncomfortable with this level of involvement in social movements. They felt it was acceptable "to do good works," but that it was dangerous to attack openly the root causes of poverty, such as unjust land distribution and government budget priorities, through revolutionary action. By 1966, at the third ISAL consultation in El Tabo, Chile, the movement asked the churches to state clearly the nature of their opposition to radical social involvement by the churches and to enter into meaningful dialogue with their members. It is important to note that revolutionary movements in the 1960s in Cuba, Colombia, Brazil, and Bolivia included Protestant students in their ranks: Frank Pais (Cuban), son of a Baptist minister; Néstor Paz (Bolivian Methodist); and Paulo Wright (Brazilian), also the son of U.S. Presbyterian missionaries. Roman Catholics were experiencing the same tensions and many of their student leaders and priests identified with the ISAL movement.

In Brazil matters became critical in 1964 when several ISAL leaders were expelled from their positions in the Department of Social Responsibility of the Federation of Evangelical Churches of Brazil. Some were jailed by military governments in the late 1960s and 1970s. At least one leader was "disappeared" in Argentina around 1973.

The contribution of ISAL to the social consciousness of the leadership of the mainline churches is unparalleled in Protestant history in Latin America. Even though the movement has been of incalculable value in the maturing of the churches, there seems to have been a loss of the sense of transcendence and mystery in religious commitment. The religious "progressives" found it difficult to balance their political projects with a vibrant and profound religious experience. This has been confirmed in a study of the Christian Student Movement in the 1960s and 1970s in that "it was restricted to a small group . . . which survived on foreign funding, but [was] not given to personal piety . . . a group of insiders which nearly fits into a 'sect' typology in the same way a sect claims a monopoly on universal meaning."[35]

Even though the historic churches held that certain ideological currents were still suspect, facing these issues brought about programs to train seminary students and pastors for more responsible social involvement and helped church members present a Christian witness in concrete situations related to social justice. By the close of the 1970s there had been a reaffirmation by historic Protestantism of a historic Protestant voice which was more prophetic. However, "the reformation in Latin America" cannot be compared in this sense to the Reformation of the sixteenth century in Europe. The context is different and many of the issues dissimilar.

HISTORIC PROTESTANT CHURCHES AND MILITARY GOVERNMENTS

There was a great diversity in the response of the churches to military regimes. In the early part of the twentieth century, the Protestant community was so small that its attitudes rarely came into conflict with authoritarian governments. In the 1930s in Guatemala, a veteran Presbyterian missionary, Paul Burgess, was called to task by President Jorge Ubico for derogatory remarks about his government in Burgess's popular tract *Tio Perucho*. The president's representative suggested to Burgess that he should let the government office check the next issue before it went to press![36]

In Venezuela in the 1920s, few Protestants spoke out against the tyranny of General Juan Vicente Gómez. It is reported that the dictator once commented: "When Venezuela becomes Evangelical, I will sleep unarmed in the public plaza!" Quite a comment on Protestant moral insensitivity to the behavior of a tyrant like Gómez!

Colombia and Civil Strife in the 1940s and 1950s

The struggle for religious freedom and the return to democracy in Colombia went hand in hand as civil war took a heavy toll in Protestant lives and church property. An eminent historian of that period wrote:

> Protestant persecution was a symptom of deeply held antagonism between Catholics and Protestants. The civil war in the countryside was carried out in the context of animosity between Liberals and Conservatives which often appeared as conflict between Catholics and Protestants. Thus, even though politically there seemed to be a confusion between Liberals and Protestants, persecution for religious motivation can not be hidden. Few forces in history are more merciless and savagely unChristian than those which arise from religious conflict and intolerance.[37]

Most Protestants were Liberals (or sympathized with their goals), and Protestants were persecuted both because of their political leanings and for their beliefs, which bothered the Conservatives. When the military government came to power in the 1950s, there was an opening for lessening the violence, not because the issues of religious prejudice went away, but because the Rojas Pinilla government was looking for a way to bridge the Liberal-Conservative split. The behind-the-scenes initiatives of North American Catholic clergy during the early 1950s played a significant role in the restoration of civil rights for non-Catholics.

Guatemala and Forty Years of Civil Strife

According to veteran missionary Dennis Smith, Guatemalan Evangelicals did not behave differently during the conflict from the general population. In rural areas, a certain sector of Evangelicals (both historic Protestants and Pentecostals) supported the insurgents. Another sector supported the counterinsurgency projects implemented by the armed forces. Both sides frequently supported their political options with their theological interpretations. Another sector, larger still, fled the conflict. In the towns and the capital city, few Evangelicals concerned themselves with the conflict, much less took sides. Fewer still chose to participate directly in the peace process. Urban Evangelicals expressed their concerns by supporting local projects to combat poverty, but few of those involved in such projects questioned the system that produced such evils. City dwellers often chose to ignore the horrible reality of the conflict, thus losing their ability to feel and relate to the pain of the others.[38]

The situation was aggravated by the questionable moral leadership of the two "Evangelical" presidents, Efrain Rios Montt and José Serrano. These leaders soured the attitudes of many Conservative Evangelicals toward the military regime, since they used the military to maintain the status quo and were discredited by most thoughtful Protestants.

Cuba and Nicaragua; Military Power and Social Change

In the rise to power of Fidel Castro, there were sharp divisions among Cuban Protestants in support of the new regime. The large majority chose to go into exile rather than adjust to the new social order. U.S. mission boards were asked to leave and their schools were confiscated. Since many of the mission boards paid the salaries of pastors and teachers, those bodies helped their former employees relocate in the United States, using refugee funds from both the churches and the federal government. Of the thirty-six Presbyterian pastors in Cuba, only ten decided to remain.

In Nicaragua twenty years later, a larger percentage of pastors remained and supported the Sandinista regime. It should be noted, however, that the international situation had changed considerably between 1959 and 1979 in terms of the fear of communism as a threat to the churches. Also, the "Contra War" was a strong deterrent to a Sandinista move farther to the political left. The historic churches also had had more experience in dealing with revolutionary governments by the 1980s and did not feel as threatened by the Sandinistas as they did by the Castro regime.

Military Governments of the Right: Brazil (1965-83);Argentina (1966-73; 1976-83); Uruguay (1968-78); and Chile (1973-90)

In Brazil the older historic churches, especially the Lutherans, gave tacit support to the military regime during the initial period of its rule. Presbyterians, Methodists, Episcopalians, and Baptists were divided in their support. Only when the military began to threaten, imprison, and torture church leaders and members who opposed the regime did some pastors and lay leaders challenge the morality of military rule. However, at least two of the major Pentecostal bodies continued to support openly the military regime until its demise. The situations in Argentina and Uruguay were quite similar in that the historic churches opposed the regime in principle but had to deal with sharp differences within their congregations and thus failed to make public statements.

In Chile after the 1973 coup it was a Lutheran bishop who spoke out against the military junta and became a unifying voice in the Committee for Peace. This committee and its successor body brought together an interfaith movement which opposed the brutality of the regime. Bishop Helmut Franz was subsequently exiled for his leadership in this movement. In the mid-1980s a confederation of Protestant churches made bold statements and held prayer vigils and public manifestations which helped strengthen public opposition and the inevitable return to democracy.

STRENGTHS AND WEAKNESSES OF HISTORIC CHURCHES

There can be little doubt that two of the strengths of the older denominations have been their record of service to the people and the preparation of their pastors and lay leaders. The educational work of Protestant schools and their social agencies of health, rural development, and child welfare have been considered by the public sector as important contributions to the public good. The historic congregations have made their presence felt in large cities and provincial centers over several generations. Many denominations, though relatively small in membership, include in their membership persons who are active in civic societies and recognized for their public service.

The historic denominations were tolerated, if not accepted, as legitimate institutions in public life. They did not usually seek special privileges because of their religious nature, as often the Roman Catholic hierarchy did. However, there were early missionaries, like the Presbyterian John C. Hill in Guatemala, who received the patronage of President Justo Rufino Barrios. It is not clear if those favors were actively sought or offered by the government. Nonetheless, the image the early missionaries projected was more of service and concern for the moral well-being of society than of a desire to seek political favors. The early denominations were observed as practicing a measure of democracy within their congregations and thus served to promote democratic practices in the body politic. They also served as a means for the poor and disenfranchised to advance to the middle class.

The councils of churches which came into being in the 1930s and 1940s served to address common issues of religious freedom and to be points of dialogue between the government and Protestant religious institutions. These councils of churches usually represented mainly the older denominations and the newly formed churches who were seeking recognition and in need of advocacy.

Many leaders in the historic churches took strong stands early in the twentieth century on issues related to child labor, women's rights, and the need for societal changes at Protestant conferences in Panama (1916), Montevideo (1925), and Havana (1929). Mexican Protestants were deeply involved in the Mexican Revolution. Moises Saenz was a key figure in the creation of the first governmental office in Mexico to address the educational and social needs of indigenous Mexicans. Protestants founded the first modern schools of nursing in Puerto Rico, Costa Rica, and Guatemala in the 1920s. In the 1950s, graduates of the Presbyterian school La Progresiva in Cuba were among the founders of the insurrection movement against Batista.

However, historic Protestant churches tended to gravitate toward the middle class and move away from the disenfranchised masses. The historic denominations also tended to facilitate upward social mobility and thus found themselves to be less in tune with the agenda of the masses.

Historic Protestants sometimes lost their potential to evangelize because they found a "safe place" in a previously hostile society and chose to rest on their laurels. The churches may also have taken for granted religious freedom and forgotten that it was a right which must be exercised through continuing evangelizing activity or be held in jeopardy. The churches have often failed to build upon the role they played in early Protestant history as heralds of new ideas and innovators of change in the religious, social, and political realms. It is yet to be seen if the historic churches will reclaim their Reformation heritage and apply it creatively to the present challenges in Latin America. No historical movement can be blamed for failing to mold future generations by its highest ideals. However, it can be judged by its understanding of what it can control, that is, its immediate history. This is the challenge of the historic churches today.

3.

EVANGELICAL CHURCHES

———————◆———————

Pedro C. Moreno

The chapter that follows provides an overview of the impact of evangelistic efforts (called by some proselytization) on church-state relations as well as relations among churches in Latin America. The first part describes the significant growth of Evangelical[1] churches in the region and the role of television in spreading the Evangelical and the Catholic messages. The chapter then reviews the frictions and conflicts created by the growth of Evangelicalism in a largely Catholic culture. Recent legal and constitutional efforts to provide for religious freedom are discussed as well as recent examples of discrimination and intolerance by Evangelicals against Catholics and vice versa.

The chapter then outlines the extent to which Evangelical churches (including Pentecostal ones) relate to so-called historic Protestant churches, mainly through the interactions of the Latin American Council of Churches (CLAI) and the Latin American Evangelical Fellowship (CONELA). The next section deals with Evangelicals' growing presence in the political realm, in the framework of Evangelicals' theological and practical considerations. Next follows an analysis of the socioeconomic impact of Evangelicals as they abandon old habits and create a new identity. Lastly, a self-critique is provided in terms of the strengths and weaknesses of the Evangelical and especially the Pentecostal movement. The chapter concludes with a note of hope that the rise of Evangelicalism in Latin America may prove to be positive for society at large, but also a sobering reminder that, as in any effort in which human beings are involved, there are serious problems in the Evangelical movement (especially among Pentecostals) that must be kept in check and corrected, if Latin America will truly benefit from this unprecedented religious resurgence.

EXPANSION OF EVANGELICAL, PENTECOSTAL, AND FUNDAMENTALIST ACTIVITY

The growth of Latin America's Evangelical (and especially Pentecostal) population has been dramatic. In 1980, Evangelicals in Latin America numbered twenty-one million, and they more than doubled to forty-six million by 1990.[2] Today it is estimated that there are close to sixty million, with eight thousand Latin American converts to Evangelicalism every day, according to the Latin American Catholic Bishops' Conference. Recent statistics show that Pentecostals account for two out of every three Evangelicals in Latin America, and that nearly 40 percent of the world's Pentecostals live in Latin America.[3] In some Latin American countries Evangelicals make up 7 to 35 percent of the population—becoming, in Guatemala, Brazil, and Nicaragua, more numerous than practicing Catholics.

TELE-EVANGELISM IN LATIN AMERICA

One of the most effective ways in which Evangelicalism has spread in Latin America is through radio and, mostly in the last five years, through television. The phenomenon is not limited to North American "tele-evangelists"; there is now a surge in "native" Latin American tele-evangelists as well. Moreover, even the Catholic church has established religion-specific television and radio networks and local TV stations in the region. A sample of evangelistic/religious ministries broadcasting via television and radio in Latin America follows.[4]

NORTH AMERICAN TELE-EVANGELISTS BROADCASTING IN LATIN AMERICA

- Pat Robertson, The 700 Club, via television in sixteen countries.
- Jimmy Swaggart, via GEM Satellite Television Network reaching all countries in Latin America, and via three individual TV stations in Brazil.
- Benny Hinn, via television to twelve countries.
- Billy Graham, mostly via radio in seven countries.
- Hermano Pablo (Paul Finkenbinder), via TV to fourteen countries, and twenty-eight countries by radio.
- Alberto Mottessi (Argentinean-born), via TV in seven countries, and eighteen countries via radio.
- Luis Palau (Argentinean-born), via radio only, in twenty countries.

Live TV satellite broadcasts in Spanish from the United States to Latin America are becoming more frequent. The largest and most recent broadcast was that of Promise Keepers' Sacred Assembly of Men that took place in Washington, D.C., on October 4, 1997.

LATIN AMERICAN TELE-EVANGELISTS

- Alberto Salcedo, Pastor of Ekklesía Church, La Paz, Bolivia, broadcasts via ENLACE satellite television network to twenty-two countries (100 individual TV stations), in all Latin American countries except Cuba. ENLACE is based in Costa Rica and was established in conjunction with the Trinity Broadcasting Network (TBN, Paul Crouch) based in the United States.
- Yiye Ávila, based in Puerto Rico, broadcasts via GE285 television satellite to ten TV stations (and about twelve radio stations) in about 10 countries in Latin America.
- Edir Macedo, Universal Church of the Kingdom of God, based in Brazil, broadcasts via twenty TV stations, mostly within Brazil. His TV network is ranked second at the national level (O Globo being the largest).
- ALAS satellite established by HCJB Radio and TransWorld Radio, based in Quito, Ecuador, broadcasts via a network of sixty radio stations (forty-five of them evangelistic and the rest commercial) reaching eleven countries. It broadcasts twenty-four hours a day.

In addition there are close to a thousand radio stations in nearly all countries and regions of Latin America broadcasting evangelistic programming.

CATHOLIC TELE-EVANGELISM

Recently, the Catholic church has established specifically religion-based radio and TV stations. There are nine Catholic TV stations in eight countries, and others are being established in other Latin American countries.

Eternal Word Television Network (EWTN) based in the United States broadcasts religious/evangelistic/doctrinal Catholic programming into Latin America. The most prominent program in this network is "Mother Angelica Live," which broadcasts via Pan Am SAT3 television satellite to all of Latin America except Cuba. EWTN also broadcasts via short-wave radio to all Latin American countries including Cuba, and through fifty-six local radio stations.

The impact of tele-evangelists (Evangelical and Catholic) is clearly felt at the religious level, with many people converting to Evangelicalism through Evangelical TV programs and others apparently renewing their faith in Catholicism through Catholic TV programs. Tele-evangelism, however, has less of an impact at the ideological/political level. When North American Evangelical tele-evangelists venture into these areas (e.g., supporting North American military strikes against Iraq), Latin American Evangelicals usually do not support, even oppose, or are indifferent to these actions. Most Evangelicals in Latin America would declare themselves conservative, not so much because of the North American tele-evangelists' influence, but for theological reasons. Of course, in terms of worship styles, theological positions, and other church affairs, there is much influence coming from the North American tele-evangelists.

PROBLEMS OF A MILITANT PROTESTANTISM
IN A CATHOLIC CULTURE

From Intolerance to Tolerance, Liberty, and Efforts toward Equality

Undeniably, religious intolerance has diminished greatly in Latin America, and unprecedented positive steps, in some instances with the active participation of the Catholic church, have been taken to secure an environment of religious freedom for all. Catholicism has been the traditional, or in some cases the state, religion in Latin American countries for hundreds of years. Its traditions have been woven into the social fabric of Latin America at both the state and local community level. As long as the fabric held, the Catholic church was secure, despite the fact that the baptized masses went largely uncatechized and that in many countries movements of radical secularism challenged church hegemony and weakened it in the process.[5] In general, the social structure has been largely resistant to change.

Church and state relations have been a controversial topic, especially after the founding of the different Latin American republics at the beginning of the nineteenth century. Many of the *"Libertadores"* (Liberators) were opposed by the traditional church because of their support of the separation of church and state.[6] Simón Bolivar, one of Latin America's greatest thinkers, in presenting his draft Constitution for Bolivia, which did not include any reference to religion, declared: "The state cannot rule the conscience of the subjects, neither by reward or punishment, because God is the only (higher) power. Religion is the law of conscience. Any law about it nullifies it, because since it imposes this duty, it takes away the value of faith which is the basis of religion."[7] He further stated: "The sacred precepts and dogmas are useful, beautiful, and of metaphysical evidence. We all know how to profess them, but this duty is moral, not political. Since (religion) is of divine jurisdiction, at first sight it seems to me sacrilegious and profane to mix our ordinances with the commandments of the Lord. To prescribe religion, thus, does not belong to legislators."[8]

Bolivar's position on church and state issues, however, changed over time: From 1819 to 1826 he held that religion should not be mentioned in the constitutional text. Thus neither his draft of the Constitution of Angostura nor of the Constitution of Bolivia mention an official religion. By 1828, Bolivar in his organic decree and his message to the "Admirable Congress" of 1830 expresses the need for the establishment and protection of the Catholic religion as the official one.[9]

José Artigas, Liberator of Uruguay, addressing the 1813 Constitutional Convention and openly favoring religious liberty for all, stated, "We shall promote civil and religious liberty to its maximum imaginable extent."[10] Vicente Rocafuerte, an Ecuador-born patriot and one of the intellectual leaders of the independence movement in Latin America, himself a Catholic, recognized that in the United States the relationship between church and state had been remarkably resolved by separating these two institutions. In 1831, in an age hostile to liberty of conscience and worship, Rocafuerte wrote his book *Essay on Religious Tolerance* in which he stated that "a dominant religion is oppressive: that is why the early Christians were also persecuted." For him the separation of church and state was "the genius of the century."[11]

In spite of the Liberators' strong conviction and support for the institutional separation of church and state, most, if not all, of the Latin American constitutions established the Roman Catholic Church as the "official church" of the state to the exclusion of any other religious faith. This was due to the strong influence the Catholic church exercised on the members of the various constitutional conventions, who for the most part professed the Catholic religion.

However, almost two hundred years have elapsed since that time, and currently only a few Latin American countries still have an "official" or established church—Argentina, Bolivia, and Costa Rica. The rest of the Latin American republics have been able to achieve a degree of church-state separation, at least constitutionally, although in practice there is still a strong state bias toward the Roman Catholic Church.

A sampling of countries categorized according to their laws and practices related to religious freedom could be given as follows:

Equality	Colombia (at the constitutional level)
Liberty	Brazil, Peru, Paraguay, Chile
Tolerance	Mexico, Argentina, Bolivia, Costa Rica
Intolerance	Cuba

Some recent examples of legal and constitutional changes concerning religious freedom include the following:

On November 6, 1996, a new law granting Protestant Christians in Chile full religious rights and equal legal status with the Roman Catholic Church, passed the Chamber of Deputies by a unanimous vote.[12] However, the Senate raised objections as a result of the Catholic church's opposition to the draft law, and its full passage is doubtful (for further details see the chapter on Chile in this volume).

In Costa Rica a law was passed in 1996 amending Articles 147 and 148 of the Costa Rican Labor Code, regarding work days and holidays. As a result, workers of different religions are now entitled to obtain permission to observe their religious holidays.[13]

In Ecuador, while Alfaro's Constitution of 1906 guaranteed freedom of thought, freedom of association, religious tolerance, and separation of church and state, it is the Constitution of 1979 and the reforms introduced on January 11, 1995, that guarantee freedom of religion. Freedom of worship is constitutionally guaranteed, as is the right to practice the religion of one's choice. The Constitution also prohibits discrimination on the basis of religion.[14]

In Argentina, despite strong support for the separation of church and state, the 1994 Constitutional Convention did not modify Article 2 of the Constitution. The Roman Catholic Church continues to enjoy "support" from the state and holds a dominant place in society. The Secretary of Religious Affairs maintains that "non-Catholic creeds have a status that is not inferior, but different."[15] However, the 1994 amended Constitution eliminated Article 76, which had required that the president and vice-president be Roman Catholic. Article 93 of the new Constitution establishes that the president and vice-president will take an oath (that invokes God) before the congress in order to take office, but that their religious beliefs will be respected. Article 14 recognizes the right of Argentineans to "profess their religion freely." Article 17 prohibits discrimination against workers on grounds of religious reasons and Article 19 exempts from the authority of the magistrates the private actions of people in relation to God that do not offend public order or morality, or harm a third person.

In Bolivia, a special Congress met in July and August of 1994 in order to amend the Constitution of 1967. Several members of this special Congress supported an amendment that would have provided for the separation of church and state. However, the amendment was never passed. Therefore, Article 3 of the Constitution still maintains that "the state recognizes and supports the Roman Apostolic Catholic Church," although freedom of religion is guaranteed.

The Catholic church enjoys special privileges in Bolivia, including a monthly salary paid by the state to all bishops and church staff disbursed by the Ministry of Foreign Affairs and Worship. Catholic bishops and church staff are thus considered public functionaries. The state recognizes the Catholic church as an "Entity of Public Law" (comparable to a municipality) thus relieving it from incorporation or registration with state agencies (as is the case for Evangelical churches and other religious associations). The organization of some official ceremonies, such as the *Te Deums* (masses that are attended by the president and other national and local authorities), is entrusted to the Catholic church.

Mexico's Constitution of 1917 discriminated against all religions, including the Roman Catholic Church. Demands for increased religious liberty were finally met by the Mexican government in 1992. More than six months after diplomatic relations were established between the Mexican government and the Holy See, the government published a new Law on Religious Associations and Public Worship, which went into effect on July 16, 1992.[16] The new law did not endorse any specific religion, but considered them all "equal before the law." It also recognized church ownership of property designated for religious purposes, the right to hold religious events outside of church structures with appropriate permits, and the right to publish freely. However, that particular law did not revoke the longstanding ban on religious broadcasts.[17] The Constitution guarantees free choice of religion and declares discrimination against persons because of their religion illegal.

The Constitution of Paraguay was amended in 1992, resulting in the separation of church and state. Interestingly, the Roman Catholic Church, arguing that its close identification with the state had done it more harm than good, joined the leaders of fourteen Protestant churches to urge the constitutional separation of church and state. The "Declaration of Christian Churches to the National Constitutional Assembly," a document formulated by the representatives of these religious denominations, called upon the Convention to end Paraguay's historic recognition of Roman Catholicism as the official state religion. The new Constitution also eliminates the requirement that the president profess the Catholic religion.[18]

Cuba is still a totalitarian state, with a Constitution adopted in 1976 and subsequently amended. Article 55 amends Article 54, establishing freedom of conscience. In July 1991, the Cuban state allowed religious believers to join the Communist Party. In July 1992, the state amended the Constitution to prohibit religious discrimination and removed references to "scientific materialism" (atheism) as the basis of the Cuban state.[19] Unfortunately, despite these legal changes, religious discrimination and persecution continue. The government still requires churches, house churches, and other religious groups to register and to obtain official recognition. The construction of new churches is prohibited, and recognition of all religious holidays ended in 1991, although in anticipation of the impending papal visit, Christmas was celebrated in 1997 for the first time in many years. According to one estimate Evangelicals are now more numerous than Catholics on the island.[20]

In Colombia, on July 18, 1991, a new Constitution was adopted recognizing freedom of conscience (Article 18) and guaranteeing freedom of worship and the equality of all churches before the law (Article 19). In May 1993, President César Gaviria signed the Religious Liberty Law,[21] which recognized the legal status of Protestant marriages and gave students the right to choose the type of religious education they receive in public schools. In addition, Protestant ministers now have equal access to patients in state-run hospitals and may be appointed to serve in the military and with the police. Concerning freedom of worship, the Penal Code punishes offenses such as preventing another person from participating in worship, insulting or causing injury to those practicing a religious rite, and generally disrupting religious activity.

Brazil has no state religion. All faiths are free to establish places of worship, train clergy, and proselytize, although the government controls entry into Indian lands. According to Article 5 of the 1988 Constitution, freedom of conscience and belief are inviolable, and freedom of worship is recognized.

The irony in all of this is that as religious freedom increases in Latin America and Evangelicals feel more comfortable with their social and legal status, they have now joined with the Catholic church to restrict the activities of newer religious movements, such as the Unification Church, operating in the region (especially in Costa Rica, Nicaragua, and Honduras).

OFFENSIVE ACTIONS OF EVANGELICALS AGAINST CATHOLICS

There have been some cases of offensive actions by Evangelicals against the Catholic church. On October 12, 1995, while preaching on a live television program, Sergio Von Helder, of the Universal Church of the Kingdom of God, kicked and insulted an image of the Virgin of Aparecida, the patroness of Brazil. The television station is owned by the Universal Church, and in his defense the bishop argued that he only "touched the virgin with his foot." He claimed that he was attempting to show that the virgin was made of clay and that the Bible prohibits the worship of images. The National Association of Evangelicals of Brazil decried the action, while the Catholic National Conference of Bishops severely criticized Von Helder's actions and declared that it "offended more than one hundred million Catholics throughout the country."[22]

The incident provoked widespread attention. The president of Brazil, Fernando Henrique Cardozo, warned of the "danger of a holy war" in Brazil and stated that the Ministry of Justice was considering making "kicking a Saint" a "federal crime against human rights." Von Helder was charged with "pre-meditated aggression against an image" as well as "religious discrimination and outrage to the image."[23] A penal court of São Paulo sentenced Von Helder to two years and two months of imprisonment. The judge did grant the bishop the opportunity to appeal, although if the conviction is upheld by an appeals tribunal, Von Helder will be imprisoned not in a regime of partial freedom, but on a penal farm.[24]

Aggressive verbal remarks against the Catholic church are common among Evangelical pastors. At one time, in 1993, the undersecretary for Religious Affairs in Bolivia "warned" Channel 27 in Bolivia (run by Evangelicals) not to attack the Catholic church anymore. An example of such statements occurred prior to the visit of Pope John Paul II to Guatemala City in 1996. During an interview, Gerardo Vileda, an elder of the Church of the Word, suggested that the committed Evangelical Christians would not welcome the visit of Pope John Paul II and declared: "The pope's visit is part of Satan's deceitful plan."[25]

Pope John Paul II's trip to Latin America appears to have further publicized the antagonistic relationship between some Evangelicals and Catholics in certain areas. Prior to the Pope's visit, members of the Universal Church of the Kingdom of God were reportedly distributing leaflets entitled "The Pope Is the Anti-Christ"[26] to individuals in Guatemala City. While this is no new phenomenon in history, such actions by Evangelicals are clearly detrimental to the Protestant movement's credibility on both a national and an international level.

DISCRIMINATION AGAINST EVANGELICALS AND OTHER NON-CATHOLICS

The recent increase in popularity of Protestantism has provided stiff competition for traditional Catholicism. But the competition has not been welcomed. As a result, derogatory statements and discriminatory actions have occurred by Catholics against Evangelicals.

The members of the Roman Catholic clergy have done a fair amount of self-criticism and have recognized their own shortcomings in terms of the lack of a sufficient number of priests for the millions of Latin American Catholics and the largely nominal character of belief among some of their faithful. Unfortunately, they have also slipped into a habit of continually terming Protestant churches and non-Catholic religious groups generally as *sectas* (which is the English equivalent of "cults," not "sects").

At their latest continental meeting in Santo Domingo, the Latin American (Catholic) Bishops' Conference (CELAM) stated in its final document that the "problem" concerning the "fundamentalist sects" has grown to "dramatic proportions and is truly worrying because of their increasing proselytism."[27] The same document supported CELAM's decision "not to dialogue" with the "fundamentalist sects," adding that "fundamentalist sects are religious groups which insist that only faith in Jesus Christ saves and that the only basis for the faith is the Sacred Scriptures interpreted in a personal and fundamentalist way, to the exclusion of the church, and the insistence on the proximity of the end of the world and the coming judgment."[28]

In 1996 Pope John Paul II called on faithful Roman Catholics to work against the expansion of "religious sects," particularly in Latin America. Speaking to a Vatican Commission responsible for the placement of priests around the world, the pope said the propagation of Catholicism faces great challenges from sects and consumerism. "In recent decades, missionary expansion has not been able to keep pace with the increase in population and is being challenged, especially in Latin America, by the destructive work of the 'sects.'"[29] During a trip to several countries in Latin America, Pope John Paul II described Latin American Evangelicals as "ravenous wolves . . . causing discord and division in our communities."[30]

On his part, Archbishop Próspero Penados del Barrio, Guatemala's highest-ranking prelate, accused Evangelicals of being "instruments of rich foreign governments," calling them "the opiate of the people." He added that Evangelicals practice "an easy faith with no social conscience and they do not have what it takes to produce martyrs."[31]

In 1992, Girolamo Prigione, Vatican Representative to Mexico, in an interview with *El Universal* newspaper in Mexico City, stated his "concern for the inroads of the Protestant sects in the country" and affirmed that "they divide the families and denationalize the country, sow confusion, and originate strife." And he added: "This is unjust and that is why we reject and condemn it. The sects, like flies, need to be thrown out."[32]

Discrimination against Evangelicals is not limited to verbal attack. Evangelicals in Chiapas, Mexico, have been beaten, raped, displaced, and even killed for their faith in the last thirty years. Though the Chamula Indians conflict in Chiapas is also related to land issues, political tensions, and inter-tribal economic disputes, a substantial part of it also relates to religious discrimination and persecution.

On November 12, 1997, two Evangelicals associated with the Organization of Evangelical Peoples of the Chiapas Highlands (OPEACH) were ambushed and murdered. Traditionalist Catholic *caciques* (local unofficial political leaders) are believed to be responsible for the murders. These *caciques* had previously opposed the enrollment of Evangelical students in the local public schools.[33] Early on October 28, 1997, Saltillo officials summoned twenty-three Protestants for a meeting at the local Catholic church and told them: "In this community, we are all Catholics. We do not accept other religions."[34] As a result of a legal complaint filed by The Rutherford Institute[35] with the Inter-American Commission on Human Rights, the Commission visited the Chiapas region in October of 1997, for the first time in its thirty-seven-year history, verifying and criticizing the situation of the persecuted Evangelicals. A solution has yet to be found.

In La Paz, Bolivia, two public hospitals posted signs in 1993 prohibiting the entrance of Evangelical groups, distribution of religious materials, proselytizing, or any other non-Catholic activity. One hospital director claimed that the hospital chaplain pressured him into posting the signs.[36] Also, in Bolivia, the commander of the army recently "prohibited" all non-Catholic religious activity in the army.[37] Other cases of sporadic religious discrimination continue to occur in other Latin American countries, but the situation of the Chamula Indians in Mexico is the worst in the region.

An attempt to influence Catholic-Evangelical relations in Latin America was made by several prominent North American Evangelical and Catholic leaders (including some Hispanics) as they signed a statement which among other things resolved to "condemn the practice of recruiting people from another community for purposes of denominational or institutional aggrandizement."[38] While encouraging Evangelicals and Catholics "in severe and sometimes violent conflict, such as in parts of Latin America" to "embrace and act upon the imperative of religious freedom,"[39] the document makes a confusing distinction between "evangelizing" and "proselytizing or 'sheep stealing.'"[40] It also asks Evangelicals and Catholics to "refrain" from proselytizing "among active adherents of another Christian community."[41] Though Evangelical tele-evangelists such as Pat Robertson and other religious leaders who are generally influential in Latin America signed the document, the impact of this statement on Latin American Evangelical-Catholic relations has been almost nil.

The evangelistic and missionary zeal, which may continue to produce religious friction in Latin America, may no longer be a trait of Evangelical churches alone. Citing the need for "renewed missionary zeal," Pope John Paul II convened at the Holy See the Synod of Bishops from North and South America in November 1997.[42] The pope noted that it was the first such synod since Columbus arrived in the Americas over five hundred years ago. Among "the great challenges of the third millennium" discussed by the synod were strategies to reach out to people who have left the Catholic church, as well as how to win new believers. Walter Altmann, president of the Latin American Council of Churches (CLAI) (a Protestant organization), one of only five non-Catholic observers, addressing Pope John Paul II and nearly three hundred bishops from the Americas, highlighted the importance of ecumenism.[43]

RELATIONS WITH HISTORIC PROTESTANT CHURCHES

There are two main organizations of Protestants in Latin America. They are CLAI—The Latin American Council of Churches (*Concilio Latinoamericano de Iglesias*)[44]—and CONELA—The Latin American Evangelical Fellowship.[45]

Each organization has a distinctive character, and at times they have had strong disagreements, in theology and practice, though they are not mutually exclusive. CLAI gathers together most "historical" Protestant churches in Latin America, such as the Methodists, Lutherans, and Anglicans. In affiliation with the World Council of Churches (WCC), CLAI has displayed an openness to all denominations and has developed a longstanding relationship with the Catholic church. CLAI's relationship with the Catholic church, however, is not always unconditional. In preparation for a historical meeting between CLAI and CELAM (Latin American Bishops' Conference of the Catholic Church), planned for May 1997, CLAI leaders stated that they would only hold the meeting if Catholics recognized and worked to solve the problems of religious intolerance against Protestants in several countries of Latin America.[46] Eventually, the meeting was held and was presented as a reaffirmation of the ecumenical relationship between the two ecclesiastical institutions.[47] CLAI has shown a certain degree of sympathy for the social content of liberation theology, which dominated theological discussion during the decades of the '60s and '70s.[48]

CONELA was founded as an alternative to CLAI, and its social, economic, and political objectives focus mainly on evangelism, missionary work, and discipleship. CONELA "was not founded to compete with, or disapprove of the work of CLAI, but to gather all Evangelical denominations that were, for one reason or another, not members of CLAI."[49] There were a great number of churches that did not feel CLAI could represent them adequately, and many of them became the founders of CONELA. CONELA attracts many denominations and independent churches, including Baptists, Pentecostals, and others, but seldom "historical" ones, with the exception of the Presbyterians. Although some members of CONELA would call themselves Fundamentalists, the majority prefer the name *evangélico*. CONELA does not pursue the traditional activities of a national Evangelical organization but seeks primarily to promote fellowship among all Evangelical denominations in Latin America.

The division between CLAI and CONELA members in Latin America has steadily increased for a number of reasons, primarily their different concepts of their mission, as well as divergent attitudes toward the Catholic church.

Politics has also provided another source of division. CLAI has leaned toward socialism and liberation theology,[50] while many members of CONELA hold conservative views and have supported military regimes. Daniel R. Miller suggests that this polarization explains why "ecumenical" (i.e., CLAI members) Protestants have been predisposed to use negative sociological categories for popular Protestantism, which, unfortunately, can damage the life of the churches at the grassroots level. In his view, Protestantism at one time was so polarized that it was unable to offer spiritual guidance in the search for new approaches to the region's social and political crises.[51]

However, a rapprochement between the two organizations took place at the Third Latin American Congress for Evangelization (CLADE III) held in Quito, Ecuador, from August 24 to September 4, 1992, which I attended. During the closing ceremony of the Congress, the president of CONELA, Juan Terranova, a pastor, invited Federico Pagura, president of CLAI, to preach in his church in Argentina. Pagura, also a pastor, immediately reciprocated. CLAI and CONELA also recognized their need to overcome longstanding theological and practical differences in order to facilitate the process of evangelization of Latin America. The event was a landmark in the history of Latin American Protestantism. More than a thousand Evangelical representatives from all countries of Latin America attended the event, which reaffirmed its basic commitment to Latin America's evangelization and discipleship, while promoting the social relevance of Evangelicals in the continent. Most important, a mutual respect for each other's work was reinforced.

INCREASING POLITICAL INFLUENCE

Despite the political apathy that has characterized most Evangelicals in past decades, participation in politics is slowly becoming more accepted within the church environment. In the early 1990s there was widespread optimism concerning the political viability of Evangelical candidates and Evangelical-led political parties. Protestant politicians had succeeded in overcoming the handicap of being a religious minority to gain public office in several predominantly Catholic nations. Brazil, the country with the largest Roman Catholic population in the world, but also one of the world's largest Protestant ones (with about twenty million Protestants), elected thirty-three professed Protestants to the Constitutional Assembly in 1987 and twenty-five to the National Congress the following year.[52]

In 1990, Peru elected an unknown newcomer, Alberto Fujimori, as president. Pollsters attributed his upset victory partially to the solid endorsement of the Evangelical Christian community. Fujimori's new Cambio 90 Party also elected seventeen Evangelical congressmen and women, and an Evangelical pastor and lawyer was appointed as second vice-president of Peru.

In 1991, Guatemala elected Pentecostal candidate Jorge Serrano Elías as president. A veteran diplomat with impeccable credentials, Serrano was the first Protestant ever elected president of a Latin American country. He was later deposed in the midst of political turmoil and charges of financial misconduct.

Also noteworthy is the creation of more than twenty Evangelical-led political parties (some insignificant, others larger and with representation in Congress) such as *Misión de Unidad Nacional Cristiana* in Paraguay, *Movimiento Unión Cristiana* in Colombia, *Partido Camino Cristiano* in Nicaragua, *Alianza Renovadora Boliviana* and *Servicio e Integridad* in Bolivia, *Partido Nacional Evangélico*, just created in Brazil, and others.

Political participation, however, has created problems with the potential for bitter intra-faith divisions (there are four Evangelical-led political parties in Guatemala, three in Colombia, and the first Evangelical-led party in Bolivia, which put one representative in Congress in 1993, has now divided into three small branches). Furthermore, experience has shown that confessional parties are not viable, because of the basic contradiction between the sectarian nature of religion and the pluralistic society of a democratic regime.

Corruption scandals in the administration of Brazilian president Fernando Collor de Mello led to his impeachment in 1992. Investigations into the disgraced president's misdeeds also exposed dishonest political deals he had made with Evangelical congressmen.

Less than two years into his term, in April 1992, President Fujimori staged a "self-coup." After disbanding Congress—which included, ironically, the Protestants who had worked so hard to elect him—Fujimori ruled by decree and suspended many constitutional rights.

In Guatemala in May 1993, President Serrano attempted similar heavy-handed tactics to gain emergency power over the government. However, the maneuver backfired, and Serrano was unceremoniously deposed and sent into exile.

All this has given renewed strength to the view that "politics is of the devil," that involvement in politics may produce self-defeating results. The mood among Protestant political activists today is decidedly less euphoric. Past successes have given way to disheartening failures during the past four years.

However, as was recently pointed out by Caio Fabio, president of the National Association of Evangelicals of Brazil, Protestants, "despite their own divisions, have managed to build a political base that, if activated, could soon become a formidable voting bloc."[53] With the statistics demonstrating that Latin America is no longer a monolithically Catholic region (Evangelicals being the second largest group after Roman Catholics) and the continual increase in the number of Evangelicals, Fabio's suggestion cannot be taken lightly.

SOCIOECONOMIC IMPACT OF EVANGELICALISM, PARTICULARLY PENTECOSTALISM

Historically, Latin America has been a region marked by great social paradoxes. It is a land of deep religiosity, but substantial official corruption; saturated with *macho* types, but not enough responsible men; with a ruling class ethnically *mestizo* (mix of Indian and European), but, out of prejudice, considering itself "white"; where the law is seldom openly challenged, but frequently disobeyed or ignored. It is a region that culturally distrusts its "own" and favors the "other" while at the same time believing itself to be the innocent victim of "foreign aggressors." Latin America is a land full of patriots, martyrs, and liberators, but too few heroes to imitate; presidents take office already divorced or, unable to handle both government and family simultaneously, divorce their wives "for the sake of the fatherland." It is a society where family, tradition, and influence take precedence over hard work, honesty, and integrity.

This latter aspect was bluntly documented in the widely read "Manual of the Perfect Latin American Idiot."[54] "The problem," say the ex-leftist authors, "is not so much being an idiot (that is, blaming others, especially the United States, for all our problems), but persisting, against all evidence, in remaining one." The manual deals with Latin American intellectual shortcomings, especially the tendency to find comfort in victimization rather than accepting responsibilities.

The British sociologist David Martin has studied the socioeconomic impact of Pentecostalism in *Tongues of Fire: The Explosion of Protestantism in Latin America*,[55] arguing that Pentecostals have created "free spaces" where a new ethos can develop. The personalized dedication on the part of the leadership and flexible structure break with the Catholic and Protestant division of clergy and laity. The Pentecostal acceptance of women in leadership, in some cases even at the pastoral level, adds to its popularity. Though most members of Pentecostal churches are poor and uneducated, an increase of middle- and upper-class members has brought the social classes together in a way unfamiliar to Latin American people. Similarly, religious services bring together racial castes—descendants of the Native Americans, the European colonists, and the African slaves—in ways rare to the usually prejudiced Latin American countries. White and black, *mestizo* and Indian, educated and illiterate, may be found holding hands and even kissing each other—a very unlikely occurrence in a highly prejudiced society in which people of Indian descent, with the "wrong" last name, the poor, and the uneducated are still considered inferior by the ruling classes.

The significance of all this according to *Forbes* magazine is "quite revolutionary" and goes beyond theology. "The old . . . order, based upon a rigid hierarchy and social immobility, has broken down. A new social atmosphere, one more flexible and more compatible with capitalism and democracy, is emerging."[56] Pentecostals find themselves not only questioning existing religious structures (both Catholic and Protestant), but also giving expression to a deep-rooted discontent with existing social and economic conditions.[57]

In Pentecostal churches across Latin America former prostitutes, drunkards, and adulterers freely testify to their conversions. Finding a sense of purpose in their new beliefs, many have developed abilities within the church (leadership, organization, public speaking, etc.) that have improved their daily work and helped them to rise economically. Pentecostal men are found to be sensitive and dedicated to their families (what the Center for Public Studies, a Chilean think-tank, has called the "feminization" of men[58]). More of their family income is spent on children's education. A recent poll of two thousand Brazilians found that they "see themselves as more optimistic and hard working than in the past" as a result of their conversion.[59] Pentecostals are generally credited with providing a sense of community to the masses migrating from the countryside to the cities and with preaching a message that concentrates on the power of God not only to comfort spiritually but also to help materially.

As Pentecostals reprioritize their lives, abandon negative habits such as excessive alcohol consumption, and develop a positive attitude toward the future, many Pentecostals are saving more and have become successful entrepreneurs. Regarding the latter, Carmen Galilea, a sociologist with the Bellarmino Center for Sociocultural Research in Chile (a Catholic organization), describes the typical Pentecostal: "He is well-regarded. He is responsible. He doesn't drink and is better motivated and better paid. As a result, he rises economically."[60] Rev. Joaquín Atenas tells the story of a man he discovered, blood-shot and drunk on the streets of Santiago, Chile. After bringing him to his church and praying for the "spirit of drunkenness" to "be gone from [his] body," the man recovered. A butcher by trade who had been unemployed for a while, the man requested and obtained a small loan from the church. A year later he had established a butcher shop, and later he set up a second butcher shop.[61] Commenting on this issue *Forbes* adds: "Upwardly striving urban poor are encouraged by religious teachings and support groups that preach the power of individuals to change their lives through faith. This contrasts sharply with the old attitude of resignation to one's fate and a glorification of poverty."[62]

Admittedly, deep-rooted cultural problems continue, hindering full democratic reform and economic advancement. Most countries in the region still operate in self-destructive ways. State officials both act and are seen to act as virtual kings and lords, while monopolies, though weakened, continue to re-emerge in the economic, political, social, and even religious realms (with a privileged and, in a few cases, official church). Tax evasion, exacerbated by governmental corruption and mismanagement of public funds, has crippled democratic reform and weakened the accountability of public officials. A career in government is still seen primarily as a way to amass a fortune.

Still, it would appear that a new basis for democracy and prosperity is being formed. The principles taught concerning self-control, giving more attention to the family, spending less on parties and more on education, and a possible emergence of a Protestant work ethic may well have a profound effect upon Latin America in due time. Any substantial socioeconomic development, however, will only come as the negative factors discussed below are overcome.

STRENGTHS AND WEAKNESSES
OF LATIN AMERICAN PENTECOSTALISM

Pentecostalism (the largest and fastest-growing sector of Protestantism in Latin America), having broken social barriers, ancestral traditions, and ecclesiastical customs, has the potential to become a transforming force in the region. However, closer analysis of the Pentecostal phenomenon raises serious questions and uncertainties about this prospect and suggests that Pentecostals themselves could be their own worst enemy.

The growth of Evangelical Protestantism in Latin America has been labeled by many as the beginning of a new Latin American Reformation, similar to the one that changed the face of Europe in the sixteenth century.[63] Others doubt whether the Evangelical revival will have any socioeconomic impact on the region.[64] Among the explanations by sociologists and other scholars of the explosive Evangelical growth are the spiritual hunger and search for spiritual responses, the desire for more participation in church life, and the expectation of less ritualized forms of worship. Furthermore, the explosive urban growth which has taken place since the 1940s has resulted in many people being stranded in unfamiliar surroundings and anonymous environments. The Evangelical church provides a sense of collective identity and of mutual support.

Another partial explanation for the phenomenal growth of Pentecostalism has been suggested by Franz Damen, a Catholic priest and missionary to Bolivia. He argues that Pentecostalism in Latin America has associated itself with the popular culture, assuming the language and even some of the religious practices (for example, vows, pilgrimages, symbols) of the people, along with folk music and dance. Together with the emphasis on practices such as non-medical healing, Pentecostalism has particularly appealed to indigenous traditions.[65] Further facilitating the growth of Pentecostal churches is the fact that 99 percent of their leaders are native Latin Americans. Pentecostalism, declares Mortimer Arias (a prominent Uruguayan Methodist bishop) is "the most indigenous and popular Protestant modality that Latin America has ever produced."[66]

A typical Latin American Pentecostal service takes place in a large, poorly furnished meeting hall, with a full-blown band leading the singing, shouting, whistling, clapping, and dancing. As the service begins, the congregants become deeply immersed, their eyes closed, some crying, others singing at the top of their voices or "speaking in tongues," and still others lifting their faces and hands toward heaven. The music moves into a crescendo, building from soft strains to a fast, arresting rhythm that after nearly two hours reaches a deafening climax and suddenly drops back again to quiet strains. With the entrance of the pastor, the whole congregation shouts and claps in praise, while he begins to preach a simple message of salvation through Jesus: You must convert now, while there is still time. No more drinking, cheating, and lying. The Lord is coming, soon. The music softly restarts while the pastor asks all who want to "accept the Lord" to come forward. As the leaders pray, the people start falling down—"slain in the Spirit"—the outward expression of the Holy Spirit come into their lives. There is no clear beginning of the service, and usually no clear end. Some because they have found what they prayed for, and others out of sheer exhaustion, begin to drift from the hall, and the service comes to an end. Nothing short of the final Rapture (being taken up to heaven before the Second Coming of Christ), for which they pray, will keep them from coming back next week, with friends and family in tow.

One could conclude that the "Pentecostalization" of Latin America promises a bright and prosperous future. Undeniably, Pentecostal churches and leaders offer a positive and integrated view of faith and the world that has had an impact. It is not clear, however, whether the explosive growth of Pentecostalism will bring forth the long-awaited and much needed economic and social transformation of Latin America.

Timothy Goodman has questioned the often assumed correlation of the rise of Evangelicalism in Latin America with cultural development. He argues that Evangelicalism tends to emotionalism and superstition, promoting "values typical of traditional society rather than 'modern' values of individualism, rationalism, achievement, and identification with the larger society beyond the immediate family."[67] A former fellow with the American Enterprise Institute, Goodman suggests, in fact, that if there is ever substantial economic improvement in Latin America, it will be not because of Evangelicals, but in spite of them, claiming that Evangelicals might well obstruct modernity rather than advance it.[68] Goodman's questioning of the real contribution of Evangelicalism to economic and social development is understandable. There is no automatic correlation of Evangelical growth with economic and social advancement. While his conclusions are too pessimistic, the fact remains that the Pentecostal contribution to social change is being hindered by Latin American Pentecostals themselves in at least three ways: with a line drawn too sharply between the religious and the secular, with an unnecessary rejection of reason in favor of emotion, and with a theological overemphasis on the "call to ministry" and the end of the world.

The pietistic notion that divides the religious from the secular and assigns more importance to the spirit than to the material world has a long history. In Latin America, this pietistic view has created what I, a Latin American Pentecostal, can only call a religious obsession—by which I mean that church members place great importance solely on "religious" matters at the expense of every other activity or aspect of life. Church takes precedence over family, work, and social life. Many believe, for instance, that they perform "spiritual things" only while reading their Bibles, attending church, or praying. Everything else—studying, working, sleeping, eating—is just "secular" or "worldly." Only that music which explicitly refers to the Bible or to Jesus is "spiritual" or "Christian." Even money spent on charity and the family may be thought to have no spiritual basis unless explicitly given to the member's church, and there has emerged in Latin American Pentecostalism a vast overemphasis on tithing. One pastor recently declared, "Ten percent of his or her income is the least a church member can give to God (that is the local church)." Expenditures on children's education, food, business, housing, and any other legitimate expense are not perceived as being given to God, and therefore are considered secondary in priority.

Concerning the unnecessary rejection of reason in favor of emotion, the excesses of secular rationalism (with its heavy reliance on the mind and disregard for Scripture) may be ultimately to blame for Pentecostals' distrust of reason, intellectuals, doctrines, and ideologies. But sole reliance on emotion forms no adequate response. The insistence on faith-healing and becoming prosperous through prayer has led many Pentecostals to believe that the "miraculous" is the rule and the "natural" is secondary. Personal responsibility disappears when all character flaws and sins are blamed on demons from whom one needs to be "delivered." A Pentecostal missionary in Bolivia was surprised when I asked why the curriculum for his New Ministerial Training Center did not include courses on church history. "We are training Christians to evangelize the people now," was his reply. "We do not need to study church history." In the attack on rationalism, all intellectual endeavor has been abandoned together with the study of systematic theology and church history, placing even the Bible in a secondary role after "experiencing and being anointed by the Holy Spirit." Indiscriminate acceptance of extra-biblical "revelations" and prophecies is also common.

Concerning the question of eschatology and theology, Pentecostal preaching rightly concentrates on the message of salvation through Jesus Christ. And yet while salvation is the fundamental message of Christianity, it can create an escapist mentality if it is not matched with an awareness of our responsibilities here on earth. The emphasis on salvation—when coupled with the belief that the Second Coming is only months away or that the Rapture is immediately approaching—has caused many Pentecostals to adopt a short-term perspective on life. Why bother participating in politics, economics, or engineering? If there is no future, why bother with the past? Well-known Latin American evangelists repeat over and over that they would not "lower themselves" to become presidents. Thus, there is a dichotomy between a reflexive rejection of politics as dirty, and the growing interest in political participation. This may be partly explained by the fact that the rejection of politics takes place at the theoretical, even theological level, while participation in political parties relates more to Evangelical interests and perceived practical needs. For example, political leverage has been found useful in order to facilitate the allocation of radio frequencies, to accelerate the registration process of churches, and even to enhance certain churches' profiles vis-a-vis other churches and the rest of society.

The emphasis on the end of the world has added a sense of urgency to evangelism, which at least partially accounts for the rapid Pentecostal growth in Latin America—particularly when joined to the comfort it gives the poor and downtrodden in the midst of dismal economic conditions. But, a constant emphasis on the end of the world can also sap the will of believers to work to improve their lot, and it may even provide a sense of bitterness at the injustices of this world.

To complicate matters, the persistent message from the pulpit stresses the importance of being "called" by God to the full-time ministry (though in many poorer areas most preachers work other jobs since they cannot afford to be "full-time" in church activities). The only people who are really doing God's work and pleasing God are evangelists, pastors, teachers, and the like. Such non-ministers as carpenters, housewives, doctors, and politicians, when they become Pentecostals, risk being second-class citizens in the Kingdom of God. Since they are not measuring up to what God wants from them, their only hope is one day to become ministers. In the meantime, and if they want to at least partially redeem their professional skills or trades, they must use them "as a tool" for evangelism. Studies, professions, and trades are good only to the extent that they allow the preaching of the Gospel in secular places.

Many of the leaders of Pentecostalism in Latin America have good intentions, much zeal for God, and a passion for evangelism, but they must consider carefully the fact that they may be helping to breed a generation of frustrated and mediocre students and professionals.

Caio Fabio, president of the Evangelical Association of Brazil, wonders if the Latin American revival is one "in the manner of God" or if it is a revival "a la Latinoamericana." If the latter is the case, Fabio predicts, "it will die in the illusion of a superficial or inoperative Evangelical joy." Fabio concludes that "we may simply become the majority in a country of immoral and miserable people, without anything changing substantially in our continent."[69] The pattern of Pentecostals despising or at least minimizing their studies or professions and the value of their work has caused an ecclesiastical atrophy, that is, a lack of growth beyond church activities. It has also diminished other areas of life, such as education, business, and especially politics (seen largely as Satan's domain).

While these issues are clearly detrimental to society and Pentecostals themselves, the potential for positive change to be initiated by this Latin American revival remains. And there are examples of Pentecostal leaders who have begun to address these problems. Over the last few years, The Church of the Word (El Verbo), a large Pentecostal church in Guatemala, has been training leaders to see every area of life as part of God's Kingdom, with the Bible not dividing the religious from the secular, but ordaining that everything done be done for the Lord. Many of its members have become involved in politics—including General Efraín Ríos Montt, a former president of Guatemala. Some time ago I had the satisfaction of witnessing the weekly meeting of Pentecostal pastors in La Paz, Bolivia, that had invited a Presbyterian pastor to train them in systematic theology. On his part, Pastor Rodolfo Sáenz Salas, until recently president of the Assemblies of God Church in Costa Rica, declared, "We need to convert our work into service to God. The quality of our work, whatever it is, will reflect what we are as people."[70]

While proper encouragement should be given to members considering ecclesiastical ministry, the same kind of encouragement should be given to all church members as they exercise their daily occupations. There is also need to balance the preaching of the imminent coming of Christ or the Rapture with an understanding that Christ in fact might delay his coming.

Real contributions of Evangelicalism to economic and social development, political and religious freedom, and the general betterment of Latin America will at the least require that all Evangelicals, and especially Pentecostals, see all areas of society, not just the church, as part of God's Kingdom, and thus worth improving; that their emotions are balanced and enriched by reason; that they see themselves as ministers of God in all that they do; and that while anticipating Christ's prompt return, they are prepared for the long run.

Pentecostals, however, will only have a fuller impact if they work together with all Latin American Christians and other like-minded sectors of society. The union of Pentecostal energy with other Protestants' theological training, knowledge of church history, and emphasis on character building would make any social effort all the more effective—particularly when it also seeks the active participation of God-fearing Catholics.

CONCLUSION

Evangelicalism in Latin America has grown explosively, especially in the last three decades in response to spiritual hunger, changing socioeconomic conditions, and other factors. One of the conduits for the expansion of Evangelicalism in the region has been the use of media—first, radio, and more recently and with greater impact, television. While the phenomenon of tele-evangelism has come from North America, "native" Latin American tele-evangelists have emerged, broadcasting via satellite in all Latin American countries except Cuba. Moreover, with Catholic television stations springing up in several Latin American countries and the use of satellite, the Catholic church has also found television to be a valuable tool for its "re-evangelization" program.

The growth of Evangelicalism in a traditionally Catholic continent has, of course, caused friction and conflict throughout the region. However, as religious diversity increases on the continent and with the inroads of democracy and structural economic reform, the environment of religious liberty has improved considerably. In many instances the Catholic church has played an active role in the separation of church and state (as in the case of Paraguay in 1992). Serious differences among the Protestant churches continue to separate the work of members of CLAI ("liberal") and CONELA ("conservative"). However, some positive steps have been taken toward rapprochement between these two organizations, especially for the sake of evangelization of the continent.

The political influence of Evangelicals in Latin America is still slight, oscillating between a "politics is of the devil" mentality and practical political participation driven by self-interest rather than a desire to transform the political and socioeconomic structure. Evangelicals still lack a comprehensive worldview about political participation and socioeconomic restructuring in Latin America. In terms of socioeconomic impact, it is still too early to predict what contribution the Evangelical-led improvements at the individual, family, and local community level will have at the national/structural level. Moreover, in order to enhance the environment of religious freedom, political participation, and the prosperity of Latin America, Latin American Evangelicalism (especially Pentecostalism) will have to address some serious internal weaknesses. If these internal problems are addressed, we may witness a positive contribution by Latin American Evangelicals to the betterment of society as a whole, as has resulted from religious revivals in other parts of the world.

Latin America is, in summary, a continent in transition, disappointed with old schemes and ideologies, and full of energy and anticipation of better days. A land spiritually hungry, with emerging markets and a keen interest in making democracy a permanent reality, Latin America eagerly awaits its future.

4.

THE ECONOMICS OF EVANGELIZATION

———————◆———————

Anthony Gill

INTRODUCTION

No one will ever deny that missionaries are motivated by faith. The typical image of a missionary is someone who travels to unfamiliar territory, braves abysmal living conditions, faces hostile audiences, and often risks loss of life, all to spread his or her religious faith. Missionaries are portrayed as persons brave in heart, courageous in spirit, and steadfastly devoted to their moral convictions. These strong character traits aside, evangelists are nonetheless mortal. They face the same constraints as all other humans; they live in a world that is characterized by limited resources and must contend with scarcity of time and personal energy. Economics—the study of choice under scarcity—can tell us a great deal about human behavior when resources are limited. This chapter views the process of religious evangelization through the lens of economic theory to reveal some often overlooked dynamics in the spread of religious organizations. While acknowledging that ideology, faith, and culture motivate the evangelization process, I argue that there are some interesting patterns of behavior that can be explained best with reference to economic (or rational choice) theory. Latin America will be used as an empirical frame of reference. This region of the world has experienced dramatic changes in its religious landscape over the past several decades, moving from a situation of virtual religious monopolization by Catholicism to a religiously pluralistic environment with the rapid growth of Protestant religions (see Cleary and Stewart-Gambino 1992; Martin 1990; Stoll 1990).

Relying upon the growing body of literature known as the religious economy school, I argue the following: First, although the Catholic Church has exercised an institutional hegemony over the region for more than five hundred years, the region never has been monolithically Catholic in religious belief

70

and/or practice. Second, given the relatively superficial penetration of "official" institutional Catholicism, the region has been ripe for Protestant growth. However, Protestants could only evangelize effectively once legal barriers to proselytizing were lowered. In effect, the ability of a religious organization to evangelize is, in part, a function of government regulation of the religious economy—high degrees of regulation impose significant costs on religious organizations and lower the willingness to evangelize. Third, once Protestantism was willing and able to enter the region, the poor represented the most receptive population for efficient evangelization. This results from the tendency of monopolistic religions to concentrate pastoral resources among the upper classes due to economic limitations imposed by the necessity of funding a large, bureaucratic organization. This does not imply that the Catholic Church was unconcerned with the needs of the poor; Catholic charities historically have assisted the lower classes. However, the ability of the Church to dole out charitable assistance was constrained by its ability to extract financial contributions from the state or upper classes. Moreover, on the spiritual front, and until the mid-twentieth century, poor neighborhoods and rural villages often went without the services of a priest for extended periods of time. Finally, I assert that evangelical organizations new to a region must offer tangible, economic incentives to their target population in order to build the trust necessary to convert people. This is because religion is a "credence good"; i.e., a good wherein the consumer cannot verify the quality of the product until a much distant point in the future. With credence goods, the more credible and trustworthy the producer (priests), the more success they will have in winning consumers (parishioners). In relation to this final point, I conclude that attempts to interpret the consequences of Protestant growth in Latin America through the eyes of Weber's "Protestant ethic" thesis are somewhat misplaced.

THE ECONOMICS OF RELIGION: A BRIEF PRIMER

Before applying economic analysis to religious evangelization in Latin America, it is imperative to understand what a rational choice perspective can *and cannot* bring to the study of religious movements. Like all theoretical perspectives, rational choice has its limitations, yet it still remains a powerful tool of analysis that can successfully explain many empirical patterns of social behavior. Many critiques of rational choice, I believe, emanate from a fundamental misunderstanding of the basic assumptions and claims of the approach. At its heart, rational choice theory is quite simple. People are assumed to pursue their goals via the most efficient means available, given a world of scarcity. Adding a few assumptions to this simple notion yields some powerful predictions about human behavior.

Rational choice theory privileges interests over ideas, culture, and psychological mindsets in explaining human behavior. Individuals are assumed to have a set of goals (i.e., interests or preferences) they wish to obtain. The content of these preferences are indeterminate and can vary from person to person. The more successful and efficient individuals are at achieving their goals, the greater their welfare. Humans are assumed to be welfare maximizers, choosing strategies that allow them to satisfy their preferences (or goals) at the lowest possible cost. Should this be the end of the story, rational choice analysis would be rather trivial.[1] What makes the perspective interesting is that people act under less-than-perfect conditions, and their welfare-maximizing actions are constrained by a variety of factors. These factors include an individual's resource endowment (i.e., wealth, skills, and power), socioeconomic and political institutions, culture,[2] cognitive limitations,[3] and the preferences and actions of other individuals. Examining how individuals behave under various constraints, and how their behavior changes when constraints change, is the central focus of rational choice analyses. To date, most work in this perspective has centered on the constraints imposed by other individuals and various institutions, often to the neglect of cultural and psychological constraints, though this is changing.

It is important to note that economic approaches to human behavior do not concern themselves with the content of people's preferences or goals. It often is claimed erroneously that rational choice theorists always posit material (financial) interests for individuals, but this is not true. Economic models are indifferent as to whether people maximize income or leisure, fortune or fame. The list of possible preferences and combination of preferences is infinite. This opens up rational choice to the accusation that it is tautologous; observed outcomes are explained as a function of a desire for that outcome. However, this methodological flaw is not inherent to rational choice alone; cultural models of human behavior are equally susceptible to the sin of tautology.[4] The way to solve this problem is to make reasonable, a priori assumptions about preferences before empirically observing behavior. This allows the rational choice theorist to account for unintended consequences of individual behavior (e.g., why do intelligent and well-meaning politicians constantly make bad policy decisions?). In fact, explaining unintended (paradoxical) outcomes is one of the favorite pastimes of economists and political economists.

In economic theory, preferences also are assumed to remain stable over the period of decision-making. This is done largely for methodological control; if preferences and exogenous constraints changed simultaneously during some choice event, then it becomes empirically difficult to sort out which element had the larger impact on behavior. This is not to say that preferences never change; they do. Rational choice theory is admittedly weak in explaining how preferences originate and how they change. This largely remains the realm of psychological and cultural studies. However, if rational choice models do well at accurately predicting social behavior, shifts in preferences probably have minimal effect. If exogenous constraints fare poorly in explaining observed behavior, then we should consider alterations in preferences.

Over the past decade, there has been an increase in the number of scholarly works examining religion, religious institutions, and religiously motivated behavior from a rational choice framework. Warner (1993) has gone so far as to declare this a paradigmatic shift in the sociology of religion. This school of thought makes a number of assumptions about preferences that are relevant for this study. First, it assumes that individuals have varying preferences in the quantity, quality, and form of religion they wish to consume. In other words, the "natural" state of the religious economy is religious diversity.[5] Given this religious diversity, parishioners will attempt to maximize their consumption of religion goods, given various constraints, by altering their patterns of religious practice—e.g., church attendance, private prayer, choice of a specific denomination, etc. On the flip side of the coin, religious producers—e.g., churches, clergy—are assumed to be pursuing the goals of parishioner maximization and revenue maximization. The former goal takes the evangelizing mission of most religions at face value—clergy want to spread their faith far and wide.[6] Some scholars argue that parishioner (or market share) maximization is the primary goal of all proselytizing religion (Gill 1998; Ekelund, Hebert, and Tollison 1989), and that churches will be willing to sacrifice financial gains in order to bring more sheep into the fold. The revenue maximization assumption—usually thought of as a secondary goal—is needed because it is observed that religious organizations need resources to survive and carry out their mission; a wealthy church is better equipped to minister to its adherents and potential converts relative to a poor church, ceteris paribus.[7] With these simple assumptions in mind, it is now possible to explore the economic dynamics of evangelization in Latin America.

THE ECONOMICS OF EVANGELIZATION

HOW CATHOLIC IS LATIN AMERICA?
THE ECONOMICS OF MONOPOLY RELIGIONS

For nearly five centuries, Catholicism has held a virtual monopoly over Latin America. Common knowledge held that the region was "solidly Catholic" with well over 95 percent of the population considering themselves adherents. In this regard, it is difficult to think of Catholicism as being a proselytizing religion; with a virtual monopoly over the religious market, its mission to gain adherents was more or less complete. However, evangelization is an ongoing process. Clergy must continually preach the faith in order to maintain depth of commitment in addition to breadth. Also, as generations pass, individuals who receive little regular contact with a religious denomination tend to fall away from that religion's belief patterns and rituals. Thus, no matter how many people claim loyalty to a given denomination, evangelization remains a central task for religious organizations. However, the economic reality of religious monopolies suggests that evangelization often takes a back seat to other institutional goals when one faith dominates a market. This appears to have been the case in Latin America.

In a highly competitive religious market (such as exists in the contemporary United States), religious producers (e.g., churches, clergy) have a strong incentive to constantly evangelize their congregations. Should they fail to do so, commitment might wane and members of their flock might become more susceptible to the calls of other denominations that promise greater attention to their spiritual needs and desires. Monopoly churches do not face those same incentives. Under a religious monopoly, neglected parishioners lack an exit option to express dissatisfaction with their current church. Given a choice between becoming irreligious—a decision many people are unwilling to make—or continuing to consume religion, most people choose the latter. They declare nominal affiliation with the dominant church even though they find it unresponsive to their needs.

The problem of uninspired evangelization efforts by the clergy of a monopoly church is further aggravated by the institutional demands of operating a large organization. As noted above, churches, like all institutions, require a constant inflow of resources to maintain their organization. As parishioners have no possibility of defection to other faiths, the clergy have an incentive of ratcheting up their revenue intake by passing the costs on to consumers. As Iannaccone has argued,

> The standard, textbook results [of monopoly production] carry over directly, and the monopoly church earns positive profits by limiting output levels and charging prices in excess of marginal cost. . . . The simple monopoly model implies inefficiency and deadweight losses, as high prices lead demanders to underconsume religious commodities (1991, 159).

In essence, revenue maximization takes precedence over parishioner maximization, the latter having been solved by the church's monopoly status. To the extent that demand for religion is inelastic, the church can maintain a nominal hold over religious allegiance in society. Then, to maximize revenue, a church will reduce input costs by diminishing the number of clergy and religious services. Quality of the clergy likely will suffer as the church devotes less time and energy to recruitment and training. However, as the quality and the quantity of religious services becomes increasingly deficient, the evangelization mission of a monopoly church is bound to suffer and religious adherents—despite nominal loyalty—will likely decrease their participation in the religion. To the extent that people want the active presence of a church to satisfy their religious needs, the level of religiosity in society will be less than optimal. Moreover, people gain an incentive to supply their own demand by developing personal religious practices unconnected to the official rites and doctrine of the institutional church.

Regardless of Latin America's image as a bastion of Catholicism, scholars and clergy alike have been noting that the population's devotion to "official" Catholicism is quite thin. The Chilean Jesuit Alberto Hurtado noted this as early as 1941 when he published his famous booklet, *Is Chile a Catholic Coun-*

try? (Hurtado 1941). This weak attachment to Catholicism relates to the high costs associated with being a practicing Catholic within the Church's institutional framework. For example, the extreme lack of clergy in Latin America meant Catholics in small towns and rural areas saw a priest only once every six to twelve months (Poblete 1965). Given the "priest-centric" nature of Catholicism, and that the sacraments require priestly mediation, this imposes a substantial burden on individuals who want to be devout Catholics. They either have to travel great distances to see a priest for various services, decrease their consumption of religious goods, or turn to another religion. With the latter option unavailable, and the former too costly for most individuals, the result has been a lack of participation in official Catholicism and the growth of "folk Catholicism," a form of "unofficial" Catholic worship. The evangelization mission of the Catholic Church—to ensure all members of the population were inextricably bound to Catholicism—suffered due to the simple dynamics of restricted supply under a monopolized religious market. Moreover, given the reasonable expectation that people will have varying preferences for the type of religion they want, it is unlikely that Catholicism—or any religion for that matter—can successfully evangelize 100 percent of the population.[8]

It is important to emphasize here that what has suffered has been participation in *institutional* church practices and belief in *official* church doctrines. Given that humans have an almost unquenchable desire to want meaning in life and death—the key, differentiating product of religion (Stark and Bainbridge 1985, 39)—people will find substitutes for religious services when those services are not being provided adequately by the dominant religion. In Latin America, the phenomenon known as "folk Catholicism" (or "popular religiosity") provides the quintessential example of this substituting behavior. Folk Catholicism is a highly individualized form of worship that usually centers around the veneration of the Virgin Mary and various Catholic saints. It occasionally manifests itself socially in the form of pilgrimages and festivals during holy days. However, such private worship, and its occasional collective manifestation, impose high costs on participants who must educate themselves in a variety of rituals, maintain elaborate private shrines, or spend substantial time organizing festivals. The practice of popular religiosity is most common in rural areas and among the outskirts of urban areas, where few priests are found. The existence of folk Catholic practice gives us a strong indication that demand for religion in Latin America has been quite high and relatively constant. It has been noted that when a religious provider enters a region bereft of Catholic priests, folk Catholicism generally declines, indicating that people would prefer to delegate the task of supplying religion to a specialist, thereby taking advantage of the gains from trade that come through specialization (see below).

The economic lesson of how monopolized religion fails to fully satisfy consumer demand has not been lost on the Catholic Church. The most recent general conference of Latin American bishops held in Santo Domingo in 1992 stressed the theme of "New Evangelization" (see Hennelly 1993). Here, the

Latin American Church publicly acknowledged that evangelization is an on-going process and merely being the dominant religion in society does not guarantee a loyal following. The Santo Domingo theme was largely a response to growing religious pluralism. Ironically, it was the rapid expansion of Protestantism that made the Catholic hierarchy aware of its tenuous hold over its flock. Even before Santo Domingo, Catholic officials increased their efforts to evangelize the population in response to religious and secular (e.g., socialism) encroachment upon their flock. Catholic Action, a movement arising in many countries during the early half of the twentieth century, was a response to these new "threats." This strongly suggests that the religious evangelization of a society is best served in a freely competitive religious market. By most accounts, participation in organized religious practice—including both Catholics and Protestants—is at an all time high. Protestants alone, taking advantage of the fact that there is a high demand for religion but a historically low supply, have doubled religious participation in the region. Stoll (1990) and others (Garrard-Burnett and Stoll 1993; Cleary and Stewart-Gambino 1992) point out that practicing Protestants equal, or even outnumber, practicing Catholics in several Latin American countries, most notably Brazil, possibly Chile, and Guatemala. The Catholic Church has responded to this spiritual encroachment by increasing the number of foreign priests and lay catechists in the region. This, in turn, has led to an increase in Catholic participation. From the standpoint of religious evangelization, religious freedom and competition make the priestly heart grow fonder.

REGULATING RELIGIOUS MARKETS:
LEGAL IMPEDIMENTS TO EVANGELIZATION

It has been noted that missionaries (or religious ministers more generally[9]) are courageous individuals, willing to brave extreme hardship to realize their goal of converting the unchurched. However, missionaries are also rational in that they will prefer to gain as many adherents as they can in the most efficient manner possible. If a colporteur can successfully reach a thousand souls in one country in one month, but only a hundred persons in the same amount of time in another country, it would be wise to choose the former country. Bearing unnecessary hardship would hinder the principal goal of evangelization—to win as many souls as possible. If this is the case, then the logical question becomes where should missionaries concentrate their efforts in order to ensure the greatest success? The simple answer is where the differential between net benefits (i.e., members converted) and net costs are greatest.

Aside from transportation and the effort associated with learning a new language, the primary costs associated with religious evangelization come from government laws and regulations, just as in industrial economies, regulated markets impose significantly higher costs on producers than unregulated ones. The regulation of religious economies includes a wide range of government policies, such as guarantees on the freedom of speech and assembly, telecommunications regulations that permit religious organizations to own or use various media outlets, property rights and taxation of church property, zoning regulations, education policy, and even laws requiring the licensing of clergy and registration of church buildings. In Argentina, the government has made it illegal for a religious minister to practice medicine simultaneously. This severely restricts the growth of a number of Pentecostal denominations that engage in faith healing. This legislation had the active endorsement of the Catholic Church, a monopoly trying to protect its declining market share. The Mexican government traditionally has placed severe restrictions on the activities of religious organizations, including the Catholic Church. Until recently, religious organizations were prohibited from owning property and needed government approval to broadcast religious services or distribute printed literature. Colombia, though declaring religious freedom in its constitution, signed a concordat with the Vatican that guarantees nearly 75 percent of the country's territory to be off limits to non-Catholic religions (including a small island inhabited by Anglicans!). Parts of this concordat were used as a legal excuse to persecute Evangelicals during *La Violencia* in the late 1940s and 1950s (Brusco chapter in this volume; Goff 1968). Protestant ministers were publicly humiliated, tortured, and often killed for exercising their constitutional right of religious freedom. As an economic analysis of evangelization predicts, Protestant growth has been slow in these three countries compared with other countries with less stringent legal codes (e.g., Chile and Brazil). This may be changing. Recent deregulation of the religious market in Mexico and Colombia has led to an increase in Protestant evangelization. Argentina, lagging somewhat behind other countries, has relaxed its regulation of religion and has experienced an expansion of non-Catholic religions.

It should be noted that many countries in Latin America liberalized their laws regulating religion as far back as the late 1800s and early 1900s. However, it was not until the 1930s and 1940s that evangelical Protestants were able to claim significant gains in the region. While this would seem to contradict the economic hypothesis just advanced, it should be remembered that missionaries were trying to maximize benefits (parishioners) net of costs. Even though costs of evangelization were lowered in Latin America during the nineteenth century in a number of countries, the most lucrative areas for evangelization were not in Latin America, but in Asia and Africa—areas largely untouched by Christianity. It was assumed by most missionaries that Latin America was already Christian (albeit Catholic), and thus it would be easier to win converts in non-Christian Asia or Africa. Indeed, efforts in the early 1900s to promote Latin America as a mission field by a few perceptive Protestants were rebuffed by other missionary groups from established churches at the 1910 Edinburgh Conference (Nuñez and Taylor 1989, 153). It took the political tumult caused by Japanese expansion in Asia and World War II in Northern Africa to significantly raise the costs of being a missionary in these regions, and hence turn Protestant attention to Latin America. In the course of my research on South American Protestantism, I have encountered numerous retired missionaries who were originally slated to preach the Gospel in China, but instead were diverted to Costa Rica or Brazil because the Asian mission fields were simply too dangerous (see Gill 1998, chap. 4). Again, a strong cost-benefit logic affecting the nature of religious evangelization is evident here: on average, evangelists prefer less costly environments to more costly ones, ceteris paribus.

But how do religious markets come to be regulated, and then deregulated? We must first begin by examining the logic behind government regulation of religious economies. In large part, the regulation of a religious market results from a bargain struck between a hegemonic church and the government (Gill 1998, 49-62). The trade-off is fairly simple: religious leaders provide an administration with legitimacy in exchange for financial subsidies and legal protection from competitors. Since religions tend to have the most successful track record of any social organization at mobilizing collective action and in inspiring people to revolt against secular governments, it is not surprising that politicians would want to control this source of ideological power for their own benefit. Religious organizations prefer government regulation prohibiting theological competitors because the production of religion is beset by low barriers to entry.[10] Furthermore, given the omnipresent problem of "free-riding" parishioners (i.e., those who make use of religious services but do not contribute to the church's coffers), religious officials would prefer the state to collect revenue from society and to distribute a portion of this to the church. Latin American history bears witness to this theoretical assertion. One way of looking at the *patronato* regulating church-state relations in the colonial and immediate post-colonial period was that the church would provide the government with legitimacy and yield substantial control over church affairs in exchange for prohibitions on Protestantism in the region and financial assistance.

Deregulation of religious economies occurs when one partner in the bargain benefits less from the bargain than it costs (Gill 1998, 62-70). Given that religions are typically in the more vulnerable position, it is usually the state that breaks the bargain and decides to deregulate religion. During the mid-late 1800s, Latin American governments facing huge debt burdens saw it as beneficial to expropriate church assets and sell them to raise revenue (Gill and Keshavarzian 1997). To further weaken the Church as a source of rival social authority, governments introduced the possibility of religious freedom. Allowing selective entrance to Protestants provided a check on Catholic power. More important, these new governments saw it as imperative to grant religious freedom to Protestants if they wanted to cultivate trade relations with Northern Europe and the United States. The opportunity costs of losing international trade contacts far outweighed the benefits of friendly relations with the clergy. In contemporary Latin America, governments are further easing restrictions on non-Catholic religions as politicians begin to realize the voting power of Protestants. The elections of Alberto Fujimori (Peru) and Ernesto Samper (Colombia) can be attributed partially to the support they received from evangelical Protestants, especially in the first rounds of their presidential elections. Chilean president Eduardo Frei attends Protestant services and listens to their concerns. Likewise, Carlos Salinas and Ernest Zedillo have tried to win the favor of Protestants in Mexico with the hope of shoring up an increasingly shaky base of social support. As religious markets become increasingly deregulated in Latin America, we should expect to see continued Protestant growth, particularly in regions where institutional Catholicism is in short supply.

A Proselytizing Preference for the Poor: The Economics of Parishioner Maximization

Once Protestants acquire access to Latin American religious markets on a national level, where are they most likely to make their greatest gains within a country? It has been observed widely that the majority of growth has occurred among the most disenfranchised sectors of society—the rural and urban poor (see Burdick 1993; Cleary and Stewart-Gambino 1992; Stoll 1990). Many scholars have attributed this to an increased *demand* for religion in the face of a growing socioeconomic crisis (Mariz 1994; Goldin and Metz 1991; Martin 1990; Poblete and Galilea 1984). The basic idea is that as industrialization, urbanization, and social violence increase rapidly in Latin America, people are uprooted from their traditional communities. Seeking to reestablish community bonds, transient individuals join new religious movements. While theoretically convincing, empirical analysis reveals that rapid urbanization and economic crisis do not correlate well with Protestant growth rates (Gill 1998). As alluded to in the previous section, factors affecting supply, most notably the degree to which the religious market is regulated, provide a better explanation for variations in Protestant growth rates across Latin American countries. Demand for religion among the poor has remained relatively constant over time as evidenced by the pervasiveness of folk Catholicism, while the supply of religion (i.e., Protestant ministers) has increased. Although it appears that religiosity has increased in society, what we are really witnessing is a greater involvement in institutionalized religion (e.g., church service attendance) brought about by the presence of more religious institutions. At a casual glance, higher involvement in organized forms of religion resulting from increased supply appears as increased demand.

This still leaves the question of why Protestants would concentrate their efforts among the lower classes. Economic theory provides a relatively straightforward answer—if new entrants into the religious market act as parishioner-maximizers, membership gains will be greatest in areas where the monopoly church is least present. Knowing a little bit about the monopoly production and capital goods can help us understand why this is so.

Economics tells us that monopolies tend to underproduce goods, charge higher prices, and distribute them to sectors that are most likely to yield them the greatest rents. Monopoly religions, such as Latin American Catholicism for most of its existence, tend to have a "preferential option for the rich." This is because religious organizations, as stated above, require revenue to survive: priests must be paid, schools built, pews purchased, etc. Wealthy individuals are more likely to contribute greater financial resources in *absolute* terms[11] than poorer parishioners. Until the mid-twentieth century, the Latin American bishops concentrated most of their pastoral resources in upper-class urban neighborhoods and on wealthier haciendas. Priests rarely visited poor urban or rural communities, and when they did it often was to administer religious services that were associated with specific fees.[12] On top of this, the Church did not invest heavily in the recruitment and training of seminarians because of decreasing marginal returns; new priests would be placed in poorer areas where financial contributions were harder to obtain, and for the episcopacy, this wasn't worth the expense.[13] (Remember, while churches tend to act as parishioner-maximizers, religious monopolies have effectively captured 100 percent of the market thus satisfying this first-order preference. The second-order preference, revenue maximization, then takes precedence in episcopal strategies.) In the early 1970s, Latin America—the most Catholic region in the world—had five to ten times *fewer* priests per ten thousand Catholics than countries where Catholicism was the minority religion (Barret 1982).

The result was that the poor did not have a great deal of contact with institutional Catholicism and hence were more likely to practice the syncretic beliefs and rites of popular religiosity. This is important given the economic notion of capital goods. Like education, religion is both a consumption good and a capital good—it provides both immediate satisfaction and can be accumulated to provide future benefits (Iannaccone 1990). Churches create religious capital in their followers through constant exposure to the faith, a process sociologists refer to as socialization. People with large stocks of religious capital are less likely to convert to another religion because they have already invested heavily in learning the doctrines and rituals of one denomination. Switching denominations imposes significant start-up costs for the convert in terms of learning new beliefs and practices, meeting new people, etc. Additionally, the theory of religious capital implies that people who do switch denominations normally will choose religions that have practices and beliefs relatively similar to their previous faith. Conversions to fringe cults are relatively rare and short-lived.

Considering that the poor in Latin America were the social sector least exposed to institutional Catholicism, it is predictable that they have been attracted to evangelical Protestantism in significant numbers. With little knowledge of the formal practices of the Catholic Church, the *opportunity costs* of learning a new religion are relatively low. Moreover, it is not surprising that Pentecostalism is the denomination of choice among the poor. Folk Catholicism, the dominant form of religion among the poor, is closer in many respects to Pentecostalism than institutional Catholicism: Pentecostalism promotes direct, unmediated relations with God, is individualistic in nature, and emphasizes the mystical aspects of Christianity more than formal Catholicism. (Interestingly, recent growth in Catholic participation has been most rapid among "charismatic" Catholic parishes that mirror the practices of Pentecostalism.) The theory of religious capital explains missionizing failures in Latin American history as well. Early efforts (c. 1890s-1910s) by missionaries to convert the upper classes were generally in vain as the elite were solidly educated in Catholic doctrine. And attempts by Anglicans, Lutherans, and Presbyterians to attract members of the popular classes proceeded much more slowly than Pentecostal evangelization because these denominations were much more staid than folk Catholicism.

Finally, when one considers the organizational costs and benefits of participating in folk Catholicism relative to evangelical Protestantism, it is no surprise that people prefer the latter. Organized religions provide a number of communal benefits (e.g., fellowship) that are not available in personal religions.[14] Even folk Catholicism with its practice of personal saint worship is manifested in communal pageants and celebrations. Ministers who specialize in organizing regular religious activities lower the costs to the consumer. Even when one considers that organized religions often require significant financial contributions, the gains from specialization and economies of scale are likely to outweigh such contributions.[15] Organized religions offer regularized companionship with fellow parishioners, something that folk Catholicism does not. Looking at the current religious landscape in Latin America, the rapid expansion of evangelical Protestantism tells us that when people are presented with the option of joining a Protestant congregation or continuing *exclusive* practice of folk Catholicism,[16] the former option usually wins out.

SELLING THE FAITH: CREDENCE GOODS AND ECONOMIC INCENTIVES FOR CONVERSION

Once evangelists choose a target population, the next question that arises is how they will attract members to their faith. Despite the fact that evangelical Protestants offer a low-cost religious alternative to the poor, conversion nonetheless imposes costs on an individual. These costs may sometimes be very substantial. For example, being one of the first to join an evangelical congregation in a town might expose an individual to social ostracism. Evangelical ministers must be able to convince prospective converts that the benefits of joining their church outweigh the costs involved. Such a task is not easy considering that religion is a credence good—i.e., a good whose real value and quality cannot be verified until a later date, possibly never. Given the uncertainty surrounding religion, prospective consumers must look for other means to judge the credibility of the minister before making a "leap of faith."[17] Producers of credence goods therefore need to invest a good deal in convincing prospective buyers of their credibility, especially if their denomination is completely foreign. This lesson was not lost on one of Latin America's first foreign missionaries—Bartolomé de Las Casas. He and several other Catholic bishops made a concerted effort to protect indigenous Americans from being abused by Spanish conquistadors in order to win their trust (de Las Casas 1992).

It is quite common for missionaries to offer unconditional economic or medical assistance to communities experiencing hardship. While this evangelizing strategy often earns the derogatory label of "ricebowl Christianity" or "disaster evangelism," it is a rational technique for establishing a trusting relationship with people who would otherwise be suspicious of "gringo" preachers. Offering long-term opportunities for self-improvement and economic advancement (e.g., literacy training, access to employment networks) is also effective in attracting parishioners. Numerous evangelists I have interviewed over the years recount how vital it is to win the trust and respect of a population before trying to convert them (Gill 1998, 88-91). It should be kept in mind that most people participate in religion not because of its instrumental value for material advancement, but because they have a thirst for God. Tangible benefits help alleviate the uncertainty surrounding a new missionary's credibility, but they do not substitute for the spiritual needs that churchgoers wish to have fulfilled.

Another commonly applied method to win converts is to indigenize the leadership of the denomination. As people typically place more trust in members of their own community over strangers, a denomination with an indigenous clergy will be more successful at establishing congregations than ones relying permanently on foreign personnel, ceteris paribus. Chilean Pentecostalism spread rapidly after a group of native Chileans broke from the foreign-dominated Iglesia Metodista de Chile to establish three new churches— La Iglesia Metodista Nacional, La Iglesia Metodista Pentecostal, and La Iglesia Evangélica Pentecostal (Sepúlveda 1987, 254-56). Typically, successful missionaries enter a town, establish a church, train a cadre of local pastors, and then move to a different site, a practice that was universal among the numerous missionaries I have interviewed over the years.

Once Evangelicals build a sizable congregation, they can take advantage of economies of scale and the recruitment process becomes easier—later converts rely upon the quality judgments of early converts in a process of informational cascading. Public testimonials are a favorite recruitment technique among Evangelicals. Realizing that people are more likely to join a church if they already know and trust some of its members, they also rely on their parishioners to recruit family members and friends, a technique employed quite effectively by Mormons throughout Latin America. Group conversions also help to lower the costs of ostracism that an individual convert would have to bear. Rev. Paul Wegmueller, known as *el misionero de las películas*, would gather several dozen people in a village for a showing of a Christian-based film. Following the film, he would have the group declare affiliation with his evangelical church.[18] Knowing that others in the community were joining helped alleviate the difficulty in making such a difficult first step into a new denomination. Having neglected the poor for so long, many Catholic clergy have found that they too must regain the trust of prospective parishioners if they are to re-evangelize Latin America (see Hurtado 1992). Not coincidentally, they have relied on techniques similar to those of Protestant missionaries. The varied activities of Ecclesial Base Communities—e.g., literacy campaigns, community improvement projects, Bible reading, etc.—mimic the early efforts of Protestants. Greater lay involvement and charismatic preachers have also been common in contemporary Latin American Catholicism.

The use of economic incentives to build trust among the evangelized and draw them into the faith sheds some light on a recent debate surrounding the socioeconomic impact of Protestant growth in Latin America (see Cavalcanti 1995). Numerous scholars have observed that Protestant converts tend to do better economically than non-converts of similar socioeconomic backgrounds (e.g., Brusco 1995). One is tempted to interpret this result as a predictive success for Weber's "Protestant ethic" thesis, wherein Protestantism is responsible for altering the mindset of individuals in a manner more conducive to capitalist development. However, when we consider the economic incentives used to evangelize parishioners we can see how material improvement is used frequently to drive religious change, not vice versa. Those joining a new faith often do so because they want to improve their life situation. In other words, the seeds for personal betterment are already sown prior to joining the evangelical church. On top of this, there is a significant self-selection bias at work. The "movers and shakers" within a community are most likely to be the ones who convert to a new religion *and* move up the socioeconomic ladder. Brusco (1995) has argued that Pentecostalism is an attractive religious choice for women because it forces males to adopt more disciplined behavioral patterns. While Protestantism may encourage certain values such as sobriety and thrift among males (thus preventing us from completely dismissing a modified version of Weber's thesis), the initial choice by the female was made with the intention of economic betterment. However new religious beliefs may help a person economically at the margins, the structural impediments to economic advancement facing the poor in Latin America are unlikely to be erased by a religious movement.

CONCLUSION

Understanding how society's religious landscape changes over time has been of great interest to social scientists. This is increasingly true in the study of Latin America, where Protestantism has exploded onto the scene in such dramatic fashion in the past several decades. Most scholarly accounts of religious change focus on the role of cultural values and worldviews. "Great Awakenings" are explained as responses to shifts in the mindset of societies undergoing great crisis. Evangelization is frequently viewed as "fanatical" behavior driven by people with steadfast morals and missionizing zeal. While partially true, a great deal of change in religion is motivated by cost-benefit calculations. Proselytizing religious organizations want to reach as many people as possible with their spiritual message. However, once a religion establishes a monopoly over the type of spiritual message preached in a society, the economic necessity of operating a hegemonic social institution prompts a church to pay more attention to enhancing its revenue base than to actively providing sufficient quantities of spirituality via constant evangelization efforts. In this case, religious participation lags in society until some new producer can crack the market and fill the void left by the lackadaisical monopoly faith. Missionary movements will tend to gravitate toward monopolized religious economies where the cost of entry is relatively low and the potential gain in converts is high. Countries with greater levels of religious freedom will witness increasing amounts of religious diversity and the expansion of new religions will most likely be located among the most disenfranchised in society. Winning converts often will require providing tangible benefits so as to build the trust of the community. This framework helps us to understand the dynamics of religion in Latin America from the time of the Conquest to present-day growth in evangelical Protestantism. While this approach cannot explain everything, the economics of evangelization illuminates a great deal about religious behavior.

Part Two

PERSPECTIVES
ON RELIGIOUS FREEDOM

———◆———

5.

Cuba

————————◆————————

Margaret E. Crahan

Religious freedom has always been an issue in Cuba.[1] From the extirpation of the religious beliefs of the indigenous peoples by the Spanish conquistadors in the sixteenth century to the attempts to snuff out the Protestantism imported by foreign merchants and seamen in the nineteenth century, intolerance was official policy and practice. Intensive efforts were also made to uproot the beliefs of the enslaved Africans who began to be imported in the sixteenth century and whose numbers increased dramatically three centuries later when Cuba became the world's principal plantation-based sugar producer. In spite of such efforts, neither Protestantism, nor Afro-Cuban spiritism, commonly known as *santería*, was wiped out. By the mid-twentieth century, Cuba was not only the most religiously diverse, but also the most secular country in Latin America.[2] Today, after four decades of Marxist-Leninist government, the island is enjoying a religious resurgence that is raising new issues of religious freedom and liberty of conscience. This essay will examine evangelization and freedom of religion in Cuba in the context of ongoing attempts to impose religious or ideological orthodoxy on a population that has historically been highly heterodox and pragmatic in its religious beliefs and practices.

HISTORICAL HERITAGE

Institutional religion was introduced into Cuba by the Spaniards in the late fifteenth century, and by the 1650s the indigenous population and their religious beliefs were virtually eradicated. In that era the Catholic church was

This chapter is a revision and expansion of "Catholicism in Cuba" by Margaret E. Crahan, *Cuban Studies* 19, ed. Carmelo Mesa-Lago (University of Pittsburgh Press, 1989). Original material is used by permission of the University of Pittsburgh Press.

intimately allied with the Spanish monarchy via the *Patronato Real* (Royal Patronage)[3] and was consequently a prime support of the crown's acquisition and consolidation of empire. Hence religion in Cuba throughout the colonial period (1492-1898) was closely identified with the exercise of political power, although the actual level of influence of the church varied over time. Nevertheless, the Catholic church was generally considered a major actor in Cuban society and a prime molder of values and attitudes.

The vitality of the Catholic church was linked to the flow of money and personnel from Spain and was affected by the fortunes of the island itself. As the mainland Spanish colonies increased in importance, Cuba became something of a colonial backwater and the Catholic church suffered accordingly. More competent and better connected clerics were generally sent to Mexico or Peru, while Cuba was, at times, used as a dumping ground for miscreant priests and friars. Ecclesiastical revenues were frequently inadequate to maintain these individuals, who sometimes abused their offices in order to survive or to enhance their living conditions. This contributed to the growth of anticlericalism in Cuba, which was reinforced by the administrative domination of Spanish priests over the Cuban clergy. Furthermore, in a relatively poor society with low organizational levels, particularly in the rural areas, the urban-centered church frequently appeared to be a distant institution. With the expansion of slavery in the latter part of the eighteenth and beginning of the nineteenth centuries, large parts of rural Cuba became strongholds of Afro-Cuban beliefs.

The Catholic church, however, did become a symbol of Cuban identity as it consolidated its institutional reach over the whole island, albeit in a rather superficial fashion.[4] Some of its intellectual leaders, most notably Father Félix Varela, contributed to the formation of Cuban nationalism and ultimately to its long struggle for independence (1868-98). However, as an institution the church tended to support the status quo in terms of both slavery and independence and hence was identified with conservative elements. The Catholic church entered the twentieth century weakened by this image and still dependent on Spain for the bulk of its personnel and funds.

It was not until the 1920s that the Catholic church began to strongly reassert itself, particularly through the organization of the *Federación de la Juventud Cubana* (1927), *Acción Católica* (1928), *Caballeros Católicos* (1929), and *Agrupación Universitaria* (1931). As in the rest of Latin America the formation of such groups was prompted, in part, by increasing preoccupation with secular and religious competitors, including Marxist political parties and labor unions, as well as Protestants. This led the church to establish competing organizations, which were strongly influenced by reformist Catholic social doctrine. However, as one Cuban Jesuit historian has concluded:

> The Church lacked any significant meaning for the peasants and the workers. In the revolution of 1933 the Church took very little part. Some

laymen occupied ministerial positions in the short-lived Grau administration (1933-1934). The Constitution of 1940, which invoked the favor of God, continued the policy of separation of Church and state,
religious freedom, and lay instruction.

All these developments would give the impression of a Church limited in its actions, and reduced to a small circle in its social relevance.[5]

For example, a 1957 survey by *Agrupación Católica* of four hundred heads of
rural families revealed the startling fact that 53.51 percent had never laid eyes
on a priest. Another 36.74 percent indicated that they only knew one by sight,
with only 7.81 percent claiming to have had any personal contact with a cleric.
The weakness of the institutional churches in the rural areas was also attested
to by the fact that 41.41 percent claimed to have no religion, while only 52.10
percent identified themselves as Catholics, 3.26 percent as Protestants, and
1.09 percent as spiritists. Of the Catholics 88.84 percent never attended mass
and only 4.25 percent did so three or more times a year. Furthermore, when
asked what institution would be of most assistance in improving the lot of the
rural worker, only 3.43 percent mentioned the church. Most named the government (68.73 percent) or employer (16.72 percent).[6] While the influence of
the Catholic church was limited, it was clearly greater than that of the Protestant churches.

Embarking on a period of strong growth in 1898, reductions in personnel
and monies caused by World War I and the Great Depression diminished Protestant expansion. In 1940, after a survey of 440 congregations, one Protestant
analyst concluded:

> The Evangelical church is not yet adjusted in program, upkeep, and lead-
> ership to the economic and social conditions of Cuba. The church is a
> middle-class and expensive institution in a largely lower-class and pov-
> erty-stricken constituency. It is an Anglo-Saxon and democratic institu-
> tion in a Latin and feudal society. It is an urbanized institution seeking to
> expand in a rural environment.[7]

There were exceptions, including *La Progresiva*, a Presbyterian school in
Cárdenas that encouraged social action, and the Baptists in Oriente who had a
strong presence among the poor.

Clearly the Protestant churches, like the Catholic church, were particularly
weak in rural areas. Both emphasized educating the Cuban upper and middle
classes as the prime means of influencing Cuban society and molding its values.

The Catholic and the Protestant churches had only just begun to seriously
experiment with programs aimed at incorporating the rural population and
urban lower classes when Fulgencio Batista staged his 1952 coup. The response of the Catholic Church to the takeover was ambiguous, according to
the historian Hugh Thomas:

Cardinal Arteaga congratulated Batista, and other bishops backed him. Two or three opposed and a Franciscan priest, Fr. Bastarrica, publicly denounced the *golpe*, as did several prominent lay leaders, such as Andrés Valdespino, president of *Juventud Católica*. . . . In June a Catholic Action meeting at Guanajay was broken up by the police. It became clear that while some members of the hierarchy and the regular clergy would tolerate the new order only too easily, most Catholic laymen and priests would not.[8]

A 1971 evaluation by the Methodist Church of the actions and attitudes of the Protestant churches in Cuba in the 1950s concluded that they had been cautious rather than prophetic.[9] This was especially true of the Baptists and Methodists, the two largest historic denominations, as well as some fundamentalists.

Up until 1957 there was a feeling within the churches that there was little possibility that Batista would be defeated militarily. Protestant tentativeness was further encouraged by their limited numbers and by continued suspicion and occasional intolerance directed at them. Catholics and Protestants feared repression by the Batista government and repeatedly proclaimed their neutrality.

The escalation of the struggle between Batista and Castro's 26th of July Movement eventually caused the Catholic and the Protestant church leadership to attempt to influence the course of events. In 1956 Cardinal Manuel Arteaga of Havana proposed a peace plan that was essentially ignored by both sides. The Methodist Church organized a vigil for peace in 1957 and considered not opening its Candler University for the academic year, in part to protest Batista's closing of the University of Havana.[10] Both Candler and the Catholic University of Villanueva were, nevertheless, opened. By and large the churches tended to limit themselves to criticizing the Castro forces for using violence to achieve their goals and Batista for suppressing democracy.

Individual church people became involved in the struggle principally on the side of the 26th of July Movement, reflecting the overwhelmingly anti-Batista sentiments of the Cuban populace. While a handful of clerics participated directly, the most active church people were youths, both Catholic and Protestant, who carried messages, helped publish revolutionary statements, raised money, and organized strikes and demonstrations.[11] Some joined Castro's forces in the Sierra, such as the Baptist youth leader Frank Pais, who lost his life in the struggle.

Overall the churches, together with the Jewish community, did not play a major role in the 1950s struggle. Although sentiment was largely anti-Batista, there was little sense that religious beliefs required taking an active part in the conflict. Rather there was an attempt to maintain the churches apart from the struggle. This did not prevent both Batista and Castro from exaggerating, for their own purposes, the contribution of the churches, particularly the Catholic, to Batista's downfall. Batista, for example, once commented to an aide that he resigned because of the opposition of the *hacendados, colonos*, the army, and the church. This was an exaggeration, as the church as a whole had been ambiguous. But it was a pleasing and flattering exaggeration. Batista did this to lessen his own responsibility. Castro, like Batista, also exaggerated the church's role—in this case to win the church's support. Castro declared that Cuba's Catholics had given the revolution "very substantial assistance."[12]

Catholics expected amicable relations with the new government and improvements in their status. Some hoped the state would expand religious instruction in the public schools. Protestants and Jews hoped for a lessening of the influence of the Catholic church in education and government. Virtually all expected a liberal democracy that would initiate an era of economic prosperity that would stimulate church growth. Few expected that within a year there would be intense conflict that would result in the departure of 70 percent of Catholic priests and 90 percent of Catholic religious. Over 50 percent of Protestant clerical and lay leaders also left, while the Jewish community was reduced to one-tenth of its 1959 size (12,000). One hundred and thirty-two priests were expelled on September 17, 1961, for alleged counterrevolutionary activities.[13] By 1963 some had returned.

The Catholic church was ill-prepared to respond to the challenge of the Castro revolution, lacking the organizational flexibility, ideological and political openness, and commitment to substantial socioeconomic change that the Second Vatican Council (1962-65) would stimulate. The church came relatively rapidly to be regarded as a counterrevolutionary institution. While the Protestant churches were more adaptable administratively and politically, their strong identification with the United States made them increasingly suspect as U.S.-Cuban tension increased in 1959-60. The situation of both the Protestants and Catholics was exacerbated by the fact that the Cuban revolution occurred at the height of the Cold War.[14] In sum, the churches in Cuba were ill-disposed to accept a Marxist revolution in Cuba, yet their institutional weaknesses, the strength of secularism in Cuban society, and foreign links reduced their capacity to offer alternatives and be accepted as legitimate critics. This was particularly true given the fact that much of their support came from those who were most likely to emigrate abroad. Hence in a struggle for the ultimate loyalty of the Cuban people, their traditional identification with the bourgeoisie and dependence on foreign personnel and funding were disadvantageous. The limited penetration of the churches in the rural areas on which the Castro government focused in the early years of the revolution further compounded the churches' dilemma.

Hence, while the Catholic and Protestant churches appeared to be gaining strength in Cuba in the 1950s with Catholic Action claiming thirty thousand members and Young Catholic Workers twenty thousand, these developments were somewhat deceptive. Church leaders were only beginning to focus on such problems as the poverty and inequality targeted by the revolution, much less to devise effective strategies to prepare the churches to respond to them. In addition, the somewhat elitist nature of groups such as Catholic Action and the Protestant Christian Student Movement meant they were ill-adapted to mobilize substantial popular support for their positions. Nevertheless, since Christianity was a pervasive cultural presence, the churches served to give expression to the generalized anti-Marxism of much of the population. The church-state struggle that occurred at the outset of the revolution was therefore quickly reduced to a single issue—communism.

The traditional weakness of the churches in the rural areas and among the urban poor meant that Castro was more able to mobilize them than the churches. This left the latter in the uncomfortable position of appearing to oppose socioeconomic reforms to benefit the poor. It also reflected a reality within the pre–Vatican II Catholic church. Traditional Catholic elites tended to view social problems "largely in terms of charity to the poor and not in terms of changing the position of the poor in the social order or changing the social order itself."[15] Thus, while the Catholic church initially responded positively to the revolutionary government's emphasis on socioeconomic change, it was not prepared to accept massive restructuring of Cuban society to accomplish it. The church's analysis of Cuban conditions was rooted in the belief that reforms flowing out of individual Christian commitment were sufficient. This belief was shared by the Protestants, but obviously not by the government. As opposition to revolutionary restructuring increased, the nature of the churches' social doctrine, in addition to their historic national and international alliances, inclined Catholics and Protestants to identify with the counterrevolution. That led to sharp conflict with the government and hostility from revolutionary elements. In this volatile atmosphere active church people became highly suspect. Church actions and the government's response will be examined in the next section dealing with the initial impact of Castro's coming to power and the consolidation of the revolution in the period 1959-61.

RELIGION AND REVOLUTION, 1959-1961

Mateo Jover, president of Catholic Action in 1959, has characterized that year as one of reciprocal acceptance and cordiality between church and state in Cuba.[16] The reality was somewhat more complex. While the Catholic hierarchy welcomed Batista's overthrow and Havana's Protestant churches held a service of thanksgiving on February 7, 1959,[17] there were reservations among both clergy and laity. Archbishop Enrique Pérez Serantes of Santiago, who had intervened on Castro's behalf when he was jailed after the failed 1953 attack on the Moncada barracks, counseled that the revolution should lead to a democratic republic devoid of "utopian egalitarianism," a catchword for communism.[18] As early as January 1959 Cardinal Richard Cushing of Boston was condemning the Cuban government for seizing church property. This prompted the Cuban bishops to issue a strong denial, adding that the church in Cuba had no properties worth taking. The following month three Cuban bishops did, however, strongly criticize the execution of some of Batista's allies and urged clemency.[19]

By March 1959 some in the Catholic church were expressing concern over an education law that would prohibit teachers from providing religious instruction in public schools as had previously been the case.[20] Tension increased when the government circulated the draft of an agrarian reform law which was adopted in May 1959. Welcomed by Bishop Evelio Díaz of Havana in the name of the hierarchy, it was condemned by the *Agrupación Católica*.[21] This helped prompt a meeting of sixty-two clerics at Castro's Jesuit alma mater, Belén, in June 1959 to review the situation. While one of the hosts, Manuel Foyacá, warned of communist elements in the agrarian reform bill, the Franciscan Friar Bíain defended the revolution. The meeting served to reinforce the preoccupations of those clerics fearful of Marxism and thereafter some priests used their pulpits to criticize the direction of the revolution.[22] Protestants shared some of the same worries and, in general, felt that the new government was more radical than warranted.[23] Overall there was an increasing preoccupation on the part of the Catholic church with the sanctity of private property. Protestants tended to divide into two groups: the majority, who withdrew from the revolutionary process and feared the loss of ties to the United States; and a minority, who began a "painful process of new ideological and theological reflection."[24]

Divisions within both the Catholic and Protestant churches limited their capacity to influence the revolution. This also caused them to be slow to react to government initiatives and hampered the offering of alternatives. Divisions within the Catholic hierarchy were exacerbated by conflicting pressures emanating from the laity.[25] Under these circumstances the churches tended to be used by various spokespersons for special interests rather than for broadly supported options.

Twenty years later a delegation of Cuban Catholics at the Latin American Bishops' Conference in Puebla would reflect:

> At the time of the triumph of the Revolution . . . the Cuban church was in a preconciliar position profoundly marked by conservatism and anti-Communism. Although it exhibited sectors with liberal and social democratic tendencies . . . it was predominantly a conservative church. For its part, international Communism during that period was marked by an acute anti-religious sentiment. This was the situation when the Cuban Revolution was declared socialist (April 1961).[26]

It was in this atmosphere that religious processions began to turn into anti-government rallies, and revolutionaries interrupted church services and raided parish houses.

The transformation of the Catholic Church into an institutional base for opposition to the revolution was symbolized by the estimated tens of thousands that attended the National Catholic Congress in November 1959. Previously no more than ten thousand had attended such meetings. As one commentator noted, the message was clear. "With the collapse of the traditional political parties, a mass demonstration had given evidence that Castro was not alone in being able to attract a great public. It was a warning, which produced no official reaction."[27] Two Catholic leaders made the message clear at the Congress. Mateo Jover, president of Catholic Action, warned against the dangers of exaggerated nationalism. José Ignacio Lasaga of *Agrupación Católica* vehemently declared: "Social justice yes; redemption of the worker yes; communism no!" The crowd responded with chants of "¡Cuba si, Comunismo no!" The Congress adopted a resolution opposing all totalitarian doctrines.[28]

Shortly thereafter two Cuban priests mounted an anti-Castro campaign in Miami, charging that the government planned to establish a state-controlled national church. This was denied by Bishop Evelio Díaz, who further asserted that no priests had been prevented from exercising their ministries as had also been alleged.[29] At that time the lay leader Manuel Artimé of *Agrupación Católica* organized a counterrevolutionary group—*Movimiento de Rescate Revolucionario* (MRR). Shortly thereafter he was put in touch with the CIA by a Jesuit priest and secretly left Cuba.[30] The lines of conflict were being drawn and the church was being sucked in as an institution. Mateo Jover characterized it as not a battle between church and state, but rather between "a revolution and a counterrevolution, and this latter kept making religious freedom one of its battle cries—at least for reasons of propaganda."[31]

Although the revolutionary government passed no laws, nor adopted any formal repressive policies with respect to religion, the increasingly Marxist orientation of the government convinced many church people that their religious freedom was in jeopardy. On May 16, 1960, Bishop Pérez Serantes declared: "We cannot say that Communism is at our doors, for in reality it is within our walls, speaking out as if it were at home."[32] This action spurred a spate of pro-government demonstrations in front of various churches. The rallying cry for the Catholics was "Cuba sí, Rusia no" and for the revolutionaries "Cuba sí, Yanqui no." By the autumn of 1960 the Cuban bishops had issued a series of pastoral letters which stated that in any conflict over Cuba between the United States and the USSR, they would support the former.[33] Coming as they did after the beginning of the nationalizations of U.S. property in June 1960 they placed the Catholic church clearly in opposition to the revolution. These documents constituted an attack on the legitimacy of the government, as well as on the revolution. They also effectively diminished the credibility of the Catholic church as a critic of the revolution, given the revolutionary credo "within the revolution everything, outside the revolution nothing."

The year 1961 was a particularly difficult one for the Cuban churches. The departure of many of the supporters of church schools resulted in precipitous declines in income for some of them, including Belén.[34] Some schools acquired reputations as centers for counterrevolutionary activities, resulting in raids of the premises to locate weapons. The National Institute of Sports, Physical

Education, and Recreation organized programs on Sunday mornings that competed with services and Sunday School classes.[35] No laws were enacted prohibiting worship, however, as has sometimes been alleged. The government nationalized private schools, religious and secular, in the aftermath of the April 17, 1961, Bay of Pigs invasion, and it prohibited religious processions in the streets after a youth was killed in a procession in September 1961 that had turned into an anti-government demonstration.[36] It was in this context that approximately 5 percent of the 2,948 priests and religious were expelled by the government.[37]

The expulsions, together with the nationalization of schools, prompted a massive exodus of church people in the summer of 1961. Some churches ceased functioning, leading to charges that the government was closing them. In reality there was a scarcity of pastors. Some Protestant churches responded by naming lay people, including women, to take over. The Catholic church did not. Nevertheless, rather than declining, the number of Catholic parishes increased from 210 in 1960 to 226 in 1965.[38]

The May 1, 1961, nationalization of private schools was justified by the government on the grounds that a number of them had been used to prepare for the insurrection that was supposed to accompany the Bay of Pigs invasion. Four Spanish priests had accompanied the invaders, and Manuel Artimé of *Agrupación Católica* commanded the force. His participation, as well as that of a number of other *Agrupados*, resulted in the closing down of the organization's headquarters in Havana.[39]

In 1970 the then-rector of the Catholic Seminary in Havana, Father Carlos Manuel de Cespedes, explained the departures in this fashion:

When the Bay of Pigs took place, many of the leaders of the invasion were Catholics, and a number of priests came with them. Everything happened very fast at that time. Fidel had admitted that our revolution was a Marxist one, and I imagine that, generally speaking, those who solidly backed the revolution looked on Catholics as their sworn enemies. For their part, Catholics felt the same: it was a Communist revolution, hence intrinsically bad. You had to fight it or flee. Only the most perceptive and tranquil minority could imagine themselves joining it. In the summer of 1961, just after the nationalization of education, most of the religious who had been teaching in Catholic schools left Cuba. Many other priests also got out—some because they had been involved in counter revolutionary activities, others out of fear; some expelled by the revolutionary government, others voluntarily. It was in that sort of atmosphere that the decision was made to send the seminarians abroad. But a year later, in 1962, seminary courses were again being held in Cuba.[40]

The Catholic and Protestant churches encouraged and facilitated such departures, a step that was later regretted by some. In 1971 a World Council of Churches' official concluded that there had been too hasty a withdrawal of missionaries and too much listening to the advice of the U.S. Embassy and the State Department.[41] This conclusion was shared by the U.S. United Methodist Board of Missions. It ascribed the departure of all but two of the forty-four Methodist ministers in Cuba to the belief that the United States would not permit a communist regime in its proverbial backyard and that it was better to sit out the coming confrontation in the safety of the United States. In addition, there was a growing fear of Marxist indoctrination of children in public schools. Inconveniences such as scarcity of basic foodstuffs also provided some stimulus, as did distaste for a loss of privilege and prestige. Overall, there was a generalized fear of the unknown. Given their ties to foreign churches, there were assurances of assistance in resettling and jobs. Finally, there was a commonality of values with their North American counterparts.[42] As one U.S. cleric phrased it, "Many of the Presbyterians and other Protestants who had left Cuba had done so because to remain in an 'anti-Yanqui' Communist land seemed to them an act of disloyalty to the stateside 'mother church.'"[43]

The departure of many clerical and lay leaders not only limited the capacity of the churches to minister to their remaining members, but it also created tensions between those who opted to go and those who stayed. A mid-1960s survey of Protestant youth in Cuba revealed that a good number of them felt that the departure of ministers had been akin to abandoning the flock in the face of the wolf.[44] Among those who left there was a sense that the church people who stayed were collaborators.[45] Fidel Castro's 1961 declaration that the revolution was Marxist-Leninist not only contributed to the exodus of church people, it reportedly left those who remained "disoriented and afraid." They turned to the church primarily as shelter, conserving the familiar and shutting out the pervasive changes being engineered in every other sector of life, such as the system of universal work, participatory education, and socialized medicine.[46]

Increasingly, church people were marginalized and alienated within Cuban society. At times they were discriminated against, particularly in schools and work places. Those regarded as "making religion a way of life" were sometimes denied admission to the universities or to certain jobs, including teaching. Although the government never mounted a broad-based campaign against the churches, the Marxist-Leninist orientation of the revolution gave it an antireligious character. Jorge Domínguez has concluded that those policies that existed in the early 1960s "probably made no difference in religious beliefs."[47] Cuba had been, and remained, a largely secular society without significant religious conflicts. Once governmental and religious elites settled their main differences by the second half of the 1960s, religion returned to its previous political unimportance. By 1962 the churches had turned in upon themselves, providing a refuge from the pervasive ferment about them. They would not begin to attempt to reinsert themselves into Cuban society until the end of the 1960s. The intervening years were not, however, totally quiescent.

FROM REFUGE TO RAPPROCHEMENT, 1963-1969

Throughout the period 1959-62 the Vatican strove to avoid serious conflict with the Castro government, frequently counseling the Cuban bishops to avoid exacerbating tensions. In 1961 Pope John XXIII sent an experienced diplomat, Monsignor Cesare Zacchi, to Havana as the papal representative. He undertook to rebuild church-state relations and had considerable success over the next dozen years. Relations with the Vatican were, in fact, more cordial than those with the Cuban hierarchy. The government assisted in the publication of the pope's 1963 encyclical *Pacem in Terris*, which was widely studied in Cuba, including by government officials.

In 1962 some of the priests who left Cuba began to return. They were joined by a few missionaries, particularly from France and Belgium.[48] Gradually government pressure and suspicion began to diminish and the churches began to turn their attention to adapting to their situation. Given the double isolation of Cuban church people stemming from the diplomatic and economic embargo of Cuba, together with that of the churches within Cuban society, the impact of international religious trends was delayed.

The adaptation of the churches was an arduous process as change was highly suspect. Even some of the reforms of Vatican II were thought by some Catholics to be government instigated to create a national church.[49] Protestant and Catholic youth were generally in the forefront in pressuring for church reforms. Their activism, however, made them somewhat suspect to both civil and ecclesiastical officials and hence their groups were generally disbanded.[50] The Protestant churches were more receptive to internal reform, particularly to more lay participation in decision making. Nevertheless, Protestant youths in the mid-1960s often felt that their churches were not well prepared to meet the challenge of the revolution and that substantial theological and structural change first had to be accomplished. This included devising a doctrinal base that would allow the church to be in the forefront of the struggle for justice. To accomplish this they felt it was necessary to promote positive aspects of the revolution. Eighty-nine percent felt that it would be useful to clarify church-state relations in law.[51]

One of the more serious problems to confront Christian youth in the mid-1960s was that posed by the adoption of universal military service. Many church people were opposed to such training and according to officials of the Cuban Council of Evangelical Churches (CIEC) they requested that such individuals be allowed to perform alternative service.[52] A few seminarians, ministers, priests, and others who made "religion a way of life" were subjected to forced labor as a result of being drafted into the Military Units to Aid Production (UMAP). Other draftees into UMAP included tramps, pimps, homosexuals, and ex-convicts. The shock of rubbing shoulders with such individuals was substantial for many church people. For some, UMAP precipitated a crisis of faith, prompting greater withdrawal from secular society and for others an increased desire to come to terms with the revolution.[53]

In 1966 a Baptist minister, Raimundo García Franco, attempted to summarize his experience and that of other Christians in UMAP. He found that while it had caused him to call upon all his psychological and spiritual resources, it had strengthened his faith. He also felt it helped him better understand nonbelievers. He reported that religious activists eventually came to occupy supervisory positions in UMAP because of their work ethic and fairness. One of the greatest difficulties was the sense of having been abandoned by their churches.[54] This feeling was seconded by a leader of Catholic Action, who claimed that priests rarely made any effort to contact lay persons drafted into UMAP.[55] A Methodist layman interviewed in Havana in 1974 stated that since his release he had been more accepted by people outside the church than those inside.[56] All claimed that their experiences in UMAP had fortified their faith and rooted it more firmly in Cuban realities. Due, in good measure, to public criticism, UMAP was disbanded by the government in the late 1960s.

By that time relations between civil and church officials were improving. Mateo Jover stated that a priest who isolated himself in his church and shunned secular officials was suspect, while the cleric who engaged in dialogue with revolutionaries was accepted. In addition, Jover held that any active Christian who "has a certain cultural level, practices some professional activity, and is scrupulously zealous in performing his work duties . . . is not only tolerated but respected."[57] Young Catholics like Jover were among those who pressured the church to initiate a dialogue with the government and build up credibility in order to be again accepted as a moral leader within Cuban society.[58] To do this, Jover felt, it was first necessary for the church to undergo substantial internal change that would make it better adapted to its existential situation. This involved rethinking the church's mission in modern society, reeducating clergy and laity, and devising mechanisms whereby the church could reinsert itself into Cuban society. Vatican II had focused on these problems, emphasizing the church's responsibility to deal with contemporary socioeconomic problems and making religious education more relevant to daily life. In addition, the council had stimulated some decentralization of authority within the church and greater lay participation. Some Catholics viewed such reforms as a means of making the church more capable of influencing the course of Cuban society. Such thinking contributed to the bishops' pastoral letters of April and September 1969.

The first document condemned the U.S. economic blockade of Cuba and urged Catholics not to stand apart from those activities which promoted the common good. The second assured Cuban Catholics that cooperation with Marxists for the betterment of Cuban society was legitimate. While these documents improved church-state relations, they also precipitated considerable discussion within the church. Some Catholics regarded them as a sellout; others felt that they did not go far enough in supporting the revolution. A sizeable group of younger Catholics felt that the bishops should have linked support for the accomplishments of the revolution with the church's assumption of the role of a critic of the process. Debate within the church was intense, and Rome sent a representative to Havana in October 1969 to meet with lay persons and clerics to discuss their differences. Ultimately the bishops maintained their control over the process of rapprochement, focusing on rebuilding the church's credibility with the government without attempting to take a critical stance. Some active Catholics who were opponents of this strategy abandoned the church at this time.[59]

The political scientist Jorge Domínguez attributes the bishops' pastoral letters to four principal motives: a desire to reinsert the church into the existing political system, the influence of developments resulting from Vatican II, the growth of progressive trends in the international church, and ecumenical dialogue.[60] All of these elements appear to have continued to prod the Catholic hierarchy to respond more directly in the 1970s to the reality of existing within a socialist society. The prelates, nevertheless, limited themselves to improving relations with the government rather than attempting to reassert strong influence within Cuban society. Hence, the Catholic church did not break out of its essentially marginal position. This strategy had some advantages, according to Manuel Fernández, editor of *Mensaje Iberoamericano*. He noted that in 1969

> the situation of the Church in Cuba, after ten years of coexistence with a Socialist regime, is far from ideal. At the same time, one should not call it a persecuted Church and even less a subterranean Church, however much some Catholics would like to use that word; for in the revolutionary context of Cuba, that would make it a conspiratorial Church, which the government would not tolerate, nor should the Church desire to be such. The government makes every effort to show that there is religious liberty . . . and Catholics make sure that their activities are always open and above board (doors and windows have literally been left wide open during certain religious meetings so that there can be no suspicion about what is being said and done). Yet it becomes increasingly apparent that the Church, though now "marginal," is no longer—as it has been till recently—"under attack." For people attack only what is a lurking threat—and Cuban Catholics are certainly no threat today.[61]

During the late 1960s the mainline Protestant denominations also sought to adapt to Cuban realities. This process was spearheaded by the Cuban Council of Evangelical Churches (CIEC), the ecumenical seminary at Matanzas, and the Presbyterian and Methodist churches, which were headed by individuals considerably more supportive of the revolution than many Cuban Protestants. CIEC initiated a series of activities aimed at encouraging dialogue within and among the churches, as well as Marxist Christian exchange. Its work, and that of individual churches, was facilitated by funds from churches in the United States transferred via the World Council of Churches. On December 24, 1963,

Secretary of State Dean Rusk approved a proposal of the U.S. National Council of Churches to send funds to the World Council for the Protestant churches and agencies in Cuba. Given their traditional financial dependence on foreign funds these monies were essential at the time. The Cuban government cooperated with the transfer from 1964 until the early 1970s when most of the churches became self-supporting. Many Cuban church people welcomed the end of this program, feeling that it limited the maturation of their churches. The Cuban government also permitted funds into the country to support the Catholic church, as well as some Protestant denominations that were not members of CIEC.[62]

Church people visiting Cuba from abroad in the late 1970s described the churches as undergoing considerable change. Most felt that there was a growing tendency, particularly among younger people, to reconcile their religious beliefs with socialism and to seek ways to contribute to the revolution. While one World Council of Churches official believed that 95 percent of Cuban Protestants continued to be ill at ease within their country, a representative of the United Methodist Board of Missions thought that Christians in Cuba were increasingly playing a significant role as reconcilers.[63] Another U.S. Protestant observer felt that the government position toward the churches was positive and that while some individual officials acted contrary to government policies, practicing Christians were not persecuted unless they were counterrevolutionaries.[64] After a 1969 visit Rabbi Everett Gendler stated:

> Today . . . signs of a new spirit are evident in Cuba's churches. Though they are hardly sufficient to place religion in the vanguard of Cuban society their importance should not be underestimated. No longer confined to a few individual clergymen, the stirrings of the spirit are now perceptible within the religious institutions. And, while the leaders' view may still be well ahead of the laity's, they bid fair to contribute significantly to the integration of some rather remote religious elements into the larger Cuban society.[65]

The Jewish community, which numbered about eleven hundred at this time, was relatively quiescent and had cordial relations with the government.

Two Chilean bishops who visited Cuba in February 1971 asserted that the lesson of Cuba was that "Christians must not stand apart from the revolutionary process. They should join it and give it the best of themselves; they should not just stay on the sidelines and carp. Because if one wants the right to criticize and suggest courses of action, he has to roll up his sleeves and get into the work. Otherwise he will have no title later to claim a hearing."[66]

RESPONSES TO THE REVOLUTIONARY CHALLENGE, 1970-1986

The Catholic, Protestant, and Jewish communities entered the 1970s having shed some of their counterrevolutionary image, although they still served to a degree as shelters for those opposed to Marxism and in some cases to the revolution. Among the leaders and younger people there was a strong desire to integrate the churches into the mainstream of Cuban life. Hence the early 1970s would witness increasing efforts to create a theological, political, and pastoral basis that would allow believers to participate in building a socialist society. Those in the vanguard of this movement, including the Cuban Council of Evangelical Churches, the faculty at Matanzas Seminary, and the Presbyterian church, frequently left the bulk of the faithful behind.[67] This reflected real impediments to change within the churches, as well as the depth of anti-Marxist feeling. Advances by progressive Christians and Jews served, however, to challenge Marxists to rethink their antireligious stance. The upshot was modification of traditional positions on both sides and an increasing admission that church people could contribute to the betterment of Cuban society. These developments resulted in greater freedom of religion and liberty of worship.

Allied with this was the growing tendency of the churches to take a more active role within Cuban society. This was, in part, the result of their becoming "uninhibited enough to discover the freedoms" they had.[68] These included contributing to the definition of a "new man" that the revolution was struggling to create, one committed to the common good rather than to individual interests. This drive struck a responsive chord among some church people. Furthermore, the increased fulfillment in Cuba of basic needs encouraged acceptance of socialism as the solution to chronic socioeconomic injustice. Ecumenical encounters, such as the *Jornadas Camilo Torres*, study groups, new seminary curriculums, and increased exchanges with church people from abroad, served to encourage greater acceptance and support for the revolution.

An example was a September 1972 meeting of over fifty Christians from diverse denominations brought together in Santiago by the Cuban Council of Evangelical Churches (CIEC) to discuss the role of the churches in the process Cuba was undergoing. This included reflection on the dual responsibility of Cuban Christians to their churches and to society. The gathering stimulated a meeting of council and government officials in order to express church interest in building better relations. Such initiatives prompted criticism by some church people, which contributed in late 1972 to the election of less prorevolutionary CIEC officials and the 1974 withdrawal of the Episcopal church.[69] Nor did these steps totally eliminate suspicion of church people on the part of revolutionaries. They did, however, represent the beginning of a coming to terms with reality on the part of both church and state.

The adaptation of the churches to the revolution required a new form of education for both clergy and laity. Such efforts were intensified in the 1970s primarily in the five Protestant and two Catholic seminaries.[70] In contrast to the prerevolutionary period, seminarians generally enter after having completed higher studies. Interviews with students at San Carlos and Matanzas in 1973, 1974, and 1976 revealed that most came from families that were not notably religious. They appeared in search of a more transcendental explana-

tion of life than that provided by atheistic materialism. All felt a strong obligation to infuse Cuban society with Christian ideals. As the rector of Nazarene
seminary expressed it: "The church is the yeast for the humanization of society."[71] The means for accomplishing this were evangelization and participation in the revolution.[72]

Progress in theological reflection and Marxist-Christian dialogue resulted
in some distancing of the seminaries from the ordinary faithful, particularly in
the case of the Protestant seminary in Matanzas, which became strongly identified as prorevolutionary and supportive of liberation theology. This reflected
the tendency for the impetus for dialogue with the government to come from
the top rather than from the base. Hence, efforts at integration into contemporary Cuban society tended to distance the leadership of some denominations
or officials within denominations from the grassroots, making convincing the
latter more difficult.[73] The Catholic hierarchy was somewhat more cautious
about distancing itself from the faithful and consequently the most experimen-
tal and internationally visible theological and pastoral developments tended
to be identified with the Presbyterian and Methodist churches, as well as the
seminary at Matanzas. Divisions within some churches impeded their inser-
tion into the revolutionary process, although official relations with the government improved. The latter development was facilitated by the evolution of
the government's and Castro's views about the role of religion in a socialist
society.

In large measure because religion ultimately did not present a threat to the
revolution and international developments suggested that dialogue between
Christians and Marxists could be useful, the Cuban government became increasingly more receptive to the churches contributing to the building of a
socialist society. Such a position was reflected in the conclusions of the First
Cuban Educational and Cultural Congress held in 1971.[74] It noted the growing progressivism of the Catholic church worldwide and its increasing tendency to separate socioeconomic from philosophic problems which allowed
Catholics to incorporate themselves into the revolution. Consequently, there
was a need for the revolution to adopt a somewhat different attitude toward
religion.

The Jehovah's Witnesses, Evangelical Gideon's Band, and Seventh-day
Adventists were, however, singled out for criticism. Some of their activities
were regarded as counterrevolutionary, in particular, the continued links of
the Jehovah's Witnesses to the United States, public proselytizing, and opposition to military service and public schooling. The Evangelical Gideon's Band
was considered to be a refuge for counterrevolutionaries.[75] Subsequently, the
Jehovah's Witnesses and Seventh-day Adventists were targeted as counterrevolutionary, antisocial, and unpatriotic in a nationwide media campaign. This
identification led to some increase in their appeal among some who were
strongly alienated from the government and hence their membership increased.
Some Jehovah's Witnesses were imprisoned for refusing military service.[76]

The next step in defining the official Cuban position on religion came with the promulgation of the 1976 Constitution. Article 54 specified:

The socialist state, which bases its activity and educates the people in the scientific materialist concept of the universe, recognizes and guarantees freedom of conscience and the right of everyone to profess any religious belief and to practice, within the framework of respect for the law, the belief of his preference.

The law regulates the activities of religious institutions. It is illegal and punishable by law to oppose one's faith or religious belief to the Revolution, education or the fulfillment of the duty to work, defend the homeland with arms, show reverence for its symbols and other duties established by the Constitution.[77]

As in the Cuban constitutions of 1903 and 1940, religious freedom was guaranteed with restrictions. In the 1940 document freedom of religious worship was to be exercised within general social mores and the requirements of public order. The restrictions in the 1976 Constitution reflect the preoccupation of the government with religious groups that offered an alternative to revolutionary loyalty and integration.[78]

The reaction of a good number of church people to the 1976 Constitution was that it was useful to have the government's position on religion clearly spelled out. An official of the Cuban Conference of Bishops stated that the Catholic church was pleased that the status of believers and churches had been defined, although it was not entirely happy with the emphasis on a materialist interpretation of life.[79] A Catholic seminarian felt that after the promulgation of the constitution there was considerable improvement in relations with the state. A fellow-student held it allowed for believers and nonbelievers to better realize themselves as persons, as well as recognized the contribution of Christians to Cuban development. Another said that the constitution "created the conditions for the full exercise of religious freedom." The rector of the seminary, Father José Manuel Miyares, added that "it is extremely . . . consoling to see that . . . all types of coercion and discrimination against believers is clearly proscribed."[80]

The intent of Article 54 was elucidated in resolutions at the First Party Congress of the Cuban Communist Party in December 1975, the 1978 Party Platform, and the Second Congress of the Cuban Communist Party in December 1980. The 1975 Congress emphasized that the struggle for a scientific view of the world was subordinated to the task of constructing a new society. In the latter struggle "believers, nonbelievers, members of religious orders, and atheists have participated, continue to participate, and must necessarily participate."[81] The construction of a new society required the efforts of all Cubans and hence believers should not be isolated or rejected, but rather incorporated into the revolution. In addition, dissemination of historical and dialectical materialism should be done in such fashion so as not to offend believers' personal or religious feelings. Membership in the Communist Party and Young Communist League, however, was to be limited to those who accepted their programs and Marxism-Leninism. This effectively excluded active church people from influential roles in government or society.

The 1978 Party Platform focused on two elements regarding religion: relations with church people and religion as ideology. With respect to the former the Party repeated its official commitment to liberty of conscience and freedom of worship within the law, but criticized the use of religion to oppose the revolution and socialism. Believers, as well as nonbelievers, had the same rights and responsibilities within society. With respect to the use of religion as an ideology, the platform reaffirmed the need for the systematic dissemination of scientific materialism, opposition to antireligious campaigns or the use of coercive or administrative measures against religion, as well as the isolation of believers. Note was taken of the increasing support of Christians for liberation movements worldwide.[82] The Second Party Congress in 1980 expanded on this theme and asserted that the support of Christians for structural transformation of unjust societies, particularly in the Western hemisphere, encouraged strategic alliances between Christians and Marxists. In order to further this, support for international exchanges involving Cuban church people was expressed.[83] This resulted in considerable increase in opportunities for Cuban church people to travel abroad or receive foreign visitors which expanded exposure to post–Vatican II trends, including the increased identification of the church on the side of the poor, and to societal change.

The idea of strategic alliances between Christians and Marxists had been raised by Fidel Castro as early as his 1972 meeting with Christians for Socialism in Chile. Castro asserted:

> There was a time when the Christian religion, which used to be the religion of the slaves, became the religion of the emperors, of the court, the religion of patricians. As we go further into history, we see how men have made serious mistakes in the name of religion. I am not going to talk about how men made even worse mistakes in their role as politicians. It was on the basis of such realities that I said we had to fight together to achieve these aims for, I ask, where do the contradictions between Christian teachings and socialist teachings lie? Where? We both wish to struggle on behalf of man, for the welfare of man, for the happiness of man.[84]

This led Castro to assert in an October 11, 1977, speech to the Jamaican Council of Churches that there are "no contradictions between the aims of religion and the aims of socialism. There aren't any."[85] When queried at that meeting why, if there were no contradictions, there was such a strong emphasis on Marxism-Leninism in Cuban education, while the study of Christianity was limited to instruction in churches, Castro replied that he thought that it was legitimate for public education to have "an orientation that opposes the religious view in the fields of philosophy or history."[86] This helps explain his opposition to church access to radio, television, and the press, although he stated that churches were free to publish their own materials. Castro also held that his government did not oppose the importation of religious publications including the Bible. When asked why there were no churches included in new housing developments, he responded that if a community requested one that it would be built. However, it was not until the late 1980s that new churches began springing up, particularly those in houses or apartments in newer communities. On the issue of political prisoners, Castro claimed that no one was imprisoned for religious beliefs, but only for counterrevolutionary activities. Castro also asserted that no revolution as thoroughgoing as the Cuban had fewer conflicts over religion. This he ascribed to the astuteness of church leaders, the growing number of progressive Christians, as well as the desire of the government not to present the revolution as an enemy of religion and thereby provide ammunition for counterrevolutionaries.[87]

Religious leaders in Cuba at the time were cheered by Castro's words and increasingly willing to engage in strategic cooperation with the government. While a good number believed that Christians and Jews could be good revolutionaries, they did not feel that they could be good Marxists. As a professor at the Catholic seminary in Havana phrased it:

> Socialism is the only economic solution available to us. As our witness to God we must work inside the process for mutual social goals. We are "Christian revolutionaries." That is possible. What is not possible is to be "Christian Marxists." That would be like putting a circle in a square. In Cuba the word "Marx" means atheism; the word "revolutionary" does not.[88]

While there was a willingness among some Cuban Christians to engage in a strategic alliance with Marxists to achieve certain societal goals, there was also a recognition of impermeability at the level of world views and ultimately of values. Strategic alliances were possible, but they did not eliminate the competition for the ultimate loyalty of all Cubans. This helps explain why the government continued to restrict the churches in their access to means of molding public opinion, including education and the media. While the individual was free to practice his or her religion, it was to be done in such fashion so as to not challenge the revolution and ultimately the government. After twenty years of revolution this was increasingly not sufficient for many churches and by the late 1970s some were increasingly ready to attempt to assume a less marginal role in society, particularly in view of what they regarded as a weakening of morality and values within society. As a result, churches and church people tended to become more assertive, and while continuing to support the overall goals of the revolution, they argued for a greater role in the reform of society and as a critic of systemic deficiencies.

The most substantial effort in this direction was the 1986 *Encuentro Nacional Eclesial Cubano* (ENEC), which was attended by hundreds of Catholic clergy, religious, and laity and was the culmination of a process of reflection begun in 1979. It focused on critically assessing the church's past, particularly its role at the outset of the revolution, in order to determine how it could best contribute to present-day Cuba. The 1979 call of the Latin American bishops at the Puebla Conference for an intensification of evangelization in order to help create more just and moral societies has struck a responsive chord among many Cubans. ENEC, as a consequence, emphasized the promotion of peace, disarmament, conservation of the environment, equitable use and distribution of consumer goods, a new international economic and social order, and greater East-West understanding. Singled out for particular concern with respect to Cuba was the need to attack corruption, fraud, theft, abuse of social property, irresponsibility of workers, abortion, sexual license, and alcoholism. The means to accomplish both the macro and micro objectives was the transformation of individuals and society through the intensification of evangelization. The task of the Catholic church in Cuba was to communicate the gospel message in the new societal reality in order to stimulate dialogue within and without the island and ultimately promote reconciliation in pursuit of the common good.[89]

What ENEC was attempting to do was to reassert a message of peace, love, justice, and the perfectibility of the individual within a context in which the pursuit of socioeconomic justice had been appropriated by a socialist revolution.

The Protestant churches and Jewish community also began to claim such a role for themselves. The waning of the Cold War, the disintegration of the Soviet Union, and the economic crisis it precipitated in Cuba caused leaders of these denominations to intensify their efforts to carve out a more substantial role for themselves. The weaknesses of the government inclined it to allow such reinsertion so long as churches continued to support the revolution, as well as socialism, and provide both material and other assistance to the government.

RELIGION IN POST-COLD WAR CUBA

Over the past ten years the repositioning of the churches in Cuba has been facilitated not only by the increasing problems faced by the government, but also by a resurgence of religion. As the economic situation worsened, as well as the capacity of the government to respond effectively to people's basic needs, there was an increased turning to religion as a source of comfort and for explanations for the suffering. All religions experienced some growth and new churches sprouted up. The house-church movement is a focus of much Pentecostal activity and *santería* is increasingly practiced. A 1994 poll conducted by CID-Gallup of Costa Rica indicated that 20 percent of the respondents claimed to have attended church the previous month.[90]

Church officials have become more inclined to speak out, including on the reasons for the religious upsurge. Methodist Bishop Joel Ajo ascribed it to the fact that "the revolution tried to make a new man and woman, and after thirty years we realized that we have failed." Catholic jurist Raúl Gómez Treto attributed it to the fact that his church had been transformed and hence is more relevant to Cubans today, particularly younger ones who are seeking answers to both practical and transcendental questions. The sociologist Laureana Cruz was of the opinion that for many Cubans "the fall of the socialist bloc meant that the world they trusted no longer exists." She further argued that many Cubans felt a great deal of stress given the economic crisis and the evangelical message that in Christ there is hope had a great deal of appeal.[91]

Still, many Cubans have not found their way to a church, a synagogue, or to *santería*. Nevertheless, there are indications of a growing generalized interest in religion and in the government's position on it. In 1993 the Cuban Ecumenical Council arranged for six hundred bibles to be put on sale in a state bookstore. Within forty minutes all had been sold, with reportedly only two going to individuals who identified themselves as Christians.[92] Prior to that a book-length interview of Fidel Castro by a Brazilian Dominican, Frei Betto, published in 1985, had reportedly sold over a million copies. In it Castro had repeated his belief that there was no necessary contradiction between Christianity and Marxism and lauded the role church people had played in revolutionary movements around the world.[93] Amplifying on those statements during a visit to Brazil, Castro told a gathering of liberation theologians that Cuba could benefit from having more Christians like them. The remark outraged some church leaders, and the Cuban Ecumenical Council protested and requested a meeting with Castro at which he admitted not only that he had ignored the contributions of many within the Cuban churches, but also that in the past some believers had been unfairly treated. He also agreed to allow house churches, although a later 1993 regulation required that they be registered with the government.[94]

Of critical importance was the 1991 elimination of the prohibition on believers being members of the Communist Party, which had generally blocked them from consideration for influential positions in government and education. In addition, a 1992 constitutional amendment changed Cuba from an atheist to a lay state. This encouraged several Protestant ministers to run for the National Assembly, where four were serving by 1998. Nevertheless, the reduction of traditional Cuban irreligion and anticlericalism has proceeded slowly. Suspicion on both sides continues, and there have been some setbacks.

This was clearly evidenced by the government's reaction to the Cuban bishops' pastoral letter of September 8, 1993, entitled "Love Hopes All Things." Responding to the escalating 1993-94 exodus of Cubans from the country on rafts and other means, the bishops issued an urgent call for dialogue, reconciliation, and moral reform. They argued that the current crisis had shown:

There are two important sides to our recent experience; namely, aid from some foreigners and interference from others. And caught in between are the Cuban people, struggling, working, suffering for a tomorrow which recedes further and further out of reach. Facing this situation, many seem to want to relieve their suffering by going somewhere else when they can; if they cannot, they fanatically idealize everything foreign or they simply take flight from the situation in a kind of internal exile. Today it is acknowledged that the Cubans who can provide economic aid are the very ones that were forced to become foreigners. Would it not be better to recognize that they also have a legitimate right and duty to provide solutions since they are Cubans? How can we approach them to ask for their help if we do not first create a climate of reconciliation among all who belong to the same people?[95]

The bishops also argued that it was time for a thoroughgoing review of Cuba's economic policies. In addition, they called for moral reform to reduce crime and fortify the family, as well as to eliminate corruption in government. Beyond this they argued that Cuba's economic situation suggested some serious political problems, including excessive centralization of power and too great dependence on ideology. They called for greater judicial independence; less surveillance by security agencies; decriminalization of opposition activities; and elimination of discrimination on the basis of political, philosophical, or religious beliefs. Basically the prelates called for a more open and competitive political system, arguing that

> [in] Cuba there is only one party, one press, one radio and one television. But the dialogue we are talking about must take into account the diversity of means and of persons, as the Holy Father says: "The social nature of man is not completely fulfilled in the state, but it is realized in various intermediary groups, beginning with the family and including economic, social, political and cultural groups which stem from human nature itself and have their own autonomy, always with a view to the common good" (*Centesimus Annus*, 13).[96]

While the bishops reaffirmed their longstanding opposition to the U.S. economic embargo, together with its tightening under the 1996 Helms-Burton law, the government strongly attacked the prelates for playing into the hands of the United States. Indeed, the magazine of the Communist youth, *Juventud Rebelde*, accused the Catholic church of treason. The Fourth Congress of the Committees for the Defense of the Revolution concluded that "the bishops defend the same anti-national thesis as the United States, with the goal of returning the country to a state of neocolonialism, something that the people— Christians and non-Christians alike—have rejected."[97] However, in a private communication to the bishops, the government reassured them that it did not want any rupture in relations and was committed to working with the church to help ameliorate the impact of the economic crisis on Cubans.[98]

On March 12, 1996, at the *Segundo Ecuentro Nacional Eclesial* in Santiago, the bishops returned to the issue of reconciliation with particular bluntness.

> When the Church in Cuba, in her prophetic mission, sets for herself the task of contributing to the growth of Cubans as persons by calling them to reconciliation, she is making a decisive choice at this juncture of our history to build the immediate and long-range future of our country.

They added:

> For this reason, we want to set our sights as a church on two painful events that weighed heavily on each and every person taking part in our Second Encounter:
>
> • The denial of permission for a gathering requested by different groups of many political persuasions brought together by the *Concilio Cubano*, followed by the detention or imprisonment of many of its members;
>
> • The shooting down of two small airplanes from the United States, particularly regrettable since it resulted in the death of four persons in those planes.
>
> We do not pretend to offer any legal or political evaluation of this sad incident. We believe in a human and Christian sense that although the repeated air incursions may have been ill-advised and stirred up bad feelings, the response was disproportionate and violent, with devastating consequences for those who support moderation as a way to resolve crises and, in the case of our Church in Cuba, reconciliation among all Cubans, including those living abroad.[99]

The reaction to this message, coming as it did in the midst of negotiations over the visit of Pope John Paul II, was somewhat restrained on the part of the government. The increasing dependence of Cuba on humanitarian assistance from such Catholic organizations as Caritas may have also been a factor. The government communicated its unhappiness with the bishops' statement via a number of channels.

Protestant leaders also spoke out in favor of exploring solutions within the context of reconciliation and tolerance at the height of the exodus and subsequently when an evangelical pastor was jailed for allegedly holding unauthorized services. In February 1994, when a number of Baptists were detained for allegedly counterrevolutionary activities, Protestant leaders urged the government to release them forthwith.[100] Such actions occurred in the context of a more general crackdown on human rights activists and dissidents. Both Catholic and Protestant officials have been criticized by some elements of both groups for not being more publicly supportive of their activities, a position seconded by some in the Cuban American community.

Catholic leaders have been quite careful not to identify themselves with such groups, apparently hoping to maintain useful relations with the government, as well as position the church as a neutral mediator if and when there is a transition from the present regime. The mainline Protestant denominations have continued to be publicly supportive of the revolution and hence have also maintained their distance from the human rights movement, as well as dissidents. They have also been positioning themselves to assume a greater role as mediators in any future transition. Some fundamentalist churches and other nontraditional religious groups, however, have been identified with the disaffected elements within society, although not necessarily with counterrevolutionary elements.

It is in this context that Pope John Paul II visited Cuba from January 21 to January 25, 1998, after years of negotiations. Both the pope and Castro had their agenda. The former was eager to stimulate the ongoing revitalization of the Catholic church and the reevangelization of the island. Preaching the gospel and disseminating Catholic social doctrine and mores in order to transform societies has been a principal goal not only of the pope but also of the Latin American church, particularly since the late 1970s. In the Cuban case the Catholic church has revived sufficiently to become much more active in evangelizing and reasserting itself as a moral leader and legitimator. The church appears committed to positioning itself in order to stabilize and influence Cuban society over the next few years. It has confidence in the appropriateness of Catholic theology, spirituality, and social doctrine to infuse any analysis of Cuban realities and hence mold solutions to the island's problems. The Cuban churches, in general, have a fear of destabilization and conflict. As the only nongovernmental institutions with a national presence, some resources, and credibility, they appear to foresee a growing role for themselves. They also want to promote reconciliation not only between Cubans on the island and elsewhere, but also within Cuba, where there has been an increase in cleavages within society, as well as growing competition for scarce resources. The Catholic church, in particular, regards reconciliation as essential for stabilizing Cuban society in the face of whatever changes may occur. In pursuing such an agenda, the churches are increasingly occupying political space that the government is involuntarily ceding.

The Catholic church viewed the papal visit as an opportunity to gain greater visibility and access in the media, thereby reasserting its legitimacy before the Cuban public, which had been imbued with a certain degree of irreligion both before and after the revolution. The church also wants a greater role in the education and formation of Cuban children and families, a responsibility that the government has long arrogated to itself. With the decreased capacity of the government to meet the basic socioeconomic needs of Cubans, including education, the churches see an opportunity to reassert themselves in this realm. They also want to promote more autonomous organizations within civil society, and hence the pope spoke out about the need to have independent labor unions, as well as political and educational organizations.

The Catholic church is also somewhat preoccupied by the growth of non-traditional religions in Cuba, including Pentecostals. Such groups have experienced considerable growth, but both the church and the state appear to be somewhat ill at ease with them. Hence, church and state appear to have a common interest in cooperating in order to reduce their influence. The government, in particular, appears much more at ease in dealing with the Catholic church, which, with its highly centralized and hierarchical organization, parallels the government. In addition, Castro clearly feels he understands the Catholic church and how it functions.

Indeed, it would appear that the government is turning to the Catholic church not only to preempt the growth of seemingly more intractable religious groups, but also to help shore up the legitimacy of the regime. The incapacity of a socialist state to meet all the socioeconomic needs of its citizens clearly undercuts its legitimacy. In addition, the "dollarization" of the economy and the strong growth of its informal sector suggest the weakness of a socialist state that has historically justified itself on the grounds of its capacity to distribute equitably the benefits of its economy. In short, in the face of the increasing incapacity of the socialist state, the Castro government is seeking more support outside of its traditional bases. Previously marginal sectors, such as church people, are being appealed to and many are responding not only because of the opportunities presented, but also because of fear of societal destabilization.

The government also viewed the papal visit as an important development in the battle against the U.S. economic embargo, whose effects have been magnified by the end of substantial Soviet economic support. The position of the Catholic, as well as the Protestant churches and the Jewish community, has been consistently that the embargo is immoral and illegal under international law. Castro was not disappointed, as the pope repeatedly called for an end to the embargo. The U.S. Catholic bishops echoed this sentiment in the aftermath of the pope's visit.

It appears that both the Catholic church and the Cuban government were reasonably well pleased with the visit. Certainly the former was strengthened, dominating TV, radio, and the print media for a week in a country where such access had been denied for close to forty years. The visuals of the pope and Castro also helped legitimize the latter's government, at least to a degree, both inside and outside Cuba. Opposition in the U.S. Congress to the embargo on foodstuffs and medicine for the island appears to have been strengthened and lobbying on the part of church people increased. The image of the Catholic church and the Cuban government working together has been strengthened and it appears that the former may have more leverage with the latter in the future.

On February 12, 1998, the Cuban bishops addressed the Cuban people in a message calling upon them to open their hearts to Christ. They also summarized the tasks that faced the church in the aftermath of the visit. These included encouraging Cubans to be the protagonists of their own history, accepting Christ as their savior, and cooperating with other religions in order to do so; increasing dialogue not only with governmental institutions, but also nongovernmental ones; and deepening the church's service to society, especially to the neediest. In addition, they committed the church to continue its efforts to educate the Cuban people to appreciate human life and the family and to oppose abortion and birth control. Finally, the prelates stated their determination to animate the laity to work with others of good will, in a spirit of reconciliation and solidarity, to find solutions to Cuba's diverse problems in accordance with Catholic social doctrine. Such work would be done in collaboration with those Cubans who have left the island but were committed to the common good of the nation.[101] In concluding they returned to words that the pope spoke in Santiago in order to summarize their message: "History . . . teaches that without faith virtue disappears and life loses its transcendent meaning."[102]

Clearly the Catholic and Protestant churches, as well as the Jewish community, are preoccupied with fortifying civil society prior to any transition and reducing the possibility that after Castro power might be seized by Cubans from outside the island. In order to avoid this the churches have been attempting to increase the preparation of lay leaders and encourage participation of civil society within Cuba. Given the continuing institutional weaknesses of the churches, this is a very great challenge. However, Cuban church people and religious institutions appear to be in a better position today to influence a transition than they were in 1959.

6.

EL SALVADOR

———————◆———————

Andrew J. Stein

INTRODUCTION

El Salvador is a country that has experienced great changes in its political, legal, and religious environments over the past decade. In 1992, a peace treaty ended the brutal civil war (1980-92) that took over eighty thousand lives. This chapter will explain the ebb and flow of church-state conflict during the war, and will trace the historical roots of church-state relations since independence from Spain. Such a long view is needed to understand previous church-state unity and cooperation, and why that pattern became untenable by the 1970s and 1980s. Second, the analysis will address the relevant constitutional provisions and government protection of Catholicism as the official faith, and the consequences of this tradition for the religious freedom of indigenous and missionary religious groups today. Finally, the chapter will discuss how the church's focus on social justice and change affected the prospects for human rights, the rule of law, and democratization in El Salvador.

THE HISTORICAL CONTEXT OF CHURCH-STATE RELATIONS

An adequate understanding of how church-state relations have evolved must begin with their origins in El Salvador during the early independence period

This chapter is dedicated to the memory of the late Enrique Baloyra, who advised many junior scholars on research about El Salvador. The author is grateful for comments on earlier drafts of this chapter and that on Nicaragua from Paul Sigmund, the other contributors to this volume, Ricardo Córdova Macías, Carlos Guillermo Ramos, Alvaro Trigueros, and José Miguel Cruz. Field work done in 1997 for this chapter was supported in part by a Tennessee Technological University Faculty Research Committee Grant.

(1821-38) and the colonial legacy. Under Spanish rule, the *patronato* system prevailed, in which church-state unity made Catholicism the official religion, granted the church special rights (such as separate law codes and property), and allowed the monarchy to appoint bishops and control internal functions of the church.

El Salvador was, like the Chiapas province in Mexico, and the other future states of the Isthmus, under the colonial jurisdiction of the Audiencia de Guatemala, based in Guatemala City. In retrospect, it is not surprising that El Salvador had a strong movement for autonomy in local government and ecclesiastical matters, given its importance as a leading population center and indigo producer, far ahead of all others in Central America except for Guatemala itself. When *intendencia* status was granted in 1786, political autonomy was followed by demands for control over church governance, as well as the right to a separate Salvadoran bishop and diocese. El Salvador also experienced rebellions in 1811-12 that were precursors to complete separation from Spain, and revolved around calls to abolish special church rights known as *fueros.*[1]

The period after independence from Spain in 1821 cannot be seen as a unified whole for El Salvador, but rather as distinct periods. The first of these involved not only the decision to separate from Spain, but also from Mexico, and then local versus regional demands under the United Provinces of Central America (1823-38). The second major period (1840-69) constituted the beginnings of a weak, independent state and the instability of frequent civil wars. After coffee became the key export crop (1870-90s), state institutions and laws were strengthened, and political stability was achieved, yet at a cost for the church.

During the initial period of independence, the new governments began a major reevaluation of the rights, privileges, and role of the Catholic Church. Certain sectors, often termed Conservatives (for their preference for protectionism in trade and maintenance of church privileges), began a decades-long clash with other elites termed Liberals. The latter were determined to rid their states of the remnants of Spanish colonialism, and influenced by European liberalism, advocated curtailing the church's political influence, property rights, and control over education, marriage, burials, and public records. Woodward has characterized the Conservatives' favoritism of the church "as a defender of their privileges and a vital element in both controlling and securing the support of the masses."[2]

At the time of independence itself, as had been the case in Mexico and elsewhere, the clergy was divided, at times on the basis of high clergy and low clergy, and whether they were Spanish born or native to the region, though the fault lines were more complex than this alone. In 1821, Father José Matías Delgado called for separation from Spain, Mexico, and Guatemala, and defended this position with arms until 1823. At that time Delgado became president of the Congress of the United Provinces of Central America, a body that began liberal reforms including the elimination of all titles of nobility and of the clergy (henceforth all clergy, including bishops, were to be called simply *padre*). Guatemalan Archbishop Casáus opposed the Central American federation in 1824-25, after the creation of the Diocese of San Salvador without his consent or that of the Vatican. The new government claimed for itself the right of royal patronage and supported Delgado when he declared himself bishop.[3]

By the 1840s, factionalism across and within member states of the federation brought it to an end. After El Salvador became a separate state, the following two decades were a period of increasing strife and Liberal-Conservative conflict that led to the expulsion of priests from El Salvador and open warfare. An indicator of the instability and weakness of the state, and the power of regional elite factions, is that the country had forty-two different presidents in the period from 1841 to 1861.[4] A concordat was signed between the government of Liberal dictator Barrios and the Vatican in 1862, but violation of the terms by both sides led to its abrogation.[5]

Subsequent decades brought alternation in power by Liberals and Conservatives, depending on their relative ability to remove the other by force, and, in 1871, El Salvador came under stable Liberal rule. Church-state conflict would resume and peak in these final decades of the nineteenth century with the production of coffee for export. The formation of state institutions, capitalist notions of private property, and the dispossession of ejidal (municipality owned) and communal (Indian) lands characterized this period.[6] This process helped to unify rival elites and Liberal-Conservative differences over confiscation of church property lessened greatly.[7] Another aspect of the consolidation of land under coffee planters' control was the move to confiscate land belonging to indigenous tribes, thereby creating a dependent labor force. This was an extremely violent process that led to several popular uprisings in 1885-99 and their bloody suppression by landowners and government troops. The Jesuits were expelled from the country in 1872 for their alleged support of resistance to the loss of communal land, yet Rodolfo Cardenal notes that most of the clergy were supportive of these changes.[8]

As part of the wave of anticlericalism, the concordat was suspended in 1874, and the Salvadoran government ceased all economic obligations to the church (such as payment of salaries and the collection of tithes). The constitutions of 1880 and 1886 did not recognize an official state religion.[9] In 1894 a law prohibiting divorce was passed, but despite church efforts, it failed to recognize Catholic religious marriage as the sole type. In addition, state officials offered little help to the church in its opposition to Masons and Protestants at this time.[10]

From the late 1870s until the 1980s, with very few exceptions, political power was transferred by coup or fixed elections, with local municipal control key to various factions' chances of governing. The church generally recognized these governments as the legitimate public authorities. According to Rodolfo Cardenal's copiously documented research, most church-state conflicts in the 1890-1931 period were on the local level. These disputes revolved around taxation, confiscation of parish houses or adjacent land, and issuance of permits to celebrate Holy Week or the various patron saint festivals.[11] On the national level, aside from its lost property or government resources, the Catholic Church was restored in practice (if not in legal terms) to the favored official religion. The style of planter-dominated politics characterized by Ciro Cardoso as "oligarchic dictatorship" continued unabated until the Depression. The 1932 massacre of thousands of middle-class and worker radicals and reformers known as *la Matanza* put an end to demands for social reform or political democratization for more than three decades.[12]

During the tenure of Luis Chávez y González as Archbishop of San Salvador (1938-77), the Salvadoran church experimented with pastoral and other reforms that antedated those encouraged by Vatican II and CELAM. There were efforts to educate the general public in the social teachings of the church and their relation to such issues as the social function of private property, the role of the state, a fair minimum wage, the right to unionize, and rural peasant cooperatives.[13] Though relations between church and state were mostly harmonious during Bishop Chávez's tenure,[14] they had started to deteriorate badly by the late 1960s and early 1970s with expulsions of foreign clergy, murder of human rights workers, and church denunciations of government actions. At this time there were efforts to promote land reform, peasant rights, and to reorient the Catholic Church in favor of service to the poor.[15] This led to increasing criticism from Salvadoran governments, distance between bishops and presidents, and eventually, open repression of the church for its assumption of what would be called at Puebla a "preferential option for the poor."

As was the case in Chile and Guatemala, in El Salvador in the early 1960s there appeared among the urban middle class (particularly in San Salvador) a strong Christian Democratic Party (Partido Demócrata Cristiano, PDC) to challenge the candidates of the military. The PDC repeatedly won municipal elections and increased its numbers in the legislature. This led to calls for land reform in 1970 and 1976 (until then a taboo for any politician), electoral fraud, and harsh government crackdowns after the elections of 1972 and 1977.[16] As part of this debate, in 1973 and 1976, death threats and demands to leave the country had been issued against Father Ignacio Ellacuría and his fellow Jesuits for their teaching and critical publications at the Externado San José High School and Central American University (Universidad Centroamericana "José Simeón Cañas," UCA), and the UCA had been bombed repeatedly.[17]

1977-1981, Government Repression and Mass Protest: The Church Faces Revolution

As Bishop Chávez retired in 1977, and his successor, Oscar Romero Galdámez, was installed as archbishop,[18] the ferment of mass organizations and guerrilla movements such as the Popular Liberation Forces (Fuerzas Populares de Liberación, FPL), came to a head, as did the savagery of government repression that left several priests, nuns, and lay catechists among the dead.[19] According to a 1978 report by the OAS's Inter-American Commission on Human Rights:

> As a result of the activities that the Catholic Church is carrying on because it considers that they are an integral part of its mission . . . it is [the] object of systematic persecution by the authorities and organizations that enjoy the favor of the government.[20]

ARCHBISHOP ROMERO, DENUNCIATION OF GOVERNMENT ABUSE AND PERSECUTION

So much has been written about Romero's period as archbishop of San Salvador that I will merely summarize some main points as they relate to church-state conflict and religious freedom. As his contemporaries have noted, it is useful to examine Bishop Romero during his period as the secretary of the Bishops' Conference of El Salvador (Conferencia Episcopal de El Salvador, CEDES) in 1967-70[21]; his time as one of two auxiliary bishops of the archdiocese in 1970-74; and the period 1974-77, when Romero was bishop of the Diocese of Santiago de María,[22] in the eastern part of El Salvador. Romero's denunciations of and conflict with the Arturo Molina (1972-77) and Carlos Humberto Romero (1977-79) administrations, and the self-styled government of the Revolutionary Junta (Junta Revolucionaria de Gobierno, JRG, 1979-82), can be understood only in part as a consequence of the growing opposition movement, government actions, and the context of the time. After General Romero was overthrown, the JRG's coup in October 1979 was the final chance to usher in peaceful reforms and avert a civil war. However, the junta represented only a faction within the military; human rights violations continued as before, and the more independent civilians on the council soon resigned. Bishop Romero and the archdiocese had no better relations with this government than with its predecessor. Reprisals against rural organizing and urban demonstrations were as bloody as before, if not more so, as were threats and violence against church pastoral workers.[23] One aspect of Romero's public sermons that eventually led to his murder in 1980, allegedly by associates of the Nationalist Republican Alliance Party (Alianza Republicana Nacionalista, ARENA) founder Roberto D'Aubisson,[24] was the manner in which he denounced the excesses of the state and dominant classes, criticisms which made church-state relations ever more precarious. His final homily had called on soldiers to disobey unjust orders from their superiors if they were called upon to murder their fellow Salvadorans.

Equally important is an understanding of Romero's evolution in terms of his views on the institution's proper relation to government authorities and his interpretation of the causes of the conflict. During his time as an auxiliary bishop, Romero was highly suspicious of what he considered "politicized" priests and theological and political ideas current among the clergy. This included such things as liberation theology, and pastoral work that included peasant training institutes.[25] However, despite Romero's concerns about obedience and unity in the church, his analysis of the conflict changed when he was in Santiago de María. Foreign clergy were expelled from the diocese without consulting Romero or religious superiors,[26] which he denounced publicly.

Romero's view on what was appropriate conduct by the clergy, and what was illicit, had evolved substantially. Widespread human rights violations, impunity, repression of dissent and freedom of assembly, and backtracking on promises of reform were reasons for a growing gulf between church and state. The outright persecution of the Catholic Church was also key. This included the murder of priests, nuns and lay catechists in the period 1977-79. Not all bishops or parish priests in San Salvador and the other dioceses (Santiago de María, San Miguel, Santa Ana, and San Vicente) had followed the pastoral and social commitment of Bishop Chávez and his auxiliary, Bishop Arturo Rivera y Damas. Some also opposed the open criticism and confrontation with the government that had occurred. As attacks on the church grew and the archdiocese's option for the poor intensified, the rift widened between Rivera and Romero on the one hand, and the remaining four prelates on the other hand (particularly Bishop Pedro Aparicio y Quintanilla in San Vicente and Auxiliary Bishop Marco René Revelo).

Crucial issues of Romero's last years (1977-80) were his views on communion and unity among bishops, priests, and the laity; the mission of the church and how to pursue it; and the consequences that disunity and pastoral action for the poor would have on church-state relations. Church unity had become ever more difficult, but Romero worked to reconcile clergy and laity, as well as splits across dioceses. The bishop rejected charges that the church had become Marxist and involved itself in political matters illegitimately. Partisan politics, he argued, was an inappropriate role for the church as an institution, but involvement in politics in pursuit of the common good was the church's right and obligation.

1980-1987, FROM CIVIL WAR WITH REFORMS AND ELECTIONS TO MILITARY STALEMATE

Independent of the church-state conflict and mutual distrust in El Salvador, several other factors made peaceful settlement of the nation's conflict in the mid-1980s unlikely. The main actors had ruled out any solution other than total military victory. The Alvaro Magaña–ARENA government in El Salvador (1982-84) had equated talks with the Farabundo Martí National Liberation Front and its civilian allies, the Democratic Revolutionary Front (Frente Farabundo Martí de Liberación Nacional and Frente Democrático Revolucionario, FMLN-FDR), as high treason, and death squads and government security forces backed this assertion by murdering and torturing those who dared to dialogue with the left. Once Christian Democratic President José Napoleón Duarte came to power (1985-89), the official argument was that El

Salvador was a democracy with elections, separation of powers, and social reforms despite the continuing impunity of security forces and death squads, and corruption in the judiciary. The left was portrayed as a band of terrorists and obstructionists who did not accept the rule of law.

On the international level, despite multilateral peace efforts by the Contadora Group, the Reagan administration's insistence on a military "solution" to the Salvadoran civil war (shown in more than $1 million in aid per day and the quadrupling of the armed forces) blocked efforts at a peaceful exit to the war.

Despite the differences between the Catholic hierarchy in the Archdiocese of San Salvador (and to a lesser extent, the Salvadoran Bishops' Conference) and the governments of Molina, Romero, the Junta, Magaña, and Duarte, the prelates were consistent in their public declarations with regard to the national situation and the conduct of the church. In the first place, following the themes of Bishop Romero, in the 1980-83 period the church claimed that negotiations and dialogue were the sole viable path, rejected violence, and advocated elections, structural change, and new values that would encourage reconciliation. The bishops called for unity within the church, obedience to superiors, and resisted political "instrumentalization" of church personnel or its mission.[27] The church's position in favor of dialogue became more consensual after the 1983 visit by Pope John Paul II, but the splits over different pastoral visions, readings of the war's causes, and the nature of the political system produced divergent understandings of which demands should be addressed, and whether to treat the FMLN-FDR as a legitimate side in future talks. Given this division within the church and the limited margins that the right, the military, and the United States provided Duarte, the talks held at La Palma in October 1984 stalled and amounted to nothing.[28]

The disunity among the members of the Bishops' Conference persisted in 1984-86, but there were increasing efforts by Archbishop Rivera to be even-handed in dealing with all participants in the conflict, including the left. The conference issued a key document in 1985 around the time of elections[29] in which it praised the democratic process and criticized priests and nuns who were influenced by Marxism. In their portrayal of the two sides in the civil war, the bishops showed a very partisan reading of the Christian Democratic government of Duarte and the FMLN-FDR as polar opposites, the former as the "fruit of the democratic process," and the latter as "[those who] claim for themselves representation of the people that cannot be clearly certified, and . . . who use violence and sabotage as an essential weapon of their struggle."[30] Blame for the war was placed much more on international communism and the guerrillas than on government and military conduct or the injustices of Salvadoran society.[31]

Rivera supported elections like the other bishops, but given his contact with the archdiocesan human rights Legal Aid organization, Tutela Legal, he was well aware of their limitations. He called for an end to arms shipments and military aid (as Romero had done), rejected armed struggle and foreign intervention (by the United States and socialist countries alike), and denounced the Christian Democratic government for a lack of good-faith negotiations and for the 1986 military offensive ("Operation Phoenix") designed by the Salvadoran army and U.S. advisors to destroy the FMLN.[32]

THE 1988 NATIONAL DEBATE, 1989 FMLN OFFENSIVE, AND 1992 PEACE ACCORDS

By August 1987, the Iran-Contra scandal and the Arias peace plan had led to a context much more favorable to dialogue, resulting in the Esquipulas II peace process that included provisions for a cease fire, the formation of a National Reconciliation Commission, and peace talks. In this instance the church (meaning both the Archdiocese of San Salvador and the Jesuits at the Central American University—UCA) played a crucial supportive role. The church had gained increasing credibility as a mediating force by the late 1980s. Repeated public declarations by UCA Rector Ignacio Ellacuría, and public opinion surveys by Father Ignacio Martín-Baró's University Public Opinion Institute (Instituto Universitario de la Opinión Pública, IUDOP-UCA) showed over a period of years that an overwhelming majority of the public did not accept what Bishop Rivera termed "the official causes" of the war (international communism) or the military "victory" desired by the government, armed forces, and United States.[33]

Archdiocesan church officials led by Bishop Rivera took the initiative in 1988 and organized a National Debate, going far beyond the minimum requirements of Esquipulas. The goal was to gather all of the representative forces of civil society to be "active agents of peace, and not passive subjects of war."[34] Church people involved were largely from the archdiocese, though the Vatican nuncio also played a key role, especially in preliminary meetings at his residence in San Salvador with the FMLN-FDR in October 1987.

The participants were to put forth an analysis of the contemporary situation, the principal causes of the war, an evaluation of proposed solutions to date (1979-88), an analysis of the Esquipulas II process as a framework for El Salvador, and each group's own proposals for a solution. A total of sixty-three groups were invited. Despite the rejection of Rivera's invitation by a few groups,[35] a broad spectrum of civil society was present, including the archdiocese; Tutela Legal; the UCA; the federation of Catholic schools; Protestant representatives from the Baptist, Episcopalian, and Lutheran churches (though Evangelical Protestants refused to take part); cooperatives; public sector unions; professional associations; social and humanitarian organizations; as well as most universities and cultural groups.[36] The church-sponsored forum helped to unify civil society in favor of a negotiated settlement to the war and major social and political reforms. As is evident in Table 1 below, organizations involved in the debate overwhelmingly rejected the notion that communist subversion caused the war, or that the most desirable outcome would be military defeat of the FMLN (as advocated by successive governments, the armed forces, and the United States).[37]

Table 6-1
Majority Planks in the National Debate of 1988

Resolution Approved by Participants	% in Favor
Main causes of war are structural injustice, maldistribution of land and wealth, government repression	100
Frequent involvement by the [Salvadoran] military in politics benefits the oligarchy and U.S.	95
Opposition to a military solution to the war as opposed to dialogue	97
Need for judicial reforms, civil liberties guarantees, and "effective popular participation in the dialogue process"	95
Churches should play important role in moral teaching, "humanization of different social sectors"	65

Source: ECA (August-September 1988), 735-48.

The issue positions summarized in Table 1 were among the central points discussed in negotiations that took place between the Alfredo Cristiani–ARENA government and FMLN-FDR in 1989-91. Many ideas regarding institutional reform were eventually reflected in the final documents of the peace accords signed in Mexico City in January 1992.[38]

At this juncture it is important to note how the Catholic Church used its moral authority and autonomy from the government to "humanize" the war, and to promote alternatives to a military victory when other sectors of civil society were allowed a very precarious and narrow degree of freedom of expression and assembly. While the role of Bishop Rivera and the archdiocese has been noted, the role of the UCA (particularly Father Ignacio Ellacuría) in bringing the war to an end merits further attention. In as small a country as El Salvador, the significance of strong personalities and of talks between individual contacts was great. From 1984 to 1989 Ellacuría had engaged in hundreds of meetings with both sides in the conflict and representative key foreign actors like the United States, the UN, and the European Union.

During this time Ellacuría's views had evolved, and he tried to maintain a "critical distance" from both the government and the FMLN-FDR, despite allegations of his sympathy for the latter.[39] In combination with the FMLN leadership's recognition of a new global and national context, from May 1988 to May 1989 Ellacuría pressed Joaquín Villalobos and other guerrilla commanders to consider negotiations and elections. The UCA rector and his fellow Jesuits Segundo Montes and Javier Ibisate conducted similar talks with President Cristiani, Armando Calderón Sol, other ARENA leaders, and some military officers. However, the obstructionist faction of ARENA and much of the military opposed negotiations vigorously. Along with a few right-wing clergy, they accused the Jesuits of being Marxist subversives, and the UCA was bombed. Threats, violence, and assassinations by the right led to polarization and a response in kind from the FMLN.[40]

Following the failure of another round of negotiations in September and October 1989, and the murders of labor leaders and others on the left, the FMLN launched its November offensive in San Salvador. It was in the midst of the fighting that the Atlacatl Battalion entered the Central American University (UCA) and executed Ellacuría, Martín-Baró, Montes, three fellow priests, their maid, and her daughter.[41] Though the order had been issued at the highest levels of the military, a coverup tried to disguise the intellectual authors of the crime. All but two officers were exonerated for killing the priests, and the 1991 convictions were overturned by a sweeping amnesty law passed by an ARENA legislative majority in April 1993.[42]

1992-1998, THE CHURCH, RELIGION, AND POLITICS IN PEACETIME

Peace came in 1992-93 with the return of former combatants, implementation of 1991 constitutional and electoral reforms, parcelling out land in FMLN areas, and the reduction in the size of the armed forces and purging of its worst violators of human rights. The six years after the Chapultepec accords marked a decreased role for the Catholic Church in national affairs. Although Lutheran Bishop Medardo Gómez and Archbishop Rivera served on the national reconciliation commission (COPAZ), the return of peace and of greater freedom of association for civil society have led to a changed context. Key to the transition were the 1994 elections, in which ARENA maintained its control over the presidency and legislative majority, and in which the FMLN participated as a legal political party for the first time.[43] By the March 1997 elections, the FMLN had improved on its previous performance so that it gained forty-eight municipalities, and nearly half of the national population was governed by it, including the capital.[44]

Within the church substantial changes have also taken place, reducing its profile. First, with the end of the war, the entire ideological spectrum is represented within existing political institutions, unlike in the 1980s. As in other countries, democratization has meant a reorientation of the Church toward issues of public morality, pastoral attention, and Protestant growth. Moreover, in November 1994, Bishop Rivera died, and his replacement, Fernando Sáenz Lacalle (a former auxiliary bishop of Santa Ana and Opus Dei member), had a background and vision of the church's mission that signified a clear break with that of nearly six decades established by Archbishops Chávez, Romero, and Rivera in the archdiocese of San Salvador. The redirection was notable in his dismissal from the national seminary of teachers with views different from his own, changes in *Orientación* (the Archdiocese's newspaper),[45] his refusal to use church forums or homilies to speak on political issues of the day,[46] and his conduct during the second visit of John Paul II in February 1996.[47] Above all, the change was clear in early 1997 in his acceptance of appointment as brigadier general and military vicar of the armed forces (from which he later resigned). His predecessor, Bishop Joaquín Ramos, was presumed to have been murdered by members of the army in 1991, and the military had been responsible for many of the murders of clergy and religious and lay catechists during the war.[48]

OFFICIAL PROTECTION OF CATHOLICISM AND RELIGIOUS FREEDOM

In literal terms the 1983 Salvadoran constitution (heavily amended since 1991) does not speak of an official faith, but a historical recognition of the predominant role of the Catholic Church is evident. Chapter II, article 26, states that the Catholic Church is automatically granted legal status (*personalidad jurídica*), and that all other churches may apply for this status in accordance with existing laws. It also guarantees freedom of religion for the individual citizen in article 25. Particularly during the Cristiani government (1989-94), Protestant churches gained access to public officials to a degree not previously attained. The church's criticism was constant in 1990-92, given government failure to prosecute the guilty parties in the Jesuit murders, along with its continuing human rights violations, and slow progress in talks with the FMLN. Scarcely a month after the massacre at the UCA, the ARENA government courted Evangelicals when it held a public "Pilgrimage for Peace," with no Catholic clergy present (despite the fact that Catholicism was the religion of 70 percent of the citizenry).[49] Now that the open rift between incumbent governments and the Catholic Church has closed, it remains to be seen whether Protestant churches will be able to maintain the access they gained during the war.

PROTESTANT GROWTH, PROSELYTIZING, AND THE POLITICS OF RELIGION

The implications of the constitutional protection of the Catholic Church are ever greater given the rapid expansion of Protestantism, particularly since the 1980s. Church-supplied data indicates that between 1956 and 1970, 93-95 percent of the population was Catholic (albeit nominally), and in the decade 1970-80 less than 5 percent of the population was Protestant.[50] Salvadoran census data from 1992 did not include information on religion. The best available data are from public opinion surveys. Trends in religious affiliation are shown in Table 2, as follows:

Table 6-2
Salvadoran Survey Data on Religious Affiliation
(numbers are percentage of total population)

Year	Firm/ sample	Catholic	Evangelical	Other	None
1988	IUDOP-UCA national	64.1	16.4	4.8	14.7
1991	Pittsburgh capital	72.3	16.1	4.9	6.6
1994	FLACSO special samples	57.0	15.8	3.1	23.4
1995	Pittsburgh national	69.5	29.3	0.5	0.7
1995	IUDOP-UCA national	56.7	17.8	2.3	23.2
1997	IUDOP-UCA		23.8		

SOURCE: IUDOP-UCA, survey of June 1988, "La religión para los salvadoreños," and "La religión para los salvadoreños en 1995," *ECA* 563 (September 1995): 851; University of Pittsburgh Central American Public Opinion Project, 1991-95; personal communications with author.[51]

Polling data is not without limitations. Philip Williams has estimated that 15-20 percent of the population is Protestant, but he notes that self-reporting by the Protestant churches often leads to overstated figures.[52]

Protestants have made the greatest inroads among the young, poorly educated, and citizens of modest means, although there is some increase among the middle class, too. The denominations that have apparently grown the most are Pentecostals, not the historic denominations that tended to hold positions closer to those of socially activist Catholics—the Baptists, Lutherans, and Episcopalians. Also noteworthy has been the ability of Protestants to attract men in equal numbers to women, in sharp contrast to Catholics.[53]

Political attitudes and participation vary between Protestants and Catholics, as Williams notes for Pentecostals, but whether one speaks of basic attitudinal patterns (ideology, partisanship, political tolerance), or concrete types of conventional participation (voting, contacting officials, community organizing) or protest action, religious denomination is not the most significant variable. The religious factor that is a more powerful predictor is religious belief. Respondents who tended to believe in literal interpretation of the Bible, for whom religion was very salient, and who had dogmatic views on doctrine displayed clear political tendencies. They voted more for parties to the right of center, rejected any kind of political protest as illegitimate, and showed high support for conventional participation.[54]

Research has shown that the stereotype of Pentecostals as apolitical and withdrawn from public life is an oversimplification. Protestants do participate in politics, yet the fortunes of exclusively Protestant parties have been dismal.

From the early 1980s until 1997, the Christian Democratic Party moved from a consistent choice of at least 30-40 percent of the electorate to less than 10 percent of the vote. This vote share has not gone to explicitly confessional parties, but to ARENA on the right and the FMLN on the left. One scholar noted that the public "did not view evangelical-inspired parties as a viable alternative," as demonstrated by the National Solidarity Movement (Movimiento de Solidaridad Nacional, MSN) getting 1 percent of the vote in 1994.[55] The MSN had to appeal to the Supreme Court to maintain its legal status, since it only garnered 0.9 percent of the legislative vote and 1.05 percent for president in 1994.[56] With the increase of the minimal vote threshold to 3 percent in order to remain on the ballot for the next election, the MSN lost its legal recognition after the 1997 polls (obtaining 0.5 percent of the vote, and no deputies or municipalities).[57] The Unity Movement (Movimiento Unidad, MU), which has ties to the Assemblies of God, emerged in 1993 and portrayed itself as a centrist alternative. The MU did gain one seat in the Legislative Assembly the following year, and showed ambivalence about its coalition for 1997 with the FMLN and center-left Democratic Convergence (Convergencia Democrática, CD), while winning three mayoral races. In those localities where the MU ran alone, it gained one deputy and four local governments, a total of over 2 percent, not enough under current law to compete in the elections of 1999 or 2000.[58] While the MU gained over twenty thousand votes spread across more than half of the country's fourteen departments (and might have a future as a coalition party), the MSN obtained only eighty-one hundred votes, mostly in San Salvador.[59]

CATHOLIC RESPONSES TO RELIGIOUS COMPETITION, ECUMENISM

Although there are still several members of the Salvadoran Catholic clergy who argue that the rapid increase of Protestants is due to a plot by the United States government (often citing the 1969 Rockefeller Report), or that it is caused by foreign missionaries "buying" the faith of desperate poor people, there is increasing recognition that part of the cause also lies with the Catholic Church itself. In two revealing documents, the Secretariat of Central American Catholic Bishops (Secretariado del Episcopado de América Central, SEDAC) notes that religious diversity is now a permanent feature of the religious landscape in the Isthmus. A 1995 study included a survey of Catholic pastoral agents and a second poll of recently converted Protestants to determine why they had left the Catholic religion in which they were raised. The main reasons were dislocation in their life (rural migrants to urban slums), unfamiliarity with Catholic doctrine, or dislike for restrictions on the priesthood, prohibitions against birth control and divorce, opposition to church involvement in political issues and its commitment to the poor and social justice, and finally, what some saw to be a cold style of worship.[60]

As for ecumenical relations, Archbishop Romero had made overtures toward the historical Protestant churches such as the Baptists, Lutherans, and

Episcopalians, and he co-founded an interdenominational organization called Diakonía. This group met for both ecumenical dialogue before the war and humanitarian assistance in the face of the crisis. Rivera continued to work in conjunction with Protestants (primarily the same three denominations) in aid programs for refugees from war zones. However, the divisions between and within Protestant churches and the Bishops' Conference were a serious limitation on cooperation (differences that were exacerbated by the war).[61] Archbishop Rivera's and Lutheran Bishop Gómez's role with the Peace Commission, COPAZ, suggests that at least in the archdiocese high-level contacts between churches continued into the early 1990s. This climate seems to have changed with the end of the war, the appointment of Archbishop Sáenz, and changes in the clergy. There is less visible effort and less contact at present.

RELIGIOUS FREEDOM, HUMAN RIGHTS, AND DEMOCRATIZATION

The conduct of Catholic bishops and priests during the periods of Chávez, Romero, and Rivera had a lasting impact on the country. First, they helped to legitimize the organization of poor Salvadorans to solve problems and address grievances (whether in Catholic Action groups, peasant cooperatives, or later unions and human rights organizations). Second, by constantly stressing a nonviolent solution to the war, the Catholic Church (particularly the Central American University) helped, along with the development of parties and (at times, flawed) elections,[62] to add new legitimacy to solving conflicts by means other than fraud or force, which had been the norm in El Salvador since the 1970s.

Human rights and the rule of law were also strengthened greatly by the input of religious actors, though today such trends are still tenuous in El Salvador. The denunciation of massacres and political murder by the security forces, death squads, and guerrillas was accompanied by physical protection of dissidents and refugees. By the 1980s, the archdiocese's Tutela Legal (Legal Aid) helped compile data and evidence in prominent cases such as the Romero killing, the Mozote massacre,[63] and the assassination of the Jesuits at the UCA. This foundation was further developed by the UN Truth Commission and helped to establish norms for the government Procurator (Ombudsman) for the Defense of Human Rights (Procuraduría para la Defensa de los Derechos Humanos, PDDH), established as part of the peace accords in 1992. These rights include not only life, personal security, privacy, expression, association, and due process, but also (still imperfectly enforced) economic and social rights. Under current law these additional rights include health, work-place rights, education, and provisions for the protection of women and children's rights.[64] While it may be the case that the Legal Aid office has not yet assumed the lower profile that it should, now that an official agency exists to carry out its original mission, it helped to create societal standards, legitimized citizen demands for such rights, and gave a forum for denunciation of human rights abuses. In the initial five years, the number of public complaints to the human rights prosecutor rose from 962 to 4,445.[65] Under Archbishop Sáenz, there is greater church cooperation with and dependence upon the state (and consequently less criticism of human rights, or the lack of compliance with the peace accords).[66]

CONCLUSION

The end of the armed conflict (and the heavy cost it had for the Catholic Church when it became a critic of governments), a new generation of clergy that did not live through Vatican II, Medellín, and repressive dictatorships,[67] and the temptation to seek the patronage and favor of the state have led the Catholic Church closer to church-state union and away from being the "voice of the voiceless"[68] as before. In San Salvador two parish priests captured the new direction:

> [Church-state ties] have changed totally, that is what is so troubling for the people, the true Church.

> Cristiani and Rivera y Damas did not get along—in the area of human rights, the Tutela [Legal Aid] criticized the government, and [the archbishop] never went to government ceremonies. [Now] the hierarchy is very much in agreement with the government (of President Calderón Sol), and they lowered their voice on human rights.[69]

What are the future prospects for Catholic-Protestant ecumenical dialogue, legal and practical religious freedom and pluralism, and church-state relations in El Salvador? There is a history of inter-church contact, but it seems that the present leadership of the archdiocese is uninterested in ecumenical efforts.

There is a large gulf between legal statutes and daily practice in terms of the separation of church and state in a nation with a limited historical tradition in this regard, and in religious freedom for non-Catholics. The future of this situation will depend on the outcome of the current efforts of bishops to gain state protection and de facto (if not de jure) favoritism of Catholicism over other religions. In the long run, this could backfire, both in terms of undercutting the prospects for ecumenism, and in terms of failing to heal deep and real divisions in the clergy and laity of the Salvadoran Catholic Church. Church-state relations under democracy are likely to be moderately contentious on individual public policy issues, but will probably not return to the polarization and open conflict of the 1970s and 1980s unless violence becomes commonplace again, and constitutional democracy breaks down. Recent surveys have shown that the Catholic Church (along with the media, the Human Rights Ombudsman, and local government) continues to be held as much more trustworthy than any other governmental or societal institution.[70] That moral authority presents it with an opportunity to contribute further to religious freedom, the rule of law, and the emergence of democracy. It remains to be seen whether Catholic leaders make use of this opening.

7.

THE NEW LEGISLATION ON RELIGIOUS FREEDOM IN MEXICO

———◆———

José Luis Soberanes Fernández

BACKGROUND

On January 28, 1992, the Official Record *(Diario Oficial)* of the Mexican Federation published a decree amending various principles of the Constitution of the Republic, relating to the fundamental right to religious freedom, religious associations, and ministers of religion. Later, on July 15 of the same year, the Official Record published the implementing legislation, *The Law of Religious Associations and Public Worship*. With this law, Mexico radically altered its legislation in these matters.[1]

In the following pages, I will try briefly to evaluate this important step in Mexico's progress in the field of human rights. The amendments were not as sweeping as one would desire, but we also must consider that it is impossible to abandon a whole laicist and sometimes persecutory—rather than secular—tradition. In addition, this new legislation corrects some outmoded situations. On the other hand, I should add that the legislation has some significant defects—as a result of internal divisions within the Mexican political system itself—due to the number of people who were involved in its writing, and above all due to a lack of experience in this matter. However, I have to emphasize that the constitutional amendments and the law represent not one but many steps forward in the area of religious freedom in Mexico.

ANTECEDENTS

As noted above, a historical explanation remains fundamental in understanding the great importance of the 1992 reform.

During the three centuries of European colonialism Mexico, like the rest of Latin America, was ruled in ecclesiastical matters by the institution of the *patronato* (patronage),[2] also called the *regio vicariato* (royal vicariate).[3] As a result, after securing independence, in the first third of the last century, all these new countries confronted the same problems with respect to the Holy See, namely, the recognition of national independence, the reestablishment of a greatly diminished hierarchy,[4] and, finally, an effort to secure papal acceptance of the continuation of the *patronato*, now called National, which caused great difficulties.[5] As a result, it was thought that since the royal rights of the colonial period were not continued, there was no sense in maintaining the ecclesiastical privileges that the old regime had created, the so-called *fueros*.

If we add to this the influence of liberal ideology, basically due to its propagation by Masonic lodges, which were very important in nineteenth-century Latin America, including Mexico, all Spanish-American countries experienced a liberal reform, which was the result primarily of the rejection of the *patronato* by the Holy See[6] and of the liberal project of the secularization of society.[7]

Returning to Mexico, the triumph of the Ayutla Revolution in 1855 brought the "pure" liberals[8] to power, initiating an authentic liberal reform that started with the so-called Juárez Law on 23 November 1855, which drastically reduced ecclesiastical and military privileges. The Lerdo Law followed on 25 June 1856, liberalizing the legal status of the holdings of civil and ecclesiastic corporations. Later, the Constitutional Congress (*Constituyente*) of 1856-57, while not establishing so-called freedom of worship, did not include the principle of non-toleration of religions other than Catholicism in the text of the Constitution of 5 February 1857, a principle that all previous constitutions had contained. By the end of the same year, conservatives carried out a coup, after which they repealed all the liberal legislation, leading to a war that would last three years: the War of Reform.

The constitutional government, headed by Benito Juàrez, eventually settled in the port of Veracruz, from which it led the liberal victory and issued the Reform Laws,[9] by which liberal reform was fully implemented. Defeated, the conservatives approached the French emperor, Napoleon III, leading in 1862 to military intervention by France, which led to the creation of the second Mexican Empire. The Austrian Prince Maximilian of Hapsburg, paradoxically of liberal background, was placed in charge of this adventure, which would last five years. In 1867, after the French troops abandoned Mexico, the empire fell and the conservatives with it. This led to the triumph of the republic, presided over by Benito Juárez and, of course, the final victory of the liberal model in Mexico. The Reform Laws were subsequently elevated to constitutional status.

A few years later, in 1876, another liberal politician rose to power, Porfirio Díaz,[10] who ruled the country in dictatorial form until 1911. His regime was appropriately labeled as one with "little politics and much administration." As was to be expected, Díaz did not abrogate the Reform Laws, but rather modified their application in a way that some think amounted to their abrogation, as part of a policy of national reconciliation called the "peace of the sepulchers," which brought with it religious toleration.

Curiously, the three liberal presidents, Juárez, Lerdo de Tejeda, and Díaz, tried to promote the development of Protestantism in Mexico[11] in order to strengthen religious freedom by expanding cultural options. During the long administration of Porfirio Díaz, two sociopolitical movements arose silently but effectively. These movements will help us to understand the reasons behind the antireligious sentiments of the Revolution that succeeded in overthrowing Díaz. I refer to the social and political activity of the Catholics and the proliferation of small political clubs of the liberal-Masonic-Protestant type.

In effect, with the publication of Pope Leo XIII's 1891 encyclical *Rerum Novarum*, Catholic Mexicans abandoned their conservative posture, discussing social issues and adopting a new political attitude in line with the thinking of Leo XIII. They had a positive influence on the formulation of labor clauses for the 1917 Constitution, which has been correctly called the world's first socially oriented constitution.[12] Politically they took a moderately critical position on the dictatorship, but they decided to act as an organization only after the fall of Díaz, through the National Catholic Party (NCP).[13] Their mistake came when President Madero was assassinated and the usurper, Victoriano Huerta, assumed power. Many of the members of the NCP decided to support him and thus, with the triumph of the constitutionalist movement which overthrew Huerta and called a new Constitutional Congress (1916-17 *Constituyente)*, the attitude of the victors became profoundly anti-Catholic.

On the other hand, many members of those liberal—Masonic—Protestant clubs were active in the revolutionary constitutionalist forces,[14] one of whose more important principles was the full implementation of the Reform Laws and an openly anti-Catholic attitude. Interestingly, former students in Catholic seminaries joined their ranks, as also occurred in the case of the Reform generation in the middle of the nineteenth century.

As a result of both these factors, the Constitutional Congress was dominated by elements that called themselves anticlerical and Jacobin, which would necessarily be reflected in five articles frankly hostile to the Catholic church (Articles 3, 5, 24, 27, and 130), demonstrating a tendency that can be described not just as lay, but as laicist.

THE 1916-17 CONSTITUTIONAL CONGRESS (*CONSTITUYENTE*)

The dictatorship of Porfirio Díaz ended with the uprising in 1911 of Francisco I. Madero, who became president in the subsequent election. He stayed in the presidency of the Republic a little more than a year, being assassinated in February 1913, bringing to power the usurper Victoriano Huerta. This last event produced an uprising in the north of the country of the aforementioned constitutionalist movement, which wanted to throw Huerta out of office and reestablish constitutional order. This movement was headed by Venustiano

Carranza, who, upon achieving the overthrow of Huerta in 1914, had to face a fight within his own revolutionary factions, from which he emerged triumphant.

In 1916, Venustiano Carranza, great victor of the Mexican Revolution, found a country in ruins, bloodied and divided by five years of civil war. He had to make sense of this apparently titanic force which lacked a purpose other than the overthrow of an illegitimate regime. Hence he decided to call a Constitutional Congress to meet in the city of Queretaro starting 1 December 1916. With the primary purpose of amending the Constitution of 1857, the framers promulgated a new constitution on 5 February 1917. Its Catholic-influenced social content made the document a legitimator of the Mexican Revolution, but at the same time, it was an anti-Catholic document, produced by anticlerical and Jacobin deputies.

The fundamental principles on this subject approved by the Constitutional Congress of Querétaro, were:

1. Secular education, in public and private schools[15];
2. Prohibition of religious groups and church ministers establishing or directing primary schools;
3. Prohibition of religious vows and of the establishment of monastic orders;
4. Religious services could only be carried out within the churches, which would always be under the supervision of the government authorities;
5. Prohibition of religious associations—churches—from acquiring, possessing, or administering real estate, with what they currently owned passing to the ownership of the state, and churches becoming national property;
6. Prohibition of ministers of worship or religious associations from sponsoring, directing, or administering institutions whose object is the help of the needy, scientific research, education, mutual aid, or any other licit purpose;
7. Repeal of the sworn oath as a requirement for binding legal proceedings, with only a "promise to tell the truth" being used in its place;
8. Removal of legal recognition from religious groups called churches;
9. Consideration of ministers as professionals subject to the corresponding legislation;
10. Empowerment of local legislatures to determine the maximum number of ministers in each federal entity (some only permitted one per state);
11. Only persons born in Mexico to be ministers;
12. Prohibition of ministers of worship from criticizing the laws, the authorities, and the government;
13. Exclusion of ministers from the vote;
14. Prohibition of ministers from associating for political purposes;
15. Prohibition of legal recognition or validation of studies in establishments dedicated to the formation of ministers;

16. Prohibition of confessional publications from commenting on political matters, or providing information about actions of the authorities, or about the functioning of public institutions;
17. Prohibition of political associations having names linked to any religious faith;
18. Prohibition of holding political meetings in churches;
19. Prohibition of ministers from inheriting by will, except in cases of relatives less than four times removed.

It is evident that these articles are opposed to the fundamental right to religious freedom. President Plutarco Elías Calles (1924-28) tried to put them into practice, issuing the corresponding statutory laws.[16] This provoked a religious persecution and a conflict that became a civil war (1926-29) known as the *Cristero War*,[17] since its battle cry was, "Long live Christ the King!" Finally, President Emilio Portes Gil signed a number of "accords" with the Catholic hierarchy, of dubious legality, that ushered in an era known as the *modus vivendi*.

THE REFORM OF 1992

After the administration of Lázaro Cárdenas (1934-40), a populist with some Marxist tendencies, President Manuel Avila Camacho took power (1940-46). Camacho had stated during his campaign that he was a believer, and he initiated a radical change in church-state relations. His policy of full religious tolerance implied the nonobservance of the constitutional principles noted above, an attitude that subsequent governments would not modify, though the constitutional text remained unchanged.

After the administration of President Luis Echevarría (1970-76), who visited Pope Paul VI at the Vatican, contacts between the Catholic hierarchy and the government were made public. President José López Portillo (1976-82) not only authorized Pope John Paul II's visit to Mexico in 1979, but also organized an official reception at the airport and received him in the official residence at Los Pinos. During the government of President Miguel de la Madrid (1982-88), the Catholic hierarchy frequently pressed for the modification of the aforementioned articles, alleging human rights violations and encountering great resistance in official sectors and, of course, among the Masons. The latter were more disposed to continue with the status quo, without modifying the basic laws, leaving them a sword of Damocles over the church.

When President Carlos Salinas de Gortari (1988-94) was engaged in the campaign that would bring him to the head of the country's executive branch, he called for the modernization of national life. In his inaugural address on 1 December 1988, he stated that he would modernize church-state relations, which touched off a great debate on this delicate matter. It is not certain whether President Salinas intended to carry out a constitutional reform on this issue, as the Minister of the Interior emphatically declared, or perhaps only to establish diplomatic relations with the Holy See. This, however, some saw as legally impossible due to Article 130 of the constitution which denied legal recognition to religious groups called churches. In fact, the government resorted to a mechanism little-known in Mexico, naming a personal representative of the president to the pope, and acknowledging the papal delegate as a personal representative to the president of Mexico, thus according him diplomatic status. Furthermore, in 1990, President Salinas invited and personally greeted Pope John Paul II at the airport—something no Mexican president has done for any chief of state—and at his official residence.

Matters having been brought to that point, during his third address to Congress, on 1 November 1991, President Salinas announced a constitutional reform relating to religion but noted three limits to this: (1) secular public education, (2) no clerical involvement in political issues, and (3) prohibition of the accumulation of property in the hands of the churches and religious groups. The governing party, PRI, was to prepare the amendments and federal deputies would be charged with presenting them to Congress (which is not common in Mexico, since the federal executive usually handles such duties).

It was thus that, after the corresponding constitutional steps and colorful discussion in the House of Deputies, the amendments to Articles 3, 5, 24, 27, and 130 were approved by a large majority (with the exception of the deputies of a small historic party with Stalinist roots, the Popular Socialist Party), and were published on 28 January 1992 in the Official Record of the Mexican Federation. With this, civil liberties were expanded in Mexico, ending years of posturing and truly modernizing an important aspect of public life. Anachronistic legal precepts that were more ridiculous than real, and inapplicable in a modern secular society, were finally eliminated. Above all, we Mexicans became reconciled with each other, ending more than 150 years of futile conflict.

The constitutional reform that took effect on 29 January 1992 left a few loose ends that needed to be specified more precisely by statutory law in order to make the reform work. Because of the imprecision of the constitutional provisions, there were many opinions and bills which made for a great quantity of options. Above all, a lack of experience with this subject left the future unclear. Finally, PRI's federal deputies presented their statutory initiatives— which still had to be negotiated by the larger parties and thoroughly discussed in Congress—to be published on 15 July 1992, with the title Law of Religious Associations and Public Worship (*Ley de Asociaciones Religiosas y Culto Bíblico*, LARCP). At the time of writing, the corresponding legal regulations are still pending.

CONTENTS OF THE REFORM

There are three main areas in Mexican legislation on this question: religious freedom, religious associations, and ministers of religion. The three can, of course, be reduced to one: the fundamental right to religious freedom in Mexico.

RELIGIOUS FREEDOM

The principle of religious freedom in Mexico is expressed in Article 24 of the constitution, which says, "Every man is free to profess the religious belief that he prefers and to participate in the ceremonies, devotions, or acts of the respective religion, as long as they are not crimes or offenses punishable by law. The Congress cannot make laws that establish or prohibit any religion." This is complemented in two other constitutional principles: the so-called historic principle of the separation of the state and the churches, along with the secular nature of that state. No political association or party can have in its name any word that would link it with anything religious. Nor can politically related meetings be held in churches. These principles are developed in Articles 2, 3, 25, and 29 of the Law of Religious Associations.

Article 3 of the law notes that the state exercises its authority over all religious manifestations, individual and collective, but only in relation to the observance of order, public morality, and as guardian of the rights of third parties. The state cannot establish any type of preference or privilege in favor of any church or religious group. Article 25 provides that no public authority shall intervene in the internal matters of religious associations, nor can it participate (except in a diplomatic capacity) in an official capacity in religious functions.

Article 2 of the law specifically adds to the content of religious freedom the following particular rights:

a) To hold or adopt the religious belief that a person prefers and to practice, individually or collectively, the religious acts or rites of his preference;

b) To profess no religious beliefs, to abstain from practicing religious acts and rites, and not to belong to any religious association;

c) Not to be the object of discrimination, coercion, or hostility, on the basis of religious belief, nor to be forced to declare those beliefs, nor can religious reasons be used to impede anybody from the exercise of any work or activity, except in cases foreseen in this and other applicable regulations;

d) Not to be forced to provide personal services nor to contribute money or its equivalent to support a religious association, church, or any other such group, nor to participate in, nor contribute in the same way to rites, ceremonies, festivals, services, and other religious acts;

e) Not to be the object of any judicial or administrative investigation due to the expression of religious ideas; and

f) To associate or meet peacefully for religious purposes.

Article 29 describes the violations of the law, thus giving additional specific content to meaning of the fundamental right of freedom of religion:

I. To associate for political ends, as well as to proselytize on behalf of, or against any candidate, party, or political association.

II. To promote conduct harmful to the health and physical integrity of the individual.

III. To exercise physical violence or mental pressure in the form of aggression or threats, to achieve its objectives.

IV. To use the property acquired by the associations for any purpose different from that foreseen in the corresponding mission statement.

V. To deviate from the goals of the associations in such a way that they lose or gravely diminish their religious nature.

VI. To convert a religious act into a political meeting.

VII. To oppose the laws of the nation or its institutions in public meetings.

On the other hand, there are five limitations to the right of religious freedom:

1) Establishing secular education as obligatory in public schools, as per Article 3 of the Constitution;

2) Prohibiting conscientious objection in Article 1, paragraph two, of the LARCP;

3) Prohibiting religious associations and ministers from acquiring and administering, for themselves or for an intermediary, communications media (Article 16), as well as the obligation to ask permission from the Ministry of Government before transmitting religious ceremonies by radio or television (Article 21);

4) Limiting religious acts of public worship outside the churches to extraordinary cases with prior authorization (express or tacit) by the proper authorities;

5) The denial of legal standing to religious ceremonies that are related to the duties of the civil registry, particularly marriages (Article 130, penultimate paragraph of the Constitution).

The guarantee of religious assistance in jails, hospitals, and homes is neither included nor prohibited.

RELIGIOUS ASSOCIATIONS

The law does not recognize the church or other religious associations. Rather, it creates the legal term *religious association,* which is the way to obtain legal standing and related benefits under the law. To register as a religious association, it is necessary to petition the Ministry of the Interior, which shall verify that the petitioning group has been substantially engaged in the observance, practice, propagation, or instruction of a religious doctrine or body of religious beliefs, has been active in Mexico for five years, and has permanent roots in the population. It is possible, interestingly enough, that the internal subdivisions of a religious association may acquire legal standing of their own, which could be the case in the Catholic church, with its dioceses and religious orders.

In Article 9, the law recognizes the following rights of religious associations:

I. To identify themselves by a particular name;

II. To organize freely their internal structures and to adopt statutes or norms that specify a system of authority and operation, including the education and designation of their ministers;

III. To perform acts of public worship, as well as propagate their doctrine, as long as they do not contradict this and other applicable regulations;

IV. To hold all types of legal activities to fulfill their objectives, as long as they are licit and do not pursue monetary gain;

V. To participate, themselves or in association with other physical or moral persons, in the establishment, administration, sustenance, and operation of institutions of private assistance, education, and health, provided that they do not pursue profit and that they subject themselves to the laws that regulate those activities;

VI. To use national property exclusively for religious ends, in the terms dictated in the respective regulations, and

VII. To enjoy the other rights that this and other laws confer.

Another very important question is related to the property of the religious associations, since Article 27, section II of the Constitution limits this to what is indispensable to fulfill the objectives of the association, so as to prevent a return to the "wealth in dead hands" (mortmain) property that could not be sold, leading to a tremendous increase in church wealth. The law thus establishes a "guiding declaration dealing with the acquisition of real estate, inheritances, and legacies; trusteeships relating to institutions of education, health, and other beneficiary organizations of the religious associations," in which case it is necessary to petition the Ministry of the Interior, with the understanding that if there is no response within forty-five days, the action is permitted. When an association is registered, the Ministry shall issue a general declaration of origin for all its possessions. The law requires four registration documents to be submitted to the authorities: that of religious association, of real estate, of national property (remember that until 1992 all the churches were property of the state) in use, as well as lists of the responsible directors and the ministers of religion.

Can a religious group that cannot or does not desire to register act freely in Mexico? Certainly—and it can even have legal standing as a civil association, for example, although it will not have all the rights of religious associations granted in sections IV, V, VI, and VII of Article 9.

Also, the representatives of religious associations must be Mexican.

MINISTERS OF RELIGION

In principle, each religious association determines its ministers. The law considers as ministers those whose principal duties are direction, organization, and representation—a definition little understood. The law only considers ministers those of registered religious associations, in practice ignoring the ministers of other groups, as well as those not belonging to any particular structure, as can indeed occur. This will have to be corrected in future legislation.

In current Mexican legislation, foreigners can act as religious ministers. Ministers can vote in elections, but they cannot run for elected office unless five years have passed between their ministry and the election, nor hold public office unless three non-ministerial years have passed for major offices and six months for minor offices. Religious ministers cannot associate for political purposes, proselytize for or campaign against candidates or political parties, oppose national laws or institutions during religious services, preach propaganda, defame national symbols in religious publications, nor can they or their relatives or religious associations inherit property from those whom they have directed or spiritually aided, with the exception of relatives less than four times removed.

Finally, it can be said that the law establishes sanctions and guides for its application; mechanisms like mediation and arbitration in the case of conflict between religious associations, as well as administrative procedures.

8.

MEXICO

Liberation Theology, Base Communities and Evangelical Protestantism

———————— ◆ ————————

Roderic Ai Camp

The most progressive elements of Vatican II and Medellín were blended to-gether into a religious/secular philosophy popularly known as liberation the-ology. The origins of what is now considered liberation theology find strong roots in the British Reformation, which also describes a God who sides with the poor.[1] Liberation theology takes on many different features, conceptual-ized as including the following significant elements. First, liberation involves freedom from the bondage of ignorance, alienation, poverty, and oppression. Second, liberation is neither spiritual nor secular but a unique combination of religious and political freedom.[2] Third, the theology of liberation implies that citizens must participate fully in shaping their own lives. Fourth, social struc-tures must be reordered to encourage human cooperation. Fifth, liberation theologians stress the value of equality, making it inseparable from freedom.[3] Sixth, its advocates pay close attention to the external causes of oppression and poverty and see external and internal colonialism as intertwined.[4] Sev-enth, liberation theology borrows conceptually from Marxist sociology, such as in stress on mass participation, but does not believe such reliance jeopar-dizes its religious roots and commitment.[5] Eighth, it alters the Church's mis-sion from a spiritualist redemption of the human race to an ethical duty to denounce injustice.[6] Ninth, it reinterprets symbols that determine the relation-ships between the individual and the community, the private and the public, and the political and the religious, challenging the ethics of public and private behavior.[7] Tenth, liberation theology attempts to view issues through the eyes

Reprinted by permission from Roderic Ai Camp, *Crossing Swords* (New York: Ox-ford University Press, 1997).

of the poor, to share their lives, and to alter the relationship between the Church and the ordinary parishioner.[8] Eleventh, the tone of liberation theology may incite retaliation and hatred toward local and international oppressors, whereas traditional Catholicism preaches love.[9] And finally, it is assumed implicitly that the presence of these conditions will produce a stronger and more influential Church than the traditional, apolitical institution.[10]

A careful examination of these concepts makes clear why widespread application of liberationist ideas would be threatening to political institutions, as well as to many groups within the Church. Higher clergy most opposed to liberation theology, however, objected to its association with Marxism. Archbishop Manuel Castro Ruiz of Mérida, Yucatán, who is often identified in the traditionalist camp, cannot be simply categorized:

> When there is a Marxist element, liberation theology cannot be accepted. The danger in liberation theology is this Marxist element, but the positive part of liberation theology is its option for the poor. I'm very much in agreement with this and, as part of this option for the poor, helping the poor to better their lot in life. When liberation theology expounds on these themes, the Church in Mexico is in agreement.[11]

In Mexico, not only did Vatican II's general flavor not pierce traditional practices as deeply or widely as occurred elsewhere in Latin America, but its most threatening concepts to traditionalists, incorporated in liberation theology, did not achieve the same level of influence in Mexico as they did elsewhere in the region. Indeed, the Church's own comprehensive survey of regular attenders at Mass discovered that only 53 percent considered themselves well informed about it in 1986.[12] The conditions inhibiting Vatican II's influence also blocked liberation theology's influence. In addition to these adverse qualities, others were also present. Some analysts have long argued that liberation theology is strongest in those regions where state-led violence is most prevalent, a situation not present, comparatively speaking, in Mexico.[13] Others believe that a weak theological tradition of praxis characterized Mexico— that is, interpreting the secular reality—as was happening in Brazil.[14] In fact, students of the movement in Mexico describe it as having few organic origins.[15] A third element is the minor presence of foreign clergy in Mexico, a group that played a significant role in countries accepting liberation theology.[16] A fourth explanation for Mexico's lower interest in liberation theology stems from the relatively small number of religious orders, those groups most receptive to this progressive thought.[17] In fact, the Latin American Conference of Religious (CLAR), composed of some 160,000 members from orders and congregations, supports a far more liberal posture than that of CELAM (the Latin American Bishops' Conference). Furthermore, the Mexican episcopate has criticized its affiliate to this group, the Conference of Religious Institutes of Mexico.[18] Finally, John Paul II tried, since his first visit in 1979, to encourage bishops to spurn this doctrine. In May 1990, he energetically condemned liberation theology before 102 bishops in Mexico.[19]

The vehicles through which liberation theology has been applied, generating the most controversy, are the *comunidades eclesiales de base*, ecclesiastical base communities. Originally, these communities developed as a response to Church concerns for pastoral care and evangelism, especially in Brazil. They drew on the French pastoral theology emphasizing small, tightly knit Christian groups and strong lay participation and training.[20] In Latin America, sufficient priests did not exist to respond to laypeople's needs, but no specific link existed between political participation, liberation theology, and the communities. Bishops viewed these communities in 1979 as

> a small group which, by reading the Bible, participating in the sacraments, and discussing common concerns and action, will internalize a new awareness of Christianity. In the CEBs, the individual is expected to find "new interpersonal relations in the faith, deepening of the Word of God, participation in the eucharist, communion with the pastors of the particular church, and a greater commitment with justice in the social reality around them."[21]

The third CELAM conference in Puebla, Mexico, in 1979, joined base communities and liberation theology in an authentically complementary way.[22] This led to a much stronger emphasis on their social mission. As Hewitt explains, they met not only to celebrate their faith but also to translate that faith into social action, to solve the material problems affecting them, and to help the poor and oppressed to achieve justice and equality.[23] It is very important to emphasize, however, that although all CEBs are involved in Bible study, they are by no means homogenous across Latin America, nor within individual countries. "The way they link spiritual understandings and group life to social and political issues ranges across the entire gamut of alternatives." [24]

Ecclesiastical base communities offer new opportunities for small groups of ordinary citizens and pose a potential for numerous religious, social, and political consequences. Contrary to the widespread impression that all of these groups are lower class, evidence demonstrates the presence of middle-class groups who are developing an awareness of their poorer counterparts' needs.[25] In a broader sense, CEBs provide an opportunity for Latin Americans to create a sense of community, to develop friendships, to share experiences, and to talk with one another. More specifically, they give individuals the opportunity to participate in a society that discourages their participation, they create new channels for making demands, and they focus on problem solving and practical local issues.[26] In the longer term, even if their direct political linkages decline, they will continue to promote new sources and styles of leaders, who in turn will affect the larger society.[27] Specifically, they have had a tremendous influence on resocializing women, who provide the majority of participants in most such communities. Not only have CEBs affected how women view their traditional roles, but they have encouraged women to take up new social roles, generating an interest in politics where none existed before.[28]

CEBs, as a representation of the new Church theology in the late 1960s, created a limited yet significant path in Mexico. They began in 1967 with the pastoral efforts under Bishop Sergio Méndez Arceo in the Cuernavaca diocese.[29] By the 1970s, CEBs existed throughout Mexico, 70 percent operating in rural regions, and the remainder in working-class urban neighborhoods.[30] In Mexico, a typical community consisted of eight to ten people and, as is true elsewhere in Latin America, although they share common characteristics, they are quite heterogeneous.[31] It is also true in the Mexican case that the vast majority of these communities are composed of lower, not middle, classes. The CEB founders, including Bishop Méndez Arceo, agree, without empirical data, that the majority of community leaders were religious order members.[32]

Although a sizable minority of bishops initially provided support for this movement or were neutral, the two Mexicans receiving the most attention as proactive CEB supporters were Sergio Méndez Arceo in Cuernavaca and Samuel Ruiz García, head of the San Cristóbal de las Casas diocese since 1960. Méndez Arceo generated considerable controversy in his diocese as a symbol of liberation theology. He represented to his supporters all that was positive about a Church of the Poor. To his worst detractors, he was known as the "Red Bishop," a scandalous sympathizer of socialism.[33] Indeed, Méndez Arceo publicly declared his support for socialism, arguing in 1970 that Christianity and socialism could coexist. Two years later, he was the only member of the episcopate to attend the Christians for Socialism conference.[34] He also attracted criticism because in 1970 he encouraged President Echeverría to form a committee of notable citizens to examine Mexico's most serious social and economic problems.[35] Echeverría himself viewed Méndez Arceo as Mexico's foremost proponent of liberation theology and favored his emphasis on redistribution of wealth and on the poor. He also believed that the clergy could help Mexicans learn the best means of organizing themselves in a capitalist society. Interestingly, both the president and Méndez Arceo considered labor unions essential to the success of base community organizing, but heavy state-controlled labor organizations limited their penetration.[36]

Méndez Arceo never was able to expand his individual influence or that of the base communities beyond a small proportion of Mexican dioceses. By becoming too controversial, he lost a sense of collegiality important to Mexican bishops and the episcopate. Expressed differently, many bishops told Dennis Hanratty that Méndez Arceo lacked sufficient commitment to the institutional Church.[37] Since Méndez Arceo's retirement in 1983, the Vatican representative used his influence to select unsympathetic bishops who reversed Méndez Arceo's impact. His initial successor, Juan Jesús Posadas Ocampo, replaced twenty-five priests in two months.[38] Nevertheless, ten years later, nearly half of the priests in the dioceses were still Méndez Arceo's followers.[39] Although many critics charged that Méndez Arceo politicized his diocese and its base communities, implying that its members opposed the government party, empirical evidence suggests no such support; indeed, religiosity in Cuernavaca is associated with increased PRI support.[40]

Samuel Ruiz replaced Méndez Arceo as the most reviled bishop by certain elements in Mexican society. The three-time head of the episcopate's indigenous affairs committee, Ruiz participated in both Vatican II and CELAM. Yet Ruiz, despite his role as the symbolic leader of liberation theology, heartily denies an interest in this philosophy. As he has stated repeatedly, "I do not have any interest in liberation theology as a theory; I am interested in liberation. It's the word of God that we must listen to. The reality that exists is not a theory, it is a Christian commitment. As baptized people we have a responsibility to deal with the reality."[41] He takes the following position on base communities:

> I myself would not encourage the formation of base communities. If they're base communities, by definition they emerge from the very bottom. As bishop I would not order their commencement or support these base communities. People will have to do that on their own. I do not think of myself as being part of a progressive Church. I only respond to the problems that are around me; I don't look behind or in front of me, I just respond to problems I see.[42]

Ruiz's defense of indigenous rights has embroiled him in many controversies in his diocese. With the uprising of the Zapatista Army of National Liberation in January 1994, his stature as a cleric sympathetic to the Church of the Poor received national and international attention.[43] Nevertheless, he long recognized the tremendous pressure on him and an attempt to portray him as a stereotype of a certain type of Latin American bishop, a portrait from which he has attempted to distance himself since the late 1980s.[44]

By the 1990s, about 20 percent of Mexico's bishops openly supported base ecclesiastical communities, and another 5-10 percent tolerated their presence.[45] Yet the influence of base communities may be more extensive in Mexico than is generally believed. For example, it has been asserted that no CEBs exist in the Mérida, Yucatán, archdiocese, whose archbishop is a traditionalist. Despite this perception, grassroots organizations perform functions typical of CEBs elsewhere in Mexico. These organizations were introduced in the Yucatán as *comunidades parroquiales* (parish communities). The archbishop opposed the language of liberation theology but not some of its essential concepts.[46]

In Mexico, activists and analysts alike agree that all CEBs, whatever their differences, typically focus on issues of social equality, social justice, and economic development rather than political democracy. In fact, generally they have little interest in political parties or partisan voting. Priests take the same posture. Overwhelmingly, they have told interviewers that poverty is a far more important issue than elections. Priests and nuns organize these grassroots groups, but unless they remain actively involved over long periods of time, the groups cease to function.[47] Although some observers predicted that committed priests would replace teachers as important local community leaders, sufficient Mexican clergy are not available to perform such functions even if every priest were willing.[48]

In reality, how do community-based organizations operate in Mexico? According to priests and nuns in Chiapas, central to their success are weekly meetings with catechists (*animadores*), who then return to their communities to deal with local issues. The groups initially started out discussing economic and social problems, combining it with analyzing the word of God and the Bible. Some members of these groups reportedly join other organizations such as peasant federations. Active clergy and religious believe, as does Bishop Samuel Ruiz, that it is essential that change occur among the people from the bottom up.[49] Indeed, some of the priests who now educate Chiapan residents in the goals and methodology of grassroots organizations are themselves products of the region's earliest base communities.

Priests and sisters in other parts of Mexico, when initially introducing the concept of base ecclesiastical communities, encounter resistance from parishioners who think of the Church only as a place for prayer, not work. They have found, however, that once they develop a sense of trust and respect, Mexicans quickly adopt new behaviors based on a pastoral philosophy described as *ver, pensar, actuar* (to see, to think, to act).[50]

Base communities are prohibited in many dioceses. Support from some bishops also appears to be conditional, based on the CEBs' political behavior or associations. Support among priests is more widespread. In Luengo's study, administered in dioceses containing few actual CEBs, one-fifth of the priests favored such community groups.[51] In the minds of some priests, a relationship exists between the growth of community organizations and the lack of priests. For example, many priests choose not to come to Chiapas, where social and political issues are very much part of the problems confronted daily in the diocese. Their decision, in turn, positively affects the growth of Chiapan CEBs that substitute for traditional parish priests and diocesan lay organizations.[52]

Over the last twenty years, Mexican priests and bishops have viewed CEBs positively but also with suspicion. In the mid-1970s, less than ten years after CEBs first arrived in Mexico, one-third of priests attending a conference in central Mexico (of all ages and from all regions) believed these communities were necessary to evangelize. About the same percentage agreed that Christianizing should include the promotion of justice.[53] By the mid-1980s, the president of the Mexican episcopate attended the CEBs' national meeting, symbolizing the hierarchy's general endorsement.[54] The increasingly positive reception of CEBs could also be attributed to the role they played in relief efforts immediately following the 1986 earthquake.[55] This open endorsement may stem in part from the hierarchy's perception that CEBs may be the Catholic Church's strongest defense in the fierce competition against evangelical groups.[56] Northern bishops addressed this issue in their pastoral letter, stating, "The witness of your lives and your missionary zeal is an evangelizing force that helps to dispel the confusion and division fostered by the Protestant sects. . . . Let the CEB help the people not to lose, or to recover their Christian historical consciousness."[57]

One bishop sagely noted that CEBs in Mexico are not well understood and that clergy often are for or against them without comprehending their actual functions. He reports that many of his colleagues openly show their lack of confidence in the vocabulary of liberation theology and likens their posture to one of ideological warfare.[58] A generation of younger priests have been influenced, generally positively, by the presence of such organizations. In Brazil, for example, priests under thirty-five typically defined the people as the poor or oppressed.[59] In Mexico, half of all priests interviewed thought CEBs were the best form of living Catholicism. Only one-fourth disagreed with that statement.[60]

Bishops throughout Latin America, and Mexico specifically, have the same reservations about religious grassroots communities as they do about political activities in general. They fear being drawn into potentially dangerous political confrontations through popular group activities, they fear the growing salience of class-based groups and demands diluting the spiritual and religious mission of the Church, they fear undercutting the authority of bishops and clergy by legitimizing such groups, and they are afraid that redefining the Church's base according to social class precludes all classes from receiving the message of salvation.[61] Clergy who are critical of this position charge that the hierarchy does not engage sufficiently in self-criticism and has not concerned itself adequately with the option for the poor.

PROTESTANTISM

One of the most dynamic social changes in Latin America in the 1970s and 1980s is the growth of evangelical Protestantism. Mainline Protestants, such as the Methodists, have not shared in this growth. Although Mexico nationally is not in the forefront of this growth, certain regions have witnessed increasingly rapid expansion among certain Protestant faiths. This has led some analysts to claim that the major challenge to the Catholic Church's influence is not the State but competition from other religions.[62] The Secretariat of Government (Interior Ministry) received 1,206 requests from Protestants to obtain legal recognition from 1940 through 1964. From 1968 through 1988, when President Salinas took office, the requests increased sixfold, to 8,199. By 1990, the states with the highest percentage of Protestants were Chiapas (16 percent), Tabasco (15 percent), Campeche (14 percent), and Quintana Roo (12 percent).[63]

Mexicans have converted to Protestantism for many of the same reasons that can be found elsewhere in Latin America. First, some observers suggest that activist Catholics have strayed too far from their pastoral responsibilities, leaving a spiritual void filled by the Protestant sects. This is a rather questionable assumption in the Mexican case. A better argument can be made for the widespread deficiencies in Catholic evangelization, extending back to the conquest, a weakness the hierarchy recognizes.[64] Second, spouses have encouraged many men to join these sects to eliminate their alcoholism and the abusive behavior it often entails.[65] Third, the typical individual who joins the Evangelicals is religiously unaffiliated rather than a practicing Catholic who converts to Protestantism. Those states with the highest percentage of increase among the Evangelicals, Baja California del Sur, Chiapas, Colima, México, Oaxaca, Querétaro, and Quintana Roo, have the highest percentage of religiously unaffiliated.[66] Fourth, Protestant converts tend to come from lower socioeconomic backgrounds.[67] Fifth, Mexicans who convert to the sects are individuals who practice their religion intensely, value home- and neighborhood-centered religious environments, are literal in their dogma, and see religion as a route to personal salvation. In particular, they are especially attracted to an organizational structure that is small and emphasizes a strong sense of community.[68] Sixth, laypersons themselves believe that Protestant groups are attractive because of the material assistance they provide, a view shared among some bishops.[69]

The increased growth of evangelical Protestants and the assertiveness of these various faiths in seeking converts engender a conflictual and tense environment among Catholic and Protestant clergy and parishioners. In fact, the level of tension between the two religions is higher than at any other point in the last three decades.[70] The Mexican population as a whole, which remains predominantly Catholic, views these Protestant sects negatively. Many Mexicans see these new religious groups as insidious, foreign influences that are infiltrating and destroying their national religious culture and unity.[71] This view predominates despite the historical fact that on occasion Catholic clergy have cooperated with various Protestant faiths, including the Pentecostals.[72] Typically, however, Catholic bishops have been uncooperative with Protestants.[73]

Catholic clergy, including the hierarchy, echo the same sentiments as the typical layperson. Interestingly, important parallels exist in how government leaders and Church leaders respond to competition. Because both have controlled their respective secular and spiritual constituencies for so long, essentially without effective competition, they confuse threats to their sovereignty and legitimacy with threats to the state and religion. This explains why representatives of the Mexican episcopate can claim that defending the Catholic religion is an issue of national security. Specifically, they charge the sects with threatening Mexico's national sovereignty.[74] Some Mexican bishops have even publicly considered the possibility of the sects being linked to United States intelligence agencies.[75] According to Dennis Hanratty,

> The church's position is that the uncontrolled proliferation of sects in Mexico is an issue which threatens not only Catholicism but the nation as well in that the sects disrupt social peace and divide communities. Perceiving the source of the threat to be the United States, the hierarchy has not hesitated to employ anti-American language.[76]

Another interpretation, however, suggests that both the government and Church leaders respond with claims of nationalism because the Protestants are introducing new values neither institution knows how to manipulate.[77]

In fairness to the Catholic perception that these sects have introduced a destabilizing element in the culture, it is true that frequent conflicts on the local level, typically in rural villages, occur between Protestant and Catholic adherents. As one scholar concluded, "The appearance of Protestant communities sometimes provokes bloody feuds with neighboring Catholic villages, and it is still dangerous to be a Protestant in many parts of Mexico."[78] Catholic priests also view Protestant groups as aggressive, as divisive, and as producing social dissolution. Some priests perceive the Protestants not only as spreading and practicing their religion but also as attacking Catholicism.[79]

The Catholic hierarchy's suspicion toward the evangelical Protestants and their view of Catholicism as the dominant religion have influenced their perceptions of the 1992 constitutional reforms. As Cardinal Posadas remarked, "It would be an injustice to give equal recognition to religious associations without taking into account the historic weight and number of members of each church and denomination." Or as the Vatican representative suggested less diplomatically, "One doesn't receive an elephant the same as an ant."[80] Some Mexicans believe that the Protestants have benefited most from the constitutional revisions because they were least likely to operate in the informal limbo during the pre-1992 church-state relationship.

A number of suppositions about the Protestant impact, based on the experience of evangelical Protestant growth in Central America and Brazil, have been suggested. In the first place, it is not true that Catholicism declines as Protestantism advances. Most Protestant converts, as suggested above, are nominal Catholics or unaffiliated. Thus Catholicism is enjoying a rebirth simultaneously with Protestantism's growth.[81] The Catholic Church, until the development of the CEBs, was not well equipped to counter the sects' influence. Because CEBs stress the same grassroots sense of community sought by those who join the sects, they provide the Catholic Church with an effective alternative. An important indirect consequence of CEBs within the Catholic Church is their ability to lay the groundwork for local democratic institutions.[82] A potentially more effective counterweight to evangelical Protestantism is the Catholic charismatic movement, which takes on many of the same features as the sects. On the other hand, at least in the case of Chihuahua, the charismatic movement establishes its own posture independent of the bishops.[83]

Originally, many theorists argued that Latin Americans were converting from Catholicism to Protestantism to avoid becoming victims of military repression. More broadly speaking, analysts made the argument that Protestants were perceived by the poor as a nonpoliticized, religious alternative. The level of converts to Protestantism potentially dampened liberation theology's most radical consequences: Catholic social activism. It would therefore be to the state's advantage to encourage evangelical growth. In Mexico, this is not a convincing argument since only in selected regions such as Chiapas did CEBs function aggressively as grassroots political and human rights advocates. Recent research, however, contradicts the politically neutral Protestant interpretation. Andrew J. Stein discovered, for example, in examining Central American Protestants, that they are no more socially passive than their Catholic counterparts and that Evangelicals attend other organizations and civic groups in numbers equal to Catholics. He also concluded that their level of support for the government does not differ from that of Catholics. However, among both Catholics and Protestants, those who are the least fundamental in their beliefs demonstrate lower levels of support for political systems. Protestants also vote in greater proportions than do the religiously nonaffiliated.[84]

In general terms, do Catholics and Protestants differ on broad social and political issues? In other countries, evangelical Catholics, distinguished from mainstream Catholics, share positions consistent with their Protestant counterparts.[85] A difference that does exist between Catholics and Protestants who share similar methodological and substantive religious beliefs stems from the importance of authority and obedience in the Catholic faith. Catholic clergy stress the importance of obedience, ranking it well ahead of intellectual autonomy.[86] However, this does not mean that laypeople follow Church directives. What it does indicate, however, at least in the United States, is that Catholic Evangelicals, if their leadership has spoken strongly on a moral-political issue, are more likely to support that interpretation than are Protestant Evangelicals.[87] Studies also demonstrate that contrary to myth, Catholics in both the United States and in Europe are more politically tolerant than Protestants.[88]

The presence of Protestant groups in Mexico does expand the number of potential social actors. Although Protestants prior to 1992 were not closely linked to the government, did not establish close ties with local politicians, and were more reluctant than priests to violate constitutional norms,[89] they provide a tremendous political potential. As one of the leaders of the Democratic Revolutionary Party, a product of an Anglican heritage, argued, "The Protestant church is a dissident church, but as an institution, it reflects the dissidence of society generally. Protestantism must be looked at not in theological terms, but as a choice stemming from the frustrations about typical social conditions."[90] Some scholars believe these new Protestant converts might be important sources of democratic values because they favor egalitarian political values. One of the few scholars of Mexican Protestantism concluded that Protestants do involve themselves in politics on the local level and are directly or indirectly threatening to local bosses.[91] The Protestant churches as institutions, regardless of their posture on temporal issues, exercise somewhat greater potential than does the Catholic Church because their faithful attend church twice as frequently as do Catholics.[92]

CONCLUSIONS

Liberation theology and the ecclesiastical base communities have already made their mark on the Mexican clergy and hierarchy. Whatever their influence, base communities as such are not likely to expand rapidly in the next decades. Rather, these influences have been incorporated into the diocesan structures of the Church, and the emphasis on the Church of the Poor is now incorporated in the visions of many priests and bishops, moderated by subsequent religious debates in the 1970s and 1980s.

Protestantism as an issue pushing the Church into the political arena is tangential to more direct influences. It will only become a significant temporal issue to the Church if the tensions between the Evangelicals and the Catholics increase to such an extent that the state is forced to mediate between them, in the same way the Church mediated the conflict between the government and Chiapan Indians in 1994. Protestantism could also become a prickly issue if nationalism increases its importance on the political agenda in the wake of the North American Free Trade Agreement and closer economic ties between the United States and Mexico. Mexican politicians and the populace increasingly could perceive these sects as associated with United States institutions, fearing threats to their national cultural sovereignty. A greater likelihood exists in the immediate future for a wave of negative reaction toward the United States as part of a longer pattern in their bilateral relations, a dispute into which the Church might easily be drawn.

Less visible, but possibly more important, is the indirect influence of base ecclesiastical communities. These grassroots organizations and their differently named counterparts indirectly contribute to laypeople's growing awareness of social and economic issues. They clearly teach people how to organize and articulate their ideas on spiritual and nonspiritual issues. Most nongovern-mental organization leaders still believe that religiously affiliated groups have not yet bridged the gap between focusing on important local social and eco-nomic issues and forging a broader political strategy for reform. Yet even their involvement in prodemocracy umbrella organizations, which have taken on the role of observing elections, introduces an entirely new civic responsibility to the average Mexican. As Daniel Levine aptly notes, in order to have any long-term impact beyond their diocese, grassroots groups need to transcend local boundaries, forging ties with other allies.[93]

The secular and religious challenges to the Catholic Church have received, as one might expect, a moderate response, but a response well grounded in many of the spiritual and political trends sweeping the region. The gradual introduction of these changing values and orientations should not be misinter-preted. Although the pace of change is gradual, the Church, long reinforcing the authoritarian culture through its own religious authoritarianism, is con-tributing just as importantly to breaking down those traditions. As Mexico faces new political and economic challenges on its developmental path, the Church's contributions are likely to expand rather than be withdrawn.

9.

GUATEMALA

————◆————

Tim Steigenga

We don't have many questions, just an answer—that Jesus Christ is Lord of Guatemala.

— GENERAL EFRAÍN RÍOS MONTT

For a number of reasons, Guatemala represents a unique and important case for understanding issues of religious freedom and Protestant-Catholic relations in Latin America. First, the Catholic church in Guatemala faced severe and lasting pressure from anticlerical Liberals to a degree unequaled elsewhere in the Americas.[1] Partly as a result of this pressure, Guatemala has a longstanding Protestant presence as well as a long history of conflict over religious freedom.[2] Reliable estimates place the current Protestant population in Guatemala between 25 and 30 percent, the highest percentage in Central America.

Protestantism has also played an important role in recent Guatemalan politics. Guatemala's first Protestant president, General Efraín Ríos Montt was placed in office for eighteen months after a military coup in 1982. Guatemala's second Protestant president, Jorge Serrano Elías,[3] was elected president in 1990 and served until his unsuccessful *autogolpe* unraveled in 1993. More than any other events or figures, these two Protestant presidents have drawn attention to the expansion of evangelical Protestantism and the political effects of evangelical growth throughout Latin America.

Guatemala is also unique in terms of the relationship between religion and the indigenous population. In a country that is one-half Mayan, competition among religious groups for indigenous converts has been fierce. Folk Catholicism, liberation theology, and various Protestant groups compete and sometimes combine with traditional Mayan religions to form a colorful and contentious religious landscape.

Finally, the peace agreements between the Guatemalan National Revolutionary Unity (URNG) and the government signed in December of 1996 marked an end to more than thirty years of civil war in Guatemala and represent a major step in a movement toward liberal pluralism. As Guatemala moves toward the consolidation of its young and fragile democracy, issues of religious freedom and religious conflict are sure to play an important role in this process.

This chapter begins with a brief overview of the political history of Guatemala, with a particular focus on the interactions among religion, politics, church, and state. We will then turn to more recent events and an analysis of survey data on religious discrimination, religious conflict, and political participation collected in Guatemala during the summer of 1993. Analysis of this data suggests that while parallels do exist between religious and political tensions in Guatemala, the popular image of an activist Catholic left pitted against a quiescent or conservative Protestant right is unduly simplified. The political effects of Guatemala's increasing religious pluralism are countervailing and complex. The political trajectories of Guatemalan Protestantism and Catholicism are far from fixed.

THE COLONIAL LEGACY

The political history of modern Guatemala was shaped by the legacy of the colonial period. Guatemala's racially divided society has its roots in a succession of economic endeavors, each of which featured a *criollo* (Guatemalans of purely European extraction) minority seeking new forms of control over an Indian labor force. Caught between these two groups, *ladinos* were rejected by the *criollo* society as a mixed race, and feared as oppressors by the Indians. In the highlands, the indigenous population resisted oppression through the creation of protective community and religious structures that acted as a buffer between village life and the intrusions of colonial and post-colonial society. These "semi-theocratic" government structures were often linked to a system of *cofradías* or religious brotherhoods in Guatemala's rural villages.[4] The political-religious system was formed by a hierarchy of religious and secular offices that were ranked in terms of prestige and social honor, creating an autonomous Indian social structure that was linked to the Catholic church but was relatively isolated from national society. According to Manning Nash, the primary link between the Guatemalan countryside and the national government was through these local chieftains who were only loosely allied to the central regime.[5]

The significance of the *cofradías* is best understood in light of the bitter and prolonged struggles for power between the Liberals and Conservatives in Guatemala. The Conservatives were made up of a coalition of landowners, bureaucrats, and religious leaders who wished to maintain the traditional Hispanic way of life in the Americas, with a continued and broadly defined role for the Catholic church. The Liberals, on the other hand, consisted of an export-oriented elite that was heavily influenced by an ideology of "enlightened liberalism" and the French revolution. For the Liberals, the Catholic church represented a major obstacle blocking their plans for progress and development in the region. As the colonial period drew to an end in Central America in the 1820s, the battle lines for political power were clearly drawn between these two groups.

From the time the United Provinces of Central America made its declaration of independence from the Mexican monarchy in 1823 until Rafael Carrera's rebel forces marched into Guatemala City in 1838, the Liberals had primary control over Guatemala and the United Provinces. During this period, the Liberals instituted a number of anticlerical reforms, including the abolishment of the tithe, the limitation of church landholding, the secularization of cemeteries, and most important, the declaration of freedom of religion in Guatemala (an act which overturned the provision of the 1824 Constitution, which declared that "the religion of the United Provinces is Catholic, Apostolic, and Roman with the exclusion of all others").[6] In 1839, with the support of Guatemala's conservative elite, Rafael Carrera led his peasant army into Guatemala City, ending fifteen years of Liberal rule. Under Carrera, the anticlerical reforms of the Liberal era were reversed, and the Catholic church was returned to its position of preeminence. However, the see-saw struggles between Liberals and Conservatives were far from over. Though Conservatives remained in power after Carrera's death in 1865, their rule came to an abrupt end when Justo Rufino Barrios and Miguel García Granados led a successful Liberal revolution in 1871. By 1873, Rufino Barrios consolidated his power as supreme commander of the Republic and the Liberals began to consolidate their rule. The fundamental goal of the Liberals under Barrios was to impose order on Guatemalan society in an effort to promote development along the lines of the "modern" nations of the nineteenth century, especially via participation in international trade.[7] In order to accomplish this goal, the Liberals felt that traditional cultural practices had to be changed, opening the way for an ideology of progress similar to that held in other developed nations, particularly the United States. Once again, the Catholic church with its large landholdings (often not in production) and its links to local leadership via the *cofradías* was considered a major obstacle to the Liberal program.

THE LIBERAL YEARS: 1871-1926

The Liberals took a number of steps in the early 1870s to undermine the strength of the Catholic church. Catholic religious orders were expelled, Jesuit landholdings were nationalized, monasteries were abolished, and on March 15,

1873, Barrios again declared the freedom of worship of "any and all religions" in Guatemala.[8] For Barrios and the Liberals, this declaration represented an attempt to convince North American missionaries to enter Guatemala. Barrios was apparently so concerned with the introduction of foreign missionaries into Guatemala that in 1882 he traveled to New York to request that the Presbyterian Board of Missions send a missionary to his country.[9]

The declaration of the freedom of religion in Guatemala, while certainly not the most important factor influencing the waning strength of the Catholic church,[10] is of note because it reflected the importance of Protestantism to the Liberal regime. The introduction of Protestantism in Guatemala fit the Liberal agenda in three ways. First, the Liberals hoped that by opening Guatemala to Protestants they could encourage both North Americans and Northern Europeans to immigrate to Guatemala.[11] The Liberals saw immigration as a key aspect in the transformation of traditional values to more modern, progress-oriented values. Second, the Liberals felt that the introduction of Protestantism could help to undermine the influence of the Catholic church on Guatemala's system of education. Beginning with Barrios, a system of quid pro quo was established between the Protestant churches and the Guatemalan government in the area of education, with Protestants receiving access to buildings for their schools and presses to publish their literature in return for their work in education.[12] Third, the introduction of Protestantism into Guatemala was perceived by the Liberals as one way they could gain greater state control over fiercely Catholic and more autonomous rural areas. Central to the Liberal plan for order and progress in Guatemala was the need to break down the autonomy of villages in order to gain access to both land and a larger labor force for the new coffee-export economy[13] A number of methods were used to change land-tenure patterns and gain greater control over indigenous rural communities, including the confiscation and sale of communal Indian lands, the expansion of the practice of forced labor, state-sanctioned debt peonage, and the introduction of Protestant groups in the hope that these groups might undermine the strength of the *cofradías*.

Soon, the reforms of the Liberal government began to have their intended effects. The traditional structure of Indian villages began to lose its strength. As David McCreery explains,

> State-enforced debt peonage, aided by Liberal land polices, broke the independence of the highland communities, instilling in the populations the habits and discipline of wage labor and creating new needs that could only be satisfied with money earned on the *fincas* [large landholdings].[14]

While Protestantism was not a primary force behind this process, Protestant missionaries did add to societal conflict in the countryside by anti-Catholic preaching.[15] The societal divisions created by Protestants, while not extremely significant on their own, added to the effects of the land tenure laws, weakening the traditional relations and political structures of Indian villages.[16] Although the Catholic church and *cofradías* remained important aspects of village life, political authority and social control began shifting toward local landowners, who controlled the Indians through forced labor and debt bondage.[17]

By the end of Estrada Cabrera's regime in 1920, *ladinos* with strong connections to the national government and the newly professionalized Guatemalan army had begun to solidify their influence at the local level. As the old societal structure broke down, a new system arose under the leadership of the *ladinos*, who controlled land and labor and had access to the coercive powers of the state. Power was transferred from the central government to local *caudillos* {leaders}. The *caudillos* maintained control through a system of repression and patronage at the local level. This system came to provide the basic structure of village politics for the next sixty years.[18]

UBICO, THE OCTOBER REVOLUTION, AND THE 1954 COUP

Following the coup that ended the Estrada Cabrera regime in 1920, Guatemala experienced a number of new leaders in rapid succession. Power was transferred from Carlos Herrera and the Unionist Party in 1920 to General José María Orellano in a 1921 coup. Following Orellano's death in 1926, Liberal Lazaro Chacón emerged victorious over Orellano's minister of war, General Jorge Ubico. When Chacón suffered a debilitating stroke in 1930, Ubico stepped in and began a period of repressive rule that would last for the next thirteen years.

Ubico managed to remain in power through political maneuvering and the unabashed use of repression against his political enemies. Circumventing Guatemala's constitutional prohibition on consecutive terms, Ubico had himself reelected through a plebiscite in 1936, and entered his third term in 1942. Under Ubico, the strict anticlericalism of the Liberals mellowed and diplomatic relations with the Vatican were reestablished. In the Catholic church Ubico saw a firm ally in his crusade against communism in Guatemala.[19]

By 1944 a growing sector of the population was beginning to resent Ubico's heavy-handed tactics and personalized style. Faced with violent student demonstrations and increasing opposition among the middle class and reformist military officers, Ubico fled the country, and power was transferred to a military junta in July of 1944, ushering in Guatemala's "October Revolution."

The basis for the October Revolution lay both in Ubico's tyranny and in the stagnation of the Guatemalan economy. Guatemala's increasingly frustrated middle class, inspired by both the democratic rhetoric of World War II and the United States' experience with the New Deal, pushed for political and economic reforms. The election of Juan José Arévalo as president in 1945 marked the beginning of a reform program that would begin to dismantle traditional power relations in Guatemala. Under Arévalo and his successor, Jacobo Arbenz Guzmán (elected in 1950), major strides were made in terms of land reform, labor reform, legal reform, and the mobilization of popular groups such as peasant organizations, labor unions, and others.

The reform process in Guatemala did not proceed without challenge. Elements of Guatemala's elite, along with factions within the military, perceived the reform process and the mobilization of popular groups as a threat to their political and economic interests. Arévalo survived multiple coup attempts during his time in office, and Arbenz faced strong opposition to his policies from the coffee oligarchy and traditionalist sectors of the military. The greatest threat to Guatemala's process of reform came, however, from more powerful sources, the United Fruit Company and the United States.

The United Fruit Company (UFCO) was both the largest employer and the largest landowner in Guatemala. With control over Guatemala's rail system, as well as the port facilities at Puerto Barrios, United Fruit exercised enormous influence over Guatemala's economy.[20] As part of Arbenz's land reform program, he took over a portion of United Fruit's land, offering compensation at its declared tax value.[21] Arbenz also undertook the construction of new roads and a new port on the Caribbean coast, policies further perceived as threats by United Fruit. Among U.S. policymakers, threats to United Fruit, Arbenz's decision to legalize Guatemala's Communist Party (bringing some Communists into his cabinet), and his purchase of arms from Czechoslovakia combined to create growing concerns about communist influence in Guatemala. Ultimately, these concerns culminated in the decision to arm and train a group of Guatemalan exiles led by Castillo Armas to oust the Arbenz regime.[22]

In June of 1954, the United States plan, "Operation Success," went into effect. Castillo Armas and his troops crossed the border into Guatemala as U.S. planes strafed and bombed the capital. By late June, after failed diplomatic efforts to end the fighting, Arbenz resigned. Guatemala's experiment with democracy and reform had come to an end. The next thirty years would be shaped by a succession of military dictatorships, the legacy of which continues to be felt in Guatemala today.

RELIGION
AND THE COUNTERREVOLUTION

While the primary force behind the 1954 coup was the United States and UFCO, Arbenz was not without enemies inside Guatemala. Once again, religion played an important role in the political struggle. Under the leadership of conservative Archbishop Mariano Rossell Arellano, the Catholic church began to reassert itself politically during the Arbenz years. Deeming "communist" the land-reform programs instituted under Arbenz, members of the Roman Catholic clergy allied themselves with landowners and segments of the military in a coalition that posed a serious threat to the autonomy of the Guatemalan state. In 1951, 200,000 Catholics attended the closing ceremony of the First Eucharistic Congress, a demonstration that was considered to be a show of church power vis-à-vis the government.[23] Two years later, Archbishop Rossell Arellano began an organized tour carrying the revered Black Christ of Esquipulas throughout the country. He stated that the Black Christ would not come to rest while communism existed in Guatemala.[24] The actions of the archbishop and other members of the clergy played a key role in undermining the Arbenz administration. Members of the clergy actively supported the June 1954 coup that brought General Carlos Castillo Armas to power. Archbishop Rossell Arellano met with CIA agents prior to the coup and gave them permission to drop thousands of copies of his pastoral letter "On the Advance of Communism in Guatemala" from planes on the day of the coup. The letter read in part:

> The people of Guatemala must arise as one man to fight the enemy of God and of their country. Our fight against communism, therefore, must be based on a nationalistic and Catholic attitude. . . . Catholics everywhere, by utilizing all means available to them as free human beings in a hemisphere not yet enslaved by the Soviet Dictatorship, enjoying the sacred freedom that is theirs as sons of God, must fight and counterattack this doctrine that is opposed to God and to Guatemala.[25]

Castillo Armas handsomely rewarded the Catholic church for aiding him in his rise to power in 1954. Archbishop Rossell Arellano was awarded the Order of Liberation, priests were appointed to positions in the National Assembly, restrictions were removed on church landholdings, and the church regained control over certain educational responsibilities and ceremonial duties.[26] Under Castillo Armas and his strongly Catholic National Liberation Movement (*Movimiento Liberación Nacional,* or MLN), Protestants lost their favored status in terms of police protection, mailing privileges, and other privileges that they had enjoyed under his predecessors. According to Virginia Garrard Burnett, some Protestants, particularly those who had been active in Arbenz's revolutionary reformism, suffered repression during this counterrevolutionary period. The violence against Protestants, however, was generally at the local level, and represented part of a general backlash against multiple forces that were undermining traditional patterns of authority in the altiplano.[27]

One of the forces that acted to undermine traditional patterns of authority was Catholic Action, a movement that began in Europe in the late 1920s and was designed, in part, to diffuse potentially radical or dangerous groups by channeling their energies into church organizations. In the Guatemalan highlands, Catholic Action was a relatively conservative organization of civil society dedicated to converting Mayan Indians into orthodox Catholics. Requirements for admission to Catholic Action often included doctrinal instruction, marriage in a church, going to confession, and prohibition from participation in the saint societies of the *cofradías*. According to David Stoll, Catholic Action appealed greatly to the youth in the Ixil communities as a means of unseating the power of the old *cofradía* hierarchy.[28] As Virginia Garrard Burnett explains, "It is clear that by the mid-1950s, traditional structures of authority and community cohesion in many locations were severely undermined, at least in a symbolic sense, and the culpability lay at the feet of Catholic Action."[29]

THE GROWTH OF A MILITARY STATE AND THE RESPONSE OF THE CHURCH

After the 1954 counterrevolution, a succession of military leaders mixed repressive economic policies with occasional elections and the trappings of democratic practices.[30] The military, boosted by United States aid and training, acted in support of the conservative elite as a buttress against the potential for a reformist return to power. Under Castillo Armas, the reforms of the Arbenz and Arévalo administrations were reversed, and those who had been involved with their administrations were severely repressed.[31] With Armas's death in 1957, Miguel Ydígoras Fuentes came to power, ushering in five years of corruption and patronage. Ydígoras's blatant corruption and close ties to the United States frustrated nationalist elements within the military, leading to an officers' revolt in November 1960. Although the revolt was not successful, some of its leaders (officers trained in the United States) escaped and later helped to form the revolutionary organizations that were precursors to the Guatemalan National Revolutionary Unity (URNG).

In 1963, with Arévalo threatening a return to the Guatemalan electoral arena, the military stepped in and took control of the government. Under coup leader Colonel Enrique Peralta Azurdía, the military became more institutionalized and increasingly involved in civilian politics. According to Jim Handy, increased United States technological and monetary aid, as well as increasing military civic-action programs and the temptation among officers to augment their salaries through government positions and business pursuits, led to the absolute militarization of Guatemalan society.[32] Despite Colonel Peralta's attempts to limit the participation of reformist groups through a reworking of the constitution in 1965, the Reformist Revolutionary Party (PR) won a substantial victory in the 1966 elections. Permitted to take office only after promising not to interfere in military affairs, PR candidate Julio César Méndez Montenegro ushered in a civilian regime that witnessed some of the worst repression Guatemala had experienced to date. In Eastern Guatemala, Colonel Carlos Arana Osorio waged a brutal counterinsurgency campaign between 1966 and 1968 that left more than six thousand dead and entire villages destroyed. At the same time a number of vigilante groups or death squads (such as the infamous *Mano Blanca*—or White Hand), made up of military personnel, engaged in widespread acts of torture and brutal killings. The activities of these groups were aimed primarily against anyone associated with popular movements and groups supporting political reform.[33]

In 1970, against a backdrop of continued guerrilla activity, military intimidations, and an opposition divided between the Christian Democrats, the Partido Revolucionário, and the Revolutionary Democratic Unity (URD), Colonel Arana was elected president as part of an alliance between the Democratic Institutional Party (PID) and the National Liberation Movement (MLN). Under Arana, levels of violence and repression in Guatemala rose to new heights with more than seven hundred political killings documented between November 1970 and March 1971. Arana's successor, General Kjell Eugenio Laugerud García, narrowly defeated the candidate of the opposition Christian Democratic party, General Efraín Ríos Montt, in an election that was tainted by fraud. Cowed into submission by Arana, Ríos Montt was quietly shipped off to a diplomatic post in Spain.

Under Laugerud's administration, levels of repression dropped, and a new opening emerged for reformist mobilization. Since the late 1960s, a number of priests, nuns, and religious lay workers had been involved in social and pastoral work in the Guatemalan countryside. According to Phillip Berryman, the efforts of these individuals and some of the more progressive bishops to coordinate their efforts and take a unified stand against political violence were repeatedly thwarted by conservative Archbishop Mario Casariego (1964-83).[34] Following the devastating earthquake in 1976 popular mobilization increased in Guatemala, as foreign missionaries, many of whom were inspired by the teachings of Vatican II and Medellín, began organizing and a new generation of popular groups emerged to meet the challenges of the natural disaster and other hardships. During the same period, labor organizations such as the CNUS (National Committee for Labor Unity) and the CNT (National Workers Federation) became more vocal in their demands and clashed with government forces. Taking advantage of Cardinal Casariego's absence from the country in 1976, the Guatemalan Bishops' Conference issued a pastoral letter that condemned violence and contained pointed social commentary on corruption, land distribution, and the abuse of power. For the first time in the history of Guatemala, popular groups and religious organizations could rally around an official statement by the bishops.

By the mid-1970s the growth of popular movements such as the Committee for Campesino Unity (*Comité de Unidad Campesina,* CUC), The Committee for Justice and Peace, labor groups, and even Ecclesial Base Communities (CEBs) was perceived as a serious threat by the Guatemalan military and the oligarchy. The emergence of the Guerrilla Army of the Poor (EGP) in 1975 in the Ixcán region and the subsequent formation of the Organization of the People in Arms (ORPA) in 1979 did little to quiet these fears. Under General Romeo Lucas García, elected in yet another set of fraudulent elections in 1978, political violence was unleashed in both the capital and in the countryside. Leaders of both the Social Democrats (PSD) and the United Front of the Revolution (FUR) were assassinated in 1979, along with more than 150 leaders and organizers for the Christian Democrats. Party leaders, union members, intellectuals, student leaders, and religious leaders all became targets of death-squad activity. In the countryside, mass killings and the destruction of entire villages became commonplace. Estimates of the number killed range into the hundreds of thousands.[35]

RELIGION, REPRESSION, AND THE ROLE OF PROTESTANTS

The political violence and brutal counterinsurgency campaigns of the 1970s and 1980s brought to light a new set of interactions between religion and politics in Guatemala. Efforts by Guatemala's more progressive bishops to promote a more activist role for the church were repeatedly blocked by Cardinal Casariego, eventually leading to the resignation of Bishop Luis Manresa of Quetzaltenango. Increasingly, as priests, lay workers, and members of CEBs began to organize and, in some cases, to make political demands through organizations such as the CUC and the Mutual Support Group (*Grupo de Apoyo Mutuo*, GAM),[36] they became the targets of both direct military action and government-sponsored death squad activity. By the mid 1980s, twelve priests and numerous other religious workers had been murdered.[37] Other priests and lay workers forced into exile by political repression joined to form the Guatemalan Church in Exile. Inside Guatemala, an increasing number of religious workers became radicalized through the experience of open violence.[38]

By 1982, Guatemala's disparate guerrilla factions had united to form the Guatemalan National Revolutionary Unity (URNG). In the March elections, another blatant attempt at fraud was met with a coup by reformist military officers. Retired General Efraín Ríos Montt, now a born-again Christian and leader of the Neo-Pentecostal El Verbo Church, was "called to power" and soon unleashed another wave of political repression in the countryside.

The rise of Ríos Montt to power in 1982 brought the issue of religion and politics in Guatemala to the fore. Hailed as the savior of Guatemala by the United States religious right and some members of the Reagan administration, and condemned as a zealot engaged in a "Holy War" by leftists, Ríos Montt pursued his agenda with dogged determination and in a charismatic style. Soon after the March 1982 coup, the military circulated a copy of the "National Plan for Security and Development," a comprehensive counterinsurgency strategy emphasizing civic action and population control through the creation of strategic hamlets and model villages in the Guatemalan countryside.[39] According to Amnesty International, more than twenty-six hundred Indians were killed by the army during the first three months of Ríos Montt's government.[40] In May, Ríos Montt declared that during the month of June there would be a general amnesty. On July 1, however, he instituted a state of siege under which military powers were expanded to an alarming degree.[41] During this period, Ríos Montt's counterinsurgency program known as *fusiles y frijoles* (rifles and beans) went into effect in the Ixil Triangle of Northeast Guatemala. This plan combined counterinsurgency with civic action in an attempt to win the allegiance of Indians living in zones where the guerrillas were active. According to Robert H. Trudeau, approximately four hundred Indian villages were destroyed during this campaign and an estimated half-million people were moved into army run "strategic hamlets" and "development poles."[42]

Ríos Montt's charismatic style, displayed in his weekly television and radio "Sunday talks" to the nation, along with his counterinsurgency campaign, drew new attention to the role of Protestantism in Guatemalan politics. While Protestants had a long history in Guatemala, the pressures of military repression, increasing landlessness, economic hardship, urbanization, and other forms of social dislocation in the countryside along with aggressive evangelization strategies and the dangers associated with being a progressive Catholic, all contributed to the rapid growth of Protestantism (especially Pentecostalism) between the 1950s and the 1980s.[43] In November of 1982, this growth was graphically demonstrated when hundreds of thousands of Protestants gathered in Guatemala City's *Campo de Marte* to celebrate one hundred years of Protestantism in Guatemala.

In much of the literature on Guatemala, Evangelicals have been characterized as either apolitical, or conservative and anticommunist.[44] In the countryside, there were a number of reports during the 1980s of Protestants acting as informants or collaborators for the army under the Ríos Montt regime. According to Virginia Garrard Burnett, one observer estimated that over 50 percent of the Evangelicals in army-controlled zones either passively supported the military or were active informers.[45] According to Deborah Huntington:

> In the newly established "strategic hamlets" they [the Protestants] became the preferred liaison between the army and the local community, leading civil defense patrols and weeding out guerrilla sympathizers. Army commanders in turn rewarded this cooperation by appointing Evangelicals to posts of authority.[46]

David Stoll's recent book, *Between Two Armies in the Ixil Towns of Guatemala,* examines this relationship, attempting to explain why Evangelicals (and many non-Evangelicals) in Guatemala's Ixil Triangle rejected calls to join revolutionary organizations, and actually supported Ríos Montt's programs and the role of the military in that region. According to Stoll, evangelical collaboration was less of a choice to side with the military against the guerrillas than an attempt to simply survive the violence and stake out a position of neutrality. As Stoll explains, "When Evangelicals are asked about their new religion and the violence, they respond with a language of neutralism, distancing themselves from the conflict rather than positioning themselves as partisans."[47] This attitude is not unique to Evangelicals, as many of the inhabitants of the Ixil region felt trapped, and did not wish to be associated with either the army or the EGP (Guerrilla Army of the Poor). According to Stoll, refugees from the region actually petitioned the army to build more model villages in the area, as these villages provided greater physical safety and improved access to the necessities of day-to-day survival (such as land, minimal health care, and potable water).[48]

Under the Ríos Montt regime, the Catholic church began to stake out a more clear position in opposition to the policies of the Guatemalan government. In March of 1982, a delegation of bishops met with Ríos Montt and leaders of the coup coalition and expressed the need to end human rights abuses and return to democracy. In May, the bishops issued another letter, vigorously condemning the continued massacres and human rights abuses.[49] Issues came to a head in 1983 when the pope asked for clemency for six men condemned to death by Ríos Montt's recently created "special tribunals." Ignoring the pope's request, Ríos Montt had the men executed three days before the pope's arrival.

In the countryside, Catholics continued to be the targets of military counterinsurgency programs and terror. According to David Stoll, government security agents, using techniques of kidnapping and torture, were able to target religious workers involved with the EGP, CUC, or organizations that reported abuses of human rights in the region. As military leaders preached of the dangers of associating with radical priests, increasing numbers of Ixil residents turned to Protestant churches for both physical safety and because the Protestants often provided relief aid.[50]

In August of 1983, after alienating the Catholic church and some sectors of the military, Ríos Montt was removed from office by another military coup.[51] In the days following the coup, police entered a number of Protestant churches in Guatemala City and interrogated members and pastors, prompting speculation that under General Humberto Mejía Víctores there would be a backlash of repression against Protestants. While rhetoric over the issue flared, no lasting pattern of anti-Protestant repression emerged.

Though only in office for a short time, Mejía Víctores advanced the military's counterinsurgency program by institutionalizing civil patrols made up of forced recruits and by creating the National Interinstitutional Coordinator (CIN), a governmental structure that placed many governmental offices and services under the control of local military zone commanders.[52] With this structure in place, Guatemala's military was willing to hold elections in order to improve its international image.

DEMOCRACY GUATEMALAN-STYLE: VINÍCIO CEREZO, SERRANO ELÍAS, AND ALVARO ARZÚ

Vinício Cerezo Arévalo, a Christian Democrat, became Guatemala's first civilian president since Méndez Montenegro when he assumed office in 1986.

During the 1985 campaign, none of the candidates raised issues of human rights, corruption, or major structural reforms.[53] Despite the shift to civilian rule, human rights violations continued. The URNG remained active in the countryside, and the military continued its counterinsurgency programs. In urban areas, death squads continued to operate, with peasant, labor, student, and religious leaders as targets.

At the same time, a peace process was beginning to emerge with the formation of a National Reconciliation Commission (CRN), as part of the broader Central American Peace plan (Esquipulas I and II) co-sponsored by Cerezo and Costa Rican president Oscar Arias. In Guatemala the peace process moved slowly forward, leading into the 1990 elections. After front runner Ríos Montt was ruled ineligible due to the fact that he had previously assumed the presidency through a coup, another evangelical, Jorge Serrano Elías, emerged as a major challenge to newspaper publisher Jorge Carpio Nicole. Serrano, the head of the conservative *Movimiento de Acción Solidaria* (MAS) and a proponent of neoliberal economic policies, won the runoff election handily with 67 percent of the vote in the second round. In the final weeks leading up to the runoff election (January 1991), the candidates traded accusations about dirty tactics and the use of religion as a political tool. In response, the bishops issued a pastoral letter warning of the danger of a "religious war" and expressing concern that votes might be cast for religious reasons rather than "in the search for the common good, justice, mutual respect, and brotherly love."[54]

Despite the escalating rhetoric, it appears as though Serrano's victory was not primarily a result of religious divisions or of Protestants voting for a Protestant. According to Anne M. Hallum, the vote for Serrano was *not* concentrated in the most Protestant departments of the country. Rather, Serrano's margin of victory was relatively stable across departments, and appears to have been more a result of effective campaigning than of a specific appeal to Protestant voters.[55]

Serrano's early popularity quickly dissipated. By 1993, charges of corruption and the effects of Serrano's neoliberal economic policies spurred a series of protests by students and workers. Pressured by key elements of the military and the right who resented the increased popular participation, and inspired by Peruvian President Fujimori's successful "self coup," Serrano organized a coup in May 1993. With backing of the military, Serrano dissolved the national congress, suspended the constitution, and proclaimed that he would rule by decree. In the face of massive protest demonstrations and threatened with international economic sanctions, the Guatemalan military quickly abandoned Serrano, shifting its support behind his vice president, Gustavo Espina Salguero. Unable to convince the Guatemalan Congress to swear him in, Espina, too, was abandoned by the military and on June 6, after a secret vote in the Guatemalan Congress, Ramiro de León Carpio, the recently appointed human rights ombudsman, was declared the new president of Guatemala. Serrano, the first elected Protestant president in Latin America, was charged with stealing government funds and now lives in exile in Panama.

As the surveys for this study were administered in July of 1993, there was guarded optimism in Guatemala about the future of de León Carpio's regime. As human rights ombudsman, he had been a fierce critic of the military and a strong supporter of the peace talks. By late June, the URNG had declared a unilateral cease-fire and the repatriation of Guatemalan refugees stepped up in the highlands. Despite these positive signs, the human rights situation in Guatemala remained bleak. On the third of July, 1993, ex-presidential candidate and secretary general of the UCN (National Union of the Center) Jorge Rafael Carpio Nicole was assassinated. In the countryside and in the capital, reports of disappearances, kidnappings, and torture continued.[56]

In Guatemala's 1995 presidential elections Party for National Advancement (PAN) candidate Alvaro Arzú emerged victorious in a contest where abstentions outnumbered votes.[57] Arzú's greatest challenge in the elections came from Ríos Montt's hand-picked candidate of the Guatemalan Republican Front (FRG), Alfonso Portillo. During the elections, campaign posters for the FRG showed Ríos Montt with his arm around Portillo, and a caption that read, "Portillo to the presidency, and Ríos to power." The FRG was particularly successful in many of the rural areas that experienced severe violence during the 1980s, again providing evidence to support David Stoll's interpretation of the popularity of Ríos Montt in that region.

CATHOLICS, PROTESTANTS, POLITICS, AND PEACE

As we noted earlier, Catholic priests and lay workers were frequent targets of state-sponsored repression under the regimes of Lucas García, Ríos Montt, and Mejía Víctores. With the death of Cardinal Casariego in June of 1983, the institutional Catholic church became much more outspoken in its criticism of the Guatemalan government. In October of 1983, the torture of one priest and the murder of another prompted the papal nuncio, Oriano Quilici, to publicly blame the security forces.[58] Under the leadership of new Archbishop Próspero Penados del Barrio (who took office in January 1984) the Guatemalan bishops have issued a number of pastoral letters that are openly critical of government-backed repression, civil patrols, and continuing structural inequality in Guatemala.[59] The Catholic church has also played a crucial role in the Guatemalan peace process through the National Reconciliation Committee (formed in 1989 and headed by Bishop Rodolfo Quezada of Zacapa) and the National Dialogue, a group of fifteen commissions from civil, religious, professional, and other groups in Guatemalan society organized to dialogue and move toward a negotiated solution to Guatemala's civil war. In 1990, Archbishop Penados del Barrio created the Social Service Office of the Archbishop of Guatemala (OSSAG) to oversee projects of human rights, social services, and migration. In an unprecedented move, the archbishop appointed formerly exiled Auxiliary Bishop Gerardi Conedera as general coordinator of OSSAG. In 1998,

Gerardi was murdered after he presented a church-sponsored report on human rights violations.

Relations between the Catholic church and the Arzú administration have been tense. Under Arzú, the Guatemalan peace process moved rapidly forward, culminating in the signing of a final peace agreement on December 29, 1996. Despite this progress, Guatemala's Catholic bishops were sharply critical of the National Reconciliation law, which provided a general amnesty for Guatemalans. Frustrated with the U.N.-mediated Truth Commission for Guatemala, which cannot give the names of human rights violators, the archbishop backed the formation of an alternative commission called the Project to Recover the Historic Memory. Sponsored by the bishops and backed by the church, the new commission is investigating the history of political repression in Guatemala and will provide names of those who participated in gross violations of human rights.[60] Stung by the bishops' criticisms, Arzú recently struck back, accusing the church of being one of the historical sources of "strife" in Guatemala.

For the most part, Protestant churches and organizations have been less critical of the Guatemalan government and military than their Catholic counterparts. While Protestants have not escaped the widespread political violence in Guatemala,[61] they have also not been targeted in the same manner as Catholics. To characterize all Protestants as apolitical or supportive of the government in Guatemala, however, would be inaccurate. Protestants have taken an active role in the National Dialogue and the Permanent Assembly of Christian Groups (an ecumenical group which urged in 1988 that the National Dialogue address issues ranging from human rights to land redistribution). According to Phillip Berryman, Catholic and Protestant members of the Permanent Assembly helped to develop proposals that framed many of the issues of the National Dialogue.[62] There has also been some shift in Protestant attitudes toward political involvement. While Serrano's candidacy is the most prominent example of the willingness of Protestants to enter into the world of politics, evidence of a greater openness toward political involvement was clear as early as 1982 under the Ríos Montt regime. In 1987, a document entitled *The Political Task of Evangelicals: Ideas for a New Guatemala* was circulated among Evangelicals by a group of Protestants known as the Christian Committee on Reflection. According to Anne M. Hallum, this document was particularly important because it "calls for believers to become active in social and political work as well as evangelism," and "recognizes government responsibility for social and economic problems in Guatemala and Christian responsibility for being involved at the local and national level in effecting change."[63]

In 1996, the Mutual Support Group (GAM) joined forces with the Confederation of Guatemalan Widows (CONAVIGUA) and other human rights groups, including some Protestant leaders, to form a new political party, the New Guatemalan Democratic Front (FDNG). In the November 1996 congressional elections, the FDNG surprised many observers by winning six of the eighty available seats in the Guatemalan congress.

The growth of Neo-Pentecostalism in Guatemala has also played an important role in increasing levels of Protestant political participation. Neo-Pentecostals are presumed to embrace "prosperity theology," the belief that health and wealth come only to those who obey God and that individuals who suffer do so because they are sinful.[64] These Evangelicals, many of whom come from the middle and upper classes of Guatemala City, are also more likely to subscribe to a version of millennialist theology known as post-millennialism. Relying heavily on the predictions of Revelations 20, post-millennialists believe that Christ will return only after Christians have built a thousand-year kingdom here on earth. Thus, Christians must work to place themselves in positions of authority in order to bring about the kingdom. Clearly, this sort of "dominion theology" represents an important theology of power for members of Neo-Pentecostal churches such as Elim, El Verbo, El Shaddhai, Maranatha, and Fraternidad Cristiana in Guatemala City.

The growth of Protestantism both in numbers and in political power has elicited mixed reactions from the Catholic church in Guatemala. Influenced by the teachings of Pope John Paul XXIII and Vatican II, some progressive clergy made ecumenical overtures to Protestant churches during the 1960s. Likewise, some Protestants (mainly those from "historic" denominations) became involved with ecumenical groups. However, these individuals represented an extreme minority among both religious movements, and by the 1970s there was no numerically significant ecumenical movement in Guatemala.

By the late 1970s, the attitude of the Catholic hierarchy toward Protestantism in Latin America had become significantly more adversarial. In 1979 when the Latin American Bishops met in Puebla warnings about the growth of conservative Protestantism were openly raised. In Guatemala, the rhetoric escalated quickly. In 1982 Bishop Mario Enrique Ríos Montt (brother of evangelical president Efraín Ríos Montt) suggested that religious conflict in Guatemala "could well turn into a religious war more serious than our political war."[65]

The Catholic church has taken a number of steps since the 1970s to address the rapid expansion of Protestantism in Guatemala, including increasing the number of priests and other religious workers, exploring new forms of religious organization and practice (ranging from Christian Base Communities to the charismatic renewal), borrowing Protestant evangelization techniques (such as the use of radio and television ministries), and improving the organizational structure and links among the archdiocese, parishes, and lay representatives of the church. Despite these efforts, evangelical Protestants have continued to make inroads in Guatemala. In particular, Protestants appear to have an advantage among the indigenous population, where they have more than a century of experience translating the Bible into indigenous languages. Evangelical churches among the indigenous population outside of the capital are often small and community-based, with Mayan ministers who preach and proselytize in the local language.

PROTESTANT-CATHOLIC RELATIONS:
EXAMINING THE DATA

Given the long and sometimes acrimonious history of Protestant-Catholic relations in Guatemala we might expect to find bitter rivalries and little tolerance for other religious groups in survey data measuring religious conflict and
discrimination. The data for this study were collected during the summer of
1993, shortly following the demise of Serrano's self-coup, a time when we
might expect such religious tensions to be heightened. Interviews were conducted with 85 Catholics, 38 Historic Protestants, 233 Pentecostals, 23 members of sects, and 25 individuals with no religious affiliation.[66]

For the purposes of this study, survey respondents have been coded into the
following six categories based on the name of the church at which the respondents report themselves to be regular attendees:

1. *Catholics* will be used as a base-line category for comparison with Protestant groups.

2. *Historic Protestants* include such groups as the Methodists, Presbyterians, Nazarenes, Episcopalians, and Lutherans. These denominations represent some of the oldest and most established churches in Central
   America.

3. *Pentecostals* are clearly the most numerous and visible of the Protestant
   groups active in Central America. Pentecostal denominations such as the
   Assembly of God, Four Square Gospel Church, the Church of God, and
   numerous other small independent denominations are characterized by
   a charismatic style of worship and evangelization. Pentecostals are presumed to stress the importance of divine healing, empowerment through
   the Holy Spirit, speaking in tongues, and a dramatic personal conversion.

4. The *Neo-Pentecostals* are hypothesized to accept some form of prosperity theology and to generally come from a higher social strata than
   most other Pentecostals. The category of Neo-Pentecostals was created
   by combining data from respondents who claimed to be regular attendees at the Elim, El Verbo, and the Fraternidad Cristiana churches in Guatemala City. While other evangelical churches in Guatemala may display
   the tendencies associated with Neo-Pentecostalism, experts on the subject agree that these three churches are clearly Neo-Pentecostal.[67]

5. The term *sect* will be used to refer to the Mormons, Jehovah's Witnesses,
   and Seventh-day Adventists included in the sample for this study. We use
   the term *sect* only as a separate miscellaneous category, not in a pejora-
   tive sense. In other words, these groups are distinct religious bodies that
   trace their roots to nineteenth-century religious revivalism in the United
   States. Each of the groups has a distinctly American flavor in terms of
   beliefs and practice.

6. According to contemporary survey data the percentage of Central Americans who profess *no religious affiliation* is significant.[68] This group has been included as a further baseline for comparison.

COMPARING RELIGIOUS GROUPS

Comparing socioeconomic indicators across religious groups in Guatemala, few significant differences emerged. There were no significant differences between religious groups in terms of occupation or income. The mean income for all respondents was approximately four hundred dollars per month. On a six-point scale ranging from the economically inactive to professional managers, the mean score for occupation was 1.7. Forty-seven percent of respondents reported themselves to be economically inactive. That percentage did not vary greatly across religious groups.

Significant differences did emerge between religious groups in terms of education. Neo-Pentecostals were significantly more educated than all other groups, while the religiously non-affiliated were significantly less educated than all other groups. Education was measured on a ten-point scale ranging from none to postgraduate education. Neo-Pentecostals also scored higher on a self-anchored scale rating social position.

The mean age for respondents was 33, with no significant differences between religious groups. The sample was split relatively evenly between genders, with the exception of sect members and the non-affiliated, who were predominantly male (approximately 75 percent of each group). Approximately 75 percent of the respondents were polled in Guatemala City, with 25 percent interviewed in more rural areas outside of the capital. All interviews with sect members were collected outside of the capital.

RELIGIOUS DISCRIMINATION
AND RELIGIOUS CONFLICT

Table 9-1 presents findings for perceptions of the experience of religious discrimination. The most striking finding is that Catholics *and* Neo-Pentecostals are the least likely to report having experienced religious discrimination with only 3 percent of the latter group reporting the experience of religious discrimination frequently or very frequently, while 70 percent of the former category report no experience whatsoever with religious discrimination. Sect members reported the most religious discrimination, with 43.8 percent claiming to have been discriminated against frequently or very frequently.[69] In this data, we can see a clear relationship between being a member of a minority religious community and the perception of more frequent religious discrimination in Guatemala. As members of more upper-class urban communities, Neo-Pentecostals represent the exception to this rule.

Table 9-1
Perceptions of Religious Discrimination by Denomination

Question: How often do you experience discrimination due to your religious beliefs?

	Catholic	Historic	Pentecostal	Neo-Pentecostal	Sect	Non-affiliated
Never	70.6%	37.8%	47.9%	45.5%	30.4%	44.4%
Sometimes	16.5%	40.5%	25.8%	51.5%	26.1%	28.9%
Frequently	4.7%	5.4%	6.1%	3.0%	26.5%	5.6%
Very frequently	8.2%	16.2%	20.2%	0.0%	17.3%	11.1%
n=	85	38	200	33	23	25

x^2=55.6   p=.0003

In order to measure levels of religious conflict, respondents were asked if the following events occurred never, almost never, sometimes, often, or very often in their community: (1) confrontations between Catholics and Protestants; (2) complaints about Protestants being too noisy or for holding services too late at night; (3) discrimination against Protestants in Catholic stores or businesses; (4) discrimination against Catholics in Protestant stores or businesses; and (5) open violence between Catholics and Protestants. These five items were combined to create a scale of community religious conflict (with potential scores ranging from 5 to 25).[70]

As with religious discrimination, Neo-Pentecostals reported the least amount of religious conflict in their communities (see Table 9-2). These findings are not particularly surprising given the fact that the Neo-Pentecostals in this study come from more upper-class urban communities.

Table 9-2
Scale of Religious Conflict

	Mean Score by Denomination	n=
Catholic	10.8	85
Historic	10.1	37
Pentecostal	9.3**	199
Neo-Pentecostal	7.8*	33
Sect	9.3	23
Non-affiliated	12.4***	15

Mean score for each group where higher scores indicate a higher decree of community religious conflict reported. Statistical test is one-way ANOVA.
*=score that is significantly lower than Historic, Catholic, or Non-affiliated.
**=score that is significantly lower than Catholic or Non-affiliated.
***=score that is significantly higher than Neo-Pentecostal, Pentecostal, or Sect
(P .05)

According to Dennis Smith, many of these individuals came to Protestantism in the late seventies and early eighties after they grew disillusioned with what they saw as the "politicization" of Catholicism.[71] Of the thirty-three Neo-Pentecostals we interviewed, nine claimed to have converted from another religion. Eight of the nine were previously Catholic.

Overall, perceptions of religious conflict among those interviewed in

Guatemala appear relatively high. The mean score for the five religious conflict items in Guatemala was 9.64. A similar study of religious conflict in Costa Rica produced a mean score of only 8.30. More than 17 percent of our Guatemalan respondents said that confrontations between Catholics and Protestants and complaints about Protestants occurred often or very often in their communities. More than 7 percent reported that open violence between Catholics and Protestants occurred often or very often.[72]

POLITICAL ORIENTATIONS
AND ACTIVITIES

If levels of religious conflict are relatively high in Guatemala, it is worth asking whether religious divisions are also political divisions. In order to get some idea about attitudes toward politics and political authority, we asked respondents if they strongly agreed, agreed, disagreed, or strongly disagreed with the following statement: "A citizen should support the government in all circumstances."

Looking at Table 9-3, we see that Pentecostals and Historic Protestants are significantly more likely than Catholics to agree that the government should be obeyed in all circumstances.[73] This finding supports the literature which describes the tendency among Evangelicals to cooperate or even collaborate with political authorities in Guatemala. Protestants, and Pentecostals in particular, appear to be less likely than Catholics to challenge political authority.

The tendency among Evangelicals to avoid potentially conflictual political action is further highlighted in Table 9-4. When asked how often they criticize public officials, Pentecostals, Neo-Pentecostals and the non-affiliated

Table 9-3
Agreement
with Political Statements
(Mean Scores by Religion)

Statement: The government should be obeyed in all circumstances.

	Agree	n=
Catholic	2.4*	83
Historic	2.7	37
Pentecostal	2.8	194
Neo-Pentecostal	2.8	33
Sect	2.5	22
Non-affiliated	2.8	25

Mean score for each group on a four-point scale where:
1=strongly disagree 2=disagree
3=agree 4=strongly agree
Statistical test is one-way ANOVA.
*=Significantly lower than Pentecostal, Historic, and Non-affiliated.
(P .05)

were significantly less likely to do so than their Catholic counterparts. In terms of the relatively non-conflictual act of voting, however, differences between groups were not significant at the .05 level.

Table 9-4
Frequency of Political Activities

Frequency of:	Voting	Criticizing public officials	n=
Catholic	2.7	1.9*	85
Historic	3.0	1.6	28
Pentecostal	2.9	1.5	199
Neo-Pentecostal	2.5	1.4	33
Sect	2.6	1.5	23
Non-affiliated	3.0	1.3	25

Mean score for each group on a five-point scale where:
1=never 2=almost never 3=sometimes
4=often 5=very often
Statistical test is one-way ANOVA.
*=Score that is significantly higher than Neo-Pentecostal, Pentecostal, or Non-affiliated
(P .05)

APPROVAL OF POLITICAL FIGURES AND ORGANIZATIONS

Respondents were asked to rate a number of political figures and organizations on a four-point scale: (1) strongly disapprove; (2) disapprove; (3) approve; and (4) strongly approve. Table 9-5 presents data for those who approve or strongly approve of attitude objects generally considered to represent the right (Ríos Montt, Serrano Elías, and Espina Salguero), the center (Ramiro de León Carpio), and the left (Grupo de Apoyo Mutuo—GAM, Comité de Unidad Campesina—CUC, Rigoberta Menchú, and the URNG). In Table 9-5 we can see that Protestants generally rated Protestant political figures higher than did Catholics or the non-affiliated. Not surprisingly, ratings for the recently exiled ex-president, Jorge Serrano Elías, and his vice president, Gustavo Espina Salguero, were the lowest, while ex-president Ríos Montt and President Ramiro de León Carpio received more favorable ratings. Historic and Neo-Pentecostal Protestants gave significantly higher ratings to Ríos Montt than did Catholics, Pentecostals, sect members, or the non-affiliated.[74] Catholics gave significantly higher ratings to Ramiro de León Carpio than did Pentecostals or sect members.

These findings on approval ratings are suggestive in two respects. First, significant differences did emerge between groups on approval of attitude objects associated with the right and center. Although overall approval of Serrano Elías and Espina Salguero was low, Protestants and sect members approved of these individuals more often than Catholics or the non-affiliated. Approval of Ríos Montt was also significantly higher among Protestants than among Catholics or the non-affiliated (though a relatively high 53.7 percent of Catholics approved of Ríos Montt as well). President Ramiro de León Carpio received the highest approval ratings, with Catholics and the non-affiliated approving at rates significantly higher than sect members.

Table 9-5
Approval Ratings
Percent Approving or Strongly Approving of Political Figures and Organizations (by Denomination)

	Catholic	Historic	Pentecostal	Neo-Pentecostal	Sect	Non-affiliated	Significance
Jorge Serrano Elías	6.0%	16.3%	17.5%	21.9%	18.8%	4.0%	$x^2=10.1$ $p=.07331$
Gustavo Espina Salguero	13.3%	29.4%	29.7%	25.8%	25.0%	8.0%	$x^2=12.3$ $p=.03041$
Efraín Ríos Montt	53.7%	70.6%	61.8%	71.9%	35.7%	40.0%	$x^2=12.5$ $p=.02894$
Ramio de León Carpio	85.4%	83.3%	78.2%	69.7%	52.6%	87.5%	$x^2=13.1$ $p=.02224$
Rigoberta Menchú Tum	63.0%	48.6%	43.5%	50.0%	47.1%	37.5%	$x^2=9.5$ $p=.09106$
Grupo de Apoyo Mútuo	59.2%	50.0%	46.9%	55.2%	35.7%	63.2%	$x^2=5.5$ $p=.35808$
Comité de Unidád	56.5%	32.3%	43.7%	42.3%	43.8%	35.0%	$x^2=6.7$ $p=.24225$
Campesina URNG	26.5%	21.9%	17.3%	21.4%	20.0%	10.0%	$x^2=3.8$ $p=.57851$

Second, differences between groups on approval ratings of attitude objects associated with the left were not significant. Contrary to the widely held assumption that Protestants are conservative, Evangelicals and members of sects do not appear to be significantly more opposed to the URNG than Catholics. It is also worthy of note that approval ratings of the URNG are relatively high for the entire sample. According to Susanne Jonas, private presidential polls showed public *simpatía* (sympathy or a favorable view) for the URNG to be between 3 and 4 percent in 1991, and up to 10 percent in 1992.[75] In our sample, this figure rose once again, with 16.6 percent of those polled approving or strongly approving of the URNG. The non-affiliated had the lowest rate of approval for the URNG, once again suggesting that these individuals may be particularly conflict-aversive in Guatemala. While Protestant approval ratings of Rigoberta Menchú, CUC, and GAM do lag behind the approval ratings of Catholics, these differences are not significant at the .05 level.

A final political variable measures respondents' self-placement on a left-right scale. Table 6 presents a distribution of religious groups across the political spectrum.

The most striking finding in Table 6 is the number of respondents who are unwilling to place themselves on a left-right scale. Sixty-four percent of the non-affiliated, 44.5 percent of Pentecostals, and 39.4 percent of the Neo-Pentecostals refused to be placed on the scale. This finding reflects both on the nature of Guatemalan politics and the nature of these religious groups. It is not particularly surprising that a relatively high number of Pentecostals would refuse to place themselves on an ideological spectrum. As noted earlier, a common theme in Pentecostal messages is that politics is "dirty" and therefore to be avoided. Association with political groups, movements, or tendencies is frowned upon in many Pentecostal circles. This finding may also be the result of the political climate in Guatemala. Frustration over a lack of viable political alternatives, combined with a fear of overt identification with challenges to the status quo, may lead to a greater unwillingness to self-identify on an ideological scale. The fact that 64 percent of the non-affiliated refused to place themselves on the ideological spectrum seems to support this hypothesis.

Table 9-6
Ideological Scale by Religion

	Catholic	Historic	Pentecostal	Neo-Pentecostal	Sect	Non-affiliated
Left	16.5%	15.8%	6.0%	0.0%	8.7%	0.0%
Center	40.0%	36.8%	30.0%	33.3%	30.4%	20.0%
Right	24.7%	26.3%	19.5%	27.3%	26.1%	16.0%
Refused	18.8%	21.1%	44.5%	39.4%	34.8%	64.0%
n=	85	38	200	33	23	25

*Refused to be placed on scale
$x^2=38.9$ $p=.00065$

For those who were willing to place themselves on the ideological scale, differences in ideological self-labels between religious groups were not as pronounced as we might have expected. A smaller percentage of Pentecostals placed themselves on the right than Catholics. Only a slightly higher percentage of Neo-Pentecostals and Historic Protestants placed themselves on the right than Catholics. The only major difference between groups is that among Pentecostals, only 6.0 percent placed themselves on the left, and no Neo-Pentecostals or religiously non-affiliated did so.

DISCUSSION AND CONCLUSIONS

What do these findings tell us about religion and politics in Guatemala? First, levels of perceived religious discrimination and religious conflict are relatively high among those we surveyed.[76] Considering the highly charged political atmosphere following the downfall of Guatemala's first democratically elected Protestant president, this finding should come as no surprise. In 1997, as Guatemala begins its experience as a post-war democracy, religious tensions may represent one among the many dangers to the consolidation of the democratic process.

Second, Guatemala's religious tensions are paralleled, to some degree, by political divisions. Our data support the notion that Evangelicals are less likely to challenge government authority or criticize public officials than Catholics. Protestants also give higher approval ratings to Protestant figures (who tended to be associated with the right) than do Catholics. Before jumping to the conclusion that Protestants in Guatemala are apolitical or right-wing, however, we must consider three important caveats. First, there were no significant differences between religious groups on approval ratings of attitude objects associated with the left, such as Rigoberta Menchú or the URNG. Second, of those who were willing to place themselves on an ideological scale, differences between Protestants and Catholics were not extreme. Fewer Pentecostals and Neo-Pentecostals placed themselves on the left than did Catholics. But more Catholics placed themselves on the right than did Pentecostals. Third, in a 1993 study of political culture in Guatemala, Mitchell A. Seligson and Joel M. Jutkowitz found that Protestantism had a significantly *positive* effect on measures of communal participation. According to these authors,

> various "non-Catholic" Christian groups, largely Protestant fundamentalists, exhibit significantly (<.001) higher communal participation than do Catholics. . . . Those with no religion had the lowest level of participation. . . . Apparently, these new groups do help stimulate local level participation.[77]

These findings suggest that simple characterizations of ideological divisions and political participation along religious lines in Guatemala are not useful. Protestants may be reticent about potentially conflictual political action, but they are not monolithically conservative and they do participate in community activities. Despite the popular image, the battle lines in Guatemala are not drawn primarily between the activist Catholic left and the quiescent Protestant right.

Third, the Neo-Pentecostals stand out as a unique group among Protestants in Guatemala. They are generally more educated, score higher on a self-anchored scale rating social position, and report lower levels of perceived religious discrimination and religious conflict in their communities. According to Anne M. Hallum, Neo-Pentecostals have remained politically active in Guatemala after Serrano's downfall, with some churches even conducting political workshops and rallies.[78] In the future, we can expect to see more political activism among Neo-Pentecostals. Despite their relative inexperience and naiveté in the game of Guatemalan politics, Neo-Pentecostals have the background, resources, and the motivation to take advantage of the democratic openings occurring in the Guatemalan political system.

It is not difficult to predict a future of continued religious pluralism in Guatemala. It is more difficult to discern the implications of this pluralism for Guatemala's democratic consolidation. Clearly, we should not assume that continuing religious pluralism represents some sort of inevitable step forward in a process leading toward political modernization or even secularization. Guatemala remains a deeply religious and a deeply divided society, facing major challenges on issues ranging from political trust, institution building, and participation, to economic growth, distribution, and race. In the short term, the growth of Protestantism has reinforced some of these divisions and exacerbated some of these problems. In the long term, however, the countervailing tendencies sparked by religious competition may become more apparent. The democratization of the Catholic church may be seen, in part, as a response to the growth of Protestantism. On the other hand, the Vatican's recent attempts to recentralize authority could be viewed simply as a different response to the same circumstances. We have already noted that Protestant groups are not monolithically conservative or apolitical and that the growth of Protestantism may actually encourage communal participation. In this sense, Protestantism may encourage the growth of a stronger and more coherent civil society in Guatemala. For this to happen, however, the vertical and authoritarian tendencies within Guatemalan Protestantism must be overcome. The disgrace of Serrano, the end of the war, and recent democratic openings may create the right circumstances to allow such political learning to take place.

10.

NICARAGUA

———————◆———————

Andrew J. Stein

INTRODUCTION

Nicaragua was one of the countries in Latin America where it was said that the Catholic Church had taken on the role of a prophetic voice against social injustice and in favor of social change in the 1960s and 1970s. The manner in which the "prophetic mission" of the Catholic Church—as defender of the poor and moral conscience of Nicaraguan society—was implemented has strongly affected patterns of church-state relations in that country. By the late 1980s there were efforts by some in the hierarchy of the Catholic Church to check the more radical clergy and laity whose actions had involved the institution in political struggles. A "Roman Restoration," indicating a sharp swing to the right, was emerging to temper and restrict the advancement of the pro-social change agenda. In cases where revolutionary movements had come to power in Latin America—in Cuba, Chile, and Nicaragua—the relationship between the Catholic Church and leftist governments had been at best strained, distrustful, and not an easy or full embrace of the new, secularly generated moral authority or changed configurations of political power.

The persistence of relations characterized by conflict under three governments that were markedly different from one another—the Somozas, the Sandinista National Liberation Front (Frente Sandinista de Liberación Nacional, FSLN), and the administration of Violeta Chamorro—is explained by the fact that the Catholic Church found it necessary to reposition itself vis-à-vis society and political power, in order to defend interests vital to its religious mission. In the 1990s there is a movement back toward church-state cooperation to a degree unseen since the 1950s, a pattern that will have significant implications for religious freedom and democracy.

This chapter is organized along lines similar to chapter 6 (on El Salvador) in this volume, and where appropriate, comparisons will be made to the experience of that country. First, it will consider how the development of church-state ties in the nineteenth and twentieth centuries were either harmonious or marked by strife, and explain why. Second, the chapter will address constitutional provisions that favored the Catholic Church over other churches, the expansion of non-Catholic Christian churches since the 1980s, and how Catholic leaders have responded toward such groups. Finally, the chapter probes the contribution of the Catholic and Protestant churches to religious freedom, respect for human rights, and democratization of Nicaragua.

THE HISTORICAL CONTEXT OF CHURCH-STATE RELATIONS

Many of the same issues that surfaced in El Salvador concerning the desirability of continuing the state's patronage relationship (with corresponding legal, property, and economic commitments) with the church after independence were also faced in Nicaragua. However, in the latter country, while Liberal-Conservative conflict was present as it was throughout much of Mexico, and Central and South America, it never assumed the anticlerical extremes that were experienced in Guatemala or El Salvador. The León-Granada split among elite factions in Nicaragua during the period 1800-58 was more over regional commercial hegemony and family-based feuds, while sharp differences over how to treat the church were, according to Burns, "mostly muted." Whether constitutions were written by Liberals (1826, 1838, 1858) or Conservatives (1848, 1854), all of the documents granted Catholicism the status of official state religion, and in the latter two instances, also promised additional government protection. Some clergy served in Liberal or Conservative governments, depending on their city of origin.[1]

Civil wars and frequent changes of government were a constant in the first half of the nineteenth century, a period marked by weak public institutions and an equally weak Catholic Church characterized as "impoverished, under-staffed, . . . and divided."[2] Bishop Jorge de Viteri y Ungo (1847-53), who had previously been expelled by Liberals in El Salvador, had conflicts with the Nicaraguan government during his tenure over such issues as patronage and government intervention in church affairs (such as the authorities' desire to name parish priests).

The invasion of Nicaragua by filibuster William Walker in 1855-57 worsened divisions among regional elites. Upon arrival Walker promised not to attack the Catholic Church (an effort to appease Conservatives based in Granada, a city he later burned to the ground).[3] A pro-slavery Tennessean who imposed English as the official language, he severely curtailed the rights of the church. Clerical response to him was not uniform, however, and what Nicaraguans call the National War (1854-56) left Catholics badly polarized. Some priests supported Walker, while others died in the fall of Granada.[4] Walker had come to Nicaragua to gain control over a trans-isthmian route, and in 1856 was recognized by American officials in the country as the legitimate president.[5]

Once foreign intervention ended temporarily, local elites signed an oligar-chic pact in 1856, and promulgated a new constitution in 1858. The next three decades (1859-93) were marked by Conservative domination, political stability, and cattle ranching by elites, accompanied by subsistence agriculture by peasants and indigenous communities. During this time the Catholic clergy helped legitimize forced labor drafts, a practice from the colonial period that was retained. The church, in turn, was the beneficiary of government-collected tithes.[6] The rapprochement between church and state was codified in the con-cordat of 1862, which made Catholicism the state religion, formalized economic obligations and church influence in education, and gave the government the right to name parish priests and present a list of candidates for bishoprics.[7]

The Catholic Church was a "power center within the oligarchic state," according to José Luis Velázquez, with both economic and ideological func-tions that were exercised through parishes, schools, universities and *cofradías* (religious confraternities). Given the status of Catholicism as the exclusive state religion, political and social status in relation to civil society, and ties to pro-duction relations of the status quo oligarchies, the Catholic Church was a central actor in the nineteenth century. The institution legitimized the existing order, and benefited from state channeling of tithes and salaries earned from export agriculture.[8]

All of the above arrangements ended dramatically with the rise of Liberal president José Santos Zelaya (1893-1909), as Nicaragua underwent the Lib-eral reforms that Guatemala and El Salvador had undergone decades earlier.[9] Equally important, the institutions of a strong national state were created, and coffee production for export became the motor of the economy. Immediately upon coming to power Zelaya abrogated the concordat, and was one of the presidents who most affected church-state relations in Nicaragua during the present century. The Liberal president made education secular, had state au-thorities displace church authorities in the areas of marriage, regulation of cemeteries, and public records. The official status conferred on Catholicism ended (and with it, government collection of tithes), the public behavior of clergy was restricted, and limits were placed on the entry of foreign priests into the country.[10] Coffee expansion was an equally brutal process of government coercion and mass resistance in Nicaragua as it had been in El Salvador, par-ticularly in the years 1881-93.[11] A consequence of this change was the expul-sion of the Jesuits in 1881 for their alleged support for native people's defense of ejidal lands in León and Matagalpa.[12] The 1893 constitution marked the hegemony of the coffee elites, and included express prohibitions against the property rights of Indian communities, as would the charters of 1905, 1910, and 1911.

Another major turning point for church-state relations was the reign of the Somoza family dynasty (1936-79). Its founder, Anastasio Somoza García, as leader of the National Liberal Party (Partido Liberal Nacional, PLN), claimed the inheritance of Zelaya. During the family's rule, four constitutions were adopted (1939, 1948, 1950, and 1974), but their differences had little to do with religious matters.[13] The documents stipulated that there was no official state religion, unlike periods of Conservative rule or in the colonial period.[14]

In practice, throughout most of the twentieth century, there has been de facto recognition of the Catholic Church hierarchy as the religious leadership of the nation. Prelates accompanied the chief of state at most public ceremonies to give their blessing, and tax exemptions were given to the church. When asked about the fact that the former archbishop of Managua, Alejandro González y Robleto (1952-68), had blessed the assassinated Somoza García as a "prince of the church" and required national memorial masses for the dictator, one prelate commented:

> May he rest in peace, but yes, [Archbishop] González was a man of his time. [Previously], there existed the image of the church married to the government *(el poder),* with little criticism of the status quo.[15]

Interestingly, the last Somoza constitution (1974, Articles 120-21) contained restrictions on the protected status of church sanctuaries, which revealed the government's distrust of some sectors of the Catholic Church and the public division of the churches over their stance toward the Somoza regime in the final years of the dictatorship. Church-state conflict in Nicaragua worsened after the 1972 earthquake and in 1974, after Anastasio Somoza Debayle remained in office by fraud.[16] This conflict would reach its peak in 1978-79 with church denunciations of National Guard massacres and use of torture, culminating in the June 2, 1979, pastoral letter by the Nicaraguan Bishops' Conference (Conferencia Episcopal de Nicaragua, CEN), in which the right to insurrection against tyranny was justified.[17] When asked what were the key factors that led to the total break with the Somozas, a retired bishop noted:

> Under Somoza we denounced abuses and pressured for [the release] of prisoners. In a [pastoral letter] we criticized stealing money, injustice, poverty, and especially the human rights situation.[18]

The 1979 revolution led to a new legal order that, at the outset, did not affect the Catholic Church substantially. The *Fundamental Statute and Law of Citizen Rights* (1979) guaranteed freedom of religion (Article 8), and had sections prohibiting the use of propaganda to foment religious hatred. An important change in this 1979 document was the granting of formal representation to the Association of Nicaraguan Clergy (Asociación del Clero Nicaragüense, ACLEN) on the Council of State (*Consejo del Estado*), the provisional legislature.[19] Formerly, contacts with the government had been handled by the bishops, not by clergy acting independently of their superiors. This change gave a greater voice to priests in political circles, and appeared to lessen their subordination to the directives of the Bishops' Conference.

When the Sandinista-controlled National Assembly adopted a constitution in 1987, there was opposition by Catholic prelates even at the symbolic level.

The preamble invoked the heroes of independence and the revolution, and referred to God in the context of revolutionary mobilization:

> In the name of . . . those Christians who, moved by their faith in God . . . committed and dedicated to the struggle for the liberation of the oppressed. . . . [20]

Bishops objected to a definition of faithful Christians that depended on the degree to which one opposed the Somozas and participated in the revolutionary struggle. Previous constitutions had merely invoked God in generic phrases like that of 1950, "under the protection of God."[21] The CEN asserted that Catholicism was the "soul and historic expression" of Nicaraguan identity, rather than being restricted to the extent of one's participation in the Frente Sandinista. The bishops also found fault with the new document in terms of the process of debate prior to ratification.

The 1987 Nicaraguan constitution (revised fundamentally in 1995) recognizes the predominant role of the Catholic Church in Nicaragua's history, but states in Title I, Article 14, that there is no official state religion. It provides for protection against legal discrimination on the basis of religion, and for freedom of individual religious belief and practice (Title III, Articles 27, 29 and 69). In the public school system there is lay education (Title VII, Article 124).[22]

Archbishop Obando and the Nicaraguan Church's Response to the FSLN, 1979–1990

How was it that the Bishops' Conference and clergy (though not uniformly) supported victims of torture and massacres by the Somoza regime and hastened its end,[23] then seemed to be in peaceful coexistence with the revolutionary junta, but finally entered into open confrontation with the Sandinista government from early 1980 until about 1986? Reviews of the substantial literature on the Catholic Church and the Sandinista government exist,[24] so I will confine myself to a few brief observations. Growing divisions among the clergy and lay persons since the late 1960s over how and whether to implement the resolutions of the 1968 Medellín Bishops' Conference, what to do about the repression and corruption of the Somozas, and attitudes toward radical social change were exacerbated by the revolution. A constant fear of the bishops was that the church would be used for political ends, a concern of the Salvadoran prelates as well.

The Sandinista leadership's desire for support for the revolution from all sectors of society led the FSLN government to favor those parts of the Catholic Church most in agreement with its policies (sympathizers or participants in the armed struggle, and high-profile priests influenced by liberation theology, especially the four who would serve as cabinet ministers of Education, Culture, Foreign Affairs, and Social Security).[25] For their part, some bishops became more intolerant of diversity and dialogue among its priests and the laity, imposing a unified opposition to the FSLN in the Catholic Church and marginalizing dissidents. The tensions between the Sandinistas and the Catholic authorities were increased by the expulsions of ten priests in 1984, and a bishop in 1986. Contrary to the insistent claims of Cardinal Obando y Bravo and the Nicaraguan Bishops' Conference, there never was the same degree of open government persecution of the church and widespread torture and murder of its clergy and pastoral workers as in El Salvador and Guatemala in the period.[26]

An institution that had once maintained generally cooperative and dependent church-state relations, and the corresponding benefits of government protection and resources, suddenly faced a revolutionary regime that questioned its centrality as a moral authority and its prerogatives in such areas as education, family law, human rights, public morality, and constitutional standing.[27] This was much more the root of the conflict than was a "persecuted church."

The perception of Sandinista government officials was that while the Catholic Church had spoken to both sides in the conflict before July 1979, it increasingly took one side in the conflict, that of the opposition parties, peak associations, and mass media based in Managua (such as COSEP, the business interest group, and *La Prensa*). Some in the FSLN even claimed that the hierarchy allied itself unambiguously with the Contra rebels composed in part of former National Guard soldiers and trained by the United States.[28] Part of the reason for the Sandinistas' restrictions on the church (monitoring and censoring its newspaper and radio station, controlling the entry of foreign clergy and nuns) was the Sandinista leaders' view, mistaken or not, that the church hierarchy and many of the diocesan priests (especially in the Archdiocese of Managua) were part of a disloyal opposition determined to undermine public support for the revolution and Sandinista Front. The issue of how church and state officials viewed each other's motives, interests, and behavior is key to understanding the conflict. A former priest who also served in the Sandinista government observed that:

> [The hostility] was due, fundamentally, to an ideological conflict that led the regime to commit a series of blunders . . . [and to] ignorance about the Catholic Church. Once in power, the leaders of the revolution saw in the Cardenal brothers, D'Escoto, and Parrales the prototype for all priests. The bishops also had a mistaken conception. They wanted the leaders of the FSLN to behave as though they were faithful members of the Catholic Church, not revolutionaries.[29]

GOVERNMENT-CHURCH RELATIONS AFTER THE REVOLUTION, 1990-1998

One scholar characterized the ties of the Chamorro administration (1990-97) to Cardinal Obando y Bravo and his fellow bishops as "active collaboration," a sharp contrast with the experience under the last of the Somozas and the

FSLN.[30] At times the diocesan authorities (and most of the parish priests throughout the country) supported the more rightist National Opposition Union (Unión Nacional Opositora, UNO) coalition and was periodically critical of Chamorro. Yet the public also noted the peaceful coexistence and a tolerant relationship between the two parties.[31] The traditional Catholic Church defense of its privileged areas of influence was evident in public policy debates, as in the period before the revolution. Education was one key area, and since the Chamorro years efforts have been made by the Catholic Church to allow for more teaching of the faith. Article 124 of the Constitution favors lay education, and voluntary religious instruction is permitted, but those who give such classes are not paid by public monies. Education Minister Humberto Belli's public statements and appearances with church officials left the impression of official favoritism toward Catholicism.[32]

While the nature of church-state relations has changed in the 1990s, the Catholic hierarchy has declared its commitment to the ideal of church autonomy from the favors and obligations of close ties with the state:

> The [Catholic] Church hierarchy should not identify itself with any ideology or regime. . . . The Church struggles always to conserve its independence with respect to temporal powers.[33]

In practice, such impartiality has been challenged, despite the good faith mediation of Cardinal Obando y Bravo and the church that took place in the crises of 1974, 1978, 1987-89, 1993, and 1995.[34] The polarization of civil society, political elites, and churches is an enduring legacy in Nicaragua at present, and the anti-Sandinista tone of the Catholic Church has been demonstrated repeatedly. This was particularly the case during the October 1996 presidential elections, which saw Arnoldo Alemán defeat Daniel Ortega, and his Liberal Alliance gain the majority of seats in the National Assembly and municipalities.[35] The role of the Catholic Church and the Evangelical denominations in the 1996 campaign was significant.[36]

The first year and a half of the Alemán government produced a profound crisis and polarization that undermined political institutions and resulted in only periodic dialogue between the two blocs on the right and left, and violent political protests.[37] In this context the Catholic leadership allied itself very explicitly with President Alemán and the Liberal Alliance to a degree not seen in Nicaragua since the 1950s. While the Bishops' Conference was careful not to ally itself with the FSLN in the 1980s, it has become more dependent on the state in the 1990s in terms of symbols (presence at government ceremonies), resources, and outright political statements. This posture could further exacerbate existing divisions among the clergy and laity that have existed since the revolution, rather than bridging the factions. In the first six months in office the Liberal president had an approval rating of 26-38 percent according to polls by Borge and Gallup.[38] If the church seeks to link itself with such an administration, the latter's political misfortunes could have lasting negative effects for the church's credibility, and make it ever harder for the church to reach out to those sectors of the laity that count themselves among the nearly 40 percent of the population that continues to support the FSLN, or other lay persons who disagree with the government in power. Multiple polls show a sharp decline in public esteem for politicians and public institutions in Nicaragua during the 1990s, but so far churches and the clergy still rank highest, along with teachers.[39]

PROTESTANT GROWTH, CATHOLICISM AND RELIGIOUS FREEDOM

The historical roots of Protestantism are much deeper in Nicaragua than is the case in El Salvador. This is particularly the case on the Atlantic Coast (long under British and American influence), where the Baptist, Episcopalian, and Moravian churches date from the period 1849-93, and have large memberships among the Miskitos Indians and creoles of African descent.[40] Some presence of the same historic denominations also was visible along the Pacific areas of the country after missionaries began arriving following World War I.[41] From the early 1960s to the present, a third wave of Protestant expansion took place in the country, particularly with Pentecostal churches throughout all regions of Nicaragua (though most strongly in Managua). Data from the 1995 Nicaraguan census, summarized in Table 10-1 below, reveal the increasing percentage of non-Catholics in the nation.

Table 10-1
Nicaraguan Census Data on Religious Affiliation
(numbers are percentage of total population)

Year	Catholic	Protestant (total)	Baptist	Anglican	Moravian	Evangelical
1995	73.0	—	—	0.001	0.1	15.1
1963	96.0	3.8	0.1	0.200	1.8	—
1950	95.8	4.1	—	—	—	—

SOURCE: Instituto Nicaragüense de Estadísticas y Censos, *Resumen censal: VII censo nacional de población y III de vivienda* (Managua, 1996), 16; 106-7.
NOTE: The response categories were not consistent for non-Catholic denominations in the three Nicaraguan censuses.

Survey data from Nicaragua suggest that the growth has occurred mostly from the late 1980s to the early 1990s.[42] An opinion poll conducted by an institute affiliated with the Central American University in Managua in 1988 stated that Evangelicals were almost one-tenth (8.9 percent) of the population, whereas 1991, 1995, and 1996 University of Pittsburgh data indicated a steady increase (12.1, 17.4, and 19 percent, respectively).[43] The share of the population identified as Catholic decreased from more than three-quarters to 70.9 percent in 1995, and a comparable level in 1996 and 1997. The percentage of respondents with no religious affiliation or respondents of other religions never reached more than a combined 15 percent.[44]

Protestant churches' own data suggest the same patterns as census and survey data: most growth happened under Sandinista rule, and Pentecostals gained more than any other type of denomination. The growth of congregations has been dramatic (see Table 10-2).

Table 10-2
Growth of Nicaraguan Protestant Congregations, 1980-1994

Year	Number of Congregations
1980	1,284
1986	2,778
1993	5,000

SOURCE: Martínez, *Las sectas*, 61; Bautz, González, and Orozco, *Política y religión*, 5.

Politics in Nicaragua during the past generation have been violent and turbulent, yet Protestant impact on elections and policy has been minimal despite an almost tenfold increase in numbers. In the 1980s, as the Sandinista government came into serious conflict with the Catholic Church hierarchy, it sought support from dissident Catholics, Baptists, Lutherans, and other interdenominational Protestant groups, such as the Evangelical Committee for Development Assistance (Comité Evangélico pro Ayuda al Desarrollo, CEPAD).[45] By the mid-1980s the polarization of the Contra War had come to influence Protestant church politics as much as it had split Catholics. Rival organizations were created for those denominations opposed to CEPAD's pro-Sandinista stance.[46]

Efforts to organize a Protestant-oriented party in Nicaragua have produced the center-right National Justice Party (Partido de Justicia Nacional, PJN, with ties to the Assemblies of God), founded in 1992 and legally recognized two years later, but it was electorally insignificant. Similarly, in 1991-93, the pro-Sandinista Popular Evangelical Movement (Movimiento Evangélico Popular, MEP) and Evangelical Convergence (Convergencia Evangélica) came into being but had little impact on national politics. Part of the failure to attract Protestants to an explicitly confessional party is due to the ideological polarization and general disgust with and low esteem for all political parties that many Nicaraguan citizens feel. Additionally, the extraordinary heterogeneity of non-Catholics makes for differences in theology, understandings of the sociopolitical and economic crises of the country, and views on the morality and desirability of direct political action including voting, community organization, protest, and church input to human rights work, social development, and church-state dialogue.[47]

A younger Protestant party that has had an important role, the Nicaraguan Christian Path (Camino Cristiano Nicaragüense, CCN), came in a distant third place in 1996 with 72,000 votes, as compared to only 5,600 for the PJN.[48] The CCN was headed by Pastor Guillermo Osorno, former director of the oldest and largest Protestant radio network, *Ondas de Luz*. The reasons this party achieved exceptional success relative to that of others include the unimpeachable personal integrity of Osorno and his credibility in calls against government corruption, his stress on a conciliatory style of politics (including Protestant-Catholic issues), and the religious images and language employed in the 1996 campaign.[49]

While repeated surveys have shown a strong willingness by most Protestant lay persons and clergy to support an Evangelical party, prior to 1996 this had not taken place. Careful analyses of Protestant voting in 1984 and 1990 indicate several trends. First, voter turnout by Protestants went from roughly half to 80-90 percent. Since voter-choice exit-poll responses are highly unreliable, particularly for Nicaragua in the 1990 vote, another area to examine is party sympathy. A plurality of the Baptists, Church of God, and Christian Mission favored the Sandinistas; others like the Four Square Gospel Church favored the UNO, and in the case of the Assemblies of God, 70 percent favored no party. There were also dramatic differences by denomination in terms of campaign involvement and preferred issue positions. The notion of a uniformly pro-UNO right-wing orientation in 1990 among Protestants is demonstrably false.[50]

On the Atlantic Coast, where, due to the particular history of the region, Baptists, Moravians, and other Protestants constitute one-third of the population,[51] five of the national deputies are Protestants. Regional autonomy has led to separate elections for the Coast in 1994 and 1998 in which Protestants have been important as candidates, but secondary to the two main parties. In the rest of the country, which accounts for 85 percent of the population, following the 1996 vote there were another five Protestant members of the National Assembly (out of 93 total), two mayors, and several city council members.

The disagreements of the Catholic Church in Nicaragua with the increasingly numerous Protestant churches are like those in El Salvador, but more severe. The bishops feel threatened and offended by the aggressive proselytizing efforts of countless non-Catholic (and occasionally, anti-Catholic) denominations and "sects," and they have no established inter-church ecumenical program on the national level (though there has been such a mechanism on the Atlantic Coast for decades). Catholic clergy admit that there is hostility, disrespect, and widespread ignorance about the doctrines and practices of the heterogeneous Protestant community in the country.[52] My survey of parish priests in Nicaragua, conducted in 1993-94,[53] indicates that there is minimal contact or cooperation between Catholics and Protestants on the parish level. When there is contact, it is with historical Protestant churches that have a formal institutional structure, seminary-trained pastors, a developed theology, and often membership in the World Council of Churches. Priests tended to classify these groups (Baptists, Lutherans) in positive terms, as "separated brethren," or "people of goodwill." In sharp contrast, the more Pentecostal religious groups and other "sects" such as the Assemblies of God, Jehovah's Witnesses, or the Unification Church were seen as "heretics," "foreign sects divorced from the national reality," or religions that gain adherents through material donations to vulnerable poor people.[54] In other words, the groups that comprise 75-85 percent of the Protestant community are seen by Nicaraguan Catholic bishops and most parish priests as being beyond the pale and not worthy partners for dialogue.[55]

DEMOCRATIZATION, HUMAN RIGHTS, AND RELIGIOUS FREEDOM

At this juncture it is important to consider the impact of the Catholic and Protestant churches on the peaceful settlement to armed conflict in Nicaragua, their contribution to democracy, human rights, the rule of law, and what the postwar context has brought in terms of religious freedom.

THE NICARAGUAN CHURCH'S ROLE IN ATTAINING PEACE, 1987-1990

In Nicaragua, the churches played a mediatory role in the peace negotiations that followed the second Central American Presidents' Meeting at Esquipulas. President Daniel Ortega requested the participation of Cardinal Obando y Bravo and Baptist minister Gustavo Parajón in the National Reconciliation Commission in the talks between the FSLN and Contras and opposition parties that resulted in the 1988 Sapoá Accord (regarding a cease fire, terms of disarmament, amnesty, and reform of the electoral law).[56] Cardinal Obando y Bravo and other members of the clergy also continued in their role of investigating human rights violations and disarmament through the mid-1990s in conjunction with the Organization of American States (OAS).[57]

Nonetheless, it is difficult to say that the church had as much impact on the course of peace in Nicaragua during 1981-87 as in El Salvador. In part this was due to the polarization between church and state, and the perception in government quarters that the church was a partisan opponent, not a neutral mediator.[58] The April 1984 Bishops' Conference pastoral letter calling for peace contained a vague description of the conflict, offered little in the way of viable alternatives, and failed to mention the role of the United States or equally distribute blame for the war.[59]

The Nicaraguan Catholic and Protestant churches did try to end the war by negotiations in the 1980s, but the polarization was such after the FSLN took power that such efforts amounted to much less than in El Salvador or Guatemala. Work with refugees remained important, but the churches were manipulated openly by both sides in the conflict (and the U.S. sponsors of the Contras). Thus the contribution to human rights protection was much weaker in Nicaragua than was that of the *Tutela Legal* in the Archdiocese of San Salvador, or the similar office of the Archdiocese of Guatemala City. The churches' impact on rule of law, elections, and democracy was limited before 1990 to the promotion of peace talks and reconciliation between former combatants.

Churches do have a potential impact on civil society-state relations, and demands for responsiveness to the public in the policy process. Catholic bishops have influenced debate on the economic policy agenda for the country, at times by criticizing the impact of such policies on income inequality, poverty, and unemployment.[60] The two governments that followed the FSLN have followed its 1988-89 policies of structural adjustment, and have privatized many state industries.[61] The churches' criticism of the social costs of these transformations, or the corruption that accompanied them, has been weak at best.

Joel Migdal describes many of the areas where state-society relations revolve around material and symbolic issues, and how mediators such as churches can help alter symbols, values, rules, and patterns of domination in a given society.[62] Catholic and Protestant churches did this often in the period of repression at the end of the Somoza dynasty (1974-79), but have not done so frequently and in a significant way since 1990. Polarization, attrition, and in the case of the Catholic Church, a reticence to promise mass mobilization in favor of the needs of the poor majority of Nicaraguan citizens (due in part to the association of the cause of the poor with revolutionary-era programs) have been the norm. As Migdal notes, the analytical and practical distinction between "society" and "civil society" is great,[63] and the church did much more to promote the latter in El Salvador than in Nicaragua.

CONCLUSIONS

The possible contributions of Nicaraguan churches to the furtherance of democracy and religious freedom are great, but as of now unrealized. Most other governmental and social institutions in the country are held in low regard, and seem to most Nicaraguans to offer little in the way of solutions to the country's pressing political, social, economic, and ecological problems. A weak Catholic Church, faced with the threat of continued Protestant expansion, may not make support for religious freedom one of its public policy priorities. Among the countries in this volume, Nicaragua shares with Mexico and Cuba the indelible social and political divisions that are a legacy of the revolution. It differs from them in the much stronger political and social influence of religion, especially Catholicism. Whether that influence will be exercised to overcome those divisions or to exacerbate them remains to be seen.

11.

ARGENTINA

Church, State, and Religious Freedom in Argentina

———————◆———————

José Míguez Bonino

The question of religious freedom in Argentina—in fact, in the whole of Spanish America—cannot be understood except against the backdrop of four interrelated historical conditions:

1. The regime of royal patronage (*patronato real*) which regulated the relations between the Roman Catholic Church (the Vatican) and the Spanish kingdom, whereby the Spanish crown exercised a controlling influence in the appointment of bishops, the authorization of religious orders, and the promulgation of papal encyclicals, letters, or decrees in Spain and its colonies.[1]

2. The characteristics of the Catholicism that came to Latin America and was the first agent of evangelization in the subcontinent. It was the Spanish Catholicism of the Reconquest (*Reconquista*), which had succeeded in 1492 in defeating the last Muslim bastion in Spain and dreamed of the establishment of a Christian kingdom in Spain and the new territories. It was also the post–Council of Trent Catholicism of the religious struggle with Protestantism from the sixteenth to the eighteenth centuries.

3. The power shift in Europe in the eighteenth century, whereby both economic and cultural initiative increasingly came to be exercised by the northern countries, particularly England, France, and the Low Countries. This shift stimulated the appearance in Latin America of *criollo* (native-born) leadership (the first generations of Spanish descendants born in Latin America), "enlightened" sectors interested in economic exchange with the new North European centers and inclined to republican and liberal ideas.

4. In relation to Argentina, the relatively "peripheral" position of this area—both economically and culturally—until the first decades of the nineteenth century.

FROM THE COLONY TO THE CONSOLIDATION
OF THE REPUBLIC

In terms of the emergence of religious pluralism and the definition of religious freedom, we have to look briefly at two historical periods: the colonial regime until 1810, and the emancipation and consolidation of the Republic from independence in 1816 through the struggles of national consolidation to the proclamation of the 1853 Constitution.

In religious terms, the colonial period was "uneventful" in the La Plata River area. Religious freedom was, of course, unthinkable in the conditions of the *patronato*, but the Inquisition, established in the colonies by Philip II in 1569, had no tribunal established in the La Plata River area because, as it was said, "criminals in matters of faith are rare in that area." Some isolated episodes show that a certain "generalized tolerance" was practiced in this region.[2]

The May Revolution (1810) presented a difficult problem concerning the church. Could the *patronato* exercised by the Spanish crown be transferred to the Buenos Aires Junta? Moreover, the Spanish-born resident Bishop Lue and some of the other bishops clearly espoused the cause of Spain. Thus, for a long period, the Catholic church in Argentina lost contact with the Holy See, which supported the rights of Spain in the "rebellious" provinces. Some of the liberal leaders of the revolution—Moreno, Belgrano, Castelli, and others—were clearly inclined to some forms of religious tolerance, if not freedom, partly influenced by liberal European republican thinkers like Rousseau or Pufendorf, partly as a condition for economic relations with Europe, particularly Britain. Thus Mariano Moreno—who had translated Rousseau's *Social Contract* into Spanish—stimulated immigration from Europe and in a draft for a possible constitution wrote that "Congress shall not adopt any law for the establishment of religion nor will it infringe on the free exercise of it."[3] Belgrano—who had published the controversial work of the Jesuit Lacunza (forbidden by the Inquisition)—wrote in the influential journal *Correo de Comercio* that there was no reason to fear "the indispensable trade with nations of diverse sects and religious opinions" and, in his mission to England in 1815 declared that foreigners would enjoy "freedom of worship and conscience" in Argentine territory.[4]

On the other hand, the "conservative" wing, partly due to its religious convictions, partly because of its interest in transferring the *patronato* to the new authorities, took a different approach, which prevailed in the early drafts of one constitution and other official decisions. In arguing that the *patronato* was related to "sovereignty" and not to the king as a person, successive local governments included it in the different constitutions and decrees. The 1811 "Decree on the Freedom of the Press" provided that the crime of "the abuse of freedom" included publications which would endanger "the preservation of the Catholic religion" (Art. 2), included "the ecclesiastical prelate" in the censorship committee (Art. 3), and indicated that "works dealing with religion cannot be printed without previous censorship by the ecclesiastical prelate" (Art. 8).[5] Using in effect the *patronato* authority, the Constitutional Assembly of 1813 legislated on a number of religious questions: it abolished the Inquisition in the national territory, invited all "enterprising foreigners" to come and reside in Argentina with the certainty that they would be able to "worship God privately in their homes, according to their custom," and established ecclesiastical regulations (including the use of warm water in baptism!).

Although no constitution was finally adopted in this Assembly, its decisions were important for future legislation, in successive constitutional drafts or partial constitutions in 1815, 1816, 1819, and 1826.[6] It is evident that, up to this point, three things seem to have been firmly established: (1) The Roman Catholic Church was considered the "established" state church. (2) Whatever other religious opinions or allegiances existed should be practiced strictly in private. (3) The state claimed the prerogatives, and assumed the responsibilities, of the *patronato* system.

Meanwhile, non-Catholic presence—almost totally Protestant—while still very limited, was more significant.[7] British residents had been establishing themselves in Argentina as consular representatives, trade agents, or owners of estates. Other immigrants of Protestant origin had established colonies, either invited or welcomed by the liberal governments of the 1820s and 1830s. In 1818 James Thompson, a Scottish minister and educator, came to Buenos Aires, sponsored by the British and Foreign Schools Society, created in 1814. He said about this trip: "The two things to which I have attended in this trip have been the education of youth and the spread of the Holy Scriptures." He was well received by the Buenos Aires municipality and appointed by the Buenos Aires municipality as "General Director of Schools." For three years he created schools, using the New Testament as a text book. Several Catholic priests cooperated in his work. In 1820, before leaving Argentina to continue his work in Chile and Peru, he was declared an Honorary Citizen of the La Plata River United Provinces.[8]

In 1825, the Buenos Aires government and England signed a treaty of friendship and trade. Under this treaty, Anglican and Presbyterian churches were authorized and built in 1826 and 1829 and a Methodist mission inaugurated in 1836. Even under the strongly Catholic government of Juan Manuel de Rosas in Buenos Aires, and in spite of the opposition of ultramontane Catholics like Tomás de Anchorena, the trade interests of the government prevailed and the Anglicans, Presbyterians, and Methodists continued their ministry, with the strict condition that they should only use the English language.

Thus, after the defeat of the Rosas government in 1852, when a series of conflicts and agreements resulted in the consolidation of the United Provinces of the La Plata River—the early name of Argentina—no serious religious conflicts had yet appeared, but religious freedom was nonexistent except as the toleration of the rights of worship of foreign communities, carried on exclusively in their own languages.[9]

By the time the 1853 Constitution was drafted, there was no lack of liberal voices advocating religious freedom. At the same time, some of these same liberals wanted to keep the *patronato* system as an instrument for controlling the Catholic church—as Rivadavia, and even Rosas and several governments afterward did. Finally, there were ultramontane Catholic sectors for whom a clear recognition of the Roman Catholic Church as the religion of the state was a nonnegotiable requirement. This explains why the question of religion played a major part in the constitutional debates of 1853.

We cannot enter into detail concerning this fascinating debate.[10] The outcome was the inclusion of Article 2, "The state supports the Roman Catholic Apostolic religion (*culto*)"[11] and Art. 78 requiring that the president and vice-president be Catholic. A number of other articles regulated the *patronato*. A few brief comments are here in order:

1. The debate between those who insisted that there should be a state religion and those who advocated the separation of church and state led to a victory of a third group which tried to define a limited form of relationship. The result was Article 2. Thus, while the author of the constitutional draft, Juan Bautista Alberdi, had developed a more comprehensive definition, "the state professes and supports," the final decision eliminated the word "professes" and left only "supports."

2. From the discussion it is clear that "supports" refers here to "economic" support. In fact, the Drafting Committee says this expressly: "This article obligates the federal state to support and maintain the Catholic, Apostolic, and Roman religion at the expense of the national treasury." Several other members of the Assembly insisted that "religion cannot be supported, protected, or regulated by any human power or regulation. . . . We have directed our attention only to the public worship that the government vows to support out of the national treasury with all majesty, pomp, and propriety." And a Catholic priest named Lavaysse (as the report indicates) maintained that "the Constitution cannot intervene in the conscience of people but only regulate external worship; the federal government is obliged to support it, and that is enough."

3. That this discussion has to do with the *patronato* is clear from the argument used by Fray Mamerto Perez to justify a religious requirement for the president: "If he enjoys the privilege of *patronato* . . . this right must be the correlate of a duty." Lavaysse makes exactly the same argument.

4. It seems clear that in this lengthy and sometimes hot debate, the members of the Constitutional Assembly of 1853: (a) wanted to establish broad religious freedom—as expressed in Art. 14, including among the rights of "all the inhabitants of the Nation" that of "freely practicing their religion; (b) even though most of them defined themselves as believers and not a few made an explicit declaration of the Roman Catholic faith, they did not want to establish a state religion; (c) they wanted to preserve the *patronato*—in fact, exhibiting a strongly authoritarian inclination; and (d) on this basis they drafted a number of articles, the main ones being Articles 2, 14, and 76. While it is true

that "support" has frequently been interpreted as nothing more than the recognition of the "official" character of the Catholic church, a historical examination of the process undercuts such interpretations.[12]

RELIGION, FREEDOM, AND THE STATE IN ARGENTINA

This brief historical sketch of the history of religious freedom and religious diversity in the early stages of Argentine society should provide the background for a more substantive consideration of the question of "evangelization and religious freedom" after the establishment of the Republic, and more specifically in the last fifty years.

THE PLURALIZATION OF RELIGIOUS LIFE: CHARACTERISTICS AND ISSUES

Shortly after 1850 a Spanish-speaking Protestantism began to grow in Argentina. In fact, the first services and preaching in Spanish took place in Buenos Aires in the Methodist church in 1867. Baptist, Methodist, and Christian church missionaries began evangelistic work in the country in the 1870s and 1880s, frequently encouraged and supported by liberal governments. Although their evangelistic work shared the characteristic religious and social critique of Catholicism common to all Protestant missionary work in Latin America, these "mainline" churches also displayed a zeal for education, social action, and a democratic and "modernizing" model of society. In this sense, they joined the efforts of the local elites in the "civilizing" project. The missions originating in the Holiness Movement of the 1920s in the United States, on the other hand, represented a much more concentrated and aggressive evangelization. While "enlightened" elites shared some of the social ideas of the missionaries and local leaders of mainline churches, it was from the worker immigrants, city workers, and peasants that both mainline and "evangelical" churches drew their converts. Numbers began to grow after the first decades of the twentieth century: from 6,850 active members in 1916, the Protestant numbers grew to 196,000 in 1937; 257,621 in 1952; 414,323 in 1962; and 1,360,000 in 1990. The increase in the 1920s and 1930s resulted from the growth of the Holiness churches and in the 1970-90 period, that of the Pentecostal movement.

A second kind of Protestant presence was represented by immigration resulting from the economic crises in some areas of Europe and the invitation of liberal governments in Argentina. Thus Lutheran and Congregationalist German colonies came to Argentina from 1859 to 1877 (and later after the World Wars), Italian Waldensians in 1850 and 1860, Baptist and Methodist Welsh in 1865, Swiss Reformed and Lutheran Danes in 1870, and Reformed Dutch in 1889. While these groups (with the possible exception of the Waldensians) usually kept their language and culture, the second and third generations have slowly but steadily become integrated into the national culture and the ecumenical movement has increasingly incorporated these churches into the larger Protestant community.[13]

Immigration from Russia, Poland, Germany and other European countries brought a significant number of Jews to Argentina in the 1810-50 period. The total Jewish population in Argentina can be estimated at between 500,000 and 700,000. Although the census in recent decades has not stated religious affiliation, there is no doubt that the great majority of this population adheres—in some cases probably only nominally—to their religious tradition in its different versions—Orthodox, Conservative, or Reformed.[14]

Anti-semitism has been a serious problem in some sectors of the Argentinean population from the 1940s onward, stimulated by Fascist, Nazi, and extreme nationalist groups but existing to some extent in the larger population.[15] The recent assaults on the Israel Embassy (1992) and the Argentine-Jewish Association (AMIA, 1994) are extreme manifestations of this problem.

The pluralization of religion has increased in the last decades with the influx of a number of new religious movements representing both the presence of world religions previously absent or invisible in Argentinean life—for instance, the Buddhists and Muslims—and of Afro-American and spiritist cults like Umbanda, Macumba, Candomblé, and of new religious or para-religious movements like the gnostics, New Age, Universalists, or Moonies.

RELIGION AND THE STATE

The relation of religion to society and specifically to the state has passed through different phases. I will only refer to some aspects which are more directly related to our subject.

The Catholic church has always felt that, on the basis of its historical relation to the origin, growth, and development of Latin American culture and identity, as well as its numerical majority, it should play a decisive role in public life, particularly in fundamental social policies concerning education, public morality, and the family. This has led to conflicts with the liberal state at different periods in history. The laicization of cemeteries, civil marriage, and *registro civil* (record of births)—established between 1820 and 1860 under the joint pressure of liberal, Free Mason, and Protestant demands—was felt by the Catholic church as a limitation on its ministry. Particularly, the education law adopted in 1882, which defined public education as "*gratuita, obligatoria y laica*" (free [not paid], compulsory, and secular [no teaching of religion]) took away from the Catholic church a sphere of public life which it considered fundamental to carrying out its role in society.

These conflicts can be viewed from different perspectives. On the one hand, it is an ideological battle which reflects the particular conditions of Argentine society and the struggle of the Roman Catholic Church against "modernity" in Europe in the nineteenth century. The influence of ultramontane French and Italian authors was very strong in Argentina and their struggle with the modernizing elites was a central issue in politics in the decades after 1850. While extreme positivistic laicism never succeeded in controlling Argentine public life or politics—as for instance in Uruguay—and conservative governments (for instance, after the 1930 military coup), or some provincial governments, reinstated at several points more pro-Catholic legislation, on the whole a moderate liberalism, which recognized the significance of the church in public life, has dominated Argentine state policies.

Historians have tended to interpret these conflicts as a question of power. This seems particularly evident in the relation of the Roman Catholic Church to the Peronist government from 1943 to 1955. In fact, the 1943 political coup led to a close alliance with the Catholic church in the early years (1945-48) of the first presidential term of General Juan Perón. The reestablishment of religious education in the schools, the emphasis on the role of the family, and the identification of Catholicism and nationalism characterized the ideology and the policies of the government. However, as the Peronist government and party increasingly claimed for themselves a monopoly on welfare and social assistance, total control of the labor movement, and the "Peronization" of education, a rift between the regime and the church widened and finally led to open conflict, the alliance of the church with the opposition and the dissatisfied elements in the armed forces, and to the church's role—still debated among political analysts and historians—in the fall of Perón in 1955.[16] It is interesting to note that, in the final phase of the conflict, certain evangelical groups, attracted by the anticlerical policies of the government, actively sided with it, while the more traditional Protestant churches, which were more identified with a discontented middle class, supported the opposition.[17]

Meanwhile, the fundamental legislation on religion contained in the 1853 Constitution was not modified at all in successive reforms.[18] The discriminatory nature of the religious clauses of the 1853 Constitution are quite evident. They were already forcefully criticized in 1853. Juan José Paso criticized the proposed requirement that the president be Catholic because it would "harm the country," which would be deprived of the possibility of "employing for such purpose [the presidency] a person of outstanding talent, ability, and morality who held different beliefs." José Ugarteche argued in the same way: "To give to a form of worship the character of a privileged religion . . . in my opinion . . . established a privilege" and "all privileges destroy equality." Moreover, the historically incorrect but widely extended use of Article 2 as recognizing Catholicism as the state religion has justified other forms of exclusion, particularly of Protestants and Jews from chaplaincies in the armed forces and hospitals and from the higher commands of the armed forces. Sometimes it has even excluded them as candidates in military institutes and schools and from different forms of representation in official acts. The prejudice involved in this paralegal discrimination has influenced public opinion in the leading spheres of society, creating until very recently real discrimination against religious dissidents in different areas of public life—the media, university, public administration, etc.

These different forms of discrimination have become very evident in the face of recent international declarations and covenants adopted and signed by Argentina. Thus, the "International Covenant on Civil and Political Rights," signed in 1966 and implemented in our country by law 23.312 in 1986, states in Articles 18 and 26 that "the law will forbid all discrimination and grant to all persons equal and effective protection against any form of discrimination for reason of race, color, sex, language, religion." On this basis the "Declaration on the Elimination of all Forms of Intolerance and Discrimination Based on Religion or Convictions," approved by the UN in 1982, specifies (Art. 2.2): "By discrimination . . . is understood any distinction, exclusion, restriction, or preference based on religion." A study published by the UN as a corollary to this declaration specifically refers to the discrimination involved in financial support given by a government to a particular religion (#393). Most post–World War II European constitutions reflect the general consensus that has developed in these and other international and inter-American documents on human rights. The recent reform of the Argentine Constitution undertaken in 1994 has tried to face the issues raised by the discriminatory aspects of our constitutional and statutory law.

The relation between religion and the state took a dramatic turn after the 1976 military coup and the establishment of a military dictatorship (self-designated as "the process of national reorganization"), infamous for its brutal repression, violation of fundamental human rights, and torture and disappearances. Thousands of people of different religious convictions were victims of repression, in many cases, precisely because of their religion. Yet members of all religious bodies were also involved as active agents in the repression. How should and would religious bodies respond and react to such a situation? The answer to this question has become a critical and delicate problem in Argentinean life which we cannot evade.

Since it is most directly linked to political power and is the most significant religious body in the country, the Roman Catholic Church has been a particular target of public examination and critique. A passionate debate has taken place in Argentina concerning the role of this church during those years. A careful, critical but considered study of this question has been done by the Catholic lawyer, professor, and scholar Emilio Mignone.[19] He examines in succession the roles of the military vicar, of the bishops and the episcopal conference, of the nuncio[20] and the Vatican, and of some particular bishops. While the ideological and practical support of the vicar to the military regime is almost universally recognized, the evaluation of the attitude of the Bishops Conference has to be clarified. There is little doubt that it decided to take a low profile, to carry out at a private level whatever action it wanted to take, and to avoid, at least during the first period, public pronouncements. Probably the first statement that points to the negative aspects of the repression—

it speaks of "illegitimate repression"—is the 1981 pastoral letter entitled "The Church and the National Community." While admitting that "in case of emergency human rights can be restricted," it calls for a rapid restoration of rights and "an urgent . . . reconciliation on the basis of truth, freedom and justice." More active and legitimizing support for the regime is documented in the case of some other bishops. Mignone's conclusion is that

> the Argentine episcopate made a purely political choice. It allied itself with temporal power, renouncing the testimony of the Gospel which demands the denunciation of crimes and of the people responsible for them and active support of the victims, even risking persecution. The episcopate knew the truth and hid it to benefit the government of the armed forces. Between God and Caesar it chose the latter.[21]

Mignone goes on to ask the reasons for such an attitude. He refers to historical conditions which have led the Catholic church to an alliance with reactionary forces in Argentine society, to the church's dependence on the financial support of the state, its prerogatives in areas like family legislation and education, and the ideological weight of the ultramontane tendencies in Catholic thinking. In my own view, to the extent that I concur with Mignone's conclusion, I would suggest that the Argentine Catholic church—more than others in the continent—developed, both for reason of the *patronato* and of other local circumstances, a strong dependence on its relation to the state for the fulfillment of its pastoral task. As a result it relied more on an indirect relation to society, mediated by its relation to political power, than on a direct pastoral relation to the people. The struggle with the liberal anticlerical regimes, as well as with the Peronist regime in its last period, reinforced this dependence. The prospect of a break with the government—even the de facto government of the military regime—made the hierarchy of the church anxious and fearful. The fact that the more "popular" pastoral activity of the "third-world priests" was seen by the military as "subversion" made it even more sensitive and hesitant.

This critical assessment of the official attitude of a significant part of the Catholic hierarchy should not hide the outstanding and courageous pioneering role of some Catholic bishops and priests and lay people. Several bishops and many priests and laypeople actively participated in the organization and action of human rights organizations. Some of them risked their lives trying to protect victims of repression or to help threatened and endangered people— whether Catholic or not. Some members of the religious orders offered protection and refuge to persecuted people—and paid for their actions with their lives. Not a few lay men and women suffered prison, torture, and death for the denunciation of repression, the public demonstration of opposition, and the defense of human rights. Devoted Roman Catholic lay people like Mignone himself or the Nobel Peace Prize winner Adolfo Pérez Esquivel, were in the forefront of the human rights struggle.

After the end of the military government many people, inside and outside the Catholic church, have expressed the desire that the Episcopal Conference make an evaluation and a public self-analysis of its role during the military dictatorship. In the context of the end of the millennium and the Pope's call for self-examination, the Conference published in 1986 a document in which it examined the role of the church. It has been generally evaluated as timid and somewhat evasive with its admissions expressed in conditional terms and ascribed to individuals.

It is more difficult, because of their variety and the lack of centralized authority, to evaluate the role of other religious communities, like the Protestant and Jewish communities. They are also much less visible because of their limited numbers and presence in Argentine public life. Some of the leadership of "mainline" Protestant churches—*La Iglesia Evangélica del Río de la Plata* (a Lutheran Reformed Church of German origin), the Methodist church, the Christian church—together with some Catholic leaders, created the Ecumenical Human Rights Movement (MEDH), which at an early point was very active in helping victims and in denouncing and documenting human rights violations. The Permanent Assembly for Human Rights, a pluralistic association of people from political parties, civic organizations, and personalities from culture and education and the trade unions, which was organized as early as 1975 as a coalition against the increasing violence in Argentine society and afterward became one of the rallying points for opposition, included in its leadership church leaders—including Catholic and Protestant bishops and presiding officers as well as several leaders of the Jewish community. In the associations of mothers, grandmothers, and relatives of victims of repression the presence of people from the different churches was also significant. While all this participation took place in personal terms, the leadership positions of many of these participants were not unnoticed.

It needs to be said, however, that large sectors of the membership of these same communities, while remaining silent, disagreed with this participation, and some actively opposed it and cooperated with the military government. The "evangelical wing" of Protestantism, partly due to the influence of the politically conservative fundamentalism that these churches had received from their mother churches in the United States, and partly due to the political and social passivity of their piety and theology, on the whole remained silent.

We do not yet have the necessary knowledge and perspective to see how the different attitudes that religious people and institutions took during this period will affect the relation of religion to society and the state in the future. If we are to judge by the signs of their attitude in the years after the fall of the military regime, it could be said that, as they examine their own immediate past, there is a tendency to pay greater attention to what is happening in society and to assume a more critical and active interest in it. This is not only true of important sectors in the leadership of the Catholic and Protestant churches but also in the increasing political awareness and interest in Evangelical and

Pentecostal churches, which were characterized by reluctance to involve themselves in public life.

THE CONSTITUTIONAL REFORM

In Argentine law constitutional reform must be authorized by Congress. Members of the Constitutional Assembly are elected by popular vote and the Assembly, when elected, is sovereign. In 1993 Congress decided to call a Constitutional Assembly in 1994 and indicated the articles that it believed should be amended. The political background for this decision was an agreement between the Peronist and the Radical parties, and the main concern of the government was to introduce a change that would authorize the reelection of the president. However, other articles came up for revision and some were introduced as connected to those indicated by Congress. The only articles concerned with religious freedom which were identified by Congress for amendment were Article 76, which required that the president and vice-president must be Roman Catholics, and Article 80, which required an oath on "the Holy Gospel." In relation to our theme I would like to make several comments.

First, both the Catholic church and the associations of Protestant and Evangelical churches expressed their expectations and concerns on the coming reforms. They had to do not only with questions specifically related to the status of the churches and their relation to the state but also included a number of issues related to justice, human rights, and democratic participation.

The document published by the Catholic Episcopal Conference early in 1994[22] underlines in its preface the importance of the reference in the Preamble to God "as the source of all reason and justice" as confirming "our deepest roots, and giving meaning to our being as a Nation, which was born and has grown in the Christian faith." It relates this to the affirmation of human dignity, the right to life, and "the fundamental . . . rights that we call human rights." The rest of the document reaffirms the role of the Catholic church in Argentine culture, and devotes a section to the affirmation of human rights and the value of democratic participation. Several sections are devoted to social issues like work, family, education, social justice, and property rights, following the lines of the social teaching of the church. Chapter VII deals with the issue of religious freedom—which it affirms in the sense of the current Constitution and the pronouncements of Vatican II—and the relation of the church to the state, which it summarizes in three points:

a) the autonomy and independence of the Church and the political community; b) the possibility of a healthy cooperation on the basis that both societies are at the service of man; and c) freedom as the regulating principle.

It refers to the agreement reached in 1968 between the Holy See and the Argentine government.[23] It simply recognizes that the question of the religion of president and vice-president is left open, "which, since it is not considered a priority, although it is important, will not be discussed in this document." It includes two possible draft proposals if the article on religious freedom is modified. Both refer specifically to the Roman Catholic Church and guarantee freedom for all other religions.[24]

Several Protestant churches made statements about their desires and concerns for the Assembly. They are very similar and can be summarized in the brief declaration signed by the three associations of churches which represent practically all of the Protestants and Evangelicals in Argentina.[25] Concerning religious freedom and the status of churches, they request the elimination of articles which are anachronistic residues of the colonial time, such as the support of a single religion (Art. 2), the religion of the president and vice-president (Art. 76), and several other articles concerning the rights of the *patronato*. While this was to be expected, it is interesting to note the inclusion of social rights among their demands—involving minorities, education, old age, protection of single mothers, abortion, housing, rights of the native population—which "rather than mere enumeration require specific articles which can be translated by Congress into legislation." In another, more extensive document, the Ecumenical Movement for Human Rights requested the inclusion in the Constitution of international declarations and conventions on human rights, questions of environment, conscientious objection, and mechanisms of direct democracy.[26]

Two things should be noticed in all these declarations: On the one hand, the large measure of consensus of the Catholic and Protestant documents (with differences on the question of the unique relationship of Catholicism to the nation present in the Catholic document); on the other, the inclusion—even the priority—given to issues of human rights. The churches do not seem to be exclusively concerned with their own status and privileges but with the best possible legislation for the whole society and particularly for the interests of the less privileged.

Second, one of the preliminary debates in the Assembly itself concerned the possibility of including in the agenda the consideration of articles which were not contemplated in the agenda set by Congress. At this point, the majority formed by the alliance of the Peronist and Radical parties blocked this possibility, admitting only the possibility of articles that they considered directly related to those included by Congress. This decision was significant in relation to two questions on religious freedom requested by the Protestant churches and supported by a significant minority in the Assembly.

One is the crucial declaration of Article 2: "the Federal State supports the Roman Catholic Religion." Although a very large number of members of the Assembly (including many members of the majority) recognized that the article was related to the *patronato*, that it referred basically to financial support that is not very significant today, and that several Catholic bishops had indicated that the church would be ready to give up this financial support, the majority refused to include this article in the agenda because it was not specifically authorized by Congress. The proposal, on the other hand, did not reflect a "lay" or "antireligious" point of view. It was concerned, not with the nineteenth-century notion of separation of church and state, but with equality and freedom for all religious groups, churches, or movements. The text proposed to replace Article 2 was the following:

> The Federal Government admits all religions, forms of worship, and conceptions of the world compatible with this Constitution and, without any discrimination and in accordance with the laws, cooperates (*coadyuba*) in their development.[27]

According to the change already suggested by Congress the religious requirement for the president and vice-president (Art. 76) and the obligation of an oath on "the Holy Gospels" (Art. 80) were repealed. A number of articles which reflected the provisions of the *patronato*, such as the prohibition of priests as members of Congress, as well as the prerogatives of the president in the appointment of bishops or the admission of religious orders into the country were also repealed. Finally, Article 67, section 15, which included the conversion of the indigenous population to Catholicism among the duties of Congress, was repealed and instead a whole article (Art. 76, sec. 17) on the rights of the native populations was included.

Although not exclusively related to the question of religious freedom, it is interesting to note that all international declarations and conventions on human rights were given constitutional status—that is, a ranking equal to the Constitution and superior to ordinary legislation. This, in fact, means that they are part of the Constitution and can only be repealed by a Constitutional Assembly. The Constitution also provided for "Advocates of the People," a widely representative Judicial Council for the naming of judges, and significant steps in the direction of greater democratic participation and control in which religious bodies as well as civic and non-governmental organizations had a significant voice.

Third, one of the issues discussed in relation to Article 2 on the "support" of the Catholic church and Article 76 on the religion of the president and vice-president was the question of "national identity." During the Assembly a number of leaflets and pamphlets were circulated defending the thesis that Catholicism was a constitutive element of Argentine national identity, or even the central core of such identity and therefore that this should be reflected in the Constitution and laws. Frequently the expression "the national being" (*el ser nacional*) was used by nationalist groups, a term that is unfortunately related to various forms of nationalist fundamentalism in many parts of the world with the tragic consequences of discrimination, repression and even "ethnic cleansing" and genocide.

This question requires more careful consideration. It is not a question of denying the concept of national identity but of reflection on what constitutes the identity of a nation and how it is developed. Social sciences seem to teach us ever more clearly that the identity of a people is not a static and supra-historical entity but a self-perception, an "elaboration of social belonging" which is generated in the consciousness of a people by the interaction of objective conditions and inter-subjective creation. Such a process can only take place in relation to an external "other" (that is, the variety of different peoples) and with internal "others" (that is, the variety within a given people). Identity, therefore, is created from "identities"; there is no one and only way of being Argentine. And the interaction among these different ways of being Argentine is what gives rise to symbols broad enough to include this diversity. It is precisely the creation of excluding symbols that threatens the dissolution of "national identity."

This is the conception that inspires the 1853 Constitution, beginning with its Preamble, which does not define the nation on the basis of some foundational myth, or of ethnic, cultural, or religious purity, but on freedom, justice, and participation. Nationality is seen as created by "the will and decision of the people," as the consequence of "agreements" and "covenants" which have resolved conflicts and differences between the different provinces. Also for this reason the Preamble invites "all men of the world who would like to live" in this country. And, interestingly enough, when it invokes God, it does not speak of some ancestral, mythological, tribal deity but of "the source of all reason and justice," precisely the ethical foundations of a historical process of creating a nation.

No one could reasonably ignore or deny the fundamental importance that the Catholic religion and the Roman Catholic Church have had and continue to have in the construction of our national identity. The church's conception of the world, values, and ethical insights have been and will continue to be—even for those who do not profess the Catholic faith because we profess another faith or no religion at all—decisive in the life of our people. As *Gaudium et Spes*, a declaration of the Second Vatican Council, so forcefully puts it: It is in this "cooperation of all in the political life" of a nation that the church is called "to spread more and more the kingdom of justice and charity . . . preaching evangelical truth and illuminating all the sectors of human action with its doctrine and the testimony of Christians," promoting "the freedom and political responsibility of citizens." This is also the perspective of the Catholic episcopate and of the evangelical documents published on the occasion of the Convention.

The task of religion is carried out, fundamentally, within civil society, which is the natural environment of the conceptions of the world that find expression in art, legislation, and economic activity, that is, in the manifold manifestations of social life. It is there where values and norms are generated. In a democracy, the state preserves the institutional framework that allows and stimulates the free and ordered exercise of this activity of civil society. If, on the other hand, the state forbids, restricts, or arbitrarily limits these agreements and differences which appear in civil society, its domination loses legitimacy and becomes "pure and simple dictatorship." Of this we have abundant experience, in our countries and in others. The correct relation between the state and religious institutions is defined in this differentiation and cooperation of civil and political society—or, if we prefer to say it differently, between the "churches" and the state. This is precisely what is stated by the Catholic bishops in the statement quoted above: autonomy and independence, cooperation and liberty as the regulating principle.

POSTSCRIPT:
THE DEBATE ON THE LEGAL REGULATION OF RELIGION

Do we need a specific law regulating activities in the religious field? Is there need for state action to acknowledge its presence, establish basic conditions, and protect the rights and determine and control the duties and limitations of religious organizations? The question had not been debated in any significant way in Argentina until the 1940s. It was taken for granted that the constitutional provisions and the codes of law were enough.

Probably two facts produced a change that resulted in 1946 in the promulgation by the military government then in power of a decree creating a National Register of Religious Groups (*Fichero Nacional de Cultos*).[28] On the one hand, there was the growth of different religious movements—as indicated earlier in this chapter. On the other hand, there was the desire of an authoritarian government to control all activities in civil society. No doubt the concern of some Catholic authorities and groups with the increase of religious groups, perceived by some as an "invasion," also played a role in this decision. Are there "undesirable" sects which threaten the moral life of society or the identity of the nation? Can any form of "proselytism" be permissible? Should any religious group enjoy the protection of the law—including, for instance, exemption from taxes? Are there specific crimes which are related to forms of religious or para-religious behavior? That this was a concern is clearly seen in the argument used in 1946 for the creation of this institution: "the proselytizing action developed in recent years throughout the territory of the Republic by religious groups other than the religion of the state."

Two years later, the Congress of the elected—Peronist—government repealed the decree. But, curiously enough, the Executive reinstated it in a "softer" version in which offensive expressions had been eliminated but the controlling functions continued to be basically the same. The National Federation of Protestant Churches, with the support of practically all the Protestant and Evangelical churches in the country, made several presentations asking for the annulment of the decree, offering juridical reasons based on the Constitution, but their requests were first postponed and then rejected.[29] The elected Radical government in 1959 did not eliminate the Register but softened its function and inaugurated a sort of "gentlemen's agreement," as Prof. Alberto Soggin argues. His conclusion, however, was that "the situation is far from being solved and one of the main factors is precisely the content of the new 1959 decree which, instead of abrogating the restrictive and unconstitutional provisions, has simply repeated them in a less polemical and restrictive language."[30]

In 1968 the military government of General Onganía produced two significant changes in the relation of the churches and the state. One was the signature of a concordat with the Holy See which in fact terminated the *patronato*, giving the church freedom from the control by the state that the *patronato* represented. In fact, such dispositions were obsolete and had fallen completely in disuse. The 1994 reform of the Constitution—as we have seen—eliminated most of the articles related to this situation.

The other change was the reestablishment of the Register of Religious Bodies (*Registro de Cultos*) in more or less the same terms that it had under previous military governments. The Register continued to operate in the Peronist government and was confirmed and strengthened by the military coup of 1976. In fact, during the military regimes it became an instrument of control and repression that particularly threatened Pentecostal churches, Jehovah's Witnesses, Mormons, and Afro-American cults like Umbanda and Macumba. In some border provinces or small villages, real persecution, arbitrary closing of worship places, and intimidation by the police were not unknown. Officially, the Roman Catholic Church did not express any opinion on this whole development. Personally, some bishops, while very critical of the role of these so-called sects and their influence in society, supported their right to enjoy religious freedom and exhorted Catholics not to respond with violence or rejection but to see them as a challenge to increase, deepen, and purify their faith and commitment.[31] Other prelates of the church and particularly some Catholic "experts" on sects, on the other hand, have frequently asked for the intervention of the state to control and limit the operation of groups which they characterized as "dangerous," *disolventes* ("dissolving," destroying the cohesion of society), or plainly immoral.

After the return to democracy in 1983 several bills were presented in Congress for laws on "religious freedom" or the "Registration of Religious Bodies." Some were clearly repressive, like that presented by Congressman Piotti, the first article of which stated: "In all the national territory the activity, of any nature or form, of any religious group other than the Roman Catholic Apostolic, unless it is duly registered in the National Register of Religious Groups (*Cultos*) of the Ministry of Foreign Affairs, Foreign Trade, and Worship, is forbidden." The introduction to the bill, after an affirmation of religious liberty, adds: "but it is different in the case of the sects . . . which constitute totalitarian groups that, under pretense of being religious entities . . . use techniques of mental control or coercive persuasion." It accuses some of these groups of "atrocities . . . generally against minors" and "perverse sexual practices." The bill did not succeed in Congress. In view of these initiatives, the "Section for Non-Catholic Religion" of the Ministry of Foreign Affairs and Worship, sometimes in consultation with Protestant/Evangelical, Anglican, Orthodox, and Jewish religious representatives, has been working on a law of

"Religious Freedom" which would take the place of the Register. The proposals have been discussed and modified several times.

Due to the limitations of space, I will make some brief comments on these proposals. It is clear that almost all the Protestant churches are critical of such a law. Although present relations with the authorities that have drafted this project are excellent and the most recent drafts have stressed the enabling aspects and carefully limited the more controlling or possibly restrictive aspects, even making registration voluntary and noncompulsory, it is difficult not to be concerned about the possibility of a less democratic administration using the law as a repressive instrument. Therefore, when organizations like the Federation of Evangelical Churches and the Pentecostal Confederation agree on the value of such a law, they are in fact choosing what they think is "the lesser evil." In fact, this has been frequently the argument of the government. It is very difficult not to see in this legislation the expression of a conscious or unconscious desire to "clean up" the religious scene. There is no doubt that the evangelistic and proselytizing activities of not a few religious groups are morally questionable and in Christian terms repugnant. It is also true that at some points some of the groups—let us say, for instance, "Satanic sects"—border on the criminal. But, attempts to codify specifically religious crimes become a very dangerous exercise. The characterizations proposed for such a law include crimes like "psychic compulsion," "contempt of, or offense to other religious beliefs," "psychic capture of people," etc., which are so close to the subjective that they easily lend themselves to abuse and persecution. The historical experience of such attempts to separate the wheat from the chaff should be enough to warn us against the attempt to define too closely the limits of religious freedom. The price paid for such "cleansing" has been too high. It is very difficult to imagine a religious crime or a religious fraud which could not be contained and punished by the secular civil and criminal codes and regulations. The rest would have to be left to the free market, the price and liabilities of which we seem to be quite ready to accept in the social, economic, or communications field as a cost of democratic, personal, and social freedom.

We may conclude, looking back on the history that we have outlined, that Argentina has moved slowly—more slowly than most other Latin American countries—but surely toward the regime of religious freedom that characterizes all of the modern nations of the West. The remaining survivals of an earlier monopolistic regime will gradually or rapidly be replaced by the pluralism and liberty that is required ethically and politically in a regime of democracy and freedom.

12.

BRAZIL

Religious Tolerance, Church-State Relations, and the Challenge of Pluralism

———————◆———————

Kenneth P. Serbin

This chapter surveys the evolution of religious freedom and church-state relations in Brazil. It begins with an overview of Christian missionary activity from the colonial period to the end of the First Republic (1889-1930). It then analyzes the prominent role of the Catholic Church in politics from 1930 to the present, especially during the military dictatorship (1964-85). The Church's political activism provides the framework for understanding current church-state relations and interreligious competition. In its relationship with the state the Church has gone through three quite different but not mutually exclusive phases: from "moral concordat" to "moral opposition"[1] to "moral watchdog." The moral concordat has been the dominant mode, and it has served as the model for other religions that have sought state ties in recent years. A third section examines the explosive growth of Pentecostalism in the post–World War II era and the onset of religious competition during democratic consolidation after 1985. It focuses specifically on competition for believers, the electoral process, attempts to win access to the state and its resources, and a recent example of religious conflict. The chapter concludes with an analysis of the structural conditions for religious freedom in Brazil.

The distinctive characteristics of the world's largest Catholic nation have equipped it better than most Latin American nations to deal with the challenges of religious freedom and evangelization in the new world (dis)order. As in Spanish America, in Brazil controversies over religious freedom and evangelization historically have revolved around the struggles between the Catholic Church and the state. But church-state difficulties of the nineteenth century did little to disrupt society. During this period religion played a role in politics, but it was not the central issue that it was in Mexico until the 1930s, for example. The predominantly conservative tenor of the Brazilian Empire (1822-89) kept the liberal-conservative division minimal.[2] Reflecting the general trend in the region, in the last half century the large growth in the number and membership of Protestant Pentecostal denominations has created religious plurality, reduced the traditional monopoly of Catholicism as a semi-official religion, and most recently, increased interreligious competition and the potential for conflict. Yet the nature of the new competing religions as products of Brazilian culture tends to work against conflict. When it has occurred, religious conflict has been the result of political struggles at the level of the leadership. These struggles are related to the "moral concordat" of the state with the Catholic Church, which is a structural limit on religious freedom. Brazil's cultural and religious syncretism, diversity, and malleability have made it a country of relative tolerance and freedom with respect to beliefs and practices. People often profess loyalty to more than one religion simultaneously, and increasingly they switch religions. Rather than reject new ideas and influences, Brazilian culture assimilates and reinterprets them. The emergence of two uniquely indigenous and syncretistic religions has exemplified the mutational tendency of Brazilian religion: the nationalistic Umbanda, which is a mixture of Catholicism, the African *candomblé*, French spiritism, and Amerindian beliefs; and the Universal Church of the Kingdom of God, a modern Pentecostal religion that includes elements of Catholicism and assumes the existence of the Afro-Brazilian spiritual universe. Both religions rose out of the culture and, in contrast with Catholicism and many Protestant denominations, were not a project of a pre-existing organization.

MISSIONARY ACTIVITY IN BRAZILIAN HISTORY

Like the Spaniards, the Portuguese colonized the Americas under a union of the cross and the sword. The settlers brought to Brazil a violent "warrior" Catholicism steeled in the reconquest of the Iberian Peninsula and embodied in a reverence for saints with martial qualities.[3] But Portuguese colonial Catholicism was less fanatical and more private than its Spanish counterpart. It revolved principally around familial, communitarian, and other popular devotions, in part because of the highly personalistic and paternalistic rule of the slave-plantation system, but also because the Portuguese crown jealously restricted the growth of the institutional Church. By the 1800s Brazil was notorious for its morally lax clergy and the institutional Church's tenuous ties to the people. Moreover, unlike Spanish America, Brazil had no permanent seat of the Inquisition. In the vacuum of ecclesiastical authority Brazil developed a highly varied and complex religious culture combining Catholicism and the religious traditions of both the natives and the Americas' largest community of African slaves.

Brazil did not experience the fierce post-independence struggles over the power of the Catholic Church fought between liberals and conservatives elsewhere in Latin America. Brazil alone remained a monarchy after independence (1822), which was achieved with relatively little violence. The smooth transition from colony to nation brought relative political stability. In general the Church supported the Empire by operating as part of the state bureaucracy and lending religious and ideological legitimacy. In the 1870s bishops and imperial officials clashed over state intervention in ecclesiastical matters, but this elite affair had little social impact. Nevertheless, severe state regulation exacerbated the Church's institutional weakness, particularly among the religious orders. In 1872 only 2,363 priests ministered to a population of almost ten million spread over Brazil's vast area. Only 107 of these men belonged to the religious orders.[4]

Imperial Brazil showed great tolerance toward Protestantism. The highly unusual transfer of the Portuguese court to Rio de Janeiro during the Napoleonic wars took place under the aegis of Britain, thus favoring the importation of Protestantism. In 1810 the two countries signed a commercial treaty that opened Brazil's ports to foreign trade and cultural influences. The agreement guaranteed religious freedom for British citizens and prepared the way for the arrival of the Anglican Church. In addition, the Constitution of 1824 maintained Catholicism as the state creed but allowed other believers to worship in unmarked churches. Missionaries from other Protestant denominations soon arrived in various regions from both Great Britain and the United States, and German immigrant communities built a strong Protestant niche in Brazil's deep south. Although some Catholic protest did occur, the missionaries were generally well received and caused little controversy. The North American Methodist missionary Daniel Kidder, who arrived in Brazil in 1837, commented that in "no other Catholic country did there exist greater tolerance or freeness of feeling toward Protestants." The relative weakness of the Catholic infrastructure, the lack of clergy, and the people's deep spirituality provided further opportunity for the missionaries. Some scholars have noted a great degree of similarity between the conditions preceding Luther's Reform and the situation in Brazil in the early 1800s, for example, the low moral status of the clergy and a growing popular interest in the Bible. Protestant missionaries freely distributed the Holy Scriptures, at times with the express support of the authorities. The epitome of Brazilian receptivity was an individual known as the "Protestant priest," Father José Manuel da Conceição. Conceição left the Catholic ministry to work as a Presbyterian missionary and embraced the ideas of the Reformation. But he also continued many of his Catholic ways, for example, his itinerant preaching in the style of St. Francis. His mixture of beliefs and practices provided an example of a uniquely "Brazilian Evangelical spirituality."[5]

The positivist-inspired military officers who toppled the monarchy disestablished the Catholic Church and guaranteed religious freedom, written into the Constitution of 1891. They ended subsidies to Catholic activities, secularized education, and generally weakened the Church's position in Brazilian society. This process was peaceful. Although the bishops opposed the loss of Catholicism's official status, they welcomed freedom from state control.

However, even before disestablishment the bishops had begun to rebuild the institutional Church in the hopes of increasing its social influence. In the 1850s they inaugurated an era of "Romanization," a Vatican-oriented campaign for the conservative modernization and moralization of Brazilian Catholicism. This movement was the second great wave of Catholic missionary work in Brazil. It flourished under republican religious freedom and lasted into the 1950s. For the first time the Brazilian Church adopted the highly disciplinary model of seminary training established at the Council of Trent in the sixteenth century. Directed by a growing corps of priests either born or educated in Europe, the new system reduced the proportion of Brazilians among the clergy and strengthened ties to the papacy. Additionally, the Church opened schools for the children of the elite and preached to the masses about moral order and obedience to authority.[6] Romanization and republican religious freedom reinvigorated the institutional Church as it created dozens of new dioceses and imported thousands of priests and nuns.[7] By the late 1920s the Church's highly educated cadres were running social assistance projects, publications, schools, convents, and seminaries. They had also become ingrained in local and regional networks of power.[8]

Romanization, however, worked against religious freedom. As the Church expanded, it attempted to impose Catholic orthodoxy on the populace. Romanization became intertwined with the Europeanizing tendencies of the First Republic. Pastors "Europeanized" religious customs by essentially seizing control of popular Catholicism and substituted uniform rituals under priestly authority for varied and numerous lay practices, including folk healing and spiritism. When total control was not possible, the clergy reformed local practices.[9] The starkest example was the 1897 massacre at Canudos, one of the formative events of modern Brazilian political elitism and authoritarianism. This large religious settlement in the backlands of the state of Bahia had an inward-looking, millenarian, monarchist worldview of popular Catholicism that contrasted sharply with the urban middle and upper classes, whose Eurocentrism meshed well with Romanization. After the local clergy failed to convince Canudos's charismatic and deeply religious founder Antônio Conselheiro to disperse the community, the military destroyed it to the applause and relief of the coastal elite.[10] In contrast with their more liberal nineteenth-century predecessors, the Catholic clergy also began to oppose Protestantism overtly.[11]

THE CATHOLIC CHURCH AND POLITICAL ACTIVISM SINCE 1930

Romanization spawned an ideology of neo-Christendom, which posited a Catholic religious monopoly and a central role for the Church through influence on the state and on the middle and upper classes.[12] As the Church grew stronger, Brazil's leaders acknowledged it as a bulwark of social stability. By the time Getúlio Vargas (1930-45, 1951-54) rose to power in the Revolution of 1930, the Church was poised to play an important role in national politics.[13]

The Revolution of 1930 defeated the old oligarchical elite, inaugurated an era of urban-based populist politics, and traced the first outline of the modern Brazilian state with its paradoxical combination of authoritarianism and democracy. In the volatile post-revolutionary political atmosphere Vargas sought Church legitimation of his regime. He publicly recognized the power of the Church and established an informal pact of cooperation, which one bishop dubbed the "moral concordat."[14] The Church offered the state ideology, moral content, and models of social discipline, and it backed Vargas's emerging corporatist system by aiming to "respiritualize culture" and foster cooperation among social classes.[15] Corporatism resonated strongly with Church teachings on social unity and against class struggle and Communism, which emerged as a political alternative in the 1930s. In return the Church received state support in the cultural and religious spheres. The Constitution of 1934, for example, contained all of the proposals made by the Church, such as, promulgation of the document in the name of God, the indissolubility of marriage, civil recognition of the legal validity of religious marriage, rights for Catholic unions, and freedom of education.[16] Vargas further granted the Church state subsidies, which helped it to expand the social infrastructure by building hospitals, charitable organizations, schools, and universities. Strictly ecclesiastical projects also benefited, for example, the construction of the National Basilica of Aparecida, which became a major symbol of devotion to Our Lady.[17] (Aparecida was recognized as Brazil's patroness by the pope in 1931. Her status among the people parallels that of the Virgin of Guadalupe in Mexico. In 1980 the government designated her day, October 12, as a national holiday.[18]) In light of Vatican concordats with Italy, Germany, and a dozen other countries, Church and state in Brazil contemplated a formal accord. None was reached, however, presumably because of Church fears that it would fall under the control of Vargas's authoritarian Estado Novo (1937-45), which repressed political organizations and closed the National Congress.[19] Nevertheless, the pact endured and continued under President Eurico Gaspar Dutra (1946-51), the second Vargas government, and the administrations of Juscelino Kubitschek (1956-61), Jânio Quadros (1961), and João Goulart (1961-64).

In the 1930s the Protestants made their first entrance into Brazilian politics in order to combat Catholic claims. In preparation for the Constituent Assembly of 1933-34 a confederation of Protestants opposed the Church's goals. For instance, they called for complete separation of church and state and opposed religious education in the schools. They also wanted to permit divorce and advocated a number of social-democratic planks that went against the more conservative Catholic program. Guaracy Silveira, a Methodist pastor, was elected to the Assembly on the ticket of the Brazilian Socialist Party. He protested Catholic influence within the state such as the use of public money for seminaries and congresses. Though far outnumbered by pro-Catholic members of the Assembly, his outspokenness kept the state from establishing even tighter ties with the Catholic Church.[20]

After World War II the Church's effort to influence Brazilian society led it on a campaign of organizational and political transformation which had profound implications for both political and religious freedom. Led by Archbishop Dom Hélder Câmara, the Brazilian Church both anticipated and revolutionized the plan for Catholic renovation and social justice laid out at the Second Vatican Council (1962-65) and its more radical Latin American sequel at Medellín, Colombia (1968). Furthermore, during these years a small but strong Catholic left emerged to participate in national and grassroots politics. Previously moderate Catholic Action groups radicalized and took leadership roles in society. The Catholic University Youth supplied cadres to the student movement and the Church's Basic Education Movement (a literacy campaign), while the Young Catholic Workers became involved in labor organizing. Another group was *Ação Popular* (Popular Action), a Catholic University Youth offshoot that grew increasingly revolutionary in the late 1960s. In the early 1960s the clergy started forming the first grassroots Church communities known as *Comunidades Eclesiais de Base* (CEBs). Like liberation theology, the CEBs inherited critical social views from Catholic Action and a grassroots political pedagogy inspired by the methods of the Brazilian educator Paulo Freire.[21] Much of the Church, however, remained traditional and rejected the innovations of reformers and radicals. (These internal differences foreshadowed the conservative reaction of the 1980s.) The political changes in the Church occurred as the armed forces prepared their 1964 overthrow of President Goulart, whom they accused of preparing a leftist takeover of Brazil. The bishops, especially the conservatives, thanked the generals for saving the country from Communism. For five years the Catholic hierarchy generally supported the regime. However, the military's attempt to modernize Brazil through rapid capitalist accumulation and a highly repressive national security policy caused the worst Church-state clash in Brazilian history. As a result, the Church came to lead the moral opposition against the regime.

The turning point came in December 1968, when hardline officers took control of the regime, closed the Congress, eliminated civil liberties and freedom of the press, and arrested members of the opposition. Brazil plunged into a small-scale civil war. Leftist guerrillas swung into action, while the security forces fiercely counterattacked, torturing thousands of people to obtain information. The "dirty war" against subversives resulted in 184 deaths and 138 disappearances. By 1973 the military had liquidated the guerrillas and relaxed the repression, although shocking incidents continued throughout the 1970s.[22] Scores of priests, nuns, bishops, and Catholic militants were targeted by the security forces. By the end of the military regime in 1985 six clerics had been killed, including one of Dom Hélder Câmara's assistants. Bishops were harassed; in one 1976 incident a squad of right-wing terrorists kidnaped and tortured a prelate. The attacks on the Church often caused the bishops to forget their theological differences and to unite in defense of their institution.

The Church frequently criticized the repression, thus making human rights a centerpiece of its moral opposition. The bishops in particular transcended their role as traditional religious leaders wedded to the elite. The National Conference of the Brazilian Bishops (CNBB) became a powerful "voice of the voiceless" by speaking on behalf of the political opposition and defending the victims of torture. Dom Hélder Câmara was highly influential in this campaign but after 1970 had to recede into the background because of harassment by the regime. Under Cardinal Paulo Evaristo Arns the Archdiocese of São Paulo assumed leadership of the human rights movement and became a major reference point for the opposition.[23] In 1975, for instance, Cardinal Arns, two rabbis, and Pastor Jaime Wright led an ecumenical memorial service for the well-known Jewish journalist Vladimir Herzog, who was tortured to death in a São Paulo interrogation center on suspicion of links to Communists. This key protest helped reawaken the opposition.[24] Working more quietly, the national Pontifical Peace and Justice Commission located in Rio de Janeiro also denounced human rights violations to the authorities. The Church's efforts culminated in 1985 with the publication of the São Paulo archdiocesan report *Brasil: Nunca Mais (Brazil: Never Again)*. Using military court records spirited away by lawyers and others, it provided detailed documentary evidence of torture and other abuses. Significantly, this was an ecumenical effort in which Cardinal Arns collaborated with Pastor Wright and received support from the World Council of Churches.[25] The 1979 amnesty law prevented prosecution of torturers, and only in 1996 did the civilian government set up an official commission to account for deaths and disappearances. Thus, the *Brasil: Nunca Mais* project was one of the most important developments in the redemocratization process.[26]

During the 1970s the Church extended the notion of human rights to cover socioeconomic oppression. As political activism among the clergy and lay militants increased, the small but highly influential progressive leadership of the CNBB worked with them to create CEBs and political programs for the poor that together became known as the Brazilian "Popular Church" or the "People's Church." The grist of liberation theology, these innovations gave rise to the "preferential option for the poor" officially adopted by the Latin American bishops at their 1979 conference in Puebla, Mexico. These developments were nothing short of a watershed in a region where the institutional Church had always safeguarded its privileges and power by supporting the status quo. The Brazilian Church in particular gained distinction among the world's religious organizations for its prophetic role.[27] As one analyst has noted, the Church's moral legitimacy and "capacity to empower civil society" greatly influenced the political liberalization that led to the exit of the military from power in 1985.[28]

Moral opposition, however, did not obviate attempts to preserve the moral concordat. From 1970 to 1974 the leading bishops and representatives of the government met in secret meetings known as the Bipartite Commission. The bishops proposed collaboration with the regime based on the Medellín Bishops' Conference document's principles of social justice. Moreover, they qualified their public opposition with private understandings in an attempt to control the radical grass roots and avoid a deepening of the Church-state fissure. To their credit they also used the Bipartite Commission skillfully to press the regime on human rights abuses. The generals reciprocated little and rejected Medellín as subversive, maintaining that the regime was already working toward social justice through its economic programs. Nevertheless, the Bipartite Commission defused Church-state crises, thereby allowing the military and the clergy to coexist during the worst moments of the dictatorship. The Bipartite Commission was especially significant because it demonstrated that the bishops were in effect proposing a modernized version of the "moral concordat." They wanted to see the Church continue in its leading political role as a semi-official religion, only now in the name of social justice and human rights rather than purely institutional and religious interests.[29]

As Brazil gradually redemocratized in the 1980s the Church receded from political activism. Several factors contributed to this trend. First, the Church did not view itself as a political organization and much less a political party. It therefore encouraged the many political groups and social movements that had emerged with crucial Church support during the dictatorship—unions, political parties, grassroots movements, and nongovernmental organizations— to take the lead in the new democracy. These groups assumed much of the work in human rights and social movements earlier carried out by the Church.[30] Second, a neo-conservative reaction within the Church rolled back or restricted many innovations of Vatican II and Medellín. A staunch anti-Communist who criticized Marxist influence on liberation theology, Pope John Paul II wanted the Brazilian clergy to sever its ties to leftist political causes. Moreover, under him the Vatican punished liberation theologians such as Brazil's Leonardo Boff, warned progressive bishops, intervened in religious orders, censored publications, nominated scores of conservative bishops, curtailed the power of the Bishops' Conference, and subdivided the Archdiocese of São Paulo, effectively undercutting Cardinal Arns's authority. At the local level bishops suspended activist priests and restricted grassroots initiatives. Significantly, in May 1995 the CNBB elected its first conservative president in twenty-five years.[31] Third, the Popular Church's prestige fell with the collapse of Communism and the resultant retreat of the Latin American left into introspection.[32] Furthermore, it is now clear that the Church of the Poor simply failed to attract most of the poor. Although low estimates of their membership have been too pessimistic, CEBs still include but a small fraction of the population. In some instances they have even proven to be *exclusionary* toward such groups as women with domestic problems, youths, and Afro-Brazilians,[33] although large numbers of the last group do participate.[34]

The Church kept the progressive legacy alive by becoming the moral watchdog of Brazilian democracy and continuing to speak out on national issues. Progressive ideas interpenetrated political structures and social movements throughout the post-1985 period. For instance, the previously unknown concepts of human rights are now part of the political landscape, thanks to the Church's campaign during the authoritarian era. Many popular and nongovernmental organizations include individuals who got their political start in religious groups such as the CEBs. The highly successful socialist-oriented *Partido dos Trabalhadores* (PT, or Workers' Party) has had a large contingent of Catholic grassroots activists. PT presidential candidate Luís Inácio Lula da Silva received key support from progressives in the 1989 and 1994 elections. After 1985 the Church continued to denounce injustice, demand a more equal economic order, and support radical groups such as the *Movimento dos Sem-Terra* (Movement of the Landless), which focused on the land conflicts that had continued unabated from the days of the military regime into the mid-1990s. The Church was also highly critical of the neo-liberal economic policies initiated by President Fernando Collor de Mello (1990-92) and carried on by President Fernando Henrique Cardoso (1995–). Furthermore, the Church demonstrated a remarkable ability to adapt to and shape the new political conjunctures and structures of the post-authoritarian era.[35] For instance, the Bishops' Conference stood in the forefront of the efforts to draft a new constitution, which was promulgated in 1988. The Church's agenda for the constitution stressed social justice and the rights and responsibilities of citizenship.[36] The Church further attempted to bolster the democratic order through voter-education programs that emphasized issues over traditional patronage politics. It also preached ethical behavior as an antidote to the myriad of corruption scandals that plagued the government, including the one leading to Collor's impeachment in 1992. Most of these ideas resonated with the Church's traditional social doctrine, which had indirectly inspired liberation theology and had the approval of the Pope.

Because the Church as moral watchdog was an updated, more socially conscious version of the "moral concordat," it kept some traditional planks in its post-authoritarian platform. It advocated the protection of the family, opposed the sterilization of women and abortion (an issue during the Constitutional Assembly that pitted feminists against the bishops), and successfully fought to keep religious instruction permissible in the public schools. In effect, the Church remained one of the major determinants of the Brazilian moral code.[37] Nor did the Church lose sight of vital institutional and religious activities. Although the Church recognized that a full return to the "moral concordat" is impossible in an increasingly pluralistic society, some bishops and clergy returned to the style of high-level political contact and lobbying that had characterized the pre-1964 era. In 1989 the Vatican and the Brazilian armed forces signed an agreement reactivating the military chaplaincy, thus sealing a peace between two of the leading adversaries of the authoritarian period. Significantly, two years later representatives of the CNBB and the Collor government quietly began negotiations on a Church-state protocol. The talks stalled under Cardoso, but specific elements of the draft agreement illustrated Church intentions, such as recognition of the legal validity of religious marriage, enactment of the constitutional provision for religious instruction in the public schools and religious assistance in public hospitals, and creation of a legal distinction between the Catholic Church and other religions. Furthermore, as European funding organizations turned away from Latin America in favor of the former Communist bloc, the Church sought state protection of its financial assets and philanthropic organizations. Because of the apparent ineffectiveness of neoliberal economic policies in alleviating social problems, the state continued to value the Church's social assistance activities.[38]

RELIGIOUS COMPETITION IN BRAZIL'S NEW DEMOCRACY

The Church's concern with institutional and religious interests must be seen against the background of increasing religious pluralism and competition from Afro-Brazilian religions such as *candomblé* and Umbanda and especially Protestant Pentecostal denominations.

At the start of the 1900s a first wave of Pentecostal missionaries had gained a foothold in Brazil. As urbanization accelerated in the 1950s and Catholicism's traditional rural parish structure began to disintegrate, a second wave of Pentecostals increased Protestant growth through the preaching of faith healing and revivals. African religions also began to grow rapidly. In the 1980s yet a third wave of new denominations increased Pentecostal growth.[39] The leading example was the fast-growing Universal Church of the Kingdom of God. According to census data, at the midpoint of this century more than 90 percent of Brazilians still adhered to Catholicism. Today the Catholic Church itself admits that as few as 75 percent of Brazil's 155 million people now belong to this faith.[40] Protestants' share of the population has grown from 2 percent in the 1930s to 4 percent in 1960 to approximately 13 percent in 1992. In 1996 the figure was estimated at 15 percent.[41] One oft-cited study states that one new Protestant church opens every day in the greater metropolitan area of Rio de Janeiro.[42]

Modern Brazil has provided a milieu in which Pentecostals have found the most effective methods for gaining new members using a variety of pastoral tactics: greater lay participation; emphasis on the Bible; exorcism; emotional spirituality; revivals and miracle healing; moralizing against drinking and adultery; and the acceptance of people with afflictions not addressed by Catholicism or traditional Protestantism. In short, Pentecostals have had greater success because they have responded more effectively to people's suffering, needs, and fears than either conservative or progressive Catholicism.[43] In contrast with the Catholic hierarchy's uncompromising stance, the Universal Church has also shown signs of greater flexibility on questions of human reproduction such as abortion and birth control.[44] At the same time, however, it should be acknowledged that the Pentecostals have grown also because of the same social forces of rapid modernization that have fostered the growth of the Catholic CEBs. CEBs and Pentecostalism lie in denominational tension but also share many sociological roots.[45]

Catholic-military conflict during the authoritarian era provided an opportunity for other religions to seek accommodation with the state. Although most of the armed forces remained Catholic, some sectors promoted Umbanda and Pentecostalism as a way to offset progressive Catholicism. Repressed during the Estado Novo and combated by the Church in the 1950s, by 1964 the nationalistic, syncretistic Umbanda had drawn 4 percent of the officer corps. During the military regime its popularity increased. The military not only allowed Umbanda to operate freely, but also helped it institutionalize by recognizing its holidays, counting its members in the census, and moving its tens of thousands of religious centers from police to civil jurisdiction.[46] Some military support also went to Pentecostals. In the Amazon region, for instance, they received open support from Jarbas Passarinho, a retired colonel who served as governor of the state of Pará and then as minister of education.[47] Nevertheless, the stereotypical image of Protestants as especially strong supporters of the regime is false. Opportunities for Protestants existed but were limited. The regime needed Protestant support for political, not religious reasons. In fact, Protestant representation did not grow in the military-controlled Congress, and three of their leaders were persecuted by the regime for working with the opposition.[48]

The new political freedom of the post-1985 era accentuated religious pluralism and competition by allowing churches new and old a greater variety of ways to spread their message and to gain access to the state. Emphasis on church-state issues shifted from the dichotomous ideological struggle between the Catholic hierarchy and the military to more traditional concerns such as state subsidies, collaboration, and electoral bargaining. Church-state dialogue became more complex because of the increasing strength and aggressiveness of the Pentecostals.[49]

While some Pentecostal denominations expanded with the aid of North American sponsors in earlier periods, causing some Brazilians to charge that an imperialist conspiracy was afoot,[50] most have gained a momentum of their own. The Assemblies of God and the Foursquare Gospel Church are two examples of imported denominations that long ago became "Brazilianized" and are now independent of their North American brothers. Recent creations are uniquely Brazilian. They are part of a more dynamic, syncretistic form of Pentecostalism referred to by some scholars as Neo-Pentecostals.[51]

The prime example is the Universal Church (*Igreja Universal do Reino de Deus*). It combines elements of Pentecostalism, Umbanda, and Catholicism. Started in 1977, by the mid-1990s it had hundreds of churches across Brazil and a membership of several million. It collected as much as $1 billion per year in tithes and owned the country's third-largest television network, thirty radio stations, two newspapers, a bank, and other business interests. The Universal Church rapidly spread overseas, setting up churches in other parts of Latin America, the United States, Europe, and Africa.[52]

Like other Pentecostal denominations, the Universal Church has attracted members from the poorest and least educated segments of the population.[53]

Accordingly, it has based its pastoral model on three theological responses to the primary needs and desires of these segments and the magical aspects of Brazilian popular culture: (1) claims of cures of any and all diseases, including cancer and AIDS; (2) exorcism, which is mainly aimed at the Afro-Brazilian spiritism which suffuses much of the populace; and (3) promises of financial success.[54] The church's "prosperity theology," in which God becomes the business partner of the individual believer, has cut away all taboos about mixing money and religion and has formed the basis of its economic empire.[55]

The success of this method has hinted at shifts in Brazilian society and culture. While Catholicism has always represented a public and civic religion to which all Brazilians had access without charge, the Universal Church has tended to privatize religion and to make it a paid service in which the believer is constantly exhorted to make donations in return for material blessings. Increasingly, Brazilians are no longer born into a religion (Catholicism) to which they will adhere their entire lives but instead are faced with the need to *choose* a religion in an ever more varied religious *marketplace*. Conversion is now a common activity, and the dissatisfied believer retains the right to switch.[56] Religion is no longer a unifying force; the tendency is toward the *separation* of the populace into distinct religious groups.[57]

Pentecostal growth and cultural change have begun changing the face of Brazilian politics. Brazilian democracy has become witness not only to competition over flocks, but to a Pentecostal effort to end the Catholic Church's status as Brazil's semi-official religion. As early as the 1930s progressive Protestants sought to keep the Brazilian state religiously neutral, though without success. In the 1980s and 1990s the Pentecostals and in particular the Universal Church have sought to *occupy* the Catholic position alongside the state. Edir Macedo, the founder and self-designated head bishop of the Universal Church, nearly achieved his goal of offering the invocation at Collor's inauguration.[58] Such an achievement would have had enormous symbolic and political impact and would have been a watershed in Brazilian history even more significant than Lutheran Ernesto Geisel's role as the first Protestant president to serve a full term (1974-78) and the (military-controlled) Congress's approval of a divorce law during his tenure.[59]

To achieve their goals the Pentecostal churches have sought formal political power. In 1986 the Pentecostals showed an impressive performance in the Constitutional Assembly election with eighteen candidates elected. Including other Protestants, the so-called *bancada evangélica* (Evangelical Coalition) totaled thirty-six representatives. They were not members of the traditional political elite but new participants in the political process who were elected because of their church connections. While the small number of earlier Protestant representatives tended toward progressive ideologies and wanted a strict separation of churches and state, the new generation was more conservative and prepared to use the state for its ends. The Pentecostal representatives openly defended the interests of their churches, sought government resources and privileges in competition with the Catholic Church, and obtained valuable television concessions in return for their support of the Sarney government, in particular his successful campaign to modify the Constitution to obtain a fifth year in power. As a result, the *bancada evangélica* gained a reputation for practicing the crass patronage politics and deal-making known in Brazil as *fisiologismo*.[60] The Pentecostals were especially successful at using their new media resources to reinforce their political strength, and vice versa. The Universal Church used its influence with Collor and Cardoso administration officials as it built its business and religious strength in the 1990s. In the 1990 election the *bancada evangélica* dropped to twenty-three members, but the Universal Church increased its representation from one to three members and in 1994 to six, including the sister of Bishop Macedo.

The Pentecostals used the media and direct appeals to the faithful to support conservative candidates in presidential and other major executive branch elections. In 1989 Pentecostals, especially the Universal Church, supported Collor. The Universal Church demonized Lula as a Communist in its publications. In subsequent elections Universal Church pastors continued to urge their followers to vote for specific candidates. In the 1990s candidates from several parties began to seek the support of Bishop Macedo and other Pentecostal churches. In 1996, for instance, José Serra, who had belonged to the radical Catholic *Ação Popular* in the 1960s, ran for mayor of São Paulo on the ticket of President Cardoso's centrist Brazilian Social Democratic Party. He was criticized by Cardinal Arns and other Catholic leaders for negotiating support from the Universal Church in exchange for alleged favors from the Cardoso government.[61] The Universal Church has also plugged into traditional patronage networks once considered the domain of the Catholic Church.

In another apparent shift in Brazilian religious competition and politics, some Pentecostals have bet on conflict as a way for gaining converts and creating political incidents. Since its inception the Universal Church has verbally and physically attacked the followers and rituals of the Afro-Brazilian religions. Like all Protestant churches, the Universal Church does not accept the special position of the Virgin Mary. Attacks on Mary became part of its repertoire against the Catholic Church. This tactic came shockingly to light in 1995 when a Universal Church pastor caused a national, media-generated scandal by kicking an image of Our Lady of Aparecida on television on October 12. The Universal Church used the incident as a theological attack on the Catholic Church and other religions but also against the Globo network, the country's largest network and an obstacle to the Universal Church's attempt to consolidate its media empire. The incident prompted the police and federal authorities to launch a major investigation of Universal Church activities and finances,[62] although bureaucratic inertia had produced little results as of early 1998. The Aparecida incident dragged on for months and caused some to speak of an incipient "holy war" in Brazil, although such a possibility was generated by media hype more than anything else.[63]

The Catholic Church's response to Pentecostal growth has been long in coming. Criticisms and exhortations against the so-called *seitas*, or sects, have been common stock in the Catholic message, but only in the 1980s and 1990s did the clergy begin to study the Pentecostal phenomenon carefully and very tentatively formulate measures to combat the flight of the faithful. It is important to recognize that the Brazilian Catholic Church, which established ecumenical relations with mainline, traditional Protestant denominations such as the Presbyterians and Lutherans in the 1970s, has not viewed its situation as one of pure competition. The life of religious institutions, especially traditional ones such as the Catholic Church, is far more complex than a zero-sum battle over the faithful. Nevertheless, Pentecostal growth, the aggressive tactics of the Universal Church, and increasing Pentecostal political influence have moved the Catholic clergy to go beyond mere denunciation of the *seitas* to outlining specific strategies.

Much of the early initiative came from the top. In the 1980s Pope John Paul II began calling for a "New Evangelization" to be carried out by the Catholic Church. This call was especially heard in Latin America, home to the world's largest bloc of Catholics. One of the major goals of the 1992 gathering of Latin American bishops in Santo Domingo was precisely to plan this campaign. Central to the New Evangelization is the revival of traditional spirituality and rituals. Many clergymen have harked back to a pre–Vatican II piety, thus leading the Church to seek its roots but also in some cases to mimic the simple yet successful techniques and spectacles of the Pentecostals and fundamentalists. The conservatives in particular have taken the lead in reacting to the new competition in this way.[64] Like the Pentecostals, some clerics have resorted to miracles and exorcism to reconquer the faithful.[65] In general, the Brazilian religious sphere has undergone a process of "pentecostalization," with Catholics and other believers borrowing practices and activities from each other.[66]

In addition, in light of Pentecostals' entrance into the media, it often goes unnoticed that the Catholic Church still maintains the largest network of religious radio stations and publishing concerns in Brazil.[67] However, the Church has recognized that it has used these tools far less successfully than the Pentecostals.[68]

The mainstay of the Catholic reaction is a group of transnational conservative movements, in particular the Catholic Charismatic Renewal, a "pentecostalized" movement born in the United States in the 1960s and brought to Brazil shortly thereafter. John Paul II has strongly encouraged these movements, which employ traditional spirituality and enjoy the support of a number of bishops. In São Paulo, for example, the Charismatics fill churches in the conservative dioceses as well as in Cardinal Arns's progressive haven. Even liberationists praise the Charismatics for revivifying faith and religious practice and building a sense of community and lay participation within the Church. Their base of support, however, is mainly middle class, thus calling into question their long-term potential for evangelizing the poor.[69] They emphasize personal salvation and shun liberation theology, although they are not necessarily averse to participation in politics.[70]

Because of the Charismatics' conservatism the Bishops' Conference waited until the mid-1990s to grant them official recognition. By this point it was clear that they were the best option for stemming Pentecostal growth. Even then, the Bishops' Conference set forth a series of strict conditions to control the movement and to prevent it from straying from official post-Vatican II beliefs and practices.[71] Such internal tensions have kept the Church from building a united front against the Pentecostals, leaving different groups to emphasize their own strategies.

CONCLUSIONS

For the first time in Brazilian history another religion (in this case, a group of Pentecostal denominations) has directly challenged the notion of the Catholic identity of the Brazilian state and Brazilian society. The Pentecostals gained electoral victories but, more important, social power through the increase in their numbers, ability to bargain with politicians, acquisition of media outlets, and the gradual reformulation of religion as a private and nonpermanent choice rather than an immutable social given. Significantly, though often painted as conservative, quackish, and manipulative, the Pentecostals have achieved what the liberation theologians and others failed to accomplish: the attraction of millions of the poorest of the poor into their flocks and the conversion of this success into political power. As one pastor perhaps cruelly but not inaccurately put it, "The Catholic Church opted for the poor, but the poor opted for the Evangelicals."[72] The poor have gained a voice in Brazil in a way that no one would have predicted a generation ago as the Catholic Church's prestige rode high in the waning moments of the dictatorship. Interestingly, as Pentecostal churches achieve power and institutional maturity, they may become part of the religious status quo and therefore gain even greater privileges but also greater responsibilities to constituents and to a general public that will not long tolerate lack of such responsibility in a democratic setting.

At the level of its people Brazil has a large historical reservoir of religious experience, diversity, and tolerance. The increase in religious and cultural diversity in recent years presents a paradoxical situation which contains the seeds of both greater tolerance and potential for conflict. Thus it can be seen as both a risky and a healthy development for Brazilian democracy. First, *risky* because competition for state benefits and the potential for interfaith religious conflict have increased. What is currently a situation of laissez-faire may require state intervention and control by the state and/or organizations within civil society—in other words, a mechanism for defense of the religious consumer.[73] The attack on Our Lady of Aparecida revealed a pastoral strategy of conflict and intolerance employed by a number of Pentecostal denominations. As distorted as it was by the media and irrational as certain sectors were in reacting to it, the Aparecida incident indicated that Brazilian society would not long tolerate high-pitched tensions over religion. Religious leaders will have to take a lead in mediating such conflict if and when it reoccurs. Second, *healthy* because diversity can help strengthen tolerance and mutual respect, two requisites for a modern democratic society, especially in a global situation in which ethnic and religious tensions have replaced the ideological conflict of the Cold War. Learning tolerance and mutual respect can reinforce other pre-requisites for improving democracy such as human rights, political debate, and social justice. While the people may easily absorb this message as a result of historical experience, it will be a special challenge for religious leaders to look beyond their purely institutional interests in their dealings in politics and with the state. The temptation exists to cut behind-the-scenes bargains, thus opening the possibility of strong inter-institutional conflict.

The Pentecostal groups per se represent a novelty in Brazilian politics. The Pentecostals have made inroads into the political system and are beginning to change the religious component of Brazilian politics in the direction of increased competition. Their long-term impact on democracy is unpredictable,[74] especially given their explosive entrance into politics. They are far from being a majority, but their *active* followers rival the number of active Catholics. Their leaders openly support specific candidates from the pulpit, something Catholic clergy have rarely done. In many ways the Pentecostals are beginning to fill traditional Catholic spaces in the political system. So far, they seem to be adapting to rather than shaping or transforming the political system. Pentecostal politicians are particularly noted for their desire for patronage and privileges. In a broad sense, they are increasing the political participation of the poor but in a conservative way. The common saying of many Brazilians is that the poor do not want revolution but to occupy the same spaces as the rich and powerful. The Pentecostal churches are perhaps reflecting this hope. Their leaders' primary concern is power, and their rather simple theologies are attuned to economic interests. Beyond this the new churches seem to have no overall vision or plan for Brazilian society and little notion of collective justice beyond the interests of the churches. Larger than a political phenomenon, they are part of long-term social, cultural, and religious changes that envelop politics: the continued modernization of Brazilian society through ever closer integration into the world capitalist economy but with the country's colonial legacy always hanging in the balance. Conflict, if and when it occurs, will have to be interpreted not only in terms of politics and church-state relations, but also more broadly to include cultural factors.

13.

CHILE

From the Patronato *to Pinochet*

———————◆———————

Martín Poblete

THE NINETEENTH CENTURY

Under Spanish colonial rule, the Catholic Church in Chile was subject to the authority of the Archbishop of Seville and of the King of Spain, who exercised the rights and privileges of royal patronage or *patronato regio*, particularly in regard to the appointment of bishops and the awarding of concessions to religious orders.

Independence brought this situation to an abrupt end. The church in Chile began a complex transfer of loyalties and obedience to the Holy See in Rome, further complicated by the ambivalence of the authorities in the newly independent republic with respect to the *patronato*. The divisions generated by the War of Independence were aggravated by Pope Pius VII's encyclical supporting the efforts of Spain to continue holding its colonies. Since a priority of the new governments was to secure their position of power, the royalist tendencies of part of the hierarchy and clergy had to be repressed, and they were.

On April 13, 1840, the Holy See recognized the independence of Chile but refused to extend the privileges of *patronato* to the government of the republic. However, it accepted the nomination of Manuel Vicuña to become Archbishop of Santiago, establishing a modus vivendi that would last eighty years. In November 1845, at the request of the government of President Manuel Bulnes, the Holy See agreed to the nomination of Rafael Valentín Valdivieso to succeed Manuel Vicuña in the Archdiocese of Santiago. Archbishop Valdivieso held the position for thirty-three years, during which time he had to deal with the paramount issue of church/state relations in Chile in the nineteenth century, the struggle of the church for its independence and freedom with respect to the republican state and the liberal ideology of some of its governments. In addition to protecting the freedom of the church, the Catholic hierarchy wanted

220

to eliminate the right to appeal to civil courts in cases decided by ecclesiastical councils under canon law. Archbishop Valdivieso also acted forcefully to protect the right of the church to own schools and offer education at all levels.

THE QUESTION OF THE SACRISTAN

In January 1856, the senior sacristan of the Cathedral of Santiago, Francisco Martínez Garfias, in consultation with the cathedral treasurer, Mariano Fontecilla, fired an employee on disciplinary grounds. Informed of this decision, the Council of the Cathedral declared it null and void, considering the consultation with the treasurer improper to the point of vitiating the procedure. The Vicar General of the Archdiocese ordered the Council to abide by the decision of the senior sacristan or face suspension of duties. Two members of the Council, Archdeacon Juan Francisco Meneses and the canon-law doctor Pascual Solís de Ovando, appealed to the archbishop and in a veiled manner indicated they would consider appealing to civil courts.

So far, it remained an internal matter, until Archdeacon Meneses and Dr. Solís de Ovando filed an appeal with the Supreme Court in April 1856. In August of that year, the Court ordered the reinstatement of the fired employee and annulled the punishment of the appellants, but Archbishop Valdivieso refused to obey and ratified the suspension of the rebellious clerics. The situation had already gone beyond legal or religious boundaries, with large crowds meeting every day in front of the residence of the archbishop to voice their support. By the end of that eventful month, the Council members withdrew their appeal, and the archbishop lifted their suspension.

The heated debates that followed the uneasy settlement led to three important politico-social developments. The landed oligarchy in the Conservative Party strengthened its Catholic allegiance, provided intellectual cadres for the church's educational institutions, and supported the hierarchy in its confrontations with liberal governments. Second, the emerging bourgeoisie in the Liberal Party distanced itself from the church and its hierarchy. Third, following the defeat of a rebellion in the northern provinces in 1858, its leaders and many of their followers, joined by defectors from the Liberal Party, founded the Radical Party, defined from its beginnings as a secular organization. This system of three major parties would last for one hundred years.

THE VACANCY OF THE ARCHDIOCESE OF SANTIAGO

Shortly after the death of Archbishop Valdivieso at the end of 1878, the outbreak of war against Bolivia and Peru in February 1879 postponed a decision on his successor until the new government of President Domingo Santa María, seeking to settle the matter, instead provoked a serious breakdown in church-state relations.

After his inauguration, President Santa María submitted to the Holy See the name of Monsignor Francisco de Paula Taforo as his choice for Archbishop of Santiago, but the Holy See turned him down. Santa María interpreted this as an insult and in a fit of rage refused to provide another name. The looming conflict evolved into confrontation when the president sent to Congress the legislation known as the secularization laws—*leyes laicas*—creating secular cemeteries, laws and regulations for civil marriage, and a new state institution, the Office of Civil Registry, taking away those functions from the church and its parishes. Congress approved the secularization laws in the legislative years of 1883-84. In the meantime, the government had declared the papal nuncio, Monsignor Celestino del Frate, persona non grata, forcing his departure and effectively downgrading relations with the Holy See.

The government of President José Manuel Balmaceda implicitly acknowledged the veto of the previous nominee, and after somewhat awkward consultations, submitted the name of Monsignor Mariano Casanova, accepted by the Vatican in 1887. All the parties involved understood the risks of situations that could be interpreted as endangering the freedom of the church. In the future, both sides refrained from attitudes or gestures that could escalate into an open conflict. In a significant indication of improved relations, Archbishop Casanova supported the proposal of Father Joaquín Larrain Gandarillas to establish the Catholic University of Chile, which was founded in 1889.

At the turn of the century, President Federico Errazuriz sought to normalize relations with the Holy See using the good offices of the Chilean Ambassador to France, Augusto Matte, who in March 1895 was received by Pope Leo XIII and his Secretary of State, Mariano Cardinal Rampolla, exchanging notes of accreditation. In March 1897, the parties signed a protocol of understanding enabling Chilean Catholics to comply with the secularization laws.

THE EARLY STAGES OF RELIGIOUS PLURALISM

On December 14, 1819, Bernardo O'Higgins signed a decree authorizing the foundation of an Anglican parish and cemetery in Valparaíso; a second parish was added in 1830, followed by the McKay School also in Valparaíso. In 1845, originally to serve American whalers and their agents, a Presbyterian parish opened in Valparaíso under its pastor, the Rev. David Trumbull.

In the 1850s, the German immigrants brought with them pastors who founded the first Lutheran parishes. During the government of President Jose Joaquín Pérez in 1865, a reinterpretation of Article 5 of the Constitution of 1833 gave legal protection to other Christian denominations in a gesture of religious tolerance. By the turn of the century, Arab immigrants brought the Catholicism of the Eastern Rite, and branches of the Orthodox Church affiliated with the Patriarchate of Athens. At about the same time, the Methodist Church began its activities in Chile, and by 1909 it was operating with a mostly native clergy.

THE SEPARATION OF CHURCH AND STATE

Chile entered the twentieth century with freedom of religion and religious tolerance anchored in its institutions. The idea of the educational duties of the state—*el estado docente*—promoted by the Radical Party and its leader Valentín Letelier, had also been socially accepted. A generation of young intellectuals, poets, and writers such as Oscar Schnake, Santiago Labarca, Eugenio González, Rudecindo Ortega, Enrique Molina, Daniel Schweitzer, Pablo Neruda, Pedro León Ugalde, Roberto Meza Fuentes, and Pedro León Loyola rejected the last vestiges of clericalism doing a great service to the country and, perhaps against their will, also to the church.

Catholics were not idle either. The founding of ANEC (*Asociacion Nacional de Estudiantes Católicos*/National Association of Catholic Students) in 1915 created the institution that would serve as standard bearer for a group of young priests known as *rerumnovaristas*, inspired by *Rerum Novarum*, the 1891 social encyclical of Pope Leo XIII. Among them were Francisco Vives Solar, Fernando Vives, Jorge Fernández Pradel, Oscar Larson, Manuel Larrain, Jorge Gomez Ugarte, and Bishop Martin Rucker.

Still unresolved was the matter of enacting the formal separation of the church from the state, but the intellectual ambiance was already favorable to its main promoter, President Arturo Alessandri. He had advanced his views in his speech accepting his presidential candidacy in 1920, and in speeches to Congress in 1922 and 1923. In 1925, President Alessandri was received by Pope Pius XI and his Secretary of State, Pietro Cardinal Gasparri. However, the Archbishop of Santiago, Crescente Errázuriz, was reluctant to support the idea. Among the other bishops, José María Caro argued for the separation, partly because he considered it inevitable, and partly because he believed it would bring greater independence to the church and the benefits of a more ascetic life.

Once the constitutional referendum was held and the ballots counted, the separation of church and state was enacted as part of the Constitution of 1925. The church retained its status as *persona jurídica de derecho público* (juridical entity under public law), a farsighted provision that would prove its value fifty years later, after the 1973 military coup. In a statement, the Chilean bishops said: "The Church of Chile begins a new era, let us look forward to it without fear."

The new relationship would be challenged in 1938 with the election as president of Pedro Aguirre Cerda, the candidate of the Radical Party, supported by the Popular Front, a coalition that included the Communist Party. It was feared that a government headed by a prominent leader of a militantly secular party, supported by Communists and Socialists, might bring back the old disputes, but the Archbishop of Santiago, José María Cardinal Caro, defused the tensions, welcoming the elected president and inviting the country to avoid confrontations. President Aguirre Cerda was peacefully inaugurated in December 1938.

Meanwhile, a young priest, Alberto Hurtado, S.J., returned to Chile after his ordination in Rome in 1936 to an apostolate that would last sixteen years. He wrote two influential books: *Es Chile un Pais Catolico?* (Is Chile a Catholic Country?), and *Humanismo Social* (Social Humanism). In 1947 he founded the *Hogar de Cristo* to provide shelter to homeless children, and in 1951 established the Jesuit monthly *Mensaje*. Father Hurtado was the bridge between the *rerumnovaristas* of the 1910s and the new forces emerging after Vatican II. Together with Bishop Manuel Larrain, he provided leadership in the pastoral action for social justice and the poor.

DECADES OF ANGER AND TURMOIL, FORGIVENESS AND RECONCILIATION

Cardinal Caro died on December 4, 1958. Although President Jorge Alessandri pointedly mentioned the precedent of his father in avoiding any attempt to influence the nomination of a successor to Cardinal Caro, he also indicated that his government expected a decision in the near future. However, the Vatican, in a surprising move, settled for appointing the auxiliary bishop, Emilio Tagle, as Apostolic Administrator on March 12, 1959, resulting in a tense relationship between President Alessandri and the nuncio, Sebastiano Baggio. After more than two years with the most important Archdiocese in the hands of a caretaker, the Holy See filled the vacancy, appointing as Archbishop of Santiago Most Rev. Raúl Silva Henriquez on April 25, 1961. Then heading the Diocese of Valparaíso, Archbishop Silva belonged to the Salesian Order; he had had a distinguished career as teacher, pastor, and president of *Caritas* (Catholic Charities of Chile). He would firmly lead the archdiocese and the church of Chile for twenty-two years, through four different governments and a traumatic institutional breakdown. He actively participated in the proceedings of Vatican Council II, in the election of three popes, and had a vital role in the protagonism of the church in times of political and social change. Archbishop Silva became a cardinal on March 19, 1962.

As the decade of the sixties began to unfold, the church faced two fronts in its relations with society as a whole. Toward the government, there was the perennial issue of education and the state's financial contribution to the operations of Catholic schools and universities. Toward civil society, whipsawed by ideologically charged demands for structural changes, the church made a consistent effort to emphasize its social doctrine and the leadership of the hierarchy. In times of political and social tensions, it was as if many forces were pulling at the seams from different directions, threatening to tear the fabric apart, while Cardinal Silva stood at the center holding the garment together.

Political changes were marked by sharp ideological confrontations, leaving no institution untouched, and the church was no exception. The bishops responded in part by writing numerous documents between March 1962 and September 1973, on behalf of either the Conference of Bishops or the Conference's Permanent Committee. These documents followed the positions outlined by the Archbishop of Santiago in his homilies and speeches.

In March 1962, under the leadership of Bishop Manuel Larrain, the Conference of Bishops produced a document, *La Iglesia y el Problema del*

Campesinado Chileno (The Church and the Problem of the Chilean Peasantry), dealing for the first time with the contentious matter of agrarian reform. On the national holiday, September 18, 1962, the Conference of Bishops released a pastoral letter, *El Deber Social y Politico en la Hora Presente (The Political and Social Duty of the Present Time)*, which outlined the bishops' approach to structural changes, ruled out collaboration with Communism, warned of the danger of Marxism, and raised concerns about morality in politics and public life. It would remain the standard reference on questions of social teaching for nine years.

As the intensely disputed presidential election of 1970 neared, the bishops asked Cardinal Silva to make clear that priests and religious should not involve themselves in partisan politics, let alone electoral activism. The cardinal responded with *Sacerdocio, Iglesia y Política (Priesthood, Church, and Politics)*, a strongly worded speech delivered on July 20, 1970. The bishops reiterated their position in a succession of statements on September 2, 1970; on September 4, the very day of the election; and on September 15, clearly indicating that the church was not a partisan in the electoral process.

During the government of President Salvador Allende, the church had to face three challenges, ideological, educational, and institutional. The first ideological challenge came from within, in the form of a movement called Christians for Socialism, whose origins can be traced back to a brief takeover of the Cathedral of Santiago by a group called *Iglesia Joven* (Young Church), on August 11, 1968. The first indication that this time things were going to be better organized came in the "Declaration of the Eighty," a statement signed by eighty priests on April 16, 1971. Under the leadership of Father Gonzalo Arroyo, S.J., the First Latin American Convention of Christians for Socialism was held in Santiago, April 23-24, 1972. It was attended by numerous international delegations including a few members of the Latin American hierarchy who arrived in Santiago without informing the archbishop and, needless to say, without seeking his permission to participate in such an event. There was an active exchange of letters involving the organizers and Cardinal Silva, and a critical memorandum drafted by Bishop Carlos Oviedo was approved at a meeting of the Conference of Bishops on January 12, 1972. The hierarchy headed by Cardinal Silva saw the Christians for Socialism as a cause of division and confusion, with a dangerous potential for questioning the authority of the bishops. Beyond the clergy and religious, Father Arroyo and his colleagues were viewed as close to a new form of clericalism, with attitudes similar to those that had been criticized in the cases of the Conservative Party and later the Christian Democrats.

In the middle of the controversy over the Christians for Socialism, on May 27, 1971, the bishops released what they called a working document, *Evangelio, Política y Socialismos (Gospel, Politics and Socialisms)*, which came close to being a pastoral letter to clarify matters of ideology and political thinking, and to offer guidance to Catholics regarding political alternatives. It was the first document of the church that described the Allende government's policies[1] as an attempt to build a "socialism of clear Marxist inspiration."

When the government of President Allende published a proposal in March 1973 for a drastic educational plan that required the teaching of socialism in all schools, including those run by the church, the bishops unequivocally opposed it in a statement published on April 11, 1973.

As the institutional crisis began to unfold, the Permanent Committee of the Conference of Bishops issued, on July 16, 1973, an Exhortation to keep the peace in Chile, the last collective statement of the bishops before the final denouement. Afterward, all the initiatives were in the hands of Cardinal Silva, who on July 20, 1973, called for a dialogue of all the political forces to find ways to avoid a violent conflict. The cardinal continued his efforts with a statement on August 10, 1973, focusing on the dangers of an alarming wave of terrorism and violence. Finally, the cardinal made a last effort when he invited to his residence both President Allende and Senator Patricio Aylwin, then president of the Christian Democratic Party, on August 17, 1973.

After the coup d'etat of September 11, 1973, the Permanent Committee of the Conference of Bishops issued a statement deploring the events and reminding the Chileans of all the bishops had done to prevent the tragedy. This statement was reaffirmed by a declaration of Cardinal Silva on September 16, 1973, and in his homily at the Te Deum ceremony of September 18, 1973. A new period in church-state relations was about to begin, a conflict that would last sixteen years with profound implications for Chile as a nation.

Defining New Pastoral Policies

The traumatic and violent institutional collapse of September 1973 had a lasting impact on the church. The option represented by the Christians for Socialism and the proponents of liberation theology was no longer viable. Their leaders were among the first to feel the harshness of the repressive onslaught carried out at that time, mostly by the intelligence services of the Armed Forces, and they left for exile. A few liberation theologians managed to remain in the country, only to realize that the situation was no longer favorable to their projects.

Almost immediately after the breakdown of democracy, the bishops began to receive information about serious abuses on the part of the Armed Forces and their intelligence services. In the early days most of the cases were related to armed confrontations with hard-line supporters of the deposed Popular Unity government, but once all forms of organized armed resistance were terminated, the incidents denounced to the bishops were related to persecution and repression of people ideologically or politically suspect of either militancy in, or sympathy with, the ousted government.

As the situation worsened, two approaches were taken by the bishops. A majority, following the leadership of Cardinal Silva, was of the opinion that some initiative should be implemented nationally, perhaps by the Conference itself, to protect those being persecuted. A significant minority, led by Bishop Emilio Tagle, argued that although they did not deny the veracity of the information regarding abuses and excesses in the repression by the Armed Forces, the military junta had concentrated in its members all the executive powers of the state, declared Congress in recess, and indicated its willingness to respect the decisions of the judiciary. Therefore, it was not for the church to question the actions of the military regime. Without consensus, it was left to the respective bishops in their dioceses to act according to their own judgment.

Cardinal Silva rose to the challenge, founding the *Comité de Cooperación para la Paz en Chile* (Committee for Peace in Chile) on October 6, 1973. Joining the cardinal as co-founders were Bishop Fernando Ariztia, Lutheran Bishop Helmut Frenz, and Rabbi Angel Kreiman. Its first director was Father Cristian Precht. Institutionally, the Committee was made up of the Catholic Church, the historic Protestant churches, the Jewish community, the Orthodox Church, the Methodist Church, and representatives of Pentecostal denominations. It was the most important ecumenical endeavor in the history of interreligious relations in Chile. Ironically, it would be the last one.

Ecumenical relations in Chile received a boost from the Second Vatican Council and Pope Paul VI's statement on ecumenism on April 21, 1964. The Chilean bishops founded a unit within their conference, the *Departamento Nacional de Ecumenismo* (National Department of Ecumenism) on April 17, 1965, chaired by Bishop Augusto Salinas and supported by Father Humberto Muñoz as secretary. In that same year the School of Theology of the Pontifical Catholic University included ecumenism in its curriculum with the courses taught every year by some of the most distinguished members of the faculty. In the same vein, Cardinal Silva made his first visit to the Synagogue of Santiago on July 29, 1965.

Five years later, a First Ecumenical Spiritual Retreat took place, with the participation of Monsignor Santiago Tapia, then pastor of the Parish of Saint Joseph the Worker, the Revs. Samuel Araya, Joel Gajardo, Samuel Vallette, and the Methodist Bishop Francisco León Garay. On October 1, 1970, biblical encounters were held in Santiago and Temuco. On November 4, 1970, Cardinal Silva presided over an ecumenical Te Deum service to highlight the inauguration of President Salvador Allende; and on August 8, 1973, Monsignor Santiago Tapia founded the Ecumenical Fraternity of Chile.

Ecumenism also was affected by the dictatorship, and the apparent unity began to show serious cracks. On December 13, 1974, about twenty-five hundred Evangelicals, among them several pastors, met with General Augusto Pinochet in the Portales Building, headquarters of the military regime. In July 1975, thirty-one Pentecostal pastors, members of a *Consejo de Pastores* (Council of Pastors) met with Pinochet, and on September 14, 1975, a solemn service, held at the large church located in Jotabeche Avenue, was attended by General Pinochet and members of his government, with the Rev. Francisco Anabalon leading the prayers and the eulogy.

THE TURBULENT YEARS OF THE COMMITTEE FOR PEACE

The promotion of human rights, the defense of the victims of repression, and the protection of their relatives were at the center of the confrontation between the church and the military regime. For the church, working for human rights was a pastoral duty inspired, as noted by Cardinal Silva on many occasions, by the parable of the Good Samaritan. However, it was also an expression of the church's freedom and independence, more valuable and valued as the passing of time continued to provide evidence of the abdication by the judiciary of its obligation to protect the citizens from abuses by those in the service of the state.

From the perspective of the government, the activities of the Committee for Peace raised questions about its legitimacy. Sometimes through middle-level officials and occasionally through its pawns in the media, the government sought to portray the Committee for Peace as a haven for assorted Marxists who had managed to infiltrate the Christian churches. The work of the Committee was a problem for the regime, which reacted to pressure concerning the whereabouts of thousands of detainees by creating the *Secretaría Nacional de Detenidos* (SENDET, National Secretariat of Detainees).

In a different area, the decision of the military regime to take over the universities added tension to the already strained relations with the church. The intervention of the Catholic University was entrusted to a retired Admiral, Jorge Swett, but Cardinal Silva as Grand Chancellor of the university complained about being bypassed regarding important administrative decisions and resigned. It could have been a serious conflict, but a deserter from the ranks, Monsignor Jorge Medina, offered himself as a replacement for the cardinal. The Holy See went along, and Monsignor Medina was appointed pro-Grand Chancellor, a defeat for the cardinal. However, large numbers of academics and researchers purged from the university needed a place to work and think as freely as possible. Making use of the provisions of the Constitution of 1925, Cardinal Silva founded the *Academia de Humanismo Cristiano* (Academy of Christian Humanism) to shelter not only the victims of repression at the Catholic University, but also others including some prominent scholars purged from the University of Chile.

Meanwhile, the Conference of Bishops managed to reach a consensus concerning the government. In a document, *La Reconciliación en Chile (Reconciliation in Chile)*, released on April 24, 1974, the bishops treated the government with respect, perhaps still expecting that some of the good words in the official language would be translated into concrete policies, but they were also critical of human rights violations and what they considered the lack of protection for the citizens at a time when the country was under a state of siege and curfew. It was fortunate that the bishops went on record with their timely criticism, for the government announced on June 14, 1974, the creation of the *Dirección de Inteligencia Nacional* (DINA, National Directorate of Intelligence) to centralize the activities of repression, opening a new stage of unprecedented violence and massive violations of human rights.

Regardless of the difficulties, the church tried to keep channels of communications with the government open, but this attitude was severely tested on two occasions during 1975. In June of that year, the government claimed to have solved the problem of people who had allegedly disappeared after detention by its security services, arguing that two lists of names published in foreign magazines attributed the deaths of those individuals to armed confrontations among rival leftists factions. Researchers for the Committee for Peace proved that the magazines did not exist, and eight detailed briefs presented to the courts by the lawyers of the Committee contained solid proof of the disappearance of those persons after their arrest.

On October 3, the government prohibited the return to the country of Lutheran Bishop Helmut Frenz. In another development, at the end of October and early November, the remaining leaders of the Movement of the Revolutionary Left (MIR) were surrounded by personnel from DINA, one of them being badly wounded. The *Miristas* managed to reach Santiago, where they secured help for the wounded and eventually assistance to find diplomatic asylum from several priests and religious. The incident broke the unity of the churches that were members of the Committee for Peace. The Orthodox and Pentecostals were the first to leave, and when Pinochet asked Cardinal Silva to close the Committee, he indicated he would do so, thus bringing to an end an exemplary ecumenical experience and opening a new chapter in the church's action for human rights and in church-state relations.

LA VICARIA DE LA SOLIDARIDAD (THE VICARIATE FOR SOLIDARITY)

Quoting from the parable of the Good Samaritan and from the church's statement of September 1925—"the Church will always be ready to serve, to work for the common good, to help all those in need without exception"—Cardinal Silva founded the Vicariate of Solidarity on January 1, 1976, to continue the work of the Committee for Peace. Its first vicar was the former director of the Committee, Monsignor Cristian Precht, joined by the lawyers, professionals, and personnel who worked at the Committee. But behind the continuity there were substantial differences. The Vicariate was an organization of the Catholic Church, founded in accordance with the provisions of the Constitution of 1925 as part of the hierarchical structure of the Archdiocese of Santiago under the authority of the archbishop, and thus qualitatively different from the Committee for Peace, but also stronger.

Under different vicars and a succession of executive secretaries and chief legal counsels, the Vicariate maintained rigorous juridical standards, earning it a unique place as a human rights organization. In the twelve years between 1976 and 1988, an average of 91,973 persons a year visited the Vicariate to request some form of assistance; of these 10,933 asked for specific legal support. In that same period, the Vicariate filed 8,706 writs of habeas corpus and recorded 38,496 cases of political arrest and 1300 cases of torture. In the social area, the Vicariate established working relations with 17,211 popular base organizations with a membership of 712,653 persons.

Since the beginning of its operations, the Vicariate was closely watched by the government and its lawyers occasionally harassed, as was the case with

Hernan Montealegre, arrested on May 12, 1976, held incommunicado for two weeks, and then detained until December of that year. The hostilities were not restricted to the Vicariate. In August 1976 a group of bishops returning from a meeting in Ecuador were ambushed at the airport by plainclothesmen of DINA who insulted and attacked them physically. The Permanent Committee of the Conference of Bishops, then chaired by the Bishop of San Felipe, Juan Francisco Fresno, strongly protested the treatment of bishops Enrique Alvear, Fernando Ariztia, and Carlos Gonzalez.

The cases of those who disappeared after detention were considered by the bishops in their statement *Nuestra Convivencia Nacional*, on March 25, 1977. In November of that same year, responding to many requests for assistance from the persecuted labor organizations, Cardinal Silva founded the *Vicaría de Pastoral Obrera* (Vicariate for the Labor Pastorate). It was headed by Monsignor Alfonso Baeza; a prestigious Catholic labor leader, José Aguilera, served as executive secretary. The new vicariate followed the institutional pattern of the Vicariate of Solidarity.

In the last years Cardinal Silva served as head of the Archdiocese of Santiago, the government continued its policy of harassment against professionals working at the Vicariate of Solidarity. The church, for its part, held an International Symposium on Human Rights November 22-25, 1978, an event that brought together representatives from human rights organizations and prominent members of the historic Protestant denominations and of the World Council of Churches. In another affirmation of the independence and freedom of the church, Cardinal Silva founded the *Banco del Desarrollo* (Bank for Development) in November 1981 to handle all the financial transactions of the archdiocese, chiefly those in foreign currency, to keep them from interference by government officials with easy access to the records of commercial banks. In January 1983, the government rescinded the visas of three foreign priests, Brian McMahon, Desmond McGillicuddy, and Brendan Ford, forcing them to leave the country.

After twenty-two years as Archbishop of Santiago, Cardinal Silva retired in April 1983. His name will be always linked to pastoral action for human rights, the struggles around the Vicariate, his uncompromising defense of the freedom and independence of the church and the authority of the hierarchy and its relationship to the pope and the Holy See. Contrary to the doomsayers on the left and the wishful thinkers in the regime, his legacy was fully assumed and enhanced by his successor.

THE FRESNO YEARS: FOCUS ON THE POLITICS OF DEMOCRATIZATION

On May 6, 1983, Juan Francisco Fresno was installed as Archbishop of Santiago amid pessimistic concerns by the left and optimistic assumptions by the government that now the pope had appointed an archbishop who would be friendly and establish a different relation from the contentious one under Cardinal

Silva. Both parties had to revise their respective prognoses. Perhaps if Archbishop Fresno had arrived in Santiago under different circumstances, he might have had a chance to try a fresh approach to the regime, but 1983 was the year of the national protests when the economic model collapsed, the regime and its leader felt in danger, and repression was again at its harshest levels.

Soon after his installation, the new archbishop appointed a new vicar to the Vicariate of Solidarity and made a personal visit to the Vicariate to emphasize his commitment to pastoral action for human rights. Afterward, he turned his attention to an effort to bring about a meeting between the opposition and the government, which took place in December 1983 without positive results. However, Archbishop Fresno persisted and was more successful two years later. In the meantime, when a visit by General Pinochet to the southernmost city of Punta Arenas on February 26, 1984, was disrupted by mass demonstrations, the government blamed the church and the local bishop, and the Conference of Bishops rallied to support Bishop Tomas González. The situation took a turn for the worse in that year, with the church and its hierarchy again at the center of tense social conflict. The protests of September 24-25 resulted in eleven people killed in numerous incidents, one of them a priest of the parish of La Victoria, Father André Jarlan. In another instance of repression, an employee of the Vicariate, José Manuel Parada, was detained by plainclothesmen on March 29, 1985. His body was found the following day with two others; all had had their throats slit.

On May 25, 1985, Archbishop Fresno was elevated to the rank of cardinal by Pope John Paul II, a gesture that undoubtedly encouraged Cardinal Fresno to try again to achieve an agreement among political groups in varying degrees of opposition to the government. Meeting separately with the leaders of those groups, Cardinal Fresno found that they had many points in common, and he invited all those consulted to meet with him. Those who were there have given witness to the impact of discovering that there was much more uniting than separating them. The immediate result of those contacts was the National Accord for the Transition to Democracy, signed by the leaders of the opposition on August 25, 1985. The government rejected the Accord, but an agreement among the opposition had been obtained and from there to the later *Concertación* opposition coalition would be a mere three years.

The perceived activism of Cardinal Fresno was a matter of concern for the government, as was the work of the Vicariate. On May 11, 1986, the military prosecutor, Colonel Fernando Torres, indicted two professionals of the Vicariate, a medical doctor, Ramiro Olivares, and a lawyer, Gustavo Villalobos, accusing them of having assisted an individual involved in the armed robbery of a bakery and the murder of a policeman. This case continued for three years, evolving into a major church-state confrontation.

As a visit by Pope John Paul II neared, the church in Chile displayed remarkable vitality. The fruits of the prophetic years under Cardinal Silva were demonstrated by seminaries and religious orders full of vocations and many ordinations; it was an authentic revival of the faithful. Pope John Paul II arrived on April 1, 1987, for a visit that lasted a week, and included a personal visit to the Vicariate. In a clear gesture of support for Cardinal Fresno, he met with the leaders of the opposition in the Nunciature. Encouraged and strengthened, Cardinal Fresno supported the establishment of two organizations, *Belén* and *Participa*, to promote political participation and electoral registration. Later, in March 1988, the Chilean bishops issued a statement outlining the requirements for the validity of the plebiscite to be held on October 5. Once the votes were counted, the bishops made a statement the next day calling on all the parties to engage in a constructive dialogue.

The military regime ended peacefully in March 1990, the transition began under Patricio Aylwin, and Cardinal Fresno prepared to depart. His final action in defense of the freedom and independence of the church was to support the vicar of the Vicariate of Solidarity in maintaining the confidentiality of its professional consultations and the integrity of its archives, defiantly challenging orders from military tribunals and even from the Supreme Court.

THE CHURCH IN THE TRANSITION: THE OVIEDO YEARS

In his first public activity as the new head of the Archdiocese of Santiago, Archbishop Carlos Oviedo visited the Vicariate of Solidarity on May 23, 1990, to demonstrate his support of the Vicariate. In his first year, Archbishop Oviedo delivered three major statements: his homily at the memorial mass for the late President Salvador Allende on September 4; his homily in the traditional Te Deum ceremony of September 18, the first under a democratic government after the dictatorship; and his first pastoral letter, *Los Católicos y la Política (Catholics and Politics)*, on September 24.

In the area of evangelization, Archbishop Oviedo launched the Mission of Santiago, mobilizing all the priests, religious, and lay pastoral agents for a year of active proselytization throughout the territory of the archdiocese. The 1990 census had just been conducted and its results released, with 76.7 percent of Chileans declaring themselves Catholics; 20.2 percent Protestants, of which 80 percent were Pentecostals; the remainder was small groups of Jews, Greek Orthodox, and nonbelievers, the last the remnants of the once powerful Freemasonry. Although there is no empirical verification, there are indications that the Catholic Church is no longer losing membership to the Pentecostals. There is a slow but noticeable return of many who had left the church, and there also seems to be an active movement of worshipers from one Protestant denomination to another. Speaking in Lima, Peru, at a meeting on October 26, 1995, Cardinal Oviedo reflected on the Pentecostal phenomenon. Taking a different view from the usual sociological approaches, he said:

> Whatever interpretation one makes, there is a profound reason that cannot be ignored. The Pentecostals define their pastoral ministry as an act

of salvation of the sinner, trusting the Word of the Gospel as the source of repentance and conversion to a life of sainthood, a conversion that is not limited to the moral aspects of life but can also have a physical and psychological dimension. If their new recruits were Catholics before, it is possible to conclude that they did not find in the church a similar vision of man and his religious conscience.

This analysis of the religious situation underlay the successful implementation of the Mission of Santiago.

Social pastoral action had to find a new center after Cardinal Oviedo announced the termination of the Vicariate of Solidarity, transferring the properly social activities to a new institution of the archdiocese called the *Vicaría de Pastoral Social* (Vicariate of Social Pastorate). Cardinal Oviedo's pastoral letter *Los Pobres no Pueden Esperar (The Poor Cannot Wait)* of September 24, 1992, called attention to the characteristic of the Chilean economic model, which while reducing poverty increases inequality, a criticism that was presented by a Chilean bishop at the meeting of the Latin American bishops with Pope John Paul II in Santo Domingo in October 1992. The end of the activities of the Vicariate of Solidarity was also the end of a period in which the church had to be the "voice of the voiceless," as an institutional alternative to political parties, the media, and social organizations in times of severe repression and restrictions on human rights, and civil and political liberties. Under Cardinal Oviedo, the church had its own transition, returning to more traditional ways to make its voice heard by the government and politicians, but this should not be interpreted as a withdrawal from politics.

Cardinal Oviedo was also active on matters of public morality. His pastoral letter *Moral, Juventud y Sociedad Permisiva (Morality, Youth, and the Permissive Society)* of September 24, 1991, dealt with delicate issues such as ethical permissiveness, the crisis of sexual morality, the dignity of women, ambiguities in sexual education, abortion, divorce, strengthening of the family, and the duties and responsibility of parents. He reiterated his views in his pastoral message *A la Iglesia de Santiago Después de Beijing (To the Church of Santiago after Beijing)* of November 5, 1995. By that time, two Christian Democratic members of the Chamber of Deputies had introduced a bill to legalize divorce, seeking to replace the somewhat farcical law of annulment. The bill remains blocked in the Senate by the opposition of conservatives and the appointed senators created by the 1980 Constitution.

On the legal framework for religion and worship in Chile, the government of President Patricio Aylwin, near the end of his term in office, sent a bill to Congress responding to the complaints of discrimination by the Pentecostal denominations. The *Ley de Cultos* (Law of Worship), providing for legal equality of all religions, remains in the Senate, partly because of the opposition of the Catholic Church to the changes it makes in its legal status, which is currently based on a 1925 concordat. A 1995 Santiago municipal anti-noise ordinance has also been criticized by some Evangelicals as directed against public preaching, but the law has not been enforced in this way.

A serious neurological illness forced Cardinal Oviedo to resign in February 1998. To succeed him, Pope John Paul II appointed Archbishop Francisco Javier Errazúuriz. In the future the Catholic Church is likely to play a less visible political role but to continue to exercise a significant influence in one of the most Catholic countries in Latin America.

14.

COLOMBIA

Past Persecution, Present Tension

————◆————

Elizabeth E. Brusco

INTRODUCTION

This chapter examines the political role of religion in Colombia, especially during the period of *La Violencia*. Overshadowed by the shocking details accompanying Colombia's global reputation for violence, political repression, human rights abuses, and endemic civil war, the chronicle of religious persecution has largely been ignored.[1] A consideration of the issue of religious freedom in Colombia must necessarily take into account the activities of the national and local governmental leaders, military and para-military groups, and the Roman Catholic clergy at all levels. Patterns of violence and repression which exist in present-day Colombia reflect in distinct ways those of the past, though their targets and overt motivations might differ. The decade of the 1990s started with a ray of hope for positive change in Colombia with the promulgation of a new constitution guaranteeing much wider political representation for previously marginalized segments of society. Sadly, near the end of the decade, the situation has deteriorated to a point where even Amnesty International has been forced by death threats to close its offices in Bogotá.

LIBERALS, CONSERVATIVES, AND THE ROMAN CATHOLIC CHURCH IN THE NINETEENTH CENTURY

In the words of Colombian scholar Francisco Leal Buitrago:

> One is Liberal or Conservative as one is Catholic, as one is Colombian—by birth. One does not even consider not being Liberal or Conservative, just as one would never think of not being Catholic or Colombian through a simple act of will (Leal Buitrago, quoted in Hartlyn 1988, 18).

This fusion of national and religious identities, as well as political party affiliation, helps to explain the reception given to evangelical missionaries when they arrived in Colombia in the middle of the nineteenth century.[2] Hartlyn (1988, 19) describes the Liberal and Conservative parties during the nineteenth century as "factional divisions within Colombia's small ruling oligarchy." The involvement of the rural peasantry in violent conflicts between the parties during that time resulted from their dependence on local landowners. Seven major episodes of civil violence occurred during the second half of the nineteenth century, and the entrenched commitment of the mass of Colombians to one party or the other (including intense animosity toward the opposite side) was solidified by the beginning of the twentieth century. Party affiliation began to be passed down from generation to generation. Despite the ethnic homogeneity of a predominantly mestizo peasantry, party affiliation often functioned as ethnic differences do in other countries, as a basis for irrational hatreds and extreme brutality.

It is difficult to neatly delineate the actual ideological differences between the two parties. Bushnell (1992, 25) has said that "one often needs a magnifying glass and an aptitude for refined hair-splitting to distinguish between the programs of the Liberal and Conservative parties." One thing is abundantly clear, however. That is the historical alliance between Conservatives and the Roman Catholic Church, and conversely, the anticlericalism of the Liberals.[3] When Liberals held power from 1863 to 1885, they enacted anti-Church reforms including the nationalization of church property and, in a new constitution, became the first nation in Latin America to decree the separation of church and state (Delpar 1980, 274). Bushnell identifies the Roman Catholic clergy as the only element of society with a reason to affiliate with just one of the two parties—the Conservative.[4] He concludes that religion was a key factor in the creation of Colombia's two-party system. During the nineteenth century, the presence of a strong institutional church was being challenged by "liberal professional men imbued with modernizing and secularizing ideas who perceived the Church to be an obstacle to the changes they hoped to bring about" (Bushnell 1992, 28).

THE CONCORDAT OF 1887

During the last decades of the nineteenth century and the first part of the twentieth, Conservatives regained control of the government, and held onto it until 1930. In 1886 a new constitution was drafted, and in 1887, a treaty was signed with the Vatican: this treaty gave the Roman Catholic Church tremendous power over the lives of Colombians. Levine (1981, 70-71) describes the arrangement as "complete Church-State integration." As a result of the Concordat of 1887, the Church played a role in the birth, marriage, and death of every Colombian. The terms of the treaty specified that education at all levels was to be carried out "in conformity with the dogma of the Catholic religion" (ibid). All subsequent debates about religious freedom in Colombia took place in the shadow of this profound state-legitimated hegemony of Roman Catholicism.

This brief examination of the history of the two political parties is important in order to understand two issues central to the topic of religious freedom in Colombia: First, the continuing strength of the Roman Catholic Church in Colombia during much of the twentieth century and its role in the "civil order," and second, official antagonism toward evangelicalism. It almost goes without saying that Evangelicals have flourished while Liberals were in power and suffered when Conservatives ruled. After the defeat of the Conservatives in 1930 up until the beginning of La Violencia in the late 1970s, evangelical organizations took advantage of the more open climate for religious pluralism and arrived in Colombia in large numbers. Reforms carried out by the government of Alfonso Lopez Pumarejo (1934-38), the Liberal president who sought to secularize the state and modernize the nation, reduced the political power of the Roman Catholic Church (Osterling 1989, 243). There was even an attempt at the time to renegotiate the Concordat with the Vatican so as to limit the control of the Church over education. Strong Conservative party opposition was, however, able to block changes to the Concordat. Thus, the bishops and priests who used their positions in active support of the Conservative party were responding to real threats from Liberal reformers, then in power. As civil chaos descended on Colombia at the end of the 1940s, and inter-party antagonisms were one of the motivations for violent conflict, all of this fed into what became a period of intense persecution of Colombian evangelical converts and Protestant foreign missionaries working with them. The details of this history are not often told.[5] In the sections that follow, the difficult recent history of Colombian evangelicalism is explored.

A BRIEF HISTORY OF EVANGELICALISM IN COLOMBIA

Evangelicalism, like Roman Catholicism in Colombia, took root as the result of the efforts of missionaries from the outside. The first Catholic friars who accompanied the Spanish conquerors of the region made efforts to supplant the indigenous Chibcha culture, including suppressing and ultimately eliminating the indigenous religious system.[6] Evangelicals in Colombia date their history to the arrival of Henry Barrington Pratt, the first Presbyterian missionary, who arrived in Santa Marta in 1856.[7] A major difference between the two faiths, however, has been their standing relative to those wielding political power in the country. While the status of the Roman Catholic Church in Colombia has been characterized as "unusually favored" (Levine 1981, 70), Evangelicals, even in the best of times, have struggled simply to attain official tolerance.

A simple view of the entrance of evangelical missionaries into the Colombian landscape portrays it as an act of ideological imperialism. Stoll (1990, xvi) has written that Catholic commentators have attributed evangelical gains in Latin America to well-funded external agents from the North. In his opinion, this vision "suggests a deep distrust of the poor, an unwillingness to accept the possibilities that they could turn an imported religion to their own purposes" (ibid). In order to understand the outcome of evangelical missionization in Latin America, it is important to see Catholicism itself as ideological—that is, not simply as a transcendent cosmology comprising an essential component of Colombian culture, but as politicized and changing over time. Colombian Catholicism should be viewed neither as a monolithic baseline against which Protestant missionaries pushed, nor as a convenient explanation for "backwardness" of segments of Colombian society. There are many faces to Catholicism in Colombia: the traditional, hegemonic Catholicism, allied with the oligarchy and viewing itself as essential to the prevention of social and political disintegration; the Catholicism of Camillo Torres, and strands of liberation theology that he began which are finally beginning to flourish as activist priests sacrifice their lives in defense of human rights in the last years of this century; and finally, the folk Catholicism that bypasses institutional structures altogether but provides meaning to the lives of the masses of Colombians. Reactions and responses to religious change, including to evangelical efforts, also vary, as do the motivations and characteristics of missionary organizations and individuals.

Religious Persecution, 1950-1957

According to the chronicles produced by evangelical historians, religious persecution has existed in Colombia for at least 375 years. The first evangelical martyr, Adam Edon, was burned at the stake by the Inquisition in 1622 in New Granada (Burford de Buchanan 1995, 27). This section focuses on religious persecution in Colombia during the years 1950-57. Events in Colombia over the past seven years, especially the formal separation of church and state in the new constitution adopted in 1991, have made this piece of history especially relevant.

Evangelical Protestants in Colombia now number about 2.5 million (out of a total population of 32 million). Since the mid-nineteenth century, when the first Protestant missionaries assembled a small group of converts, discrimination and exclusion from the political process have accompanied identification with Protestant evangelicalism. Despite this fact, the conversion rate has grown through time, often accelerating during times of the most pronounced repression. The most important period, in terms of explosive growth in evangelicalism, was the time of the most severe repression during the late 1940s and throughout most of the 1950s.[8]

La Violencia

Violence has been chronic in Colombian history, a fact of life, although there are episodic eruptions that stun even those long habituated to it. Colombian scholars and journalists have elaborated a specialized vocabulary surrounding types of violence, including terms like *magnicidio* (magnacide, referring to the assassination of illustrious individuals), and *neonarcoterrorismo* (neo-narcoterrorism). In the past it was *la corbata* (the necktie) and *la canoa* (the canoe), names for types of wounds inflicted with a machete. There is even a specialized academic subdiscipline focusing on the topic: scholars called *violentólogos* (violentologists). This group of historians, political scientists, journalists, and philosophers, endeavor "to destroy the Violence by understanding it" (Peñaranda, in Bergquist et al. 1992, 294).

Key to this understanding is the link between the contemporary Colombian situation and a single historical antecedent. Specialists in Colombian violence always return to the "obligatory point of reference" (Sánchez, in Bergquist et al. 1992, 76), which is the period from 1946 to 1958. In Colombia, this period is known simply as *La Violencia*.

It is estimated that up to 300,000 Colombians were killed during the decade or more of *La Violencia*. Peñaranda describes this "complex political and social phenomenon" as "a mixture of official terror, partisan confrontation, political banditry, pillage, and peasant uprising" (Bergquist et al. 1992, 294). Primary explanations for the phenomenon range from viewing *La Violencia* as a class war or peasant uprising, to attributing the problems to a breakdown of the state. Not surprisingly, the scholarly treatment of *La Violencia* has paralleled contemporary social issues and agenda. As Peñaranda puts it: "Works on the Violence . . . have followed a tortuous path closely tied to the political situation in the country" (Bergquist et al. 1992, 295). Between 1964 and 1982, Colombia was officially a country at peace and "in an attempt to erase what has happened, successive governments and the information media decided that the best thing would be not to talk about it" (ibid.). It was not until 1985 that the first international symposium on the Violence in Colombia was held in Bogotá. At this point the relationship between the phenomenon known as *La Violencia* and the contemporary crisis enveloping the country became an issue.

Notably understudied have been the religious dimensions of violence during that period and subsequently. In a recent collection of articles by some of the most distinguished researchers on violence in Colombia (Bergquist et al. 1992), atrocities committed against Protestant converts are reduced to only one sentence. Colombian historian Gonzalo Sánchez, in his interpretative synthesis of the Violence, says, "In a display of religious intolerance, whole communities of Protestants in central Tolima (in the towns of Ibagué, Rovira, and Armero) were decimated and their churches destroyed" (Bergquist et al. 1992, 89). As dramatic as this sentence is, it misrepresents the scope of religious persecution, which was by no means confined to central Tolima. Nor does it adequately specify who was behind the destruction of these communities.

When I first conducted fieldwork on Protestant evangelical conversion in Colombia during 1982-83, I was surprised to learn from my older informants about the severity of the persecution they had suffered during the years of *La Violencia*. Within the chaos and ferocity that characterized that epoch there were multitudinous motivations for violent acts, ranging from party animosities to vendetta feuding. And Colombian Evangelicals informed me that religious intolerance, often instigated from the top down, was yet another motivation. During *La Violencia*, hundreds of Protestant churches were damaged or destroyed, and Protestants were attacked and killed or detained and tortured by police. Protestant churches and schools were forced to close.

Throughout the seven years of the worst violence, CEDEC amassed information on cases of violence against Protestant converts and distributed it in special bulletins. The bulk of these monthly bulletins was prepared by a Presbyterian missionary, James Goff, who was based in the Caribbean coastal city of Barranquilla and served as the secretary of the Office of Information for CEDEC. Goff eventually published a book on the subject (Goff 1968). CEDEC was an interdenominational group organized in 1950; it represented seventeen evangelical denominations in Colombia.[9] This section is based, in part, on the collection of these "persecution bulletins."[10]

Detailing incidents which occurred beginning in December 1951 and continuing through December 1957, forty-three separate mimeographed bulletins report hundreds of cases of violence against and harassment of Evangelicals, ranging from the destruction of religious books to murder. The compilers of the bulletins estimate that these published accounts represent only about 25 percent of actual incidents of persecution against Evangelicals. None of the oral accounts that I collected from Evangelicals in the region of Boyacá who had survived this period are documented in the reports, perhaps owing to the remoteness of that region during the time. The reports are varied and extremely detailed, including the names of all individuals involved. The accounts were based on signed statements made by eyewitnesses and victims, or by people with firsthand knowledge of the events.

The total number of incidents reported in the bulletins as of the July 1956 issue was as follows: forty-seven churches destroyed by fire and dynamite; seventy-five individuals murdered because of their religion; two hundred schools closed by the government (CEDEC Bulletin #30-4).

The persecution of Evangelicals took a distinctive form fostered by the Roman Catholic clergy. In addition to promoting outright physical violence against Evangelicals, the priests advocated that Evangelicals be ostracized by their communities. The pattern recounted in the bulletins is substantiated in a statement I collected from a prominent lawyer in the municipality of El Cocuy, Boyacá, in 1983. He said,

> In those days, the Roman Catholic priests had a method of frightening the people, and that was excommunication. The guy whom they excommunicated did not even deserve to live in society, and no one would accept him because they knew that he was already body and soul, from this life onwards, in hell. And actually, you could see how those people began to decay, because everybody began to look badly upon them and no one wanted to have anything to do with them, and they would stop helping them in every way. Then the priests would say from the pulpit,

"You see what excommunication does to you? There you have it, now you see how it is."

A frequent theme of Catholic indictment of the Evangelicals was that they lived in concubinage and bigamy. This accusation was based on the refusal of the Roman Catholic clergy to recognize civil marriage. The control of the Catholic church over matters relating to the family and the life cycle of the individual, including baptism, education, marriage, and burial, was guaranteed in the Concordat, making it impossible for evangelical converts to evade the clergy's authority. Hence, devout evangelical couples who refused to say their vows in the Catholic church were considered unmarried, regardless of the fact that their union had been legitimated both by civil authorities and by their own (evangelical) churches. Catholic clergy were relentless in their allegations against Evangelicals in this regard. In Catholic publications from the time, an oft-mentioned characteristic of Martin Luther was his purported lewdness and debauchery. A booklet issued by the archbishop of Antioquia in 1953 entitled *Protestantism, Its History and Errors*, states that Luther "kidnapped a nun and lived in sacrilegious concubinage with her" (CEDEC Bulletin #12-13).

Another powerful weapon used by the Catholic clergy against those who strayed from their flock was refusing to allow Evangelicals to bury their dead in the church cemetery, or allowing the interment of deceased Protestants only in the part of the cemetery designated for suicides. One CEDEC bulletin recounts the case of a man in the department of el Valle who was denied permission to bury his father, a 78-year-old Protestant and one of the founders of the town. He eventually had to take his father's body to another city to bury it (CEDEC Bulletin #3-12). This policy was particularly cruel and amounted to a kind of ostracism of the dead, desacralizing them at precisely the time when their families most needed to perceive them as linked to the divine.[11]

The destruction or confiscation of evangelical property was common, especially books (prayer books, hymnbooks, and Bibles). Possession of a Bible was considered a heretical act.[12] Houses and churches were burned and bombed as well. These actions took place largely in the small towns or in the countryside, and victims often responded by fleeing to the cities to hide from their tormentors. *La Violencia* led to a great deal of dislocation of people, and it was during that period that Colombia changed from a predominantly rural country into an overwhelming urban one.

THE ROLES OF THE POLICE, PUBLIC AUTHORITIES, AND ROMAN CATHOLIC CLERGY IN THE PERSECUTION OF EVANGÉLICOS

> Las cuentas de mi rosario
> Son balas de artillería
> Que tiemblan los protestantes
> Cuando digo, "Ave María."

(The beads of my rosary
Are balls of artillery
That shake the Protestants
When I say, "Ave Maria.")
—Verse of a song taught to Catholic school children during
La Violencia (CEDEC Bulletin #2-23)

The CEDEC bulletins painstakingly document the role of the police, public authorities, and especially the Roman Catholic clergy in inciting violence against Evangelicals. During the year 1952, for example, the CEDEC bulletin reported 150 cases of acts of persecution against Protestants. Priests were involved in 35 percent of the cases, while police and other government officials figured in 58 percent of them (CEDEC Bulletin #7-11).

Below I include the transcript of an incident that typifies the roles of the local priest and authorities in harassment of Evangelicals during *La Violencia*. This account comes from the first bulletin, compiled in February 1952. It illustrates both the types of situations that were recorded as well as the particular style of the bulletin. Reports were distributed both in English and in Spanish. This account was taken from an English version:

On January 1, 1952, Sr. José Quintero Gómez, Adventist of Chucarima, municipality of Chitaga, Norte de Santander, was summoned to the office of the parish priest, Father Carlos Barrera. The priest ordered him to bring his wife and children to the Catholic church on January 6, 1952, to publicly denounce his Protestant faith, under oath, and to have his children baptized in the Catholic church. The priest told Sr. Quintero Gómez that if the order was not obeyed he was ready to continue the persecution authorized by the departmental governor.

A year ago, in February of 1951, the same Adventist had been ordered by the sheriff, Sr. Juan Pablo Santafé, to discontinue family worship in his house. The sheriff called the parish priest, Father Barrera, and the two of them forbade Sr. Quintero to have any more Protestant meetings in the region. They told him that if he did not abandon his beliefs it would go bad with him. "The priest asked me what authorization we had to conduct religious meetings," said Sr. Quintero to CEDEC's representatives, "and I replied that God had given us souls and bodies and that we had to surrender to Him, and that we were Temples of the Holy Spirit, and that He authorized us. The priest then shouted, 'What Holy Spirit?'"

On November 10, 1951, Father Barrera with a group of men, including the new sheriff, Sr. Mario Prada, arrived at my house to take me prisoner. However, only my wife and children were at home. The priest insulted my wife with vile language and ordered her to take the children out of the house because he was going to burn it. He asked her where I was, and when she did not reply he grabbed her by the hair and shook her violently. Then the priest and his friends left.

At six o'clock the following morning, four men arrived with orders from the priest and the sheriff to arrest me. They took me to town and as the sheriff was at mass they left me in the jail, with hands and feet tied and with guards at the door. When the mass was over, I was carried to the door of the Catholic church. The sheriff came out and said unspeakable things about me to the people. He authorized the people to persecute Protestants, saying that they could kill up to a thousand Protestants and it would not be a sin. Much of his language cannot be mentioned because of its vileness and obscenity.

The priest came out of the church and said that I was being fined 100 pesos for having had Protestant services in my house. Two agents of the sheriff then tied me again and putting me on the ground in front of the Catholic church caused the school children to walk over me. (This same punishment had been meted out to two other Adventists the previous day. They had been tied hand and foot and stretched out on the ground and beaten with whips. Then the children of the Catholic school had been led out to walk over them.) In this treatment I fainted.

Others told me that while I was unconscious I had been hung up and whipped. When I came to, I found myself tied up in a very dusty room. My clothing was soaked, as though I had been carried there through a heavy rain. The priest, Father Barrera, let me go under the condition that I would attend mass every Sunday. He threatened the owner of the farm where I lived with a fine of 100 pesos if he should let me flee.

The next entry recounts the murder of a Seventh-day Adventist man, also in the Santander region, by the police. After repeated threats from the priest and the police, some one hundred Adventists had abandoned their homes and farms. It was noted that this happened right at the time of the coffee harvest, and that these farmers would have to default on payment of loans to the Farm Credit Bank (CEDEC Bulletin #1-12).

In case after case reported in the bulletin, the victims or representatives of CEDEC went to the authorities, including police chiefs, mayors, and governors, to report the crimes, and received no support.[13] What is clear from the reports is that the violence against Protestants was not simply a grassroots development. People were incited by the Roman Catholic clergy, the police took action against Protestant churches and individuals of their own volition, and municipal mayors harassed Protestants. For example, on March 16, 1952, two young Seventh-day Adventists came to the town of Bolívar, Antioquia, to sell Bibles and other religious books. A short time after they had begun, the parish priest went up into the tower of his church and began to shout through a megaphone:

> People of Bolívar, some Protestants have arrived and are strewing the corrupted seed of Protestantism by means of books. But this is an apostolic, Roman Catholic town and we must not, by any means, permit these wicked men to be in our midst. Without loss of time we must defend our religion. These men are rapacious wolves who have come to destroy your souls, but we must drive them out, and it doesn't matter how we do it" (CEDEC Bulletin #2-12).[14]

Eventually the two men were driven out of town, and their books were all confiscated.

A lengthy account of the events which occurred in Genova, Caldas, documents the efforts of the parish priest, Father Angel de Jesús Arteaga, to turn public sentiment against local Protestants. Many statements he made over the public loudspeaker in the town square were reported, including: "That shack of the Protestants must be burned down! Don't be cowards! Why not destroy the Protestant Church? If you aren't capable of doing it, I am." On May 16, 1952, the Protestant Church in Genova was burned down. Two of the attackers died in the flames, apparently caught inside the building while soaking it with gasoline when the vapors exploded (CEDEC Bulletin #4-2, #2-6). With one exception, departmental governors refused to investigate the acts of persecution reported to them (CEDEC Bulletin #4-21). Eventually, even national-level government officials joined in the battle against Protestantism, as when, in March 1952, the Ministry of Communications suspended Protestant radio programs in Bogotá. When the CEDEC investigator visited the chief censor in the offices of the Ministry, he admitted having given the order to block broadcast of the programs, but would not explain his actions or provide a written copy of the order he had received from the Ministry (CEDEC Bulletin #2-13). A debate ensued about the constitutionality of religious freedom, and efforts were made to legally limit the activities of Protestants and missionaries. These developments are discussed below (see "What Is Meant by Religious Freedom?").

EXPRESSIONS OF ANTI-U.S. SENTIMENT

Most religiously motivated acts of violence were committed against Colombian evangelical converts, but foreign missionaries were also attacked, and the language used in justifying these acts reveals a strong anti-U.S. sentiment. For example, a Catholic priest led a group of his parishioners in the stoning of the newly constructed Baptist Church in Bogotá. In his sermon, he said:

> "These foreigners have come to destroy the true faith and to lead the people away from the true Church. While Colombian soldiers are bleed-

ing and dying in Korea in defense of freedom and democracy, heretical Protestant millionaires are pouring their money into Colombia in an effort to steal the true faith from the careless, behind the backs of the clergy" (CEDEC Bulletin #1-5).

The building was stoned, breaking out 131 stained-glass windows. The Colombian pastor, Gustavo Padilla, was struck on the head by a stone. A police patrol car arrived during the demonstration but did nothing to disperse the crowd.

In a pastoral letter at the same time, Monsignor Miguel Angel Builes, bishop of Santa Rosa de Osos, wrote:

> Protestantism in Colombia and in all of Latin America is nothing more than a "fifth-column" which looks forward to the economic conquest and absorption which it hopes to accomplish through its Protestant propaganda. . . . Protestants seek an earthly and imperialistic dominion over the Latin-speaking peoples, and the pretext is evangelization. . . . The Good News they bring is that of slavery (CEDEC Bulletin #4-22).

Protestant missionaries were often denounced as foreigners who were in Colombia to steal "our faith, and with it our nationality, our freedom, and our independence (CEDEC Bulletin #14). Ironically, this accusation was sometimes made by Catholic priests who were themselves foreigners.

In January 1953, a "Treaty on the Missions" was signed which gave Catholic bishops total authority over education in the Indian territories. In September 1953, the national government directed departmental governors to stop every form of religious activity other than that of the Roman Catholic Church in eighteen parts of the country designated as Catholic Mission Territories. This area amounted to three-quarters of Colombia and included the predominantly Protestant, English-speaking islands of San Andrés and Providencia, Colombia's possessions in the Caribbean. Stoll (1982, 166) speculates that there is a link between this development and the success during the same month of Cameron Townsend in gaining access for the Summer Institute of Linguistics (SIL) in Peru. For years, Townsend had been trying to gain entry for the SIL into Colombia, but had found the 1887 Vatican Concordat an obstacle. It was not until almost a decade later (February 1962) that SIL signed a contract with the Colombian government under Liberal president Alberto Lleras Camargo.[15]

COLOMBIA'S COLD WAR

Yet, in striking contradiction to the anti-U.S. rhetoric, Catholic denunciation of the Protestants often employed the language of the Cold War. Protestants were routinely accused of being Communists, of distributing Communist literature, or of opening the door for a Communist takeover in Colombia. Protestantism was referred to as "religious subversion." People were denounced as being Liberal, Protestant, subversive, and Communist in the same breath (CEDEC Bulletin #8-13).

President Rojas Pinilla, who was greeted with great hope by Liberals and Conservatives alike (who felt that only the military could put an end to the violence), articulated the assumptions behind the link between Communism and Protestantism in his inaugural address in 1953 (CEDEC Bulletin #43-1). His logic was that Protestantism eventually leads to the loss of all religious faith and hence inevitably to Communism:

> "As one can see not only from the history of the Reformation but also from daily experience, the dissemination of Protestantism in Latin American countries leads not so much to the increase in sincere and respectable Protestants as to the loss of all religious faith and to the inevitable adherence to Communism of those who have been exposed to teachings fundamentally contrary to the essential dogmas of Catholicism" (CEDEC Bulletin #34-1).

The bulletin reports frequent instances of the denunciation of North American missionaries as Communist agents. On February 21, 1953, two U.S. women missionaries working in Quinchia, Caldas, were accused of giving out Communist literature. Their house was searched, some gospel tracts were confiscated, and the postmaster was ordered not to deliver or send out mail for them without the mayor's consent (CEDEC Bulletin #8-11). On March 2, 1953, a North American woman missionary living in Piedecuesta, Santander, was awakened by a mob of twenty men at 1:30 in the morning. They broke into her house, and she was struck on the hand and chest with crowbars. The men said they were attacking "because you are Communists" (CEDEC Bulletin #9-2). They stole and wrecked everything they could, and threatened the missionary, saying that if she did not leave within two days they were coming back to set the building on fire.

There is a connection here between understandings at the time about the origins of the civil chaos and this somewhat surprising link between Protestantism and Communism. The onset of the worst part of *La Violencia* is often dated to the assassination of Liberal Party populist leader Jorge Eliecer Gaitán in April 1948. The ensuing riots in Bogotá (referred to as the *Bogotázo*) resulted in the destruction and looting of buildings that symbolized the power structure. The Presidential Palace and many Catholic churches were attacked, and the archbishop's palace was burned to the ground. The bishops issued a pastoral letter, condemning attacks on the church and its representatives. In it, they laid the blame for violence on "anti-Catholic propaganda, moral disintegration, and the inflamed passions of those who sought to undermine the social order, of which the Church was an integral part" (Levine 1981, 84).[16] For its part, the government blamed a Communist conspiracy to disrupt the Ninth Inter-American Conference then taking place in Bogotá (Hartlyn 1988, 39).

Subsequently, Colombia suspended diplomatic relations with the Soviet Union in the belief that Russian agents had worked in collaboration with Colombian Communists. There are many permutations to the logic behind the link between Protestantism and Communism. In March 1953, a newspaper article entitled "Protestantism or Communism," quoted in Bulletin #9, stated that Protestantism's "poor and disorganized ideology creates in the mind of the people a favorable condition for the propagation of dialectical materialism, which has a firmer structure and is more convincing" (CEDEC Bulletin #9-14). The author goes on to claim that "the conversion of a convinced Catholic to a Communist is an almost impossible task."

For its part, the Colombian Communist Party denied any association with Protestant groups. When Gilberto Vieira, the secretary general of the Communist Party in Colombia, was accused of inviting Protestant missionaries to the region where he lives, he denied the charge, saying that "he had nothing to do with Protestant missionaries, as they were agents of Yankee Imperialism" (CEDEC Bulletin #9-14).

Colombia's First Human Rights Reports: The CEDEC Bulletins

CEDEC's campaign to document the persecution and bring it to the attention of the international community was diligent and well thought out. The CEDEC bulletin can be seen as Colombia's first human rights reports. Copies of the bulletins were distributed to, among others, the United Nations Commission on Human Rights, the Organization of American States, the Pan American Union, U.S. President Harry S. Truman, Secretary of State Dean Acheson, The World Council of Churches, the Associated Press and United Press, International News Service, Pope Pius XII, Vatican officials, Cardinal Spellman, and editors of leading secular and religious publications throughout the world. The diligence with which CEDEC reported incidents of violence against Evangelicals was rewarded with international recognition of the situation and efforts on the parts of many groups within the United States to put pressure on the Colombia government to put a stop to religious persecution.

What Is Meant by Freedom of Religion?

A key question in the discussion of the religious persecution of Protestants during the 1950s was its legality. The question of the meaning of religious freedom was hotly debated in the popular and religious press. At the time *La Violencia* broke out, a contradiction existed between the Concordat (the treaty between the Colombian government and the Vatican) and the Colombian constitution. One of the significant outcomes of constitutional reforms of 1936 was the establishment of religious freedom. Article 53 reads: "The State guarantees freedom of conscience. No one shall be disturbed because of his religious opinions, or obliged to profess creeds or to observe practices which are contrary to his conscience. Freedom of religious worship is guaranteed where it is not contrary to Christian morals or to the law" (CEDEC Bulletin #5-27).

The police, mayors, public authorities, and Catholic clergy on one side and the evangelical converts on the other repeatedly invoked the Constitution of Colombia as their justification in support of, or condemnation of religious freedom. During 1952, a well-known Jesuit named Eduardo Ospina published an article in the Bogotá newspaper, *El Tiempo*, stating that although the Constitution granted Protestants the freedom to worship inside their temples, it did not give them the right to make propaganda (CEDEC Bulletin #9-13). By August 1952, this position was accepted as the official government interpretation of the constitutional rulings on religious freedom. The inspector of public education, who had closed evangelical primary schools in August 1952, stated: "In Colombia there is no liberty of worship. There is liberty to profess, but not to preach or propagate, and that is not liberty, it is tolerance. Tolerance is what there is in Colombia" (CEDEC Bulletin #5-21).

This new distinction, between freedom of worship and freedom of propaganda, began to appear in statements from national government officials in 1952 (CEDEC Bulletin #5-25). The CEDEC bulletin records the increasing alarm with which Evangelicals responded to this new development. Goff observes in Bulletin #9: "Where a few years ago no government official considered that Protestant propaganda was unconstitutional, now every mayor and policeman had a legal excuse to jail or fine anyone found distributing tracts, holding street meetings, or making publicity concerning the Protestant church" (CEDEC Bulletin #9-13).

The Catholic hierarchy responded enthusiastically to this new distinction, saying, for example: "The civil law cannot impede a man from having certain beliefs, but it can surely prohibit him from propagating his evil ideas." In his 1952 Lenten pastoral letter, Monsignor Miguel Angel Builes, bishop of Santa Rosa de Osos, Antioquía, articulates the belief that religious freedom ensured by the Constitution will lead to civil disorder:

> The national Constitution recognizes liberty of worship, but it does not give the heretics liberty to express their faith outside of their chapels. By so expressing their religion, Protestants are endangering national unity and they will carry us, gradually, to religious war, the greatest evil which can come upon a nation" (CEDEC Bulletin #2-27).

In a time of increasing chaos and civil unrest, the Roman Catholic Church was sending the clear message that Roman Catholicism was not only the sole legitimate religion of Colombia but that the state recognized it as an essential element in the social order and was thus obliged to protect it and make it respected. The logic for laying the blame for the violence on the back of the Protestants was impeccable: If Roman Catholicism was essential to the social order, then whatever and whomever challenges it also challenges the social order.

The rhetoric conflating religious unity and social order increased as time went on. In a radio address (reprinted in *El Siglo*) in May 1952, Monsignor Botero, rector of the Catholic University in Medellín, made the statement:

"The peace of the country has to be first of all a religious peace. The Protestants and enemies of the Church dissolve national unity and create extremely serious problems for the Government and for the public order. A country which has religious cohesion is more easily governed than a country where different creeds are rampant" (CEDEC Bulletin #3-21).

The rich corpus of material available in the CEDEC bulletins adds a crucial dimension to the study of the history of *La Violencia*. Much more analysis of them is needed. Many patterns which carry over into the present day can be identified. The connection between this material and the contemporary situation in Colombia is considered in the next sections.

RECENT DEVELOPMENTS IN THE ROMAN CATHOLIC CHURCH

The Roman Catholic Church worldwide experienced dramatic changes during the 1960s and 1970s, but by and large, the Catholic Church in Colombia was less affected by those changes than many other areas. The 1968 Latin American Bishops' Conference (CELAM) held in Medellín, Colombia, is often viewed as the turning point, when the established church in Latin America recognized its need to be more responsive to issues of social injustice and the struggle of the poor. Colombian bishops rejected some of the more dramatic conclusions of the Medellín conference and published a treatise outlining their objections to the statements emerging from that conference. During the decades following *La Violencia,* the Roman Catholic hierarchy, for the most part, was resistant to ideas of social change that challenged its authority. As the ideas of liberation theology became influential in other regions of Latin America, Colombia's Church became a major center of opposition to its more radical elements. Despite this, Camilo Torres, a young Colombian Jesuit of upper-class origins, became one of the first martyrs of liberation theology. He was killed in 1966 shortly after he left the priesthood to fight with the Ejército de Liberación Nacional (ELN). During the decade of the 1970s, the Roman Catholic Church in Colombia did produce a few progressive bishops, among them Raúl Camader Zambrano and Gerardo Valencia Cano, both of whom were killed in plane crashes at the beginning of the 1970s. Wilde has stated that the Roman Catholic Church in Colombia entered the 1980s deeply divided "with an unparalleled internal conflict, sharply divided between longings toward a stable past, associations with a reformist present, and hopes for a transformed future."[17]

In the 1990s, this conflict within the Roman Catholic hierarchy has continued. Responses from Catholic leaders to the government's war on left-wing rebels demonstrate a deep split. Bishop Leonardo Gómez Serna, from the Santander region, reportedly "begged the government and the army to back off from their declaration of all-out war against the leftist groups on the basis that it would put the poor and defenseless at risk." At the same time, Archbishop Pedro Rubiano Saenz, president of Colombia's episcopal conference, supported the government's actions and asked it to "put the house in order" by taking a tough stance against the rebels (Wirpsa 1997).

Leading the conservative response to radicalizing tendencies in the church was Alfonso López Trujillo, first as a secretary and president of CELAM, and then as cardinal archbishop of Medellín. His departure for Rome has been linked to greater openness to change within the Church, and the Church has clearly taken on a greater role as an advocate for the poor. Priests and Catholic workers have been murdered for their role in attempting to mediate conflicts and put a stop to the activities of paramilitary death squads (Wirpsa 1997), and Jesuits and other Catholic leaders have been at the forefront of the efforts to put a stop to human rights abuses in contemporary Colombia.

CURRENT ISSUES IN CHURCH-STATE RELATIONS IN COLOMBIA

There are some striking parallels between developments in Colombia during the 1990s and the history outlined above. In 1990, an evangelical educator, Jaime Ortiz Hurtado, rector of the Biblical Seminary in Medellín, won a seat in the National Constitutional Assembly that drafted the new constitution. The inclusion of Evangelicals in the Assembly was a first in Colombian politics.[18] It was something of a stunning debut: Ortiz received so many votes (the sixth highest of 116) that his Unión Cristiana Party won an additional seat in the seventy-member Assembly, which was occupied by Arturo Mejía Borda, a university professor in Bogotá. The news media took a sudden interest in Ortiz, who is considered one of the top Protestant systematic theologians in Latin America. He apparently bears a striking physical resemblance to Mikhail Gorbachev, and the press rapidly dubbed him "Colombia's Gorbachev." Articles in El Tiempo spoke of an evangelical perestroika, noting that Evangelicals, who at that time numbered about 2.5 million, might have captured as many as sixteen seats had they organized their campaign sooner and voted in bloc. However, the Unión Cristiana had coalesced only about a month before the election. Since the Assembly, Colombian Evangelicals have become increasingly politically active. By 1992, three Evangelicals had been elected to Congress.

A new constitution, promulgated in 1991, replaces the 1886 Colombian Constitution, which was the oldest uninterrupted constitution in Latin America. (See Morgan and Alzate Buitrago 1992 for an excellent discussion of the recent constitutional reform in Colombia.) Among its many significant legal reforms, the new constitution separates church and state and declares all religions equal.[19] In August 1992, the Colombian Attorney General's office released a seventy-page document declaring that Colombian laws relating to the Concordat were unconstitutional. Bishops and priests responded to this document with anger, claiming that the Constitution itself violates the Concordat (*New York Times*, Sept. 6, 1992, 11). Reports in 1993, however, stated that the constitutional court declared that ruling on the Concordat was beyond its legal jurisdiction *(New York Times*, August 8, 1993 10: 1). A renegotiated treaty was discarded, unsigned after the court's decision in July 1993.

Colombian Evangelicals hope that the official government arrangement that has designated them as second-class citizens will fade into history. The head of the Unión Cristiana, Rev. Héctor Pardo, has been one of many voices urging the government to do away with the Concordat. In the *New York Times* (Sept. 6, 1992), he made the following statement about the privileged position of the Catholic Church in Colombia: "They have held the reins of power for centuries, and the results are evident: A nation with fewer moral values and more out of control every day."

When a rumor spread during the Colombian presidential elections in 1994 that the Liberal Party candidate, Ernesto Samper Pizano, had secretly promised to name a Protestant as his education minister, the archbishop of Bucaramanga, using language reminiscent of the 1950s, called upon Catholic Liberals to cast blank ballots in the election. A vote for Samper, he claimed, would support the "diabolical Liberal-Protestant alliance" and would "damage the religious unity of the republic" (Brooke 1994, 9) For his part, Samper accused his Conservative opponent, Andrés Pastrana, of inciting a religious war. At a "tolerance banquet" in Bucaramanga, Samper stated, "We have come [to the city of Bucaramanga] to say no to the religious war, no to fanaticism, and yes to tolerance" (ibid.). In support of Samper's stance, a dozen Colombian intellectuals, including the Nobel laureate Gabriel García Márquez, released a manifesto for religious freedom.

In January 1997, the Mennonite Central Committee reported that the Colombian government had moved to close the Mennonite seminary *Hacedores de Paz* (Peacemakers). The program offers an alternative to military service for conscientious objectors, with about seventy students. In addition to instruction in nonviolence, human rights, and ecology, students at the seminary learn Anabaptist theology. The *Hacedores* program invoked a Colombian law which exempts youth who are enrolled in theological seminaries from military service. The Colombian military refused to exempt the Mennonite seminary students from military service, claiming that the seminary did not meet the educational requirements established by law. The National Police recommended the closure of the *Hacedores* seminary, and began investigations of the Colombian Mennonite Church and its reconciliation program, Justapaz. The case received a good deal of international attention, was covered on CNN, and some three hundred North Americans wrote letters in support of the seminary.

On April 25, a Bogotá court ruled that the seminary may remain open (NISBCO 1997).

CONCLUSIONS

The foremost authority on Colombian Catholicism, Daniel Levine, argues that from the beginning the Colombian Roman Catholic hierarchy has been determined to preserve its authority and unity, reaffirm hierarchy, and thus control and limit popular groups. This situation, he writes, results in "unrelenting pressures and sustained attacks on internal democratization and radical activism" (Levine 1986, 20). Their conservatism is a contrary example to the view that the Roman Catholic Church is a progressive force all over Latin America, and that Protestant converts are conservatives who collaborate with government. In Colombia, as elsewhere in Latin America, evangelicalism has been a movement of the poor. Whatever else evangelical conversion may accomplish for individuals, it removes them from the direct authority of the Catholic hierarchy, and by doing so, may be perceived as a threat to both religious and civil power structures when they are closely linked.

Studying the details of religious persecution during the years of *La Violencia* sheds new light on processes unfolding in Colombia during those years. In particular, this history highlights the way the state, with the aid of the Roman Catholic clergy, tried to compensate for fragmentation by forging an ideological guise of unity. Protestants were convenient scapegoats. Numerically, there were not enough of them to have been the real reason why violence erupted during the 1950s, but they represented deep-seated dissatisfaction with the status quo (couched in religious terms readily intelligible to the clergy). The equation of national unity with religious unity during a period when the authority of the state was being challenged represents perfectly the symbiosis of church and state in Colombia, and underscores the role the church has played in sustaining the oligarchy. The contemporary drive to eliminate or weaken the government's treaty with the Vatican, then, logically follows the restructuring of government growing out of the new constitution, which in turn was a response to new social and political currents in Colombia, among them that of evangelical Christianity. As evangelicalism grows, one can expect further challenges to the dominant position of Roman Catholicism.

15.

PERU

Evangelization and Religious Freedom

————————◆————————

Jeffrey Klaiber, S.J.

The debate as to whether the evangelization of Peru occurred in the sixteenth century or is just beginning to happen in the late twentieth century is as much a question of religion and theology as it is of social control and cultural pluralism. The Catholic bishops who raised the voice of alarm over growing Protestant influence during the Fujimori presidential campaign in 1990 were the same ones who led the battle against liberation theology within their own church. In the sixteenth century bishops and priests also anguished over what appeared to be deviant forms of Christianity, but the various campaigns to extirpate idolatries frequently had more to do with asserting control over the Indians than with evangelizing them. In this sense, it is well to keep in mind that the Peruvian church, like the pre–Vatican II Catholic church in general, was never a uniform monolith, although Rome and some bishops often wished it were.

The sixteenth-century church harbored both open-minded humanists and narrow-minded zealots. The humanists would include José de Acosta, the Spanish Jesuit who admired the cultural achievements of the Incas, as well as the mestizo Jesuit Blas Valera, who, along with certain lay mestizo chroniclers like Garcilaso de la Vega, believed that they saw the hand of God in the culture and history of the Incas long before the conquest. For them the Indian cultures were fundamentally good, and evangelization represented not a major break but rather the final step in a process of maturation (Klaiber 1995, 37-62). Along with these humanists other churchmen like Gerónimo Loayza, the first archbishop of Lima, and his successor, Toribio de Mogrovejo, accepted the fundamental theses of Bartolomé de Las Casas that the Indians had basic rights that could not be violated, and that Spain had no legitimate right to be in the New World if it did not evangelize the Indians and treat them as human beings. At the other end of the spectrum were churchmen and political authorities, imbued by sixteenth-century nationalism and fired up by the militant neo-orthodoxy of Trent, who saw evangelization as an instrument of domination. Their best representative was Viceroy Francisco Toledo (1569-81), who zealously sought to reorder Peru and reevangelize it. This mentality may also be seen in the many archbishops, bishops, and priests who throughout the sixteenth and seventeenth centuries enthusiastically destroyed idols, forever discovering new evidence that the Indians were not real Christians. This contrast, between the humanists with a wider view of Christianity and culture, and those with a narrow and more sectarian view, was strikingly highlighted in the anti-idolatry campaigns of the seventeenth century.

THE ANTI-IDOLATRY CAMPAIGNS

The evangelization of Peru began in 1532 with the arrival of Pizarro. Franciscans, Dominicans, Augustinians, and Mercedarians worked hand in hand with the *encomenderos*—the beneficiaries of royal land grants which required them to convert the Indians—to set up Indian parishes. The Jesuits, who arrived with Viceroy Francisco Toledo, were the last of the major religious orders that carried out the evangelization of Peru. But their coming also marked the beginning of a second stage in that process. Toledo, who had heard reports about the ineffectiveness of the first attempt to evangelize the Indians, arrived with clear orders to reorganize the viceroyalty and to reevangelize it. In the 1560s, for example, in the region of Huamanga the Indians, in the belief that the *huacas* (idols) had come alive, broke out in a frenzied dance called Taki Onqoy. Furthermore, it was not until 1571 that the last Inca, Túpac Amaru, who had hidden away in the inaccessible fortress of Vilcabamba, turned himself over to the authorities in Cuzco.

In the background of Toledo's concerns was the Catholic Counter-Reformation and especially the Council of Trent (1545-63) which imposed a new and more demanding orthodoxy on Catholic Europe. The Jesuits, who stood out for their theological contributions at the council, seemed best fitted to apply the new orthodoxy to the New World situation. Indeed, José de Acosta and other Jesuits played a prominent role at the Third Council of Lima (1582-83), presided over by the great reorganizer of the Peruvian church, Archbishop Toribio de Mogrovejo. Finally, in 1608, following the outcry of Francisco de Avila, a priest of Huarochirí outside of Lima, the first of the anti-idolatry campaigns was set into motion. Avila revealed that he had discovered innumerable idols and mummies among his Indian charges. This crisis could not be handled by the Inquisition, founded in Lima in 1569, because the Indians were exempt from its jurisdiction. The anti-idolatry campaigns became therefore a sort of substitute for the formal Inquisition.[1] In 1621 Archbishop Villagómez appointed seven visitor-generals to visit the villages and root out the old idols. The most famous of the visitors, the Jesuit Pablo de Arriaga, described in detail in his chronicle, *The Extirpation of Idolatries in Peru* (1621), how he rounded up mummies and idols and had them burned in bonfires in the main square of each town.

These denunciations of idolatry, if taken at their face value, certainly supported the claim that the first evangelization had failed. Yet recent authors have presented new interpretations which question that thesis. Upon closer examination one can find widely diverging interpretations of the state of the Indians' Christianity among the very witnesses of the process. In 1626 Archbishop Gonzalo de Campo of Lima reported to the king: "I have found much idolatry in many places in this archbishopric." Three years earlier, in 1623, the bishop of Cuzco made this startling statement in his report to the king: "I give infinite thanks to God that I have found this land free of idolatrous abuses and rites."² Was the bishop of Cuzco naïve and unaware of the subtleties of native cultural resistance, or was he a broad-minded Christian who believed that what others called idolatrous ways were simply harmless cultural remnants that had been absorbed and woven into the Indian's new Catholic religion?

There is no doubt that government and church officials were genuinely concerned about the authenticity of the Indians' religion. But in order to avoid arriving at hasty conclusions about the truth of their reports, it is well to keep in mind the many vested interests that some of those officials had in carrying out the anti-idolatry campaigns. In the first place the king and Viceroy Toledo were particularly concerned about the damage caused by Bartolomé de Las Casas's campaign in favor of the rights of the Indians. In his campaign Las Casas questioned the legitimacy of Spain's right to be in the New World. In order to reestablish that claim to legitimacy, Toledo rounded up Indian informants who conveniently revealed that the Incas, in fact, had been tyrants and were therefore not the legitimate lords of the land. Furthermore, as long as idols were to be found, Spain's fundamental mission to the New World, which was to evangelize it, was still justified. It can be argued that Toledo, who created the Indian reductions or resettlements, did not single out religion per se as the object of his concern, but rather the entire cultural memory of a people that looked to the Inca, living in their midst or in some far-away land, as their real lord.

In the second place, church authorities, and especially the archbishops of the secular clergy who followed the first wave of the religious orders, could point to the persistence of idols as proof that the religious had not done a good job. It is somewhat curious that Saint Toribio de Mogrovejo, archbishop of Lima from 1581 to 1606, and a member of the secular clergy, visited hundreds of Andean villages during his four lengthy visits and did not seem to be unduly worried about a resurgence of idol worship. Most of his criticism was directed at the local magistrates (*corregidores*) who exploited the Indians.³ But many of Toribio's successors were gravely concerned about the apparent widespread presence of idols, although, like the archbishop of Lima in 1626, they did not always point to concrete instances to support their claim. During that very period the bishops were in the process of removing the responsibility for catechizing the Indians from the religious orders and handing them over to the secular clergy. On a variant note, Toledo also turned over some of the Domini-can responsibilities to the Jesuits. As one author observed, the timing of the anti-idolatry campaigns had more to do with inner church politics than with a "measurable recrudescence of native beliefs" (Griffith 1996, 39).

In the third place, individual priests and other authorities in charge of the anti-idolatry campaigns had good reason to emphasize and even exaggerate numbers. One of the informants on the Taki Onqoy phenomenon, Cristóbal Albornoz, made scant mention of it in his first report. But in a later report, written to advance his ecclesiastical career, he emphasized the great number of idols he personally had destroyed.[4] The bishop of Huamanga, Francisco Verdugo (1621-37), refused to let the visitors into his diocese because they "distress" the Indians (Griffith 1996, 58). Finally, local priests had their own motives for fostering the campaigns. In some cases the Indians accused them of exploitation and mistreatment. The best defense in that situation was to counter by accusing the Indians of having lapsed into idolatrous ways. In fact, Francisco de Avila, the priest who touched off the first anti-idolatry campaign, had been accused by his Indian wards of robbing them (Duviols 1977, 405).

By mid-seventeenth century the anti-idolatry campaigns had been termi-nated. Apparently the church was satisfied that the basic work of evangeliza-tion was done, and political authorities believed that the Indian population was safely under control. But the debate about the anti-idolatry campaigns remains quite open. Were they really necessary, or, as the new interpretations suggest, did they cover over power plays carried out by viceroys, archbishops, secular and religious clergy as they vied to assert their authority and enhance their prestige?

THE BOURBONS, REBELLIONS, AND THE INQUISITION

In the eighteenth century the Spanish Bourbons were faced with two new dan-gers: growing creole (Peruvians of European extraction) pride and the resur-gence of a neo-Inca nationalism. The Indian rebellions were incited in part by Bourbon reformism, which in the practice meant more taxation and forced labor work in the *mita* (public works) and the mines. In 1742 Juan Santos Atahualpa led a movement which engulfed a major section of the eastern jungle region of Peru. Juan Santos claimed to be the new Inca sent by God to rectify injustices and restore Peru to its legitimate owners. He disappeared in 1756 in the same mysterious way in which he had appeared (Castro Arenas 1973, 11-12). In 1780, in the area south of Cuzco, Túpac Amaru ignited the greatest Indian rebellion in South America. Bishop Moscoso of Cuzco excommuni-cated him, and the visitor, José Antonio de Areche, formally denounced him as a traitor and an apostate, guilty of leading the Indians back along the path of idolatry. Túpac Amaru, a pious Catholic who had studied under the Jesuits in Cuzco, responded by citing the Bible to justify his revolution.[5]

The other problem—growing creole consciousness—was first felt within the church. Even before the Crown faced that problem it had already imposed many restrictions on the religious orders in order to eliminate abuses and irregularities. Of special concern was the overpopulating of convents and monasteries, a problem that had affected the church in Europe on the eve of the Reformation. In 1653, for example, a royal decree forbade the founding of new convents, and in 1734 a moratorium was placed on the admission of candidates to religious life. But the greatest concern for the eighteenth century Bourbons was growing creole influence in both the religious and secular clergy. For the religious orders the Crown devised the *alternativa*, a measure by which every other superior or provincial had to be a *peninsular*, i.e., Spanish born, no matter how many creoles belonged to the order or the convent. In 1680 the imposition of a new Spanish provincial on the Franciscans in Lima led to a street battle between friars and soldiers.[6] Increasingly, measures such as the *alternativa* produced friction between creoles and Spanish in religious life. The expulsion of the Jesuits in 1767, which represented the high point of Bourbon absolutism, was done in large part to send a warning to all other religious orders. Finally, the Inquisition, which dealt mainly with lapses in public and clerical morality, turned its attention increasingly to subversive literature and attitudes. In a breakdown of all the cases dealt with by the Lima Inquisition, only 10 percent dealt with heresy. The rest concerned Jewish-Portuguese merchants accused of being "Judaizers"(17%), bigamy (20%), witchcraft (12%), and solicitation by clergy (7%).[7] In the eighteenth century, the Inquisition paid particular attention to books and other written materials arriving from Europe. One important precursor of Peru's independence, Toribio Rodríguez de Mendoza, the priest rector of San Carlos, Lima's principal *colegio* (high school), was warned by the Inquisition about forbidden works he kept in his office.[8]

INDEPENDENCE, LIBERALS, AND ROMANIZATION

The church's role in the independence in Latin America is a well-known story, and Peru was no exception to the rule. The upper clergy condemned the movement, while the lower clergy sympathized with or openly supported it. In effect, the official church lost control over large numbers of priests and patriotic laypersons who were not moved by papal and episcopal exhortations to return to obedience to Spain. Under pressure from Ferdinand VII both Pope Pius VII and Pope Leo XII exhorted disobedient Latin Americans to obey their legitimate sovereigns. All bishops in Peru save one condemned the rebels. The exception was the bishop of Cuzco, José Pérez de Armendáriz, who not only did not condemn the movement but was even suspected of being a conspirator during the Pumacahua rebellion in 1814.[9] Ildefonso Muñecas, a creole priest, led a separatist army up to the Bolivian highlands where he was killed by the Spaniards. In Arequipa another local priest, Mariano José de Arce, called for outright separation from Spain. Many of these liberal priests were elected to the first constitutional assembly (1822-23), which was presided over by Francisco Javier de Luna Pizarro, a priest from Arequipa and future archbishop of Lima. One measure of the liberal atmosphere that reigned during those years was the fact that James Thompson, a Baptist minister who was invited by San Martin to establish the system of instruction of Joseph Lancaster, the English educator, in Peruvian schools, received full cooperation from several priests (Mecham 1966, 162).

Peru, like the rest of Latin America, experienced a process of "Romanization" during the initial decades of the century. Most of the bishops at the time of independence were Spaniards who either fled or were forced to leave. Rome refused to recognize the new republic's claim to enjoy the same rights of patronage as the king. After several years of a mutual standoff, the Vatican finally consented to allowing the government in Lima to present candidates, but Rome would make the final choice. The Archdiocese of Lima, vacant since 1821, received its first archbishop—Jorge Benavente—in 1835. Soon all the other dioceses had new bishops. But the new bishops were named by Rome on the condition that they demonstrate their loyalty to the papacy, which was deeply concerned about liberalism and anticlericalism in Europe. The new bishops were all Peruvians, but noticeably more conservative than the liberal clergy who had raised the banner of independence. In 1851 Archbishop Luna Pizarro, once a liberal but then a firm spokesman for the new Roman line, published a brief excommunicating Francisco de Paúla Vigil, a liberal priest who called for a national church freed from the interference of the Roman curia. By the middle of the century, the generation of liberal priests at the time of independence had been successfully marginalized.[10]

It would be simplistic to present this story only in terms of a liberal-church struggle. In fact, the real difficulty that the church had to face after 1821 was the authoritarian mentality of many liberals, who were no more tolerant than the Bourbons. One early manifestation of that mentality was the reform of religious orders of 1826. Lay liberals respected the liberal clergy because most of them were Peruvians and members of the secular clergy. But they did not favor the members of the religious orders because they did not seem to offer any useful service to the new republic. Furthermore, because many religious orders were missionary in character, there were many more Spaniards among the religious. In 1824 Simón Bolívar himself closed down the Franciscan monastery of St. Rose of Ocopa in the central highlands and expelled all the friars. When General Santa Cruz published the Reform of Regulars in 1826, in reality he simply republished a decree that had already been prepared by the Bourbons. The decree ordered thirty-nine convents and monasteries throughout Peru to be confiscated by the state because they did not have a sufficient number of residents, or because there were two convents of the same order in the same city (Tibesar 1982, 205-39). The Reform also placed all the members of religious orders under their local bishops, thus cutting them off from communication with their own superiors in Europe. As a result of this blow, as well as internal problems that the orders had been experiencing since well before independence, religious life fell into a deep crisis from which it recovered only in the second part of the century.

LIBERALS, ANTICLERICALS, AND THE END OF PATRONAGE

By mid-century the liberals took on the church. In the 1856 constitutional convention they eliminated tithes and the ecclesiastical liberal privileges (*fueros*), and attempted to separate church and state. Their measures were deemed too radical for the times, and in the midst of protests the more pragmatic-minded caudillo, Ramón Castillo, sought a middle course. In a new convention, held in 1860, the assembly members retained the elimination of tithes and the *fueros*, but maintained Catholicism as the exclusive religion of the state. But peace between liberals and the church was far from secured and many more skirmishes followed. Two notorious examples of government heavy-handedness concerned the bishop of Puno and the Jesuits. In 1866 the new bishop of Puno, Ambrosio Huerta, provoked the ire of the attorney general, José Gregorio Paz Soldán, when he failed to asked for official authorization to hold a local synod. He compounded his error when he went off to Rome to attend the First Vatican Council without asking for the necessary permission. Under pressure, he resigned as bishop in 1874. Later, he was restored to grace and became bishop of Arequipa.[11] The Jesuits, who returned to Peru in 1871, also provoked the wrath of the liberals when one of their members, Father Ricardo Cappa, a Spaniard, wrote a history of Peru placing the Peruvians in a bad light. The Peruvian parliament voted to expel the order in 1886. The Jesuits quietly returned a year later.[12]

On more legitimate grounds, liberals passed legislation curtailing the church's control over secular society. In 1869 the government removed the cemeteries from the church's control and allowed municipal government to provide for lay cemeteries. In 1897 non-Catholics were granted the right to have a civil marriage.

The high tide of anticlerical liberalism was reached in the constitutional congress of 1932-33. In the previous decade Archbishop Emilio Lissón of Lima had established very close ties with President Augusto B. Leguía, who curried the church's favor in every way possible. Lissón responded by enthusiastically embracing the dictator on every public occasion. On one of those occasions Leguía was declared a "Knight of the Supreme Military Order of Christ."[13] The archbishop's discreet silence when Leguía deported or silenced his enemies proved to be his downfall. In the wake of Leguía's overthrow in 1930 Lissón was called to Rome under a cloud and never returned to Peru. The memory of the church's close association with Leguía highly influenced liberals, Apristas, socialists, and right-wing nationalists at the constitutional convention held under President Sánchez Cerro in 1932. The Apristas in particular remembered that their leader, Haya de la Torre, had been deported as a consequence of his role in leading a protest march against the consecration of

Peru to the Sacred Heart in 1923. Although the Apristas were expelled from the assembly in 1933, there were still enough anticlericals on the right to push through legislation which the church found objectionable.

In 1930 Sánchez Cerro decreed obligatory civil marriage for all and allowed for divorce. The 1932 assembly ratified those decrees. In the constitution which was promulgated in 1933, Article 85 deprived members of religious orders of the right of citizenship, which in practice meant the right to vote, and Article 100 declared that members of the clergy could not be elected to congress.[14] Although these measures were a pale reflection of the anticlerical provisions of the Mexican constitution of 1917, they clearly underlined the antidemocratic double standard that anticlericals practiced with regard to the church. Víctor Andrés Belaunde, who defended the Catholic cause in the assembly, proposed to give the vote to women. But his opponents rejected the proposal, reportedly on grounds that women would be dominated by clerics. They did, however, allow women to vote in municipal elections.[15] In 1940, a new law took the power of nominating bishops out of the hands of congress and gave it to the president of the republic, who alone exercised the right of presentation until the constitution of 1980 ended the system of national patronage.

The atmosphere surrounding the 1978-79 constitutional assembly was strikingly different from the heavily charged anticlerical atmosphere of the thirties. The Peruvian church had emerged from the Second Vatican Council (1962-65) and the Bishops' Conference of Medellín (1968) as one of the most progressive in Latin America. Under the leadership of Cardinal Juan Landázuri Ricketts, Archbishop of Lima (1955-90), the church underwent a radical transformation. Gustavo Gutiérrez influenced the Medellín conference with his theology of liberation, which became a rallying banner for progressive clergy, religious women, and lay pastoral agents throughout the country. The Peruvian Episcopal Conference took the initiative to propose to the constitutional assembly—elected in 1978—the formula which put an end to the last vestiges of state patronage. The assembly, presided over by Victor Raúl Haya de la Torre, accepted the church's formula without debate, and turned it into Article 86 of the new constitution. The formula states simply:

> Within a framework of independence and autonomy, the state recognizes the Catholic church as an important element in the historical, cultural, and moral formation of Peru. The state offers it its cooperation. The state may also establish different types of cooperation with other confessions.[16]

In essence, the article puts an end to state control over the naming of bishops (*patronato*). At the same time church and state signed a mutual agreement regarding particular points in their new arrangement. For example, the church agreed to notify the government before creating any new ecclesiastical jurisdictions or naming any new bishops.[17] The same general agreement stipulates that the church and religious orders are exonerated from paying taxes.[18] The church's right to found schools is formally guaranteed. Finally, military chaplains must be Peruvians by birth.[19] The latest constitution, written by the congress elected in the wake of Alberto Fujimori's closing of his first congress in 1992, included the 1980 church-state formula as Article 50.[20]

One of the most important areas of church-state cooperation is education. The military junta of 1962-63 adopted a policy of allocating a portion of the education budget to church schools for the poor. This was done to alleviate pressure on the public school system, which already felt the strain of the country's burgeoning youth population. It was also perceived as a way of extending quality education to the poor. All successive governments have renewed this practice. From a financial point of view, the Catholic educational system, which includes approximately 8 percent of the entire primary and secondary student population, is divided into three categories: private, self-financed schools; mixed state and privately financed schools; and schools which are nearly totally financed by the state. The schools belonging to this last category are really state schools which are administered by the church.

A major block within this third category are the Faith and Joy (*Fe y Alegría*) schools run by the Jesuit fathers. In 1997 there were 107 Faith and Joy schools throughout the country, with a total student body of 61,169.[21] According to the church-state agreement, the state pays the salaries of the teachers and the Jesuits have the right to name the teachers and the school directors. These schools also differ from normal state schools in another way: the Jesuits require a high degree of parental participation, which includes working on the weekends to build the schools and participating in all important decisions affecting the schools.

PROTESTANTS AND RELIGIOUS TOLERATION

James Thompson, the Baptist minister who went to Peru in 1822 to set up schools according to the Lancaster method, was impressed by the atmosphere of relative freedom in Peru. At the first constitutional assembly (1822-23) the liberal clergy supported the granting of toleration to non-Catholic religions. But conservative laymen insisted on inserting the provision in the constitution "and the practice of any other religion is excluded."[22] The few Protestants who lived in Peru in those years—mostly British diplomats and merchants—practiced their religion in private and lived in harmony with their neighbors. By mid-century the Catholic clergy was "Romanized" and no longer favorable to toleration. But liberals, arguing that the lack of toleration inhibited immigration, took up the cause of granting religious liberty.

In the meantime the small Protestant population grew steadily. The first Anglican church was founded in Lima in 1849 and the first Methodist missionary from the United States arrived in 1877. An American Presbyterian mission began in 1882 but lasted only a short time. The first Protestant missionary to defy Peruvian law openly was Francisco Penzotti, an Italian-born carpenter who had lived in Uruguay. Penzotti, who worked for the American Bible Society, first arrived in Peru in 1884 and returned in 1889. He preached in public and distributed bibles, leading to his arrest first in Arequipa, then in Lima in 1890; these arrests set off a storm of protests from liberals, Masons, and American and British diplomats. In March 1891, a Peruvian judge released him. Even though the article forbidding toleration remained unchanged, after the Penzotti case Protestant missionaries were no longer harassed by the government.[23]

Penzotti's work was continued by Thomas Wood, an American Methodist, and his daughter Elsie. By 1893 there were five Methodist schools operating in Lima and Callao.[24] The most famous Methodist school, Lima High School, was founded in 1906. In the meantime, the Seventh-day Adventists began missionary work in 1898 in the southern altiplano region of Peru and Bolivia. Under the energetic leadership of Frederick Stahl and his wife, Anne, both from the United States, the Adventists founded churches, schools, and clinics among the Aymara Indians. By 1924 the Adventists had founded eighty schools and counted 4,150 Indians among their faithful.[25] A clash between the Catholic church and the Adventists finally led to religious toleration. In 1913 the bishop of Puno, Valentín Ampuero, led a group of Indians to the little town of Platería, where the Stahls lived. The bishop's party threatened and harassed the newly converted Adventist Indians. This incident ignited stormy debates in the national congress in Lima, and in 1915, much to the displeasure of President José Pardo, the congress abrogated the clause of Article 4 which prohibited the practice of non-Catholic religions.

In the meantime, Protestants of other denominations established missions and schools. John Ritchie, who arrived in 1906, founded the nondenominational Peruvian Evangelical Church, associated with the Christian Missionary Alliance until the two groups split in 1954. The most famous missionary of that period was John Mackay, a Scottish Presbyterian who had studied at Princeton and in Madrid. He arrived in Peru in 1917, studied at San Marcos University, and founded the Anglo-Peruvian High School. Mackay courted the friendship of many reform-minded thinkers, especially Haya de la Torre, who taught in his school until he was deported by Leguía in 1923. Through their schools the Methodists and Mackay won recognition from many middle-class Peruvians. In 1930 Leguía visited the Anglo-Peruvian School when it opened a new building—a sign of official approval.

But Protestant growth was still relatively slow. By 1940 Protestants numbered around 54,818.[26] That same year mainline Protestants joined together to found the Peruvian National Evangelical Council, known by the Spanish acronym CONEP. However, the Adventists, who until recent times constituted the largest Protestant group in Peru, never joined. In the postwar years Protestants continued their quest to gain social respectability. One constant irritant was the question of religion courses. Peruvian law since the thirties had established mandatory religion classes in all schools. On several occasions the ministry of education rebuked the Protestant schools for not teaching Catholicism in the classroom. In 1956 Jorge Basadre, Peru's national historian, became minister of education and quietly shelved that ordinance (Stoll 1982, 320).

In the decade of the sixties Protestant-Catholic relations steadily improved, especially after Vatican II. Although progressive Catholics, inspired by liberation theology, were more interested in the social question than in ecumenical relations, all welcomed cooperation with Protestants who were equally interested in human rights and development. But both progressive Catholics and mainline Protestants looked somewhat askance at fundamentalist Protestants and other Christian groups that did not seek ecumenical ties. One such group, the Summer Language Institute, became the center of a stormy debate and came close to being asked to leave the country. The Summer Language Institute, founded by William Cameron Townsend in 1936 as an educational branch of the Wycliffe Bible Translators, began working in Peru in 1945 and by the late sixties had 262 persons in its employ (ibid., 206). Its principal base was in Yarinacocha, near Pucallpa, but it also had offices in the Ministry of Education in Lima, and even enjoyed a modest government subsidy. The Institute devoted itself to the task of putting into written form the languages of the jungle tribes, an apparently innocent and laudatory mission. Yet Catholic missionaries complained that the Institute was really a facade for a fundamentalist organization, the real purpose of which was to proselytize. By the late sixties neo-leftist indigenists joined in denouncing the Institute for duplicity and false claims about its real intentions. Critics also observed that the Institute did not employ Peruvian linguists or anthropologists. The military government of General Juan Velasco established a commission to reexamine the Institute's contract with the government. Velasco was overthrown in 1975 and his successor, General Francisco Morales Bermúdez, possibly concerned about leaving a vacuum in the jungle that might be filled by leftist guerrillas, decided to allow the Institute to stay.[27] Peruvian intellectuals in general were divided on the subject. Catholic progressives, although they agreed that the Institute was not what it claimed to be, defended its right to remain on the grounds of religious freedom.

HUMAN RIGHTS TENSIONS

During the second administration of Fernando Belaúnde (1980-85) and the Alan García government (1985-90) church-state relations oscillated between relative calm and visible turbulence. This period was marked by two papal visits (1985 and 1988), which were celebrated as festive, national events. The first visit included an ecumenical breakfast during which the pope played host to Protestant and Jewish leaders. Political leaders, of course, basked in the light of the presence of the pope, who drew the biggest crowds in Peruvian history. However, this display of good will between political and religious leaders covered over underlying tensions caused by human rights violations and accusations of complicity between liberation-theology Catholics and guerrilla subversives. The background of this new tension was the emergence of the Maoist Shining Path terrorist movement in 1980, and the Túpac Amaru Revolutionary Movement in 1984. In January 1983, President Belaúnde accused various church-connected research centers and charitable foundations of giving aid to the subversives.[28] Similarly, on many occasions during the García period Apristas accused liberation-theology clergy of giving aid and comfort to the revolutionaries.[29] None of these accusations was substantiated. In fact, the Shining Path directed its wrath especially against the progressive clergy, particularly if they were foreigners. In its bloody wake two priests, five nuns, and dozens of catechists who organized peasant defense bands were murdered. *Sendero* (its popular abbreviated form in Peru) was no less violent in its treatment of Evangelicals. *Senderistas* murdered many pastors in the small towns in the Ayacucho countryside. But the anti-subversive forces frequently responded by rushing into local situations without distinguishing between victims and subversives. In 1984 navy marines killed six members of the Presbyterian church in the small Andean town of Callqui. In this and in many other similar situations the military were blinded by racial and cultural prejudices. For them all Quechua-speaking peasants were suspected of harboring pro–Shining Path sympathies.

In 1985 President García created a National Peace Commission and the Catholic church designated Augusto Beuzeville, a Catholic auxiliary bishop of Lima, as its representative. But in 1991, when Alberto Fujimori formed the National Peace Council, a successor to García's commission, Bishop José Dammert, a leading progressive, declined the invitation to be either president or a member of the council. In truth, Dammert and the other bishops believed that the government was using the church for its own ends and did not seriously intend to investigate charges of government violation of human rights.

FUJIMORI, EVANGELICALS, AND OPUS DEI

Alberto Fujimori's unexpected election as Peru's president in 1990 also proved to be a watershed in Peruvian politics and social history. A year before the elections, Fujimori, a first generation Japanese-Peruvian who had risen to become president of the National Agrarian University and president of the Council of University Presidents, founded a new party, Cambio 90. Sensing that the electorate was discontented with the traditional parties, Fujimori hoped that his new party would attract dissidents and independents. His candidacy drew the attention of small businessmen and, with his message of work, honesty, and discipline, he also interested many Protestants (*Evangélicos*). As he had no real hope of being elected president, Fujimori was also a candidate for the Senate—a more realistic goal. The frontrunner was Mario Vargas Llosa, the world famous novelist who had founded his own political coalition, FREDEMO (Democratic Front), which also aimed to defeat the traditional parties and usher in the age of neoliberalism in Peru. Next in line came the candidates of the APRA, the United Left, and Popular Action. Fujimori was not perceived to be a serious candidate until the last few weeks of the campaign, when he began to rise steadily in the polls. On election day Vargas Llosa garnered a disappointingly low 27.6 percent of the vote, and Fujimori followed with 24.62 percent. By law, a runoff election was required. Observers quickly realized that if APRA (Center-Left) and the Left voted for Fujimori, he would have a good chance of winning the second round, scheduled for June 10.

Two issues that had not surfaced in the race until then began to loom large: race and religion. Unseemly expressions of anti-Japanese sentiments were uttered in fashionable restaurants in Lima. Upper-class Peruvians stressed the importance of being a "real" Peruvian in order to be president of the country. However, the lower classes voted for Fujimori, who by dint of hard work had risen from poverty to prominence, because he was much closer to their ideal of a Peruvian than Vargas Llosa, who belonged to the upper class and did not spend much time in Peru. Then the political opposition discovered the presence of a significant number of Protestants among Cambio 90's congressional candidates: 50 out of 240. The candidate for second vice president, Carlos García, was a Baptist minister and a former president of the National Evangelical Council. The other candidates included members of the Methodist church, the Christian Missionary Alliance, the Peruvian Evangelical Church, and the Assemblies of God.

For most of the twentieth century the majority of Peruvian Protestants had looked to the Aprista Party as their channel of expression. But they had become quite disenchanted with the corruption-ridden administration of Alan García and began looking elsewhere. Beyond disenchantment with a particular party, many Protestants, aware of their growing presence (7 percent of the population according to the 1992 census), had been thinking for some time of organizing their own political party. In 1980 a group of pastors and lay leaders founded *Fe* (Evangelical Front), and in 1985 another group emerged, *Asociación Movimiento Cristiano de Acción Renovadora* (Association of the Christian Movement of Renovating Action). The association joined forces with National Convergence, an alliance between Andrés Townsend, expelled from the Aprista Party, and Luis Bedoya Reyes, of the right-wing Christian Democrats. The search for political representation was also a response to the climate of violence in the eighties. Pentecostal church leaders in the highlands were being subjected to attacks by both the Shining Path and the security forces. The violence of those years forced many lower-class Evangelicals to become aware of human rights issues and to defend themselves by recourse to politics. In fact, in the pre-election phase of the 1990 election, two different Protestant groups emerged: UREP (Reform Union), made up mainly of fundamentalist Pentecostals; and the group of pastors that decided to support Fujimori. The Pentecostals hoped to establish a purely Evangelical party which would fight for educational and other rights that they believed were still denied them. The group that followed Carlos García was more mainline and ecumenical, and did not mind that Fujimori himself was a Catholic. In fact, in November 1989, in preparation for the campaign, the group invited Catholic intellectuals to address them on the relationship among religion, ideology, and politics.[30]

During the month preceding the runoff election, Peru took on the air of a circus, with a number of bizarre sideshows. Cardinal Augusto Vargas Alzamora, the Jesuit archbishop of Lima, paid what was supposed to be a secret visit to Mario Vargas Llosa, presumably to encourage him to stay in the race. Cardinal Vargas, a conservative who was named archbishop in 1990, was concerned about the influence that Protestants might wield in a government presided over by Fujimori. He did not seem to be concerned about the fact that Vargas Llosa was an agnostic. Then, a mysterious one-page flier addressed to Protestants began circulating. In the name of "Jehovah our Father" it encouraged them to vote for Fujimori to "save Catholics from Lucifer." That the flier, a crude attempt to anger Catholics, was probably fabricated by the "dirty tricks" office of FREDEMO was obvious to knowledgeable Catholics and Protestants. Indeed, Protestant leaders visited Cardinal Vargas to deplore the use of such tactics. In spite of that visit, the cardinal published a public statement decrying the attacks on the Catholic faith and announced that a procession would be held in reparation. The Lord of Miracles is the most venerated image in Lima, and the procession in honor of the image is traditionally held in October. Nevertheless, on May 31 the image was taken in procession, and anti-Fujimori fliers were distributed to the unwitting faithful. Other conservative bishops held similar processions in their own dioceses. Bishop Luis Bambarén in Chimbote published a pamphlet warning of the dangers of the "sects." The pamphlet made explicit reference to Cambio 90.[31] Luis Cipriani, an Opus Dei bishop, wrote a public letter condemning Protestants who "support the candidacy of Fujimori."[32] Progressive Catholics, dismayed by this flagrant manipulation of religious sentiment for political purposes, warned their faithful to stay away from such politically charged religious acts. Bishop José Dammert of Cajamarca, a strong supporter of liberation theology, declared that he would not have any such procession in his diocese.[33]

Fujimori won the runoff election with 57 percent of the vote to Vargas Llosa's 34 percent. If the conservative bishops hoped to influence Peru's lower classes with their processions and dire warnings about voting for anti-Catholics, they certainly failed. If anything, the election demonstrated what little influence they did have. After the election the cardinal and other Catholic bishops visited Fujimori to express their congratulations. But the damage was done, and relations between Fujimori, the church, and Cardinal Vargas in particular, have oscillated between awkward and openly hostile.

When the dust settled after the stormy polemics, it soon became apparent that, in reality, Evangelicals were not destined to have a significant role in Fujimori's government. Seats in congress were determined by the results of the first round, not the second. According to the results, of 60 senate seats, Cambio 90 won only 14. In the House of Deputies, of 180 seats, Fujimori's party was apportioned 32. The total number of Evangelicals was 18: 4 in the senate and

14 in the lower house. Finally, when Fujimori named his ministers and top advisers, not a single Evangelical was to be found among them. Simply put, the Evangelicals who supported Fujimori, many of whom were from the lower classes, did not have the educational background or the professional experience to assume important roles in the government. Fujimori mainly ignored the Protestants who had worked to support him. In April 1992, frustrated over the inability of the congress to face the rising terrorist menace, he used military force to disband it and called for new elections. Carlos García, the second vice president, was unceremoniously dismissed. For the presidential elections of 1995, the majority of Protestants switched allegiance and supported Javier Pérez de Cuéllar, leader of the Union for Peru coalition. Most Protestant leaders looked back on their brief experience in politics as a reflection of their own naïveté. One group, however, did not learn that lesson. In 1994 Víctor Arroyo, one of the Evangelical senators, founded Christian Presence, an Evangelical party which declared that it would "moralize political practices."[34] It had little influence in the 1995 elections.

Fujimori's relationship with the Catholic church was further strained by the question of human rights violations during the continuing war against terrorism, and by the birth-control issue. The most dramatic flareup of tensions occurred in September 1995, when the Peruvian congress amended a 1985 law which excluded abortion and sterilization as birth-control methods. The new law dropped the reference to sterilization and added: "the adoption of methods depends on the free decision of each person."[35] The bishops and Catholic institutions denounced the amendment as an incentive to health workers to impose sterilization on the unwitting poor. Fujimori exacerbated the debate by declaring in public: "The state defines demographic policy. . . . The church has no say in this matter."[36]

If Fujimori's relations are strained with most bishops, he enjoys very good relations with the conservative Catholic organization Opus Dei, and especially with Juan Luis Cipriani, the Opus Dei archbishop of Ayacucho. With seven bishops and two thousand members, Opus Dei in Peru is especially strong and influential. Among known members are important politicians, journalists, and businessmen. Two highly visible members in the Peruvian congress are Martha Chávez, of Cambio 90, who served as president of congress in 1995, and Rafael Rey, leader of his own party, Renovation. What draws Fujimori and Opus Dei together is a mutual appreciation of neoliberalism and modern efficiency, which in practice often translates into the use of authoritarian methods. Archbishop Cipriani, who closed down the church's human rights office and other social programs in his archdiocese, publicly supported Fujimori's call for the death penalty and the imposition of censorship on journalists.[37] On one point he does not see eye to eye with Fujimori, and that is the government's aggressive birth-control campaign. Until he resigned in March 1998, Cipriani was also a member of the board of directors of *Foncodes* (Fund for Compensation and Social Development), the government organization to help Ayacucho and other depressed areas.

Cipriani gained worldwide prominence when he acted as a mediator in the hostage crisis in the Japanese ambassador's residence in Lima (December 1996–April 1997). In fact, Fujimori had appointed his education minister, Domingo Palermo, to that task, but the minister and Fujimori decided to invite Cipriani as an additional mediator. Although the papal nuncio announced that Cipriani was the official representative of the church, the Peruvian Episcopal Conference was only informed of Cipriani's new role when it was a fait accompli. Not a few observers believe that the nuncio and powerful supporters in Rome would like to see Cipriani become archbishop of Lima, and hence Opus Dei's first cardinal in the world. But Cipriani and Opus Dei also have many critics among intellectuals and journalists and do not enjoy a popular following.

As Peru nears the end of the twentieth century, it is tempting to draw parallels between this and the sixteenth century. To be sure, there are no more anti-idolatry campaigns to control the hearts and minds of the Indians. But the efforts of the conservative bishops in 1990 to influence election results make one wonder if there is not more continuity than change. Although Peru enjoys full religious liberty, it does not enjoy religious harmony. Conservative bishops work steadily to marginalize progressive Catholics, and conservative Catholics in general only grudgingly admit religious pluralism. On the other hand, certain fundamentalist Evangelicals do not hide their anti-Catholicism. On a brighter note, for years progressive Catholics and mainline Protestants have engaged in dialogue and collaborated on common human rights projects. That, as well as other signs of vitality, suggests that the humanism of the sixteenth century also lives on in new forms.

16.

VENEZUELA

Nationhood, Patronage, and the Conflict over New Religious Movements

◆

David A. Smilde

INTRODUCTION

Since it was a difficult, infertile terrain containing myriad groups of mainly non-sedentary Indians, the Spanish never focused their colonizing efforts on Venezuela. Indeed, Mary Watters argues that the Spanish never achieved political or ecclesiastical control of the territory. As a result, by the end of the colonial period, the Catholic Church in Venezuela shared the decentralization and factionalism characteristic of Venezuelan society in general (Watters 1933). During the years of the revolution, the Church was divided in its loyalties to the Crown and the independence movement, and it appears not to have had a decisive influence (ibid., 70).

In the consolidation of *La Gran Colombia* (what is now Colombia, Ecuador, and Venezuela), however, the question of the relationship between Church and state became a key source of conflict (ibid., 71). With the end of Spanish rule, the Church looked forward to freedom from the relations of "patronage" (*patronato*) that had given the Spanish kings control over the Church. The founders of the Republic, however, assumed that they would inherit the

---

This chapter is dedicated to Padre Hermann González Oropeza, who passed away during its writing. He has been of unfailing assistance in my research in Venezuela, and graciously opened his personal files for this chapter. He will be missed by all who knew him. I would also like to thank Pedro Moreno for calling to my attention the stalled legalization requests, and Angel Bermúdez of *El Universal* for assisting in my interpretation of it. Godofredo Marín, Néstor Luis Alvarez, Daniel Oquendo, Pedro Prado, Jacobo García, and Robert Gómez all interrupted their busy schedules to answer my questions.

arrangement. On July 28, 1824, the executive of *Gran Colombia* confirmed this inheritance by signing the Law of Patronage, which declared that the state would "maintain the rights that it possesses as protector of the Church," delineated far-reaching state control over the operation of the Church, and prohibited the publication of ecclesiastical bulls and briefs "that in any manner are opposed to the sovereignty and prerogatives of the nation" (in ibid., 232-37).

Despite this movement toward civil control of the Church, by the end of the 1820s, increasing social turbulence led Simón Bolívar to seek to strengthen the Church's social influence. Reactionary decrees made by Bolívar—such as the prohibition of the teaching of the philosophy of Jeremy Bentham, mandating religious studies instead; and the inclusion of a provision hostile to non-Catholic religions in the constitution of 1830—produced an anticlerical reaction in the province of Venezuela, as well as the fear that renewed clerical power would discourage non-Catholic immigration. Bolívar's decrees were among the many factors that led to Venezuela's secession from *Gran Colombia* in 1830 (ibid., 108-9; Mecham 1966). The new republic declared the Law of Patronage in effect. Indeed, throughout the nineteenth century a succession of Conservative and Liberal governments had in common the continual consolidation and extension of civil control over the Church. This tendency reached its apex with the presidency of Antonio Guzmán Blanco in the 1880s. By the beginning of the twentieth century, the Church was poor, weak, and no longer exercised significant influence in Venezuela.[1]

The Venezuelan Church has slowly recovered its position during the course of the twentieth century by focusing on education, serving the religious needs of the upper-middle classes, and exercising a cautious but consistent political voice.[2] In 1964 negotiations between the Vatican and the democratic government of Romulo Betancourt resulted in the signing of a *Modus Vivendi* that annulled the Law of Patronage of 1824. It also ratified the state's recognition of the Church's legal personality; reduced the state's control over the organizational operations of the Church; gave the Church the freedom to publish bulls, briefs, decrees, and pastoral letters; as well as affirming the state's continuing support for Catholic missions with indigenous peoples, and financial support in the form of annual ecclesiastic allocations.[3] This new autonomy and financial support—projected allocations for 1998 are close to $100 million[4]—has facilitated the growth of the Church as an institutional presence and social voice in recent decades.[5] However, the Church still suffers from a scarcity of native-born clergy[6] and of committed adherents and is finding that state financial support can politically threaten the autonomy it has achieved legally.[7]

This increasing presence of the Catholic Church has come at the same time that the religious landscape has diversified. Mainline Protestant churches and Baptists consolidated their presence in the 1940s, 1950s, and 1960s. The decades since have seen the dramatic growth of Pentecostals, Jehovah's Witnesses, Seventh-day Adventists, Mormons, and other New Religious Movements (NRMs).[8] This has produced uncertainty and tension regarding the relationship between the state, the Catholic church, and these new religious competitors. Already in the 1940s, mainline Protestant and Baptist churches organized to oppose state financial support for the Church, and in the 1960s publicly opposed the signing of the *Modus Vivendi* with the Vatican.[9] However, tension has developed into overt conflict as a result of the challenge posed by the New Religious Movements. Their growing presence challenges, on the one hand, the state's contradictory status as patron of the Catholic Church and guarantor of religious freedom for non-Catholic religions; and on the other, Venezuela's tenuously imagined "nationhood." In this chapter I will explore the sources of this tension and the terms of the conflict by examining the battle over the evangelization of indigenous groups, the controversy created by the state's attempt to monitor the new religions, and the struggle between Pentecostal plaza preachers and municipal authorities.

THE CONFLICT OVER THE EVANGELIZATION OF INDIGENOUS GROUPS

Though small compared to that of other Latin American countries, Venezuela's indigenous population is dispersed throughout the vast southern frontier that, since the birth of the Republic, governments have wanted to incorporate into "the life of the nation." To do so, "reducing" the Indians and bringing them the "advantages of civilization," has been considered a top priority. Bolívar's reaffirmation of the role of the Church in the post-independence period included a declaration of the "absolute necessity" of reestablishing Catholic missions among the indigenous people in order to "instruct them in religion, morality and the arts necessary for life."[10] Fray Cesáreo de Armellada writes that the philosophy behind state support of Catholic missions has always been that they are "the best means for protecting and incorporating indigenous peoples, cultures, and territories into the life of the Nation; and at the same time, are the best remedy for the faults and deficiencies of these territories and their inhabitants."[11]

The ambiguity created by the presence of non-Catholic missionaries in Venezuela began early in this century. In 1911, prompted by the growing presence of non-Catholic religions in Venezuela, dictator Juan Vicente Gómez issued a decree extending the Law of Patronage to them.[12] In 1915, the passing of a new law on the missions brought inquiries by U.S. Protestant missionaries as to whether foreign missionaries could themselves select the territory they wanted to evangelize, and whether a territory already conceded to a mission was exclusive to it. The government responded, in effect, that it was not in the position of regulating an open arena of mission activities, but rather had the indigenous areas of the country under its tutelage and contracted missionaries on its own initiative.[13]

At mid-century, the exclusivity of the agreements made by the executive branch and Catholic religious orders was upheld in several cases. In 1945, then Minister of the Interior Arturo Uslar Pietri wrote to the governor of the southern state of Bolívar about the presence of a Seventh-day Adventist pastor in the territory of a Capuchin mission. He stated that there was no problem with an Adventist church in the town of Santa Elena, but that under no circumstances were they to be allowed to evangelize within the areas exclusively conceded to the Capuchins. He reasoned: "Freedom of religion does not apply to the uncivilized indigenous tribes and groups of our territory who, because of their lack of culture and civilization are placed under the tutelage of the state, which, for its part, delegates this difficult labor to the [Capuchin] missionaries."[14]

Nevertheless, by the end of the 1940s the situation became more complex as the government designated an Indigenous Commission to carry out its indigenous policy—an obligation Venezuela had acquired in 1946 by becoming a member of the Interamerican Indigenist Institute—which was confirmed by a decree from President Romulo Betancourt in 1959.[15] The Indigenous Commission granted legal entry to numerous Protestant groups into indigenous areas, resulting in protests on the part of Catholic officials, who argued that the state's indigenous policy was to be exercised exclusively by means of missions, and that these missions were to be operated exclusively by Catholic religious orders.[16] We can see the nature of the objections in a letter written by de Armellada attempting to convince the archbishop of Caracas, Monsignor Arias, of the gravity of these developments. He argues that the Commission

> violates the laws [of Venezuela] that order the incorporation [of Indigenous peoples] to be carried out by means of religious orders (as expressed in the Law of Patronage by order of Bolívar). Like the serpent in the Garden of Eden it asks, "Why this, and why not with missionaries without robes; and why not by means of Protestants, who would even help economically instead of asking for [economic] help?"

Reviewing the text of the 1915 Law on Missions and later amendments to it, de Armellada points to their distinctly Catholic language. "All of them speak of priests, secular or religious, of parishes, convents, ecclesiastical prelates." He also argues that the 1911 extension of the Law of Patronage does not give Protestants an equivalent foothold in the work of missionizing but rather intends to establish state inspection of them. "Nothing would be more opposed to the spirit of the Law of Ecclesiastical Patronage than to compare the special status of the Catholic Church, with other merely tolerated religions."[17] These positions seemed to have had little effect on government policy, and when one examines the relevant texts, they receive little support.[18]

In the 1970s, Marxist intellectuals—led by anthropologist Esteban Monsoyi and organized as the National Identity Movement (NIM)—began to publicly criticize the work of missionaries associated with the New Tribes Mission (NTM), a mission organization founded by Southern Baptists that works with indigenous groups throughout Latin America. The NIM fought to make changes in the state's indigenous policy in general, but especially focused on the work of North American missionaries.[19] A pamphlet from the "Indigenous People and the National Identity" meetings the NIM held in 1979 portrays the Southern Baptist missionaries as imperialist agents and destroyers of indigenous cultures. "To political and cultural espionage can be added the destruction of indigenous cultures . . . by these missionaries who propagate a terrifying idea of sin and the end of the world." They warn against permitting the New Tribes Mission to repeat the colonial Catholic Church's identification of the will of the Crown with the will of God. "We should be sufficiently cautious in this respect to make sure that Evangelicals do not confuse the exercising of their religiosity with North American interests in this country."[20]

In 1979, in response to the public controversy, the Congress named socialist congressman Alexis Ortiz to head a commission to investigate the charges. Six months later, the commission's report recommended the expulsion of the New Tribes Mission based on three basic accusations: the use of coercive methods of evangelization; the carrying out of economic espionage in favor of transnational corporations; and the illegality of their functioning in territory conceded to Catholic missions.[21] Shortly after the presentation of the report, Luis Antonio Montilla, the head of the Directorate of Religion (*Dirección de Justicia y Cultos,* DJC) of the Ministry of Justice—the government organ responsible for monitoring religious activity in Venezuela—announced that the NTM was operating legitimately in Venezuela according to a permit granted in 1953. Ortiz resigned from the congressional commission in July, disillusioned by the inaction of the dominant political parties.[22] However, the National Identity Movement (NIM) remained active. In August 1980, the Second International Meeting for Community Development took place in Caracas. Members of NIM, along with like-minded international representatives, dominated the Indigenous Commission of the meeting and fought to include a condemnation of all evangelization of indigenous peoples in the text of the resolutions to be adopted. The initiative did not succeed, however, because of the opposition of the representative of the Netherlands.[23] Instead, the document calls for a prohibition of groups whose work threatens indigenous communities and cultures, and calls for a recognition "that the indigenous people represent the true ethnic root of our nationality."[24]

The response of interested parties within the Catholic Church to this public debate over the New Tribes Mission ranged from a clear desire to add fuel to the fire,[25] to defense of the NTM,[26] to cautious concern that public ire could become channeled toward missions and evangelization in general. A Salesian missionary gave eloquent expression to the last impulse in a meeting organized to describe the cultural sensitivity of the Salesian missions. "What we want to make clear is that we and the New Tribes Missions should not be stuck in the same bag."[27]

Through the 1970s and 1980s, the New Tribes Mission astutely responded to specific charges and described its work as combining ideas of cultural sensitivity with "civilizing" discourse. In his 1974 report to the Ministry of Justice,

Director Jaime Bou stated: "This is one of the goals we put into practice: to bring civilization to the Indians and adapt it to their necessities and customs so that it can be useful to them and not destructive of their thoughts, action, and culture, which have been formed over many centuries."[28] In a paid advertisement in the late-1980s, he argued that the mission "has facilitated the action of the regional government toward these groups of Venezuelans that before lived on the margins of the dominant culture" and "has contributed to the formation of human resources for the government and for private enterprise."[29] National Evangelical organizations also came to the defense of the New Tribes Mission's work in Venezuela. In 1979, the Evangelical Council of Venezuela (CEV) organized the First National Evangelical Congress on Indigenous Missions and produced a document explaining and defending the work of the NTM.[30]

Beyond the occasional obstruction of missionary visas, the state has never taken any official action against the New Tribes Mission. Nevertheless, complaints still flow from all of the protagonists.[31] The military periodically publishes memoranda expressing worries about Venezuela's territorial sovereignty, given that the NTM has a more developed network of telecommunications and airstrips than the state itself, and operates with little state supervision in areas with resources that can be used for the production of arms.[32] As a result of the continuing polemic, attempts to resolve the situation are being developed in different state organs. In 1995 a bill was presented in the Congress, the Law on Indigenous Communities, Peoples, and Cultures. Among other things it establishes a new Indigenous Institute consisting of an indigenous representative, a social scientist specializing in indigenous groups, a member of the Catholic hierarchy, and a member of the military. It also annuls all previous permits to evangelize indigenous groups, requiring that the permits be reviewed and validated by the Indigenous Institute.[33] This would in effect subject the permits under which the NTM and other groups evangelize to the approval of a commission dominated by representatives of those sectors that oppose their presence. This bill was defeated in December 1997 but was immediately followed by a similar bill that is currently under consideration.

The Directorate of Religion of the Ministry of Justice has also become interested in the situation. A 1996 newspaper report quoted its current director, Néstor Luis Alvarez, as seeking the cancellation of the NTM's 1953 permit.[34] When I asked about the report he said he had been misquoted but admitted that his Directorate had recently asked the New Tribes Mission to respond in writing to accusations and complaints it had received over the years. In our conversation he mentioned a case in Zaire in which the presence of Protestant missionaries in an area of vast gold deposits resulted in intensification of interethnic rivalries and a secessionist movement. In Alvarez's opinion, the presence of the NTMs in Venezuelan territory has not received the attention that it deserves. "[Venezuela's leaders] lack a vision of the lofty and sacred interests of the state. Since they don't have a sense of nationhood, they have not understood the importance and seriousness of these foci of social disintegration."

When asked to elaborate he argued: "Any religious group that undermines the national identity of a society is dangerous because it can divide that society because of religious passion. . . . We have no reason to think that the NTM is one of these cases. . . . We simply have to make sure that it is not."[35]

THE CONFLICT OVER STATE SUPERVISION
OF NEW RELIGIOUS MOVEMENTS

THE STALLED LEGALIZATION REQUESTS

Venezuela's constitution guarantees not only the citizen's religious freedom, but also expresses the state's obligation to monitor religious practice as to its compatibility with "public order and good morals" (see constitutional provisions below). This monitoring is done by the Directorate of Religion of the Justice Ministry (DJC) and is enforced using its ability to grant, deny, or revoke the registration of a group as a nonprofit religious association. Duly registered, a religious organization obtains legal personality, can buy property and open accounts with special tax privileges, receives exemptions from import duties, and can bring missionaries into the country.[36]

In 1996 and 1997 important battles were waged over this registration process, and will likely result in changes in the legal system. Beginning in 1992, a backlog of registration requests began to develop in the DJC, amounting to over six hundred by mid-1997.[37] In early 1996, Evangelical umbrella groups tried to get the DJC to move these documents along, producing considerable tension between the two sides. In mid-1996, the Director of the DJC, Néstor Luis Alvarez, sought the mediation of Godofredo Marín, the lone congressman of Venezuela's one Evangelical party: the Authentic Renewal Organization (ORA). Six months of dialogue resulted in Alvarez's signing a resolution nullifying the procedure that had been in effect since 1982, in order to establish a commission—including representatives of the major Evangelical organizations—that would develop a new one.[38] However, six months later the resolution had not been implemented, and the backlog remained.

In response, Godofredo Marín filed a complaint with the *Comision de Mesa* (standing committee) of the Congress, which in turn requested the president of the Congress and Marín to meet with the Director. As a result of this meeting—in which Marín says Alvarez expressed his hostility to the Evangelical community, a claim Alvarez denies—the president of the Congress and Marín asked the *Comision de Mesa* to request the removal of Alvarez, which it did. Minister of Justice Hilarión Cardozo did not respond to this request and when confronted by a congressional subcommission said that such an action would be impossible since Alvarez had the personal support of President Rafael Caldera.[39]

In October 1997, Marín requested and was granted the opportunity to speak to the Congress. On the day of Marín's speech in the Congress, representatives of more than 140 Evangelical organizations demonstrated outside the Congress in support.[40] Marín summarized the problem and the events of the previous eighteen months, and requested the interpellation (formal questioning) of the minister of justice. The Congress unanimously approved the request and the questioning of the minister of justice took place on November 4. In it, Cardozo argued that the delay was a problem of internal bureaucracy and promised to clear it up—indeed, the next day he announced that 676 religious associations were legalized. He also expressed the need for a law to govern the administration of the constitutional provisions on religious freedom.[41]

The DJC maintains that the problem of "internal bureaucracy" was the lack of a "single representative," a hierarchy, organization, or other entity that represents a religion in its interactions with the state. Alvarez says that this requirement is fulfilled by other religions

> but not by Evangelicals and Protestants. They refuse to provide the government with a single representative, saying that their organization is horizontal and that they all are pastors. I have someone who can verify who is a rabbi, because the Central Rabbinical Department of Israel certifies him. The same is true of Moslems and Catholics, but not with Evangelicals. Many of them introduce themselves as pastors and there is no way to identify them as such.[42]

The previous policy had been to permit any church to define who its governing body is. However, administrative chaos had developed, says the DJC, because of the rapid growth in numbers of new Evangelical churches seeking registration and because many churches failed to keep the DJC informed of changes in leadership. Thus individuals would arrive at the DJC identifying themselves as pastors of a given church in order to, for example, request a tax exemption for their church, but their names would not appear in the church's file. Without a single representative with whom to verify these transactions— as well as the registration of new churches—each case needs to be investigated individually; hence the backlog.[43]

Evangelical groups reject this explanation, arguing that the DJC never made a serious attempt to resolve the problem. Jacobo Garcia, current president of the Evangelical Council of Venezuela, points out that while Alvarez sent them all copies of the December 1996 resolution, it was never legalized and "there was no execution or fulfillment of what he had written and signed."[44] Robert Gómez, president of the Pentecostal Evangelical Confederation of Venezuela (CEPV), says they designated a representative but that the DJC did not want to collaborate.[45] The DJC responds that the situation became unworkable when each of the Evangelical organizations wanted to be *the* representative of Venezuelan Evangelicals but would not agree to be represented by another Evangelical organization.[46]

A New Law on the Freedom of Religious Expression?

Currently, the only legislation in effect is a 1911 extension of the 1824 Law of Patronage (itself annulled by the 1964 *Modus Vivendi*) to non-Catholic groups. The DJC itself says that in the current situation it has too much discretionary power and that there needs to be a clear set of rules.[47] But while Congressman Godofredo Marín is looking forward to a bill, the Evangelical umbrella groups are suspicious of the intentions of the DJC. Robert Gómez sees a simple desire "to control religious practice to such a degree that the [Evangelical] Church cannot function."[48] Jacobo García predicts that the DJC is "going to put forward a compulsory set of rules in which the Venezuelan state continues to have the power to do whatever it wants with regard to religious practice. This kind of bill does not interest us."[49] The CEPV, after prodding by some congressmen, is working on the elements it would like incorporated into a bill and is getting legal advice on it. However, its members are skeptical. "I'm sure that the director has something up his sleeve," commented Robert Gómez.

The DJC provided me with a copy of the bill that it has developed. The proposed law contains relatively unobjectionable clauses focusing on the procedure for obtaining and maintaining legal recognition, and the establishment of an Advisory Council on Religious Practice consisting of representatives of various governmental organisms as well as representatives of the three largest religious federations in the country. However, glancing at the preamble to the bill we see a clear desire on the part of the DJC to decide both what is "truly religious" and what is compatible with the "Venezuelan character."

> The proliferation of "cults," religious groups and sects understood as the negative or misinterpreted side of the freedom of religious practice; not having a religious character, having only false religious values, or which are led by a false prophet, and which seek to take advantage of the faith of followers that have been "attracted" in a forced manner by having seen or heard of "miracles;" taking advantage of the material goods of these followers or fanatics . . . is not consonant with the spirit and character of the Venezuelan people."[50]

The Functions and Jurisdiction of the Directorate of Religion

Evangelical leaders tend to view government institutions as strongly influenced by the Catholic Church and the DJC as directly controlled by it. In my interview with him, Jacobo García explained the situation in Venezuela, saying, "In Venezuela there is religious toleration but not genuine religious freedom because the majority of government authorities have responded to and respond to the interests of the Catholic Church." He sees the DJC as a case in point. "The present Director of the DJC [was] put in that position in a covert, direct, premeditated way by the Catholic Church, with, of course, the help of the president of the Republic." This view and its delegitimizing implications are only reinforced by frequent statements from the Catholic hierarchy that seek to argue for the Church's historically privileged relationship to the state. During the congressional proceedings regarding the removal of Alvarez in July 1997, Monsignor Hernán Sánchez Porras, general secretary of the Venezuelan Episcopal Conference, sent a letter of support to the president of the Congress that included the following:

> It is important to be clear that freedom of religion cannot be understood as the "equality of religions," giving privileges to an Evangelical minority to the detriment to a nation that in its majority is Catholic. We support the actions of Dr. Néstor Luis Alvarez, for we understand that he is working not only for the Church, but also for the country.[51]

It is public knowledge that Alvarez is a close personal acquaintance of President Rafael Caldera, considers him his political mentor, and shares his fervent Catholicism.[52] However, Alvarez denies any favoritism to the Catholic Church, says that he considers Evangelicals to be "very honorable people and excellent citizens," and argues that all religions must fulfill the same requirements for legal recognition. He points out, however, that the DJC not only administers the constitutional provisions on the freedom of religion, but also administers part of the state's financial transfers to the Church.

When I asked Alvarez about his frequent statements[53] regarding Venezuelan "identity" and "character"—such as in the bill on religious freedom above—he explained as follows:

> "We [Latin Americans] are a people that have our own character and identity, a personality since the Discovery and the evangelization. If there is any essential part of the identity of our countries, it is precisely the religious-cultural aspect. Without attempting to be a confessional country . . . we must have a sense of nation and the responsibility and courage to protect those factors inherent to our peoples, that is to say, that which, were it to be lost, would diminish our nations and leave us prisoner of any international or global process that gains force."[54]

These considerations have led him to say that the presence of religious groups is "an issue of national security, because it has to do with the national identity, which is indispensable to the security and defense of the country."[55] This tendency to identify the national identity with Catholicism and regard it as essential to the perpetuation of the nation is not confined to this mid-level bureaucrat but is common within Venezuelan leadership circles. When Reverend Sun Myung Moon's Unification Church had its permit revoked in September 1997, Monsignor Sánchez Porras sent a letter to the minister of justice supporting the decision "to put a stop to this pseudo-religious sect that seeks to destroy the base of our Venezuelan values."[56] In addition, an *El Nacional* editorial applauded the decision, but criticized the DJC for having granted a permit to the Unification Church in the first place, given "the danger represented by the presence of sects—not only religious but political and for Latin American unity."[57]

I asked both Alvarez and sub-director Daniel Oquendo whether protecting the "national identity"—this religious-cultural aspect common to Latin American countries—was a legitimate function of a modern state. Oquendo immediately responded that the state's jurisdiction was simply to carry out the law, and that the "national identity" was not specified by the law. Alvarez, however, responded as follows:

> "I believe that it is a legitimate function of every Venezuelan. . . . If, for some reason, Venezuela is incapable of fulfilling this responsibility because the law does not permit it, then the law must be violated. What you must have very clear is that the most serious and important interests of the country are above the law. If not, the law becomes nothing more than a perverse instrument that goes against the interests of the country when in principle the law is an instrument that society creates to order life in common, channel the rights and obligations of citizens, and guarantee peace and harmony. . . . We cannot bow down to the law over and against the interests of the nation."[58]

PLAZA PREACHERS AND MUNICIPAL AUTHORITIES

The most visible manifestation of the New Religious Movements in Venezuela is the presence of Pentecostal preachers in city plazas across the country. Despite popular stereotypes of these preachers as itinerant vendors of their own personal creed, there is actually a sustained, organized effort behind them. Plaza services generally happen every day at the same time, are organized by specific churches or Pentecostal organizations, and are carried out with the permission of the municipal government. Obtaining these permits, however, is a constant source of conflict.

Pedro Prado is one of the founding members of the Christian Coalition Front (FCC)—a group he and several other Evangelicals formed about ten years ago to bring the Gospel to *Caraqueños* during the course of their daily routine. They hold their services at noon in the *Plaza El Venezolano*, at the geographical heart of Caracas. In the middle of the plaza there is a fountain, and on the north side, above three steps, is a large shade tree, a space the FCC has made into its amphitheater. Starting at noon, services begin with singing and prayer, then a preacher preaches until 1:00 P.M., followed by an altar call. Then the process is repeated with a second preacher, ending at 2:00 P.M.

I asked Prado for an interview about the procedure for obtaining permits to carry out plaza services, and we agreed to meet during the services the next day. When I arrived he quickly pulled from his bag a worn copy of the constitution of 1961, with dozens of folded-up documents in its pages, and began to show me the parts that he had marked off.[59] In the constitution's statement of purpose, two paragraphs were blocked off with red pen. The first read:

> To maintain social and juridical equality, without discrimination on the basis of race, sex, *creed,* or social condition.

The word *creed* had been highlighted in yellow. The penultimate paragraph of the preamble had also been blocked off in red pen. The italic text represents the words that Prado highlighted.

> To support the *democratic* order as the *sole* and *irrevocable* means of assuring the *rights* and *dignity of the citizens*, and *peacefully favor* their extension to all the *peoples* of the *Earth*.

In the section entitled Individual Rights three other paragraphs had been blocked off with red pen and highlighted in yellow, with the number of the article circled in blue.

> Article 65—Everyone has the right to profess their religious faith and carry out their worship, privately or publicly as long as it does not go against public order and good customs.
> Article 66—Everyone has the right to express their thoughts verbally or in writing and to make use of any means of dissemination for this purpose, without being subject to previous censorship; but they remain subject to punishment, in conformity to the law, for any expressions that are criminal.
> Article 71—Everyone has the right to associate, publicly or privately, without previous permission, for legal ends and without arms. Meetings in public places will obey the law.

Prado then began to unfold documents from different moments in the Christian Coalition Front's battle to conduct its plaza services. Most important was a September 1995 decree from the governor of the Federal District prohibiting "public meetings of civil, political, or religious character in public plazas and boulevards."[60] Several pamphlets had been distributed among the area's Evangelical churches in order to raise consciousness about the decree. One document has in large bold letters at the top: KNOW AND DEFEND YOUR RIGHTS. At the side it has the subtitle: "Freedom of Religion: An Innate Right, Given by God to Man." It contains copies of the relevant individual rights and the articles in the penal code of Venezuela that treat "Crimes against established religions." The last page ends with the following[61]:

NOTE:
Circulate this information in all of the Churches of the Lord, letting all Venezuelans know that these articles of the law of Venezuela are being violated every day in our national territory.
CHRIST IS COMING SOON

The governor's decree was not implemented because the Christian Coalition Front obtained the help of a candidate for governor who took legal action resulting in a stay on its enforcement. Nevertheless, every three months the FCC needs to renew its permit and frequently meets with difficulties. Prado interprets this as an orchestrated attempt to suppress the Gospel.[62] "They bounce you around, from here to there, making you run around in circles. That's the way they operate. . . . The persecution continues." He summed up, "Thank God, we are ready for it, know what our rights are, and who we are fighting against. The truth is that we are not fighting against the mayor, nor the governor, but against Satan, the devil who has possessed their minds and hearts."[63]

January 1997 was one of the times when the Christian Coalition Front failed to obtain the necessary permits. In the first couple of days the regulars showed up and simply talked among themselves, sang songs in a circle, and shared "testimonies." When I talked to him on the first day without the permit, Ramiro, one of the preachers, referred to St. Paul's Epistle to the Romans, chapter 13, and explained that they were not preaching because God placed worldly authorities in their position and Christians must obey them. Within a couple of days, however, the preachers began to preach without the sound equipment. This went on for a few weeks until, in early February, the municipal police came and told them they could not preach, even without the sound equipment. Arriving at the plaza the next day, I asked Ramiro what had happened. "The Devil again," he said, visibly upset. "The Bible commands us to be subject to the law. [But] I can't when they are violating my rights," he said, throwing his arms up in the air. "The Bible says that the law is for the transgressor. So they come and silence those who are doing good. I can't subject myself to this." Another regular came up and Ramiro continued, now speaking to both of us. "The problem is that the Gospel is a molotov [cocktail] that explodes in the hearts of people. They [those in authority] know that to continue doing evil, they have to silence Evangelicals."

CONCLUSION: NEW RELIGIOUS MOVEMENTS, AND THE CHALLENGE TO PATRONAGE AND NATIONHOOD

Mainstream Protestants, Jews, Moslems, and representatives of other world religions have had little trouble practicing their religion in Venezuela. Besides their greater willingness and ability to fulfill government obligations, they spend little time evangelizing and have experienced little growth. The NRMs, on the other hand, evangelize relentlessly, have grown explosively, and represent creeds that do not meet with the respect provided by centuries of history. Their presence exposes the tension between the state as guarantor of the freedom of religion—which the minister of justice recently defined as the task of assuring to all citizens the right to worship, without favoring or promoting any particular religion[64]—and the state as provider of multimillion-dollar subsidies and "special support" to one particular religion.

However, the conflicts outlined above have a special emotional charge insofar as the growing presence of NRMs also challenges a tenuously imagined nationhood.[65] In Venezuela the secular concern for building the territory and its inhabitants into a modern nation, combined with the stubborn persistence of premodern social conditions, has resulted in a widely diffused, self-critical discourse about nationhood.[66] The presence of NRMs enters easily into the terms of this discourse. Their overseas origins combined with Venezuela's vast oil and mineral resources have made them the target of continual accusations of political and economic espionage. Their distance from the dominant forms of social and cultural association also produces suspicion that they could represent centrifugal forces in the attempt to maintain the nation's boundaries. Furthermore, NRM growth has coincided with processes that have increasingly exposed Venezuela to global forces. Through oil revenues, Venezuela was once able to pursue state-led modernization programs to a degree envied by other developing countries. But the decline in oil prices and resulting debt crisis have compelled the state to open its internal policies to international lending agencies and to open its economy to global capitalism.

Many of those currently in positions of leadership in Venezuela—not only within the government but also in the mass media and educational institutions—were trained under, and still hold to, the idea that collective well-being depends on a nation-state that is economically self-sufficient and politically sovereign over a territory with a culturally unified population. They often perceive the presence of New Religious Movements as a direct challenge to the nation-state's unquestioned goal of "monopoly sovereignty."[67] Apart from concern about political or economic espionage, their alarm over this challenge is frequently expressed as a perceived threat to a "national identity" that ranges from an identification of Catholicism with the Venezuelan or Latin American "character," to the postulation of a mythical indigenous heritage.

Initiatives to provide clear legislation on the freedom of religion and the question of evangelization of indigenous groups are currently underway and have the potential to reconcile the interests of the different parties to the conflict. However, there has been little show of good will and willingness to compromise among them. Furthermore it should be mentioned that, in the long run, attempts to reconcile conflicting interests through legal instruments are complicated in Venezuela by the generalized view of the law as a stratagem of those in power rather than as a guarantor of equality—a view expressed in the popular Venezuelan saying, El que hace la ley, hace la trampa (He who makes the law, makes the way to get around it). As a result, the inevitable tension between substantive and formal justice[68] is consistently resolved by favoring the former over the latter. As can be seen in the data, if a given law, say, limits a group's freedom to evangelize, threatens a hypothetical "national identity," or results in time-consuming bureaucratic requirements, the tendency is to see it as illegitimate and to defy it, rather than dutifully to comply or attempt to change it.

NOTES

1. The term *evangelization* has specifically Christian roots since etymologically it means the spreading of the gospel (*evangelium*), but it has come to mean missionary activity in general. Etymologically, *proselytism* means conversion, literally, "coming near," which seems to be a more neutral term. For some Christian critics, however, it has acquired negative connotations involving the use of force or manipulation. See the discussion in the Cleary and Moreno chapters in this volume.

PART ONE
PERSPECTIVE ON THE CHURCHES
AND EVANGELIZATION TODAY

1 THE CATHOLIC CHURCH / EDWARD L. CLEARY

1. In 1994 Raymond L. Flynn, then U.S. Ambassador to the Holy See, urged President Clinton to establish an office of Assistant Secretary of State for Religious Affairs. In November 1996 the State Department established an Advisory Committee on Religious Freedom Abroad.

2. "Policy" here refers to a definite course of action selected from alternatives and under given conditions guiding acceptable procedures. While some political scientists reserve discussion of policies to government or business, churches have laws and directives that guide procedures in a similar fashion.

3. W. Eugen Shiels, S.J., *King and Church: The Rise and Fall of the Patronato Real* (Chicago: Loyola University Press, 1961).

4. Understanding Latin American religious issues requires a careful appraisal of the national period, from 1808 on. Recent scholarship, such as that of David Bushnell, Neill Macauley, John Lynch, Ralph Woodward, Frank Safford, and many others has illuminated a period whose understanding was obscured by patriotic exaggerations. A much smaller group of scholars, including Kenneth Scott Latourette, delved into historical church-state issues during the period.

For church-state issues J. Lloyd Mecham produced a work whose authority has been largely unquestioned. His masterpiece, *Church and State in Latin America*, first published in 1934 and updated in 1966, long dominated the field. The *Journal of Church and State* and similar publications have continued to add refinements to Mecham's work. For church-state relations in the period immediately before Vatican Council II, John J. Kennedy provides a useful summary in "The Legal Status of the Church in Latin America: Some Recent Developments," in *The Church and Social Change in Latin America*, ed. Henry Landsberger (Notre Dame, Ind.: University of

Notre Dame Press, 1970), 162-65. For more recent national situations, see Fernando Retamal Fuentes, "La libertad de conciencia y la libertad de las religiones en los grandes sistemas contemporáneos—América Latina," *Teología y Vida* 37 (1996): 307-39, and Jesús González López, ed., *Relaciones Iglesia-Estado: Análisis Teológico-Jurídico desde América Latina* (Bogotá: Consejo Episcopal Latinoamericano, n.d.).

    5. Kenneth Scott Latourette, *Christianity in a Revolutionary Age* (Grand Rapids, Mich.: Zondervan, 1969), 3:350.

    6. Mecham, *Church,* 1966 ed., 60.

    7. Ibid.

    8. For the evolution of royal patronage, see Shiels, *King,* passim.

    9. Latourette, *Christianity,* 3:297, quoting Mecham, *Church,* 1934 ed., 97.

    10. Mecham, *Church,* 1966 ed., 68.

    11. Rome began dealing directly with church agents from Latin America under Leo XII, but formal recognition of the Spanish-American republics only began with Gregory XVI in 1831.

    12. John Lynch, *The Spanish American Revolutions 1808-1826,* 2d ed. (New York: Norton, 1986), 350.

    13. W. Eugen Shiels, "Church and State in Latin America," *New Catholic Encyclopedia* (Washington, D.C.: Catholic University of America, 1967), 3:740.

    14. Mecham, *Church,* 1966 ed., 62.

    15. See Pius IX, allocution, *Numquam fore* (Dec. 15, 1856).

    16. Shiels, "Church," 741.

    17. The first internuncio to Nueva Granada was named in May 1836.

    18. Rome established what would become a nunciature in Rio de Janeiro in 1830, with a larger mission to most of Latin America. See William J. Coleman, "The First Apostolic Delegation in Rio de Janeiro and Its Influence in Spanish America: A Study in Papal Policy, 1830-1840" (Ph.D. diss., Catholic University of America, 1950).

    19. For the Vatican's views on liberalism, see esp. Roger Aubert, *Tolérance et Communauté humaine: Chrétiens dans un monde divise* (Paris: Casterman, 1952), 75-103.

    20. John Henry White, *Catholics in Western Democracies* (New York: St. Martins Press, 1981); John A. Coleman, *The Evolution of Dutch Catholicism, 1958-1974* (Berkeley and Los Angeles: University of California Press, 1978); Lord Acton, *Essays on Church and State* (New York: Thomas Y. Crowell, 1968); and Frances Lannon, *Privilege, Persecution, and Prophecy* (Oxford: Clarendon Press, 1987).

    21. Mecham, *Church,* 1966 ed., 416.

    22. Mecham, *Church,* 1934 ed., 370; and Mary P. Holleran, *Church and State in Guatemala* (New York: Octagon, 1974).

    23. Adrian A. Bantjes, "Idolatry and Iconoclasm in Revolutionary Mexico: The De-Christianization Campaigns, 1929-1940," *Mexican Studies* 13, 1 (1997): 87-120.

    24. Latourette, *Christianity,* 3:300.

    25. Ivan Vallier, *Catholicism, Social Control, and Modernization* (Englewood Cliffs, N.J.: Prentice-Hall, 1970).

    26. Other cases of separation include Uruguay, Ecuador, Cuba, and Panama.

    27. E. Bradford Burns, *A History of Brazil,* 3d ed. (New York: Columbia University Press, 1993), 236. Separation did not, however, create the equivalent of the situation of the churches in the United States.

28. See Thomas C. Bruneau, *The Church in Brazil: The Politics of Religion* (Austin, Tex.: University of Texas Press, 1982), 11-16.

29. Conferência Nacional dos Bispos do Brasil, *Rumo ao Novo Milênio: Projeto de Evangelização da Igreja no Brasil em Preparação ao Grande Jubileu do Ano 2000* (São Paulo: Editorial Salesiana Don Bosco, 1996), nos. 51, 18.

30. Mecham, *Church*, 1966 ed., 217.

31. Luis Galdames, *Historia de Chile: La evolución constitucional 1810-1925,* vol. 1, *1810-1833* (Santiago, Chile), 493, cited by Mecham, *Church*, 1966 ed., 217-18.

32. See Brian H. Smith and Michael Fleet, *The Catholic Church and Democracy in Chile and Peru* (Notre Dame, Ind.: University of Notre Dame Press, 1997), 36-39.

33. Ibid.

34. See, for example, Michael Lowy and Jesús García-Ruiz, "Les sources francaises du christianisme de la libération au Brésil," *Archives de Sciences sociales des Religion* 42, 97 (Jan.-Mar. 1997): 9-32.

35. A succinct view of this process is presented in Daniel Levine and David Stoll, "Bridging the Gap between Empowerment and Power in Latin America," in *Transnational Religion and Weak States*, ed. Susanne Hoeber Rudolph and James Piscatori (Boulder, Colo.: Westview, 1997), 76ff.

36. For military governments and their legacies, see Edward L. Cleary, *The Struggle for Human Rights in Latin America* (Westport, Conn.: Praeger, 1997).

37. For a historical account of the church's view of democracy, see Antonio Acerbi, *Chiesa e democrazia: Da Leone XIII al Vaticano II* (Milan: Vota e Pensiero, 1991).

38. Samuel Huntington, "Religion and the Third Wave," *The National Interest* (Summer 1991): 35.

39. Cleary, *Struggle;* idem, "The Catholic Church and Nation-Building in Brazil," paper for American Political Science Association national meeting, August 28, 1997.

40. See Cleary, *Struggle*, 62ff.

41. For a description of the Christendom and New Christendom models, see Enrique Dussel's reflections on Latin American church history in his introduction to *The Church in Latin America 1492-1992*, ed. Enrique Dussel (Maryknoll, N.Y.: Orbis Books, 1992), esp. 1-13.

42. Edward L. Cleary, "The Brazilian Catholic Church and Church-State Relations: Nation-Building," *Journal of Church and State* 39, 2 (Spring 1997): 253-72.

43. Ibid, 253-72.

44. The most consistent and forceful message of John Paul II on his numerous journeys has been human rights protection. See David Hollenbach, "Both Bread and Freedom: The Interconnection of Economic and Political Rights in Recent Catholic Thought," in *Human Rights and Global Mission of the Church*, ed. Arthur Dyck (Cambridge, Mass.: Boston Theological Institute, 1985), 31. John Paul's comments on human rights during his journeys through 1992 fill two volumes thus far. See *Juan Pablo II y los derechos humanos (1978-1981)* (Pamplona: Ediciones Universidad de Navarra, 1982) and *Juan Pablo II y los derechos humanos (1981-1992)* (Pamplona: Ediciones Universidad de Navarra, 1993). For the church as transnational human rights actor, see Cleary, *Struggle*, 128-32.

45. Petrus Huizing provides a careful survey in his "Religious Freedom: A Bibliographical Survey," *Concilium* (New York: Paulist Press, 1966), 18:111-39.

46. See esp. Thomas Aquinas, *Summa Theologiae* 2a2ae, Questions 10-12 and 3a, 68.10.

47. Eric D'Arcy, "Freedom of Religion," *New Catholic Encyclopedia* (Washington, D.C.: Catholic University of America, 1967), 6:109-10.

48. Interviews by author, esp. at Protestant seminaries in Guatemala, Costa Rica, Bolivia, Chile, Argentina, and Brazil, 1981 to 1997.

49. Mexico and Cuba are special cases. Ambiguities about government control continue in Mexico. See esp. Roberto Blancarte, "Church-State Relations: From Debate to Disarray," in *Rebuilding the State: Mexico after Salinas*, ed. Mónica Serrano and Victor Bulmer-Thomas (London: Institute of Latin American Studies, University of London, 1996), 99-109; chapters in this volume; and Roderic Ai Camp, *Crossing Swords: Politics and Religion in Mexico* (New York: Oxford University Press, 1997). For Cuba, see the chapter by Margaret Crahan in this volume. For key national situations, see other country chapters in this volume and Kevin Boyle and Juliet Sheen, eds., *Freedom of Religion and Belief: A World Report* (New York: Routledge, 1997), 89-153.

50. For a noteworthy account of Vatican II debate, see Teodoro Jiménez Urresti, *La libertad religiosa. Declaración del Concilio Ecuménico Vaticano II*. Edición bilingue latino-castellana (Madrid: Colección de Pastoral Aplicada, 1965). See also John Courtney Murray, "La déclaration sur la liberté religieuse," *Nouvelle Revue Theologique* 88, 1 (Jan. 1966): 41-67.

51. In the vast literature of histories and commentaries about religious freedom and Vatican Council II, see esp. Pietro Pavan, "The Right to Religious Freedom in the Conciliar Declaration," *Concilium* (New York: Paulist Press, 1966), 18:37-52.

52. The shift was not as abrupt as sometimes portrayed but evolutionary, as shown by Pius Augustin, *Religious Freedom in Church and State: A Study in Doctrinal Development* (Baltimore: Helicon, 1966).

53. This was recognized even as the declaration was being disseminated. See John Courtney Murray, ed., *Religious Liberty: An End and a Beginning: The Declaration on Religious Freedom: An Ecumenical Discussion* (New York: Macmillan, 1966).

54. Many Latin American Protestants reacted in shock to the changes at Vatican II. See, for example, W. Dayton Roberts, *Strachan of Costa Rica* (Grand Rapids, Mich.: Eerdmans, 1971), 129.

55. One instrument is the United Nations Declaration on the Elimination of All Forms of Intolerance and of Discrimination Based on Religion or Belief (1981).

56. Roland Minnerath, "Church-State Relations and Religious Liberty Issues: A Catholic Response," paper (Exhibit XVI) prepared for meeting of Conference of Secretaries of Christian World Communions, Oslo, Oct. 24, 1996.

57. Tiny countries, as Monaco and Malta, still constitutionally maintain Catholicism as their official religion.

58. Joel-Benoît D'Onorio provides a postconciliar overview in his "Les concordats et conventions postconciliaires," in *Le Saint Siege dans les relations internationales*, ed. Joel-Benoît D'Onorio (Paris: Cerf-Cujas, 1989), 193-245.

59. Inter-church policy can be found in Vatican Council II's *Unitatis Redintegratio* and later statements such as John Paul II's *Ut Unum Sint*.

60. Fundamentally different processes result from relating to different publics: ecumenism (among Christians), interreligious dialogue (among world religions), and preaching/evangelization among non-Christians.

61. *Unitatis Redintegratio*, no. 3.

62. Joint Working Group between the Roman Catholic Church and the World Council of Churches, "The Challenge of Proselytism and the Calling to Common

Witness," *Information Service* [Rome, The Pontifical Council for Promoting Christian Unity] 91, 1-2 (1991), 81.

63. Numerous commentaries have been made in Latin America that Pentecostals are even more of a problem for historical Protestants than for Catholics. Roberto Blancarte, a leading Mexican sociologist and counselor to the Mexican embassy to the Holy See, confirms this assessment for Mexico. (Interview, Rome, May 2, 1997).

64. Joint Working Group, "The Challenge," 77-83.

65. Edward Cassidy, "The Christian Mission in the Third Millennium: Evangelizing and Reevangelizing Latin America With—Not Against—One Another," *First Things* 79 (Jan. 1998): 26.

66. John Paul II, "Opening Address to Fourth General Conference of Latin American Episcopate," English trans., *Origins* 22, 19 (Oct. 22, 1992), esp. No. 12. For the conference's statement on ecumenism and a Catholic and a Protestant commentary, see Alfred T. Hennelly, *Santo Domingo and Beyond* (Maryknoll, N.Y.: Orbis Books, 1993).

67. Interview with Samuel Escobar, Protestant mission scholar, Oct. 20, 1992.

68. Cardinal Ernesto Cirripio Ahumada of Mexico explicitly identified Pentecostals and sects in "Regional Reports of Latin America" (Apr. 5, 1991), in *Sects and New Religious Movements: An Anthology of Texts from the Catholic Church, 1986-1994* (Washington, D.C.: U.S. Catholic Conference, 1995), 4.

69. Santo Domingo, Final Document, no. 135.

70. James S. Torrens, "Here Comes the Synod for America," *America* (Nov. 1, 1997), 3.

71. Edward L. Cleary, "John Paul Cries Wolf," *Commonweal* (Nov. 20, 1992), 7-8.

72. Pontifical Council for Promoting Christian Unity, *Information Service* 84, 3-4 (1993), 122.

73. *Veja* 1415 (Oct. 25, 1995), 104-5.

74. Ibid, 98.

75. Cecil Robeck, *Commonweal* (Dec. 18, 1992), 30-31.

76. Cecil Robeck, "Pentecostals and Ecumenism in a Pluralistic World," paper for Globalization of Pentecostalism Conference, San José, Costa Rica, June 10-14, 1996.

77. Cecil Robeck, "Evangelization or Proselytism of Hispanics? A Pentecostal Perspective," *Journal of Hispanic and Latino Theology* 4, 4 (1997): 42-43.

78. John A. Rodano, "Pentecostal-Roman Catholic International Dialogue," *Mid-Stream* 31, 1 (Jan. 1992): 26-31; Jerry L. Sandidge, *Roman Catholic/Pentecostal Dialogue (1977-82): A Study in Developing Ecumenism,* 2 vols. (Frankfurt und Main: Verlag Peter Lang, 1987); and Peter Hocken, "Dialogue Extraordinary," *One in Christ* 24, 3 (1988): 202-13.

79. Guillermo Cook, "Interchurch Relations, Exclusion, Ecumenism, and the Poor," in *Power, Politics, and Pentecostals in Latin America,* ed. Edward L. Cleary and Hannah Stewart-Gambino (Boulder, Colo.: Westview, 1997), 80-81.

80. Interview, Rome, April 28, 1997.

81. Interview given on condition of anonymity, May 2, 1997.

82. Brian H. Smith, "Pentecostalism and Catholicism in Contemporary Latin America," paper prepared with support by National Endowment for the Humanities, Sept. 1996, 53.

83. Paul Marshall, *Their Blood Cries Out: The Worldwide Tragedy of Modern Christians Who Are Dying for Their Faith* (Dallas: Word Publishing, 1997), 137-38.

84. Jean-Pierre Bastian, "Minorités religieuses et confessionnalisation de la politique en Amérique Latine," *Archives de Sciences Sociales des Religions* 42, 97 (Jan.-Mar. 1997): 103.

85. Paul Freston, "Brother Votes for Brother: The New Politics of Protestantism in Brazil," in *Rethinking Protestantism in Latin America*, ed. Virginia Garrard-Burnett and David Stoll (Philadelphia, Pa.: Temple University Press, 1993), 100-102.

86. Leandro Piquet Carneiro, "The Church as Political Context: Civic Culture and Political Participation among Protestants," paper presented at Latin American Studies Association International Congress, 1997.

87. Robert K. Zub, "Relaciones iglesia y estado en Nicaragua: Una perspectiva protestante," unpublished paper, August 1994.

88. For a summary of views of Pentecostals and their political involvements, see Edward L. Cleary, "Introduction: Pentecostals, Prominence, and Politics," and Edward L. Cleary and Juan Sepúlveda, "Chilean Pentecostalism: Coming of Age," in Cleary and Stewart-Gambino, *Power*, 1-24, 97-121.

89. Pentecostals have been shown to be neither uniformly apolitical nor conservative in voting or in their political views. Further, they have supported revolutionary politics in Chile and Nicaragua. See Cleary, "Introduction," and Cleary and Sepúlveda, "Chilean Pentecostalism"; Timothy Steigenga and Kenneth Coleman, "Protestant Political Orientations and the Structure of Political Opportunity: Chile, 1972-1991," *Polity* 27, 3 (1995): 465-82; Christian Smith and Liesl Ann Haas, "Revolutionary Evangelicals in Nicaragua: Political Opportunity, Class Interests, and Religious Identity," *Journal for Scientific Study of Religion* 36, 3 (1997): 440-54; and Daniel Míguez, "Pentecostalism and Politics in Argentina: The Role of Pentecostals in Clientelistic Politics," unpublished paper.

90. Smith, "Pentecostalism," 83.

91. Marshall, *Their Blood*, 138.

92. See Cleary and Sepúlveda, "Chilean Pentecostalism," 97-121.

93. Subsecretariado de Culto, *El fenómeno religioso no católico en Bolivia: Una primera aproximación* (La Paz: Ministerio de Relaciones Exteriores y Culto, 1996), 51.

94. Interview with Mark Glover, Brigham Young University, who for many years has surveyed Mormons in Latin America, Washington, D.C., May 19, 1997.

95. *Latinamerica Press* 24, 2 (Jan. 23, 1992), 7.

96. Subsecretariado de Culto, *El fenómeno*, 74.

97. Interview with Armando Loaiza Mariaca, Rome, May 2, 1997.

98. Ibid.

99. *Latinamerica Press* (May 22, 1997), 6.

100. Jeffrey Gros, "Dignitatis Humanae and Ecumenism: A Foundation and a Promise," *Symposium on Religious Liberty: Paul VI and Dignitatis Humanae* (Brescia: Istituo Paolo VI, 1995), 143.

101. Ibid, 145.

102. Segundo Galilea, "Latin America in the Medellín and Puebla Conferences: An Example of Selective and Creative Reception of Vatican II," in Giuseppe Alberigo et al., *The Reception of Vatican II* (Washington, D.C.: Catholic University of America Press, 1987), 72.

103. Torrens, "Here Comes the Synod," 3.

104. Thomas J. Reese, "Synod for America," *America* (Dec. 13, 1997), 4.

105. *The Tablet* (Dec. 20-27, 1997), 1667.

106. Franz Damen, "Las sectas, avalancha o desafío?" *Cuarto Intermedio* [Cochabamba] 3 (May 1987): 44-65; and Roger Aubrey, *La misión siguiendo a Jesús por los caminos de América Latina* (Buenos Aires: Editorial Guadalupe, 1990).

2 HISTORICAL PROTESTANTISM / JOHN H. SINCLAIR

1. An excellent summary of the seven waves of Protestant growth and missionary activity is found in Daniel R. Miller, ed., *Coming of Age: Protestantism in Contemporary Latin America* (New York: University Press of America, 1994), 177.

2. See J. P. Bastian, *Historia del Protestantismo en América Latina* (Mexico: Casa Unida de Publicaciones, 1990), 46-57.

3. See G. Baez Camargo, Colección "Documentos," in *Protestantes enjuiciados por la Inquisición en Iberoamérica*, vol. 4 (Mexico: Casa Unida de Publicaciones, 1960).

4. See Bastian, *Historia*, 85-92.

5. Ibid., 90-91; see also W. Stanley Rycroft, "The Protestant Churches and Religious Freedom in Latin America," *Journal of Church and State* (Summer 1966): 263ff.

6. Símon Bolívar, quoted in J. L. Mecham, *Church and State in Latin America*, rev. ed. (Chapel Hill: University of North Carolina Press, 1966).

7. See Bastian, *Historia*, 102-16.

8. See W. Villapando et al., eds., *Protestantismo y Inmigracion en la Argentina* (Buenos Aires: Casa Pubicadora "La Aurora," 1970).

9. I. Paul, *A Yankee Reformer in Chile: The Life and Works of David Trumbull* (South Pasadena, Calif.: William Carey Press, 1963), 63.

10. Ibid., 104-7.

11. Ibid., 58-60.

12. Bastian, *Historia*, 124-25.

13. See T. S. Goslin, *Los Evangélicos en América Latina: Siglo XIX los comienzos* (Buenos Aires: Casa Pubicadora "La Aurora," 1956).

14. Bastian, *Historia*, 126.

15. See J. Stam, "La Mision Latinoamericana y el imperalismo Americano: 1926-1928," *Contribuciones para una historia del Protestantismo en America Latina*, no. 9 (Mexico: Comunidad Teológica, 1981).

16. R. S. Storr, in Bastian, *Historia*, 133.

17. G. Cook, "Contrasting Visions," in Miller, *Coming of Age*, 125.

18. See A. Rembao, *Discurso a la Nación Evangélica* (Buenos Aires, Casa Publicadora "La Aurora," 1949).

19. J. Sepúlveda, "Avanza el Protestantismo en América Latina," in *El Estandarte* (Buenos Aires, 1991).

20. See Walter Wink, "Prayer and Power," *Sojourners* [Washington, D.C.] (1990).

21. See D. Levine, *Protestants and Catholics in Latin America: A Family Portrait* (Chicago, 1991), 31.

22. G. Cook, "Contrasting Visions," in Miller, *Coming of Age*, 133.

23. D. Smith, "Algunos Rasgos y Desafíos de la Conyuntura Centroamericana," *Centro Evangelico de Estudios Pastorales* [Guatemala City] (October 1997), 8.

24. See E. Cleary, in Miller, *Coming of Age*, xviii.

25. See J. A. Mackay, *Ecumenics: The Science of the Church Universal* (Englewood Cliffs, N.J.: Prentice-Hall, 1964).

26. See commentary on this Catholic Action Congress at Chimbote, Peru, by William J. Coleman, *Latin American Catholicism: A Self-criticism* (Maryknoll, N.Y.: Maryknoll Publications, 1958).

27. See J. H. Sinclair, "Conversations between Protestants and Roman Catholics and the Latin American Churches," in Buck Hill Falls Conferences of the Committee on Cooperation in Latin American series (New York, National Council of Churches of Christ, U.S.A., 1963).

28. Cleary, in Miller, *Coming of Age*, 213.

29. Ibid., see chap. 8.

30. See "Ecumenical Challenges," *Princeton Seminary Review* (Princeton, N.J.: Princeton Theological Seminary, 1997), 19.

31. G. Diekmann, *Minneapolis Star Tribune* (March 19, 1997).

32. D. Sabanes Plou, *Caminos de Unidad* (Quito: CLAI, 1993), 95-99.

33. See D. Smith, "Reflexiones de un evangelio desencantado . . . ," *Centro Evangelico de Estudios Pastorales* [Guatemala City] (November 1997).

34. D. Sabanes Plou, *Caminos de Unidad* (Quito: CLAI, 1993), 95.

35. E. Abumanssur, quoted in Cook, "Contrasting Visions," in Miller, *Coming of Age*, 127. See also Rubén Alves, *Protestantism and Repression: A Brazilian Case Study* (Maryknoll, N.Y.: Orbis Books, 1985).

36. A. M. Almquist, *Burgess of Guatemala* (Langley, B.C.: Cedar Books, 1985), 130.

37. J. D. Martz, *Colombia: A Contemporary Political Survey* (Chapel Hill: University of North Carolina Press, 1962).

38. See P. Jeffrey, *Guatemalan Churches and the Challenges of Peacemaking*, unpublished manuscript (1997).

3 EVANGELICAL CHURCHES / PEDRO C. MORENO

1. For purposes of this chapter, the term *Evangelical* is used for the Protestant churches that emphasize personal transformation, the Bible as the basis of faith, and the religious requirement to spread the Gospel to others (evangelization). However, note that in Latin America all Protestants are described as *evangélicos*.

2. Patrick Johnstone, *Operation World* (Grand Rapids, Mich., 1993), 65.

3. Ibid.

4. Information obtained by author from the evangelistic/religious ministries themselves as of December 1997.

5. Joseph E. Davis, "The Protestant Challenge in Latin America," *America* (January 19, 1991), 37.

6. See generally John W. Whitehead and Pedro C. Moreno, *Iglesia y Estado en Las Américas* (La Paz, Bolivia, 1994).

7. Luis D. Salem, *El Dios de Nuestros Libertadores* (Argentina, 1977).

8. Ibid.

9. Eduardo Rozo Acuna, *Bolívar y la Organización de los Poderes Públicos* (Bogotá, Colombia, 1988), 117.

10. Arnoldo Canclini, *La Libertad de Cultos* (Buenos Aires, Argentina, 1987), 75.

11. Alejandro Soto Cárdenas, *Influencia de la Independencia de los Estados Unidos en la Constitución de las Naciones Latinoamericanas* (Washington, D.C., 1979), 159.

12. David Miller, "Chile Expected to Approve Law Guaranteeing Religious Equality," *Compass Direct* [California] (February 21, 1997).

13. Law 7619 of 24 July, 1996, amends Articles 147 and 148 of the Labor Code concerning working days, holidays, and weekend rests; lists holidays; and regulates absence from work for religious reasons.

14. Pedro C. Moreno, ed., *Handbook on Religious Liberty around the World* (Charlottesville, Va., 1996), 238-39.

15. Author's interview with Dr. Angel Centeno, Secretary of Religious Affairs (Buenos Aires, Argentina, July 22, 1994). See also *La Nación* [Buenos Aires], April 12, 1992.

16. "Finalizó monopolio católico en México," *El Bravo* [Tamaulipas, Mexico] (March 12, 1992), 1.

17. "Externan Evangélicos su Apoyo a la Nueva Relación Estado-Iglesias," *La Jornada* [Mexico] (March 1992).

18. Author's interview with Dr. Oscar Facundo Ynsfrán, President of the Constitutional Convention of Paraguay (Asunción, June 1992).

19. U.S. Department of State, *Country Reports on Human Rights Practices for 1996* (Washington, D.C., 1997).

20. There are 250 Catholic priests and 450 nuns in Cuba, compared to over 1,000 Evangelical pastors and close to 3,000 house churches. *Verdad y Vida* [Venezuela] (September 1997).

21. Pedro C. Moreno, *Constitutional Reforms in Latin America Promoting Religious Freedom*, XXXI Annual Conference of the Inter-American Bar Association (Puerto Rico, June 25-30, 1994), 15.

22. "Secta declara guerra santa contra el gobierno en Brasil," *El Nuevo Herald* [Miami] (December 3, 1995), 29A.

23. Ibid.

24. "Brasil: La justicia condena a obispo que pateó imagen de la Virgen de Aparecida," *Agencia Latinoamericana y Caribeña de Comunicación* [Lima, Peru] (May 12, 1997).

25. "John Paul Goes to War," *Newsweek* (February 12, 1996), 39.

26. "John Paul Woos Straying Flock," *Christianity Today* (April 8, 1996), 94.

27. Point 139, CELAM, October 1992. See also "Catholic Bishops Renew Missionary Efforts to Stem Growth of Sects," *Christianity Today* (December 14, 1992), 46.

28. IV General Conference of the Latin American Bishops (held in Santo Domingo, Dominican Republic), *Documento de Conclusiones Ediciones Paulinas* (La Paz, Bolivia, 1992), 102-3.

29. *News Network International—News Service* [California] (January 19, 1995), 15-16.

30. See "John Paul Goes to War."

31. See "John Paul Woos Straying Flock."

32. *El Universal* [Mexico City] (March 18, 1992).

33. "Two Evangelical Lay Workers Killed in Chiapas, Mexico," *Compass Direct* [California] (November 18, 1997).

34. "Indigenous Leaders in Chiapas Force Evangelicals from Their Homes," *Compass Direct* [California] (November 21, 1997).

35. The Rutherford Institute is an international legal and educational organization dedicated to the defense of civil liberties, especially religious freedom.

36. Author's telephone interview with Hospital Obrero's director (La Paz, Bolivia, September 1993).

37. "Prohiben terminantemente ingreso de ministros no-católicos al ejército boliviano," *Rutherford* [Spanish ed., La Paz, Bolivia] (December 1994), 2.

38. *Evangelicals and Catholics Together: The Christian Mission in the Third Millennium* (Cincinnati, Ohio, 1994), Point 52.

39. Ibid., Point 33.

40. Ibid., Point 52.

41. Ibid., Point 53.

42. "Pope Asks Bishops in Americas to Renew Zeal," *International Herald Tribune* (November 17, 1997), 7.

43. "Presidente del CLAI Presenta Mensaje al Sínodo de las Américas," *Agencia Latinoamericana y Caribeña de Comunicación* [Lima, Peru] (December 3, 1997).

44. CLAI, the Latin American Council of Churches, was officially founded on November 16, 1982, in Huampaní, Peru.

45. CONELA, the Latin American Evangelical Fellowship, was founded during the Latin American Consultation that took place in Panama from April 19 to April 23, 1982.

46. *Rápidas* [Quito] (April 1997).

47. *Rápidas* [Quito] (June 1997).

48. See "Martirio y Esperanza," *Memoria del Encuentro Continental* [CLAI's official document] (Cochabamba, Bolivia, August 9-15, 1992). Also, a telephone interview was conducted by The Rutherford Institute with Bishop Rolando Villena, CLAI's secretary for the Andean Region, based in La Paz, Bolivia, August 4, 1997.

49. Telephone interview conducted by The Rutherford Institute with CONELA's executive secretary, Rubén Proietti, based in Buenos Aires, August 4, 1997.

50. See Paulino Montejo and Xuaco Arnaiz, "Los Pueblos de la Esperanza, Frente al Neoliberalismo," *AELAPI* [Articulación Ecuménica Latinoamericana de Pastoral Indígena] (Ecuador, 1997). See also "Comprometidos con el Reino 3, Declaraciones, Resoluciones y Cartas Oficiales del Consejo Latinoamericano de Iglesias 1988-1994," (Ecuador, 1994). On this subject, Cardinal Ratzinger, prefect of the Sacred Congregation of the Faith at the Vatican, has accused the WCC and Protestants affiliated with CLAI of having supported subversive movements in Latin America. Ratzinger claimed that the WCC gave financial support to the liberation theology and the guerrilla movements in Latin America from the 1960s to the 1980s. "Italia: Cardenal Ratzinger Embiste Contra los Protestantes," *Agencia Latinoamericana y Caribeña de Comunicación* [Lima, Peru] (June 12, 1997).

51. Daniel R. Miller, ed., *Coming of Age, Protestantism in Contemporary Latin America* (Lanham, Md., 1994), 9.

52. David Miller, "Protestants Assess Progress of Political Activist Movement," *News Network International—Special Report* (October 20, 1995).

53. Tropic Supplement, *Miami Herald* (January 29, 1995), 18.

54. Plinio Apuleyo Mendoza, Carlos A. Montaner, and Alvaro Vargas Llosa, *Manual del Perfecto Idiota Latinoamericano* (Mexico, 1996).

55. David Martin, *Tongues of Fire: The Explosion of Protestantism in Latin America* (Oxford, England, 1990).

56. John Marcom Jr., "The Fire Down South," *Forbes* (October 15, 1990), 56.

57. Julio Córdova, "Élites, Religiosidad y Pluralismo," *La Razón* [La Paz, Bolivia] (April 7, 1996).

58. Arturo Fontaine Talavera, "Retrato del Movimiento Evangélico a la Luz de las Encuestas de Opinión Pública," *Estudios Públicos* 44 [Santiago, Chile] (Spring 1991), 63-124.

59. *EP News* (March 1996).

60. Quoted in Daniel Wattenberg, "Gospel Message of Getting Ahead Inch by Inch," *Insight* (July 16, 1990), 16.

61. Ibid., 15.

62. See Marcom, "The Fire Down South."

63. See Martin, *Tongues of Fire.*

64. Timothy Goodman, "The Latin American Reformation," *The American Enterprise* (July/August 1991), 41.

65. Author's interview with Franz Damen, 1993. See also Franz Damen, *El Desafío de las Sectas* (Oruro, Bolivia, 1989).

66. Mortimer Arias, "El Protestantismo," *Presencia* [La Paz, Bolivia] (August 6, 1975), 184.

67. Timothy Goodman, "A Force for Modernization," *Rutherford* (May 1994), 13.

68. Ibid.

69. Caio Fabio D'Araújo Filho, *El Verdadero Avivamiento* (Buenos Aires, Argentina, 1993), 22.

70. Author's telephone interview with Pastor Sáenz Salas based in Costa Rica, winter 1996-97.

4 The Economics of Evangelization / Anthony Gill

1. Chaves (1995) criticizes the rational choice assumption of welfare maximization as being trivial and makes the logical jump that rational choice adds little to our understanding of human behavior. He correctly notes that the maximization assumption is trivial, but is remiss in claiming this assumption comprises the whole of rational choice theory. Chaves fails to recognize that the key to rational choice analysis is examining how changes in environmental constraints affect maximizing behavior. See Laurence Iannaccone 1995, 76-88, for a response.

2. Rational choice theorists do not necessarily deny that culture is important. However, rational choice theories differ from cultural theories in that they see culture (values, norms, and ideologies) as constraints on, rather than the principal cause of, human behavior. See North 1981 for an economic treatment of ideology as a means of lowering transaction costs.

3. Critics assert that human beings simply do not possess the mental capacity to process all the information needed that most economic models imply, and that they are fooled by shifts in how information is framed (see Stepen Tversky and Daniel Kahneman, "The Framing of Decisions and the Psychology of Choice," *Science* 211 [1981]: 453-58). However, in some instances—when the stakes are high or when there are repetitive interactions between actors—people are more likely to engage in calculating behavior (Barbara Geddes, "Uses and Limitations of Rational Choice," in Smith 1995).

4. A common example of this can be found in explanations for the rise of progressive Catholicism in Latin America. It is claimed that progressive Catholicism results from shifts in a church's worldview. But how do we know that a church has shifted its worldview (especially if we do not have recourse to survey data that control for confounding factors)? We can only know if there has been such a shift if we observe progressive Catholicism. The observation on the dependent variable (progressive Catholicism) becomes evidence for the presence of the independent variable (shift in worldview).

5. A religious economy is any environment where religious goods and services are exchanged between consumers (parishioners) and producers (priests). Religious goods and services are those things that religious uniquely specialize in, namely, supernatural answers to life's grand questions (see Stark and Bainbridge 1985). The religious economy is somewhat unique in that consumers also serve as producers, via individual prayers and participation in communal rituals.

6. This could be qualified by noting that some religious organizations are not proselytizing (e.g., Judaism). Nonetheless, retaining members is still important to all religions to my knowledge, and particularly ones active in Latin America. This assumption of preferences thus can be relaxed to "avoidance of parishioner loss."

7. The ceteris paribus clause is important here in that a poor church may be able to use its meager resources more efficiently, and thus will be more successful than a relatively inefficient wealthy church.

8. It is somewhat counterintuitive to note that the Catholic Church, despite being the world's largest bureaucracy, is very effective at incorporating a wide array of religious beliefs and practices (e.g., liberation theologians, charismatic Catholics, Opus Dei) under a single organization. Protestantism tends toward schism when faced with internal diversity, while the Catholic Church has been more flexible historically in dealing with internal, theological divisions. Images of the Catholic Church as a rigid bureaucracy are very misleading.

9. It should be noted here that while *foreign* missionaries have been responsible for bringing Protestantism to Latin America, the spread of non-Catholic religions is now primarily an indigenous affair for a variety of strategic reasons (see below). In this essay, I refer to missionaries as anyone who is bringing a new form of religion to a population previously unfamiliar with that denomination. In this regard, Catholic catechists are missionaries.

10. For an argument that religions cannot maintain a monopoly without the help of state coercion see Stark 1992, 261-71, and Anthony Gill, "Protestant Growth in Latin America: A Supply-Side Explanation," paper presented at the Twentieth International Congress of the Latin American Studies Association, Guadalajara, Mexico (1997).

11. Laurence Iannaccone, "Skewness Explained: A Rational Choice Model of Religious Giving," *Journal for the Scientific Study of Religion* 36 (2) (1997): 141-57, points out that there is no correlation between one's class standing and the *percentage* of one's income contributed to religious organizations. However, basic algebra informs us that 10 percent of a millionaire's income yields greater *absolute* resources for a church than does 10 percent of the income of a person at the poverty line.

12. This helps to explain why illegitimacy was so high in rural areas. If only the Catholic Church could officially sanction marriage, and the Church was never around to marry people, it was a natural outcome that most children would be born out of wedlock. Also, lacking a legally and morally binding contract with their female partner, men had an incentive to be profligate. Economics thus offers an alternative to cultural explanations of this same phenomenon (e.g., the culture of *machismo*).

13. It is interesting to note that when religious competition started increasing in the mid-twentieth century, the Catholic Church expended more effort in putting clergy into areas it previously had neglected. This included the importation of foreign priests from the U.S. and Europe, as well as an attempt to recruit seminarians. Many Catholic organizations (e.g., human rights groups) also benefited from international sources of funding during the 1970s and 1980s thereby reducing pressures on the Church's

budget and allowing the Church to devote more resources to more segments of the population.

14. This would seem to support the demand-side hypothesis of Protestant growth that people are seeking new forms of community when joining new religious movements. While this is true, one wonders why disenfranchised individuals did not seek out Catholic parishes to rebuild their sense of community. After all, Catholicism supposedly would be more familiar and help to alleviate social alienation and anomie.

15. To my knowledge, no study has been conducted comparing the consumer costs of folk Catholicism with evangelical Protestantism. It is not obvious that the former would be less expensive to practice than the latter. Practitioners of folk Catholicism frequently spend significant portions of their annual income on annual religious feasts.

16. People who join Protestant congregations sometimes continue to venerate Catholic saints. As the religious capital model predicts, past religious practices are hard to give up. Practicing multiple forms of religion is also consistent with the economic theory of portfolio investment.

17. It is common for people to assume that religious belief does not imply rational calculation, only "blind faith." If this were strictly true, anybody professing any doctrine, no matter how unconventional, would be able to win a following. However, we know from experience that fringe religions have a hard time attracting a following, largely because their claims are not credible. People make rational decisions when they choose to avoid non-credible religious claims.

18. Author's interview with Paul Wegmueller, 29 May 1992, Pasadena, California.

PART TWO
PERSPECTIVES ON RELIGIOUS FREEDOM

5 Cuba / Margaret E. Crahan

1. For the purposes of this study *religious freedom* and *liberty of worship* will be defined as they are in Article 18 of the Universal Declaration of Human Rights (1948), i.e., "Everyone has the right to freedom of thought, conscience and religion; this right includes freedom to change his religion and belief, and freedom, either alone or in community with others and in public or private, to manifest his religion or belief in teaching, practice, worship and observance."

2. This essay will focus primarily on institutionalized religion, although it has been estimated that one-tenth to two-thirds of Cuba's population engage in some spiritist practices. In 1960 nominal Catholics constituted approximately 70-75 percent of the total population of Cuba (7,500,000) and Protestants 3-6 percent. According to the 1982 *Anuario Pontificio* there were 3,944,522 Catholics in Cuba or 40 percent of the total population (9,844,168), albeit most nonpracticing. Protestant estimates ranged in 1959 from 25,000 to 80,000 with actual strength probably about 40,000-45,000. The Jewish community numbered approximately 12,000 in the 1950s. In the late 1980s and early 1990s religion was experiencing a resurgence. Catholic baptisms increased from 14,440 in 1988 to 70,081 in 1994. Expressions of popular religiosity also grew, with 68,000 visiting the Sanctuary of *El Rincón* on San Lázaro's feast day in 1988 and 97,000 in 1995. The cult of San Lázaro attracts Catholics, Protestants, adherents of *santería*, and nonaffiliates alike. In recent years Pentecostals have gathered strength in Cuba. In the late 1980s the Center for Psychological

and Sociological Studies of the Cuban Academy of Sciences estimated that 65-85 percent of Cubans believed in the supernatural while 13.60 percent did not. Jorge Ramírez Calzadilla, "Religión, Cultura y Sociedad in Cuba," Departamento de Estudios Socioreligiosos (DESR), Centro de Investigaciones Psicológicas y Sociológicas (CIPS), Academia de Ciencias, mss., 1996. See also René F. de la Huerta Aguiar, "Espiritismo y otras Supersticiones en la Población Cubana," *Revista del Hospital Psiquiátrico de la Habana* 2 (1) (Jan.-Mar. 1960), 46-47; D. P. Noonan, "Religion in Cuba: Christianity in the Catacombs," photocopy, United States Catholic Conference Files (1982), 7; Alice L. Hageman and Philip E. Wheaton, eds., *Religion in Cuba Today: A New Church in a New Society* (New York, 1971), 30-31; Joseph Beckman, "The Future of Religion in Cuba," *LADOC* 9 (5) (May/June 1979), 27; Jacinto Ordoñez, "Informe sobre una visita a Cuba, 20 a 28 de junio 1974," photocopy (15 de agosto de 1974), 4; Jim Wallace, "Christians in Cuba," *Cuban Research Center Newsletter* 3 (1) (April 1973), 6; James M. Wall, "A New Use for the Miramar," *Christian Century* 97 (November 12, 1980): 1083-84; Interviews IH97326 and IH67328. (In 1973, 1974, 1975, 1976, 1979, and 1984 I conducted extensive interviews with fifty Cuban church people on the island, in Spain, and in the United States. These interviews were updated in 1988, 1996, 1997, and 1998, and additional interviews conducted.)

3. The *patronato real* was a system of patronage whereby the crown enjoyed certain privileges concerning ecclesiastical appointments, benefices, and finances in return for financial support for church institutions and personnel. In addition, the monarchs assisted the church in its evangelizing mission. The alliance between church and state that resulted was closer in the colonies than in Spain and led to overlapping authority and occasional jurisdictional disputes. Both civil and ecclesiastical officials were, at times, sharp critics of their counterparts, giving rise in the seventeenth and eighteenth centuries to conflicts between church and state. Liberal ideas, including anticlericalism, were transmitted to the colonies in the eighteenth and nineteenth centuries by both Protestants and Catholics, including priests. In Cuba, Masons helped stimulate the independence movement, which also involved some priests. Manuel P. Maza, S.J., *El Clero Cubano y la Independencia: Las Investigaciones de Francisco González del Valle (1881-1942)* (Santo Domingo, 1993).

4. Manuel P. Maza, S.J., "The Cuban Catholic Church: True Struggles and False Dilemmas: The Historical Characteristics of the Cuban Catholic Church and Their Impact on the 1959-1960 Episcopal Documents" (master's thesis, Georgetown University, 1982), 34-35.

5. Ibid., 55.

6. Oscar A. Echevarría Salvat, *La Agricultura Cubana, 1934-1966: Régimen Social, Productividad y Nivel de Vida de Secto Cola* (Miami, 1971), 14-16, 25.

7. Merle Davis, *The Cuban Church in a Sugar Economy* (New York, 1942), 133. This study, commissioned by the International Missionary Council, officially surveyed all the Protestant churches in Cuba, some 440, in an effort to devise more effective missionary strategies. Davis recommended increased social-welfare and evangelizing efforts in the rural areas, together with decreased dependence on the "mother" churches in the United States. It was not until the 1950s that most Protestant churches intensified their efforts in rural areas and in the late 1960s and early 1970s most became self-supporting and legally independent of U.S. mission agencies. Since the late 1980s with increased economic stringency in Cuba, some churches have again turned to foreign support.

8. Hugh Thomas, *Cuba: The Pursuit of Freedom* (New York, 1971), 793.

9. United Methodist Board of Missions, Minutes of March 1, 1971, meeting, Cuba Sub-Group, Latin American Task Force, 2.

10. Ibid., 3.

11. Alfred L. Padula Jr., "The Fall of the Bourgeoisie: Cuba 1959-1961" (Ph.D. diss., University of New Mexico, 1974), 438-39.

12. Ibid., 439.

13. In 1960 there were approximately 723 priests in Cuba; in 1965 there were 220. Female religious declined from 2,225 in 1960 to 193 in 1965. In 1980 there were 213 priests and 220 nuns in Cuba. It is estimated that 75-80 percent of the Catholic clergy in 1960 in Cuba was Spanish. While the bulk of the Protestant clergy was Cuban, important administrative decisions were made by the U.S. mission agencies, which provided most of the funds for the churches. Leslie Dewart, *Christianity and Revolution: The Lesson of Cuba* (New York, 1963), 95; *Anuario Pontificio*, 1982. In 1988 there were approximately 110 secular and 82 order priests, together with 214 nuns. Baptist clergy were more numerous than in 1959 while the clergy of the other mainline Protestant denominations were fewer. Enrique López Oliva, "La Iglesia que Vive en Cuba: Entrevista al Presidente de la Conferencia Episcopal de Cuba," *Boletín Informativo sobre la Religión en Cuba* (1) (Jan.-Feb. 1988): 5; United Methodist Board of Missions, 3; Theo Tschuy, "Responses to Questions in Mr. Davis' Letter of February 11, 1971, Tannay, Switzerland" (April 25, 1971); Rivas, Minutes of the Cuba Sub-Group, 7; Raúl Gómez Treto, *The Church and Socialism in Cuba* (Maryknoll, N.Y., 1988), 45-46; John M. Kirk, *Between God and the Party* (Tampa, 1989), 103.

14. Dewart, *Christianity and Revolution*, 15.

15. Daniel H. Levine, "The Meaning of Politics to Catholic Elites in Latin America," paper presented at the Ninth World Congress of the International Political Science Association, Montreal, Canada (August 19-25, 1973), 4.

16. Mateo Jover Marimón, "The Church," in *Revolutionary Change in Cuba*, ed. Carmelo Mesa-Lago (Pittsburgh, 1971), 403.

17. Theo Tschuy, "The Cuban Miracle and the Church's Prison," *Cross Currents* 11 (2) (Spring 1961): 187.

18. Claude Julien, "Church and State in Cuba: Development of a Conflict," *Cross Currents* 11 (2) (Spring 1961): 187.

19. Ibid.

20. Ibid.

21. Julien, "Church and State," 187; François Houtart and André Rousseau, *The Church and the Revolution* (Maryknoll, N.Y., 1971), 11-19.

22. Padula, "The Fall of the Bourgeoisie," 143, 453-54.

23. Rivas, Minutes of the Cuba Sub-Group, 6.

24. United Methodist Board of Missions, Minutes of May 14, 1971, meeting, Cuba Sub-Group, Latin American Task Force, 6.

25. Padula, "The Fall of the Bourgeoisie," 58l; Mateo Jover, "The Cuban Church in a Revolutionary Society," *LADOC* 4 (32) (April 1974): 18; Interview IM5771112.

26. Maria Teresa Bolívar Arostegui et al., "Cuban Christians and Puebla," *LADOC Keyhole Series* (17) (1980): 41.

27. Julien, "Church and State," 188.

28. Padula, "The Fall of the Bourgeoisie," 459.

29. Julien, "Church and State," 188.

30. Padula, "The Fall of the Bourgeoisie," 466.

31. Jover, "The Church," 21.

32. As quoted in Julien, "The Church and State," 188. For the full text, see Enrique Pérez Serantes, "Por Dios y Por Cuba," May 6, 1960 (Santiago), in *Historia Eclesiástica de Cuba*, ed. Ismael Teste (Barcelona, 1975), 5:562-68.

33. Conferencia Episcopal de Cuba, "Carta Abierta del Episcopado al Primer Ministro" (December 4, 1960), in Teste, *Historia Eclesiástica*, 5:569-77, 585-90, 603-6; Enrique Pérez Serantes, "Ni Traidores, Ni Parias" (September 24, 1960); "Roma o Moscu" (November 1980); "Con Cristo o Contra Cristo" (December 24, 1960).

34. Padula, "The Fall of the Bourgeoisie," 480.

35. Jover, "The Church," 23.

36. Interview IH47413.

37. Houtart and Rousseau, *The Church and the Revolution*, 124.

38. *Anuario Pontificio,* 1982.

39. Dewart, *Christianity and Revolution*, 1,65; Houtart and Rousseau, *The Church and the Revolution*, 122; Padula, "The Fall of the Bourgeoisie," 491-92.

40. Antonio Benítez Rojas, "Fresh Air Blows through the Seminary," *LADOC Keyhole Series* (7)(n.d.): 53.

41. Tschuy, "Responses to Questions," 1.

42. United Methodist Board of Missions, Minutes of March 1, 1971, 7-8; Rivas, Minutes of Cuba Sub-Group, 6; United Methodist Board of Missions, March 1, 1961, 3.

43. Dean Peerman, "Church-Hopping in Havana," *Christian Century* (December 8, 1971), 1435.

44. Cépeda, 27-28.

45. Harry Genet, "Cuba: The Church Finds Its Role in a Socialist State," *Christianity Today* (23) (December 21, 1979), 40.

46. Ibid.

47. Jorge I. Domínguez, "Political Culture in Cuba: Continuity and Change," paper presented at the National Meeting of the Latin American Studies Association, Atlanta (March 25-28, 1976), 13.

48. Houtart and Rousseau, *The Church and the Revolution*, 124-25.

49. Piero Gheddo, "What I Saw in Cuba," *LADOC Keyhole Series*, 7 (n.d.): 13.

50. *El Equipo Diocesano de Jóvenes de Camagüey*, "Estadística Socioreligiosa de la Diocesis de Camagüey," mss. (1967), 19-21; Interview TM5771112; Wallace, "Christians in Cuba," 7.

51. Cépeda, 26-28.

52. Interview ISM67516.

53. Jover, "The Church," 23; Wallace, "Christians in Cuba," 4.

54. Raimundo García Franco, "Pastores en la U.M.A.P.: Diálogo en la U.M.A.P.," mss. (10/2/66), 1-8. See also United Methodist Board of Missions, Summary of the Meeting of April 2-3, 1971, Cuba Sub-Group Latin American Task Force, 2.

55. Interview IM5771112.

56. Interview IH4701181.

57. Jover, "The Church," 23.

58. Ibid., 27-34.

59. Cuban Christians for Socialism, "How Christians in Cuba See Their Future," and Episcopal Conference of Cuba, "Pastoral Letter, April 10, 1969," *LADOC Key-*

hole Series 7 (n.d.): 76-77, 46-49; Houtart and Rousseau, *The Church and the Revolution*, 125; Wallace, "Christians in Cuba," 4-5; Interview IM5771112.

60. Jorge I. Domínguez, "Cuban Catholics and Castro," *Worldview*, 1 (5) (February 1972), 25.

61. Manuel Fernández, "The Church in Cuba, Eleven Years Later, " *LADOC* 1 (5) (June 1970): 7.

62. Cépeda, 29; Iglesia Metodista de Cuba, *El Evangelista Cubano* 57 (2) (Jan. 1965), 7; United Methodist Board of Missions, May 14, 1971, 5; Theo Tschuy, "Cuban Protestantism: A Historical Sketch, Memo to Faith and Order Team to Cuba, March 1971, Geneva" (February 3, 1971), 8; Tschuy, April 25, 1971, 2; Wallace, "Christians in Cuba," 8; World Council of Churches Archives (WCCA) 280.57291 (Box 1), Cuban Council of Evangelical Churches, "Informe del Secretario Ejecutivo, Alolfo Ham, 1967," 2; WCCA, 425, Division of Interchurch Aid, DICARWS Divisional Committee, Projects Subcommittee, Tutzing, July 22-26, 1964, 2-3.

63. Tschuy, April 25, 1971, 4; Joyce Hill, "Report of Trip to Cuba" (March 31, 1971), 6.

64. Wallace, "Christians in Cuba," 3-4.

65. Everett E. Gendler, "Cuba and Religion: Challenge and Response," *Christian Century* 86 (July 30, 1969), 1013-14.

66. Raúl V. Gutierrez, "What I Saw in Cuba: Interview with Auxiliary Bishop Fernando Ariztia, of Santiago, Chile, and Bishop Carlos González of Talca," *LADOC* 2 (5c) (October 1971): 4.

67. A 1971 survey of four thousand members of the Presbyterian church revealed that a majority continued to harbor anti-government attitudes and oppose the efforts of church leaders to dialogue with Marxists. Wallace, "Christians in Cuba," 9.

68. Hill, "Report of Trip to Cuba," 5.

69. Wallace, "Christians in Cuba," 10.

70. The five Protestant seminaries were the Nazarene in Punta Brava, Western Baptist in Havana, Eastern Baptist in Santiago, the Pinos Nuevos in Placetas, and the Evangelical Seminary in Matanzas. The Catholics had a minor seminary in Santiago and a major one in Havana.

71. Reverend Eduardo Valdéz, as quoted in Doug Hostetter, "Cuba Trip: September 1-10, 1976," mss., 11.

72. Ordoñez, "Informe sobre una visita a Cuba," 9.

73. José María González Ruiz, "La Iglesia Católica en Cuba," *Sabado Gráfico* 795 (August 19, 1972), 13.

74. National Congress on Education and Culture, "Declaration, April 30, 1971," *LADOC Keyhole Series* 7 (n.d.): 51.

75. Ibid., 50-51.

76. Interviews IH67038; IH47412-2; IM57711-12.

77. Constitution of the Republic of Cuba (Havana, 1975), 30.

78. Leonel-Antonio de la Cuesta, "The Cuban Socialist Constitution: Its Originality and Role in Institutionalization," *Cuban Studies* 6 (July 1976): 18-20.

79. Interview IH67328.

80. Elmer Rodríguez, "Cuba: Who Said There Is No Religious Freedom in Cuba?" *Prensa Latina Feature Service* 168 (Nov. 1, 1977): 2-3.

81. Center for Cuban Studies Archives, D888, "Resolution on Religion: First Party Congress of the Cuban Communist Party, December 1975," 35.

82. Partido Comunista de Cuba, *Plataforma Programática: Tesis y Resolución* (Havana, 1978), 100-102.

83. Partido Comunista de Cuba, Segundo Congreso, "La Construcción del Socialismo y la Libertad de Consciencia" (1980), photocopy, n.p.

84. Fidel Castro, Transcripts (November 20, 1977), 5.

85. Ibid.

86. Ibid., 8.

87. Ibid., 3-9.

88. Dow Kirkpatrick, "U.S. Christians in Cuba," *Christian Century* 94 (August 3-10, 1977), 687.

89. Encuentro Nacional Eclesial Cubano (ENEC), *Documento Final* (Miami, 1987), 99-100.

90. Sandra Levinson, "Gallup Poll in Cuba: First Independent Poll in More than 30 Years," *Cuba Update* 15 (1) (February/March 1995), 9.

91. Paul Jeffrey, "A Rebirth for Cuba's Church," *Sojourners* 21 (10) (December 1992), 30-31.

92. Bill Yoder, "Cuban Methodist Churches Thrive Despite Setbacks: Economic Crisis Spurs Growth of House Church," News Network International—News Service (November 24, 1993), 49.

93. Fidel Castro, *Fidel y la Religión: Conversaciones con Frei Betto* (Havana, 1985).

94. Marc Frank, "Cuba's Religious Renaissance," *Latinamerica Press* 27 (12) (April 6, 1995), 1.

95. Cuban Bishops' Conference, "A Call for True Dialogue," *Origins: CNS Documentary Service*, 23 (1-6) (September 30, 1993): 275.

96. Ibid., 278.

97. "Cuban State Press Lashes Out at Catholic Church," *CubaINFO* 5 (13): 12.

98. Personal communication from a Cuban bishop.

99. Cuban Episcopal Conference, "A Call to Reconciliation and Peace," Santiago, Cuba (Mar. 12, 1996), photocopy.

100. "Cuban Christians Worried by Arrest of Baptist Leader: Other Arrests, Beatings Reported," News Network International—News Service (March 15, 1994), 30.

101. The Catholic Bishops of Cuba, "¡Abran sus Corazones a Cristo! Mensaje de los Obispos Católicos de Cuba despues de la Visita del Papa Juan Pablo II" (Open Your Hearts to Christ: Message of the Catholic Bishops of Cuba after the Visit of Pope John Paul II), Havana (Feb. 12, 1998), 4-5.

102. Ibid., 6. Translation by the author.

6 EL SALVADOR / ANDREW J. STEIN

1. Ralph Lee Woodward Jr., "The Aftermath of Independence, 1821-c.1870," in *Central America since Independence*, ed. Leslie Bethell (New York, 1991), 2-4.

2. Ibid., 10, 15. Peasants were deeply opposed to the anticlerical measures taken by Liberals such as the expulsion of priests.

3. Ibid., 10-13; see also Jesús Delgado, *Historia de la Iglesia en El Salvador* (San Salvador, 1821-85, 1992), 2:15-36, 64-77, 155-67; Frederick B. Pike, "The Catholic Church in Central America," *Review of Politics* 21 (1) (January 1959), 86-91.

4. Robert G. Williams, *States and Social Evolution: Coffee and the Rise of National Governments in Central America* (Chapel Hill, 1994), 203.

5. Delgado, *Historia de la Iglesia*, 2:188-207, 213-25.

6. Williams, *State and Social Evolution*, 73-74, notes that both types of land constituted as much as one-fourth of total holdings, and were legally proscribed in 1881-82; Rodolfo Cardenal, *El poder eclesiástico en El Salvador* (San Salvador, 1980), 26-30, 54-63.

7. Williams, *State and Social Evolution*, 246.

8. Cardenal, *El Poder Eclesiástico*, 179.

9. Ibid., 116, 145-63; J. Lloyd Mecham, *Church and State in Latin America* (Chapel Hill, 1934), 386-87; Ciro F. S. Cardoso, "The Liberal Era, c.1870-1930," in Bethell, *Central America since Independence*, 61.

10. Cardenal, *El Poder Eclesiástico*, 206, 210-17.

11. Ibid., 310-23.

12. Thomas P. Anderson, *Matanza: El Salvador's Communist Revolt of 1932* (Lincoln, Neb., 1971).

13. Rosa Carmelita Samos, *Sobre el magisterio de Mons: Luis Chávez y González* (San Salvador, 1992), 102-19.

14. Chávez's period as archbishop covered thirteen different governments. Fraudulent elections, military rule, and growing middle class and grassroots mobilization marked the final years of his era. See Enrique Baloyra, *El Salvador in Transition* (Chapel Hill, 1982), 1-30, 56-57.

15. Jorge Cáceres Prendes, "Political Radicalization and Popular Pastoral Practices in El Salvador, 1969-1985," in *The Progressive Church in Latin America*, ed. Scott Mainwaring and Alexander Wilde (Notre Dame, Ind., 1989), 104-11.

16. Stephen Webre, *José Napoleón Duarte and the Christian Democratic Party in Salvadoran Politics, 1960-1972* (Baton Rouge, 1979).

17. For background on how the UCA was founded and the central role it had, see Francisco Javier Ibisate, S.J., "Los treinta años de la UCA," *ECA* 565-66 (November-December 1995): 1150-51; Ignacio Ellacuría, *Veinte años de historia en El Salvador: escritos políticos (1969-1989)* (San Salvador, 1995).

18. On Romero, see James R. Brockman, *Romero: A Life* (Maryknoll, N.Y., 1989); Jon Sobrino, *Monseñor Romero* (San Salvador, 1989); Jesús Delgado, *Oscar A. Romero, biografía* (San Salvador, 1995); *Archbishop Oscar Romero, Voice of the Voiceless* (Maryknoll, N.Y., 1985); Arnoldo Mora, ed., *Monseñor Romero* (San José, 1981); María López Vigíl, *Piezas para un retrato*, 3d ed. (San Salvador, 1995).

19. For the events leading up to the start of the civil war, see Baloyra, *El Salvador in Transition*, 86-113; Tommie Sue Montgomery, *Revolution in El Salvador* (Boulder, 1995), 71-79, 127-36.

20. Cited in Americas Watch and the American Civil Liberties Union, *Report on Human Rights in El Salvador* (New York, 1982), 110.

21. See Delgado, *Oscar A. Romero*, 32-58.

22. Zacarías Diez and Juan Macho, *"En Santiago de María me topé con la miseria": dos años en la vida de Mons. Romero (1975-1976)* (San José, 1994).

23. Brockman, *Romero*, 200-248.

24. United Nations, Truth Commission Report, "De la locura a la esperanza, la guerra de doce años en El Salvador: Informe de la Comisión de la Verdad," *ECA* 533 (March 1993): 269-75.

25. Diez and Macho, *"En Santiago de María,"* 46-52.

26. Ibid., 23, 67-81, 182-89. The expulsions of 1975-76 curtailed the pastoral abilities of the Diocese of Santiago de María, since twelve of twenty priests were

foreigners. Forty order priests were expelled by the Molina and Romero govern-ments, at a time when nearly half of the estimated 189 priests the archdiocese had in 1979 were members of foreign religious orders. See Ivan D. Paredes, "La Situación de la Iglesia en El Salvador y su influjo social," *ECA* (July-August 1979), 602-5.

27. CEDES, "No a la violencia, sí a la paz," San Salvador, September 15, 1980, and "Comunicado de la Conferencia Episcopal de El Salvador alusivo a las elecciones," *ECA* 399-400 (January-February 1982): 136.

28. Phillip Berryman, *Stubborn Hope: Religion, Politics and Revolution in Central America* (Maryknoll, N.Y., 1994), 80-81.

29. CEDES, "Reconciliación y Paz," August 6, 1985, in *ECA* 443-44 (September-October 1985): 743-50.

30. Ibid., 746-47.

31. An FMLN-FDR response accused the bishops of a double standard for reject-ing violence and yet failing to mention massacres and assassinations of civilians by the military and right-wing death squads, or the preponderant degree of U.S. inter-vention. "Respuesta del FMLN-FDR a la carta pastoral de la CEDES," *ECA* (Sep-tember-October 1985), 748.

32. Arturo Rivera Damas, "Quinto aniversario de la muerte de Monseñor Romero. Homilía del 24 de marzo de 1985," in *ECA* (March 1985): 178, and "El difícil camino de la paz," letter of January 4, 1987, in *Cartas del Arzobispo 1983-1994: Monseñor Arturo Rivera Damas* (San Salvador, 1996), 339-41.

33. More than 60 percent of the public favored the church's role in the peace process, and less than 5 percent thought that it favored the left, as extremist critics of the Jesuits and the archdiocese often alleged. See Ignacio Martín-Baró, *La opinión pública salvadoreña, 1987-1988* (San Salvador, 1989), 47, 74-75.

34. Introductory letter by Bishop Rivera, "Debate Nacional 1988, convocado por el Arzobispado de San Salvador, del 17 de junio al 4 de septiembre de 1988" (San Salvador, 1988).

35. For instance, the College of Architects, the Salvadoran Chamber of Commerce and Industry, and two Evangelical universities did not take part on the grounds that the FMLN members were terrorists and that the group convened by the archdiocese was biased in favor of the left. See original letters of refusal reproduced in "Debate Nacional, 1988," n.p.

36. "Debate Nacional 1988, documento final," *ECA* 478-79 (August-September 1988): 764-65.

37. For a discussion of the military during the war, see Philip J. Williams and Knut Walter, *Militarization and Demilitarization in El Salvador's Transition to Democ-racy* (Pittsburgh, 1997), 114-50.

38. United Nations, *The United Nations and El Salvador, 1990-1995* (New York, 1995); Ricardo Córdova Macías, *El Salvador: las negociaciones de paz y los retos de la postguerra* (San Salvador, 1993), 14.

39. Teresa Whitfield, *Paying the Price: Ignacio Ellacuría and the Murdered Jesuits of El Salvador* (Philadelphia, 1994), 207-8, 214-22. This book discusses their views on Marxism, liberation theology, violence, and the relationship of the church to popular organizations.

40. Ibid., 321-35.

41. UN Truth Commission Report, "De la locura a la esperanza," 200-206; Jon Sobrino, *Companions of Jesus: The Jesuit Martyrs of El Salvador* (Maryknoll, N.Y., 1990); Whitfield, *Paying the Price*, 365, 385-89.

42. Whitfield, *Paying the Price*, 365; 375-390.

43. Enrique A. Baloyra, "Elections, Civil War, and Transition in El Salvador, 1982-1994," in *Elections and Democracy in Central America, Revisited*, ed. Mitchell A. Seligson and John A. Booth (Chapel Hill, 1995), 45-61; Ricardo Córdova Macías and Andrew J. Stein, "National and Local Elections in Salvadoran Politics (1982-1994)," in *Urban Elections in Democratic Latin America*, ed. Henry Dietz and Gil Shidlo (Wilmington, Del., 1998).

44. "El mensaje en las urnas," *ECA* 581-82 (March-April 1997): 203-58; Tommie Sue Montgomery, "El Salvador's Extraordinary Elections," *LASA Forum* 28:1 (Spring 1997): 4-8.

45. *Sentir con la Iglesia* [San Salvador] (March 15-April 15, 1996), 4; *Sentir con la Iglesia* (August 15-September 15, 1996), 9-10.

46. Bishop Fernando Sáenz Lacalle, "Homilía en la toma de posesión canonica de la arquidiócesis de San Salvador," *ECA* 559-60 (May-June 1995): 604. Sáenz did come out and say that, under certain circumstances, a proposed bill that would expand the crimes punishable by the death penalty could be acceptable. Others in the archdiocesan clergy, the Jesuits, and public opinion polls were in strong disagreement with this stance. See IUDOP-UCA, "Los salvadoreños evaluan el año 1996," *Boletín de Prensa*, 9:7.

47. Rodolfo Cardenal, "La segunda visita de Juan Pablo II," *ECA* 567-68 (January-February 1996): 29-46. Of the 12.3 million colones spent for the pope's visit, the church paid only 70,000, with the rest coming from the ARENA government and the private sector (*Sentir con la Iglesia* [March 15-August 15 1996]: 4).

48. "El asesinato del obispo salvadoreño Mons. Joaquín Ramos," *Carta a las Iglesias* (UCA Pastoral Center) 307 (June 1-15, 1994): 8-9; "Jerarquía y fuerza armada: grave situación eclesial," *Carta a las Iglesias* 370: 2-3, 8-10; "Diócesis de Chalatenango: Dudas, confusiones y escandalo en las comunidades de Chalatenango" (communiqué by priests, nuns and laity), in *ECA* 597-80 (January-February 1997): 174-77; "Nuevo administrador del Ordinariato Militar," *Carta a las Iglesias* 381 (July 1-15, 1997): 16.

49. Juan Luis Recio, "La incidencia política de las sectas religiosas: el caso de Centroamérica," *ECA* 531-32 (January-February 1993): 84.

50. James Wilke, ed., *Statistical Abstract for Latin America* (Los Angeles, 1977 and 1993).

51. The seemingly inflated Protestant figure from the 1995 Pittsburgh poll is due in part to coding of non-Catholic categories.

52. Philip J. Williams, "The Sound of the Tambourines: The Politics of Pentecostal Growth in El Salvador," in *Power, Politics, and Pentecostals in Latin America*, ed. Edward L. Cleary and Hannah Stewart-Gambino (Boulder, Colo., 1997), 183; Juan Luis Recio, "Las iglesias evangélicas en El Salvador," *ECA* 512 (June 1991): 587.

53. Ibid; Martín-Baró, *La opinión pública salvadoreña*, 29-32; Edwin Aguilar, José Miguel Sandoval, Timothy J. Steigenga, and Kenneth M. Coleman, "Protestantism in El Salvador: Conventional Wisdom versus the Survey Evidence," *Latin American Research Review* 28 (1993): 2; IUDOP-UCA, "La religión para los salvadoreños en 1995," 850.

54. Andrew J. Stein, "Religion and Mass Politics in Central America: Conventional Participation in Nicaragua Compared to Its Neighbors," paper presented at the Annual Meeting of the Midwest Political Science Association, Chicago, 1996; Timothy Steigenga, "Protestantism and Politics in Costa Rica: The Religious Deter-

minants of Political Activities and Beliefs," paper presented at the Annual Meeting of the Midwest Political Science Association, Chicago, 1995; IUDOP-UCA, "La religión para los salvadoreños en 1995," 857 table 8.

55. Williams, "The Sound of the Tambourines," 192-93.

56. Carlos Guillermo Ramos, "Los partidos políticos en las elecciones 1997," in *El Salvador: Elecciones 1997* (San Salvador, 1997), 83-84.

57. CIDAI, "Las elecciones del 16 de marzo de 1997: quiebre de la hegemonía de ARENA," *ECA* 581-82 (March-April 1997): 221 table 1.

58. Ramos, "Los partidos," 86; CIDAI, "Las elecciones," 221.

59. Tribunal Supremo Electoral, "Escrutinio final para concejos municipales," reprinted in *ECA* 581-82 (March-April 1997): 339-58.

60. SEDAC, *El paso de algunos católicos a las sectas fundamentalistas en Centroamérica* (Guatemala City, 1995), 145-51, and SEDAC, *Estudio pastoral sobre el protestantismo fundamentalista en Centro América* (Guatemala City, 1992).

61. Margaret E. Crahan, "Religion, Revolution, and Counterrevolution: The Role of the Religious Right in Central America," in *The Right and Democracy in Latin America*, ed. Douglas A. Chalmers et al. (New York, 1992), 166-67.

62. Baloyra, "Elections, Civil War, and Transition," 60-61.

63. Mark Danner, *The Massacre at Mozote* (New York, 1993).

64. Procuraduría para la Defensa de los Derechos Humanos, PDDH, *Evolución de los Derechos Humanos en El Salvador: 1996, Informe Anual* (San Salvador, 1997); PDDH, *La seguridad ciudadana, la Policía Nacional Civil, y los derechos humanos* (San Salvador, 1997).

65. PDDH, *Evolución*, 13.

66. This is the case despite the fact that death threats were issued against Bishop Gregorio Rosa Chávez, UCA professor Rodolfo Cardenal, and human rights violations continued in 1996, the majority committed by the new National Civilian Police. Oficina de Tutela Legal del Arzobispado, *Situación de los derechos humanos en El Salvador durante 1996* (San Salvador, 1997); PDDH, *Evolución*.

67. See Andrew J. Stein, "The Consequences of the Nicaraguan Revolution for Political Tolerance among the Mass Public, Catholic Priests, and Secular Elites," *Comparative Politics*, in press.

68. *Sentir con la Iglesia* (August 15-September 15, 1996), 10. There are still minority voices in favor of an option for the poor. See "Sínodo católico analizará avances en la solidaridad humana," Internet service of *La Nación*, "Noticias de El Salvador," <www.nacion.co.cr>, September 29, 1997.

69. Author's interviews with parish priests, San Salvador, July 1997.

70. IUDOP-UCA, "Los salvadoreños y las expectativas hacia las autoridades del país," *Boletín de Prensa* 12 (September 17, 1997): 6 table 4.

7 MEXICO / JOSÉ LUIS SOBERANES FERNÁNDEZ

1. I think that prior to 1992, real religious freedom did not exist in Mexico, but only a poor imitation of it. Now it has not been fully secured, but it has been advanced, as we will see in this essay.

2. There is much literature about this; for example, see Cayetano Bruno, S.D.G., *El Derecho Público de la Iglesia en Indias* (Salamanca, Consejo Superior de Investigaciones Científicas, Instituto San Raimundo de Peñafort, 1967); Pedro Vicente

Cañete, *Syntagma de las Resoluciones Prácticas Cotidianas del Derecho Real Patronazgo de las Indias* (Buenos Aires: Talleres Gráficos, Mundial, 1973); Jesús García Gutiérrez, *Apuntes para la Historia del Origen y Desenvolvimiento del Regio Patronato Indiano hasta 1857* (Mexico City: Ed. Jus-ELD, 1941); María del Refugio González, "Patronato Real," *Diccionario Jurídico Mexicano*, 2d ed., vol. 4 (P-Z) (Mexico City: Ed. Porrúa-Instituto de Investigaciones Jurídicas, 1988), 2365-68; Alberto de la Hera, *Iglesia y Corona de la América Española* (Madrid: Ed. Maptre, 1992); Guillermo F. Margadant, *La Iglesia ante el Derecho Mexicano: Esbozo Histórico-jurídico* (Mexico City: Miguel Angel Porrúa, Librero-Editor, 1991); Ismael Sánchez Bella, *Iglesia y Estado en la América Española* (Pamplona: Ediciones Universidad de Navarra, 1990).

3. See Alberto de la Hera, *El Regalismo Borbónico* (Madrid: Rialp, 1963).

4. Some of the bishops, particularly those of Spanish birth, returned to Spain. Due to natural losses from deaths and lack of appointments, and imprisonment in the wars of independence, but above all because of the physical impossibility for the king to exercise his rights (since he did not control his old colonies in the Americas), the hierarchy found itself enormously reduced. In Mexico, of ten prelates (an archbishop and nine bishops), only the old bishop of Puebla, Mons. Antonio Joaquín Pérez, was left.

5. See Roberto Gómez Ciraza, *México ante la Diplomacia Vaticana: El período triangular 1821-36* (Mexico City: FCE, 1977); Jean Meyer, *Historia de los Cristianosos en América Latina, siglos XIX y XX* (Mexico City: Vuelta, 1989).

6. The first Mexican constitutions established the duties of the president of the Republic, including the president's role as titular of the National *Patronato* and negotiator with the Holy See; among the duties of the Legislature, the power of ratification of Church-State agreements; and among the duties of the Judiciary, the power of considering papal letters.

7. Besides the so-called freedom of religion, this included a change in the legal status of religious groups, the civil registry, civil marriage, the dissolution of religious orders, and the termination of ecclesiastical involvement in public education.

8. In Mexico, during the first fifty years of independence, the "pure" liberals differentiated themselves from the "moderates" by the more radical nature of their proposals regarding Church-State relations.

9. The Reform Laws included the nationalization of clerical property, the separation of Church and State, the suppression of religious orders and other ecclesiastic associations, and the closing of novitiates (all this on 12 July 1859), civil marriage (23 July), the civil registry (28 July), the cessation of clerical involvement in the business of cemeteries and monuments (31 July), and the law of freedom of religion (4 December 1860).

10. There was an interregnum involving the presidency of a relative of Porfirio Díaz, General Manuel González (1880-84), who prepared the reelection of Díaz in such a way that from 1884 he continued to be reelected indefinitely.

11. See Jean Meyer, *Historia de los cristianos*.

12. See Jorge Adame, *El Pensamiento Políitico y Social de los Católicos Mexicanos 1867-1914* (Mexico City: UNAM, 1981); Manuel Ceballos Ramírez, *El Catolicismo Social: un Tercero en Discordia, Rerum Novarum, "la cuestión social" y la movilización de los católicos mexicanos (1891-1911)* (Mexico City: El Colegio de México, 1991); Alicia Sedano Olivera, *Aspectos del Conflicto Religioso de 1926 a 1929: Sus Antecedentes y Consecuencias* (Mexico City: INAH, 1966).

13. See Eduardo J. Correa, *El Partido Católico Nacional y sus Directores: Explicación de su Fracaso y Deslinde de Responsabilidades* 2d ed. (Mexico City: FCE, 1991).

14. See Jean-Pierre Bastian (comp.), *Protestantes, Liberales y Francmasones, Sociedades de Ideas y Modernidad en América Latina* (Mexico City: Siglo XXI,FCE-LEHILA, 1990).

15. In 1934, as a result of the accession to power of a populist regime headed by General Lázaro Cárdenas, Article 3 was amended in its discussion of secular education in favor of "socialist education." The amendment noted: "The education given by the State shall be socialist, and further to exclude all religious doctrine it will combat fanaticism and prejudice, so that the school shall organize its teachings and activities in a manner that will allow it to form in the youth a rational and accurate concept of the universe and of social life." It further stated, "Private individuals may be authorized to teach . . . in accordance in every case with the following: . . . they must without exception follow what is mandated in the initial paragraph."

16. The Regulatory Law of Article 130 of the Federal Constitution, on 18 January 1927; Law Regulating the Seventh Paragraph of Constitutional Article 130, Relative to the Number of Priests that can Work in the Federal District and Territories, on December 30, 1931; and the Law of Reform of the Penal Code for the Federal District and Territories, on July 2, 1926.

17. Jean Meyer, *La Cristiada*, 3 vols. (Mexico City: Siglo XXI, 1972).

8 Mexico / Roderic Ai Camp

1. John H. Yoder, "The Wider Setting of 'Liberation Theology,'" *Review of Politics* 50 (1988): 291.

2. Daniel H. Levine, *Religion and Politics in Latin America: The Catholic Church in Venezuela and Colombia* (Princeton: Princeton University Press, 1980), 46.

3. Michael Dodson, "The Christian Left in Latin American Politics," *Journal of InterAmerican Studies and World Affairs* 2, no. 1 (February 1979): 53.

4. Edward L. Cleary, *Crisis and Change: The Church in Latin America* (Maryknoll, N.Y.: Orbis Books, 1985), 55.

5. Daniel H. Levine, "Assessing the Impacts of Liberation Theology in Latin America," *Review of Politics* 50 (1988): 246.

6. Cornelia Butler Flora and Rosario Bello, "The Impact of the Catholic Church on National Level Change in Latin America," *Journal of Church and State* 31, no. 3 (Autumn 1989): 532.

7. Claude Pomerlau, "The Catholic Church in Mexico and Its Changing Relationship to Society and the State," unpublished manuscript, December 1980, 17.

8. Levine, "Assessing the Impacts of Liberation Theology in Latin America," 243.

9. Frederick Sontag, "Liberation Theology and Its View of Political Violence," *Journal of Church and State* 31, no. 2 (Spring 1989): 286.

10. Hannah W. Stewart-Gambino, "New Approaches to Studying the Role of Religion in Latin America," *Latin American Research Review* 24, no. 3 (1989): 198.

11. Personal interview between Sharman Mattiace and Archbishop Manuel Castro Ruiz, Mérida Archdiocese, Mérida, Yucatán, August 21, 1989.

12. Comisión Episcopal para el Apostolado de los Laicos, *Qué piensan los laicos mexicanos del sínodo '87* (Mexico City: CEM, 1986), 17.

13. See, for example, Penny Lernoux, *Cry of the People: The Struggle for Human Rights in Latin America-The Catholic Church in Conflict with U.S. Policy* (New York: Penguin, 1982).

14. Dennis Goulet, "The Mexican Church: Into the Public Arena," *America* (April 8, 1989): 322.

15. Martín de la Rosa, "La Iglesia católica en México, del Vaticano II a la CELAM III," *Cuadernos Politicos* 19 (January-March 1979): 102.

16. Sharman Mattiace, "The Social Role of the Mexican Catholic Church: The Case of the Yucatán Base Community," senior honors thesis, Central University of Iowa, 1990, 29.

17. Personal interview with Brother Jesús Vergara Aceves, Mexico City, June 29, 1989.

18. George Grayson, *The Church in Contemporary Mexico* (Washington: CSIS, 1992), 31-32, also notes that several of the most important religious research centers in Mexico City, such as the Jesuit Reflexión Teológica or the Dominican Estudios Dominicanos, favor liberationist themes, as do important religious publications such as *Christus* and *Cencos*.

19. *El Nacional* (May 13, 1990), n.p.

20. Brian Smith, "Religion and Social Change: Classical Theories and New Formulations in the Content of Recent Development in Latin America," *Latin American Research Review* 10 (1975): 9.

21. Thomas G. Sanders, "The Puebla Conference," *American Universities Field Staff Reports* 30 (1979): 7.

22. Yoder, "The Wider Setting of 'Liberation Theology,'" 286.

23. W. E. Hewitt, "Christian Base Communities (CEBS): Structure, Orientation, and Sociopolitical Thrust," *Thought* 63, no. 249 (June 1988): 164.

24. Daniel H. Levine, "Religion and Politics: Dimensions of Renewal," *Thought* 59, no. 233 (June 1984): 132; Thomas C. Bruneau, "Basic Christian Communities in Latin America: Their Nature and Significance, Especially in Brazil," in *Churches and Politics in Latin America*, ed. Daniel Levine (Beverly Hills: Sage Publications, 1980), 226; Hewitt, "Christian Base Communities (CEBS)," 173-74.

25. W. E. Hewitt, "Christian Base Communities (CEBs)," 174.

26. Thomas C. Bruneau, "Basic Christian Communities in Latin America: Their Nature and Significance, Especially in Brazil," 227, 235.

27. Daniel H. Levine, "From Church and State to Religion and Politics and Back Again," *World Affairs* 150 (Fall 1987): 104.

28. Carol Ann Drogus, "Religious Change and Women's Status in Latin America: A Comparison of Catholic Base Communities and Pentecostal Churches," unpublished paper, Kellogg Institute for International Studies, University of Notre Dame, 1993, 3, 7, 21-22; Katherine Anne Gilfeather, "Coming of Age in Latin America," in *The Church and Women in the Third World*, ed. John Webster (Philadelphia, Pa.: Westminster Press, 1985), 69. Gilfeather reports that 66 percent of women working in slum areas showed a marked tendency to reinterpret doctrinal affirmations.

29. Claude Pomerleau, "The Changing Church in Mexico and Its Challenge to the State," *Review of Politics* 43, no. 4 (October 1981): 554.

30. Miguel Concha Maio, "Tensiones entre la religión de pueblo y las CEB's en México con sectores de la jearquia: implicaciones eclesiológicas," *Ciencia Tomista* 114 (May-August 1987): 309; Martín de la Rosa, "Iglesia y sociedad en el México de

hoy," in *Religión y Política en México,* ed. Martín de la Rosa and Charles A. Reilly (Mexico City: Siglo XXI, 1985), 279.

31. Matilde Gastalver and Lino F. Salas, *Las comunidades eclesiales de base y el movimiento popular en México* (Mexico City: Ibero-American University, 1983), 4.

32. Personal interviews with Sergio Méndez Arceo and Miguel Concha.

33. This label was often used in the press during the 1980s. Yet when I interviewed a leading entrepreneurial figure in 1992, he criticized the "terrible damage" the "Red Bishop" Méndez Arceo, allegedly a Communist, introduced in his diocese. Personal interview with Antonio Madero Bracho, Mexico City, August 7, 1992.

34. Lauro López Beltrán, *Diócesis y obispos de Cuernavaca, 1875-1978* (Mexico, 1978), 284.

35. Personal interview with Sergio Méndez Arceo.

36. Personal interview with ex-president Luis Echeverría Alvarez, Mexico City, August 2, 1992.

37. Dennis Hanratty, "Change and Conflict in the Contemporary Mexican Catholic Church" (Ph.D. diss., Duke University, 1980), 255.

38. Enrique Maza, "En su compromiso con los pobres, don Sergio prefirió ser parte y no juez," *Proceso* (February 10, 1992): 8.

39. Rodrigo Vera, "La jerarquía en combate contra seguidores de Méndez Arceo y su obra en Morelos," *Proceso* (April 3, 1989): 18.

40. Charles L. Davis, "Religion and Partisan Loyalty: The Case of Catholic Workers in Mexico," *Western Political Quarterly* 45 (March 1992): 280.

41. Personal interview between Sharman Mattiace and Bishop Samuel Ruiz García, San Cristóbal de las Casas Diocese, San Cristóbal de las Casas, Chiapas, August 15, 1989; personal interview with Bishop Samuel Ruiz García, Lago de Guadalupe, Cuautitlán, México, April 20, 1992.

42. Personal interview with Sharman Mattiace.

43. For example, an advertisement in *El Nacional,* written by Gustavo de Anda, condemns Ruiz as an international agitator who used his position to obtain funds to support the Zapatistas. "El Verdadero Samuel Ruiz," *El Nacional* (July 19, 1994), n.p. President Salinas asked Cardinal Corripio to denounce the Zapatistas on January 4, 1994. Corripio flatly turned down his request. See Michael Tangeman, *Mexico at the Crossroads: Politics, the Church, and the Poor* (Maryknoll, N.Y.: Orbis Books, 1994).

44. His self-description squares with that of a sister who has worked many years in his diocese as a base-community organizer. She described him as follows: "He experienced a great personal change at Medellín when he realized the plight of the poor and the social situation that he was facing as bishop of San Cristóbal. . . . Bishop Ruiz walks in the jungle with the people. He lives with them, sleeps where they do, and doesn't presume anything for himself or take personal credit. Ruiz gives all the credit to religious and laypeople who work with the poor. . . . He just animates the clergy and gives them support, but it's their job." Personal interview between Sharman Mattiace and Sister Efigenia Vásquez, San Cristóbal de las Casas Diocese, San Cristóbal de las Casas, Chiapas, August 15, 1989.

45. Cindy Anders, "No Power, No Glory," *Proceso* (June 15, 1989): 20.

46. Mattiace, "The Social Role of the Mexican Catholic Church," 40-41.

47. Hewitt, "Christian Base Communities (CEBs)," 174; Cleary, *Crisis and Change,* 142.

48. Soledad Loaeza, citing Pablo González Casanova in "La Iglesia y la Democracia en México," *Revista Mexicana de Socidogia* 47, no. 1 (January-March 1985), 163.

49. Personal interview between Sharman Mattiace and Sister Efigenia Vásquez.

50. Personal interview by Scott Pentzer and Meg Mitchell with Father Ochoa Aguilar and layworker Faviola Díaz Elías, San Luis Potosí Diocese, July 14, 1993.

51. Enrique Luengo, "Los Párrocos: una Visión," unpublished manuscript, Ibero-American University, December 1989, 62.

52. Personal interview between Sharman Mattiace and Father Ramón Castillo Aguilar, San Cristóbal de las Casas Diocese, San Cristóbal de las Casas, Chiapas, August 14, 1989.

53. José María Díaz Mozaz and Vicente J. Sastre, "Una Encuesta de Opinión al Clérigo Mexicano, Aproximación a la Realidad Socioreligiosa Mexicana," *Vidal Pastoral* 2, no. 2 (August 1976): 14, 16.

54. Dennis M. Hanratty, "The Church," in *Prospects for Mexico,* ed. George W. Grayson (Washington: Center for the Study of Foreign Affairs, 1988), 116.

55. Tangeman, *Mexico at the Crossroads,* 119.

56. Dennis M. Hanratty, "Church-State Relations in Mexico in the 1980s," *Thought* 63, no. 250 (1988): 212.

57. *Documentación e Información Católica* 13 (June 13, 1985): 429-30. David L. Clawson, in his case study of a Mexican village, also has remarked that the only way for the Catholic Church to compete against the Protestant faiths is to develop a small-church ambience duplicating the sense of community among the Protestant churches. He believes CEBs could conceivably perform such a function. "Religion and Change in a Mexican Village," *Journal of Cultural Geography* 9, no. 2 (1989): 69.

58. Bishop Jorge Martínez Martínez's diary is full of significant insights. *Memorias y Reflexiones de un Obispo* (Mexico: Editorial Villicafia, 1986), 27, 36.

59. David Lehmann, *Democracy and Development in Latin America: Economics, Politics, and Religion in the Postwar Period* (Philadelphia: Temple University Press, 1990), 138.

60. Luengo, "Los Párrocos: una Visión," 90.

61. Levine, "Religion and Politics: Dimensions of Renewal," 134; Daniel H. Levine, "Religion, Society, and Politics: States of the Art," *Latin American Research Review* 16, no. 3 (Fall 1981): 199; Levine, "Assessing the Impacts of Liberation Theology in Latin America," 259.

62. Bernardo Barranco Villafan and Raquel Pastor Escobar, *Jerarquía Católica y Modernización Política en México* (Mexico City: Palabra Ediciones, Centro Antonio de Montesinos, 1989), 29.

63. Grupo Consultor Interdisciplinario, "Carta de Política Mexicana, las otras Iglesias, las Razones del Cambio y lo que Viene," March 20, 1992, 2, 4. See also Secretaría de Gobernación, "Catálogo Nacional de Cultos Religiosos en México," unpublished manuscript, 1991, n.p., which lists the number of Protestant churches in each state. This is deceptive because large numbers of churches are not indicative of the percentage of residents who are Protestant. For example, Tamaulipas and Baja California have more Protestant than Catholic churches.

64. *El Nacional* (July 8, 1992): 11.

65. Personal interview with Manuel Carrillo, former adviser to the subsecretary of government in charge of church-state affairs, Mexico City, August 4, 1992.

66. Rodolfo Casillas and Alberto Hernández, "Demografía y religión en México: una relación poco explorada," *Cristianismo y Sociedad* 105 (January-April 1990): 80.

67. Edwin Eloy Aguilar et al., "Protestantism in El Salvador: Conventional Wisdom versus the Survey Evidence," in *Rethinking Protestantism in Latin America*, ed. Virginia Garrard Burnett and David Stoll (Philadelphia: Temple University Press, 1993), 9.

68. Ibid., 16; Clawson, "Religion and Change in a Mexican Village," 61.

69. Catholic Church, Diocese of Tijuana, *Plan Pastoral, 1989-1994, hacia una Iglesia Nueva* (Tijuana: La Diocese, 1989), 245.

70. Chris Woehr, "Catholic, Protestant Tensions Rise," *Christianity Today* 34 (March 19, 1990): 44.

71. Rolf Lahusen, "The Encounter between Church and Marxism in Mexico," in *The Encounter of the Church with Movements of Social Change in Various Cultural Contexts*, Part 2, ed. Gerd Decke (Geneva: Department of Studies, Lutheran World Federation, 1977), iii.

72. For an example as early as 1914, see Guillermo Floris Margadant, *La Iglesia ante el Derecho Mexicano, Esbozo Histórico-Jurídico* (Mexico City: Miguel Angel Porrúa, 1991), 196.

73. An excellent example was provided by Eduardo Bustamante, Secretary of Government Properties under President Adolfo López Mateos (1958-64). The president's wife was a Protestant. "She had many close ties with Protestant groups in the United States. Once she went to a meeting in Oaxaca with a large group of Protestants, and during this meeting it came out that they wanted to bring gifts for needy children for Christmas. They asked her to come and present the children with the gifts, but the president's wife did not want to do this because she might have offended Catholics in the state. Instead, she called the Catholic bishop and asked him to give out the toys. However, the bishop adamantly refused because the toys were coming from Protestants rather than from Catholics." Personal interview, Mexico City, May 29, 1987.

74. Marta Eugenia Garcia Ugarte, "Las Posiciones Políticas de la Jerarquía Católica, Efectos en la Cultura Religiosa Mexicana," in *Religiosidad y política en México*, ed. Carlos Martínez Assad (Mexico City: Ibero-American University, 1992), 98; Allan Metz "Protestantism in Mexico: Contemporary Contextual Developments," *Journal of Church and State* 36, no. 1 (Winter 1994): 65-66.

75. Their assertions have some basis in historical fact. For evidence of this, see Gerard Colby and Charlotte Dennett, *Thy Will Be Done: The Conquest of the Amazon—Nelson Rockefeller and Evangelism in the Age of Oil* (New York: HarperCollins, 1995).

76. Hanratty, "Church-State Relations in Mexico in the 1980s," 211. Father Gabriel Medina Mavallanes told Scott Pentzer and Meg Mitchell that the Protestants were a "noxious U.S. import," that Catholicism and Mexican nationality were inseparable, and that the United Nations was plotting to destroy Mexican families with disinformation about birth control, sex education, and women's roles. Personal interview, Zacatecas Diocese, July 19, 1993. Catholic officials in Zacatecas, including Bishop Javier Lozano Barragán, have declared publicly that the sects threaten national sovereignty and that they are an attack against Mexican culture. See Lucía Alonso Reyes, "Función social de la iglesia en Zacatecas," Memorias, segundo informe de investigación sobre el estado de Zacatecas (Zacatecas, 1989), 192.

77. This has been suggested by Julio Faesler, personal interview.

78. Mario Méndez Acosta, "Belief and Unbelief in Mexico," *Free Inquiry* (Winter 1986-87): 28.

79. Personal interview between Scott Pentzer and Father Rafael Ramírez Díaz, abbot of the Basílica of Guanajuato, Guanajuato Diocese, Guanajuato, Guanajuato, July 9, 1993.

80. David Scott Clark, "Mexicans Debate the Structure of New Church-State Relations," *Christian Science Monitor* (May 19, 1992), n.p.

81. Edward L. Cleary, "Politics and Religion—Crisis, Constraints, and Restructuring," in *Conflict and Competition: The Latin American Church in a Changing Environment*, ed. Edward L. Cleary and Hannah Stewart-Gambino (Boulder, Colo.: Lynne Rienner, 1992), 215.

82. Ivan Vallier, "Religious Elites, Differentiations, and Developments in Roman Catholicism," in *Elites in Latin America*, ed. Seymour Martin Lipset (New York: Oxford University Press, 1968), 196; Anthony J. Gill, "Rendering unto Caesar?: Religious Competition and Catholic Political Strategy in Latin America," paper presented at the Latin American Studies Association, Los Angeles, September 1992, 27.

83. See Vikrani Khub Chand, "Politics, Institutions, and Democracy in Mexico: The Politics of the State of Chihuahua in National Perspective," Ph.D. diss., Harvard University, May 1991, 247-61.

84. Andrew J. Stein, "Religion and Mass Politics in Central America," paper presented at the New England Council of Latin American Studies, Boston University, October 1992, 25-26; Timothy Steigenga and Kenneth Coleman, "Protestantism and Politics in Chile, 1972-1991," paper presented at the New England Council of Latin Americanists, Boston, October 1992, 21.

85. Michael Welch and David Leege, "Dual Reference Groups and Political Orientations: An Examination of Evangelically Oriented Catholics," *American Journal of Political Science* 35, no. 1 (1991): 45.

86. Gerhard Lenski, *The Religious Factor: A Sociological Study of Religion's Impact on Politics and Family Life* (Garden City, N.Y.: Doubleday, 1963), 270.

87. Welch and Leege, "Dual Reference Groups and Political Orientations," 51.

88. John L. Sullivan et al., *Political Tolerance and American Democracy* (Chicago: University of Chicago Press, 1982), 136; Andrew M. Greeley, *The Catholic Myth: The Behavior and Beliefs of American Catholics* (New York: Collier Books, 1990), 51.

89. Susan Eckstein, "Politics and Priests: The 'Iron Law of Oligarchy' and Interorganizational Relations," *Comparative Politics* 9 (July 1977): 470.

90. Personal interview with Ricardo Pascoe, secretary of communications, Party of the Democratic Revolution, Mexico City, May 5, 1992.

91. Jean-Pierre Bastian, "Disidencia Religiosa en el Campo Mexicano," in de la Rosa and Reilly, *Religión y política en México*, 190-92.

92. Eloy Aguilar, "Protestantism in El Salvador," 12.

93. Levine, "Assessing the Impacts of Liberation Theology in Latin America," 259; idem, "Religion and Politics: Drawing Lines, Understanding Change," *Latin American Research Review* 20, no. 1 (1985): 199, where he further argues that the future path of change lies less with their ideas than with what they actually practice.

9 Guatemala / Tim Steigenga

1. See John Lloyd Mecham, *Church and State in Latin America* (Chapel Hill: University of North Carolina, 1934), 370.

2. Freedom of religion in Guatemala was first declared under the Liberals in 1832.

3. Serrano left the Elím church to join the El Shaddai church during his electoral campaign.

4. See Jim Handy, *Gift of the Devil: A History of Guatemala* (Boston: South End Press, 1984), 46; Adrian C. Van Oss, *Catholic Colonialism: A Parish History of Guatemala: 1524-1821* (New York: Cambridge University Press, 1986), 109.

5. See Manning Nash, "The Impact of Mid-Nineteenth Century Economic Change upon the Indians of Middle America," in *Race and Class Relations in Middle America* (New York and London: Columbia University Press, 1970), 177-79.

6. See Virginia Garrard Burnett, *A History of Protestantism in Guatemala* (Ph.D. diss., Tulane University, 1987), 14.

7. In the case of Guatemala, this was primarily through the new coffee-export economy.

8. Burnett, *A History of Protestantism in Guatemala*, 27.

9. See Kenneth Scott Latourette, *Christianity in a Revolutionary Age: The Nineteenth Century outside Europe* (New York: Harper and Brothers, 1961), 115-16. Also see Richard Millet, "The Protestant Role in Twentieth Century Church-State Relations," *Journal of Church and State* (Autumn 1973): 372.

10. Far more damaging to the power of the Catholic church were the loss of income from corporate landholdings and the disbanding of religious orders, which led to severe shortages of clergy. See Hubert J. Miller, "Church-State Relations in Guatemala, 1927-1944—Decline of Anticlericalism," presented at the 1997 meeting of the Latin American Studies Association, Continental Plaza Hotel, Guadalajara, Mexico, April 17-19, 1997, 3.

11. Burnett, *A History of Protestantism in Guatemala*, 28.

12. See James C. Dekker, "North American Protestant Theology: Impact on Central America," *The Mennonite Quarterly Review* 58 (August Supplement 1984): 378-93. Under Liberal strongman Manuel Estrada Cabrera (1889-1920) the relationship between Protestant churches grew even stronger. Estrada Cabrera provided Protestants with free mailing privileges, police protection, the right to preach in public schools, and tax exemptions on imported equipment. See Burnett, *A History of Protestantism in Guatemala*, chaps. 3 and 4, for a complete history of the growth of the Protestant church in Guatemala during this period.

13. John Weeks, "An Interpretation of the Central American Crisis," *Latin American Research Review* 21 (1986): 37. Also see Robert G. Williams, *States and Social Evolution: Coffee and the Rise of National Governments in Central America* (Chapel Hill: University of North Carolina Press, 1994).

14. David McCreery, "Debt Servitude in Rural Guatemala, 1876-1936," in *Readings in Latin American History,* Vol. 2, *The Modern Experience,* ed. John J. Johnston and Peter J. Bakewell (Durham: Duke University Press, 1985), 242.

15. See Burnett, *A History of Protestantism in Guatemala*, for descriptions of conflicts between Protestants and Catholics.

16. See Virginia Garrard Burnett, "Tearing a Hole in the Sacred Canopy: Religious Conflict in Guatemala, 1944-1960," presented at the 1997 meeting of the Latin American Studies Association, Continental Plaza Hotel, Guadalajara, Mexico, April 17-19, 1997, 13.

17. Handy, *Gift of the Devil*, 69.

18. Ibid., 70-72.

19. According to Hubert J. Miller, there is even some evidence to suggest that Ubico may have had some influence on the selection of conservative Mariano Rossell Arellano as archbishop in 1939. See Miller, "Church-State Relations," 16.

20. Steven Schlesinger and Steven Kinzer, *Bitter Fruit: The Untold Story of the American Coup in Guatemala* (New York: Anchor Press/Doubleday, 1983), 70.

21. Reports of the exact amount of compensation offered differ. See Morris J. Blachman, William M. LeoGrand, and Kenneth E. Sharp, eds., *Confronting Revolution: Security through Diplomacy in Central America* (New York: Pantheon, 1986), 26.

22. For a detailed account of the events surrounding the coup, see Piero Gleijeses, *Shattered Hope: The Guatemalan Revolution and the United States, 1944-1954* (Princeton, N.J.: Princeton University Press, 1991).

23. Philip Berryman, *Christians in Guatemala's Struggle* (Nottingham: Russell Press Ltd., 1984), 7.

24. Thomas D. Melville, "The Catholic Church in Guatemala, 1944-1982," *Cultural Survival Quarterly* 7 (Spring 1983): 24.

25. Quoted in Frederick B. Pike, *The Conflict between Church and State in Latin America* (New York: Alfred A. Knopf, 1964), 178.

26. Berryman, *Christians in Guatemala's Struggle*, 9. These privileges were also reinforced twelve years later in the 1966 constitution.

27. See Burnett, *A History of Protestantism in Guatemala*, 167-69. Also see Burnett, "Tearing a Hole," 8-11, for examples of Catholic against Protestant violence.

28. See David Stoll, *Between Two Armies in the Ixil Towns of Guatemala* (New York: Columbia University Press, 1993).

29. Burnett, "Tearing a Hole," 13.

30. See Robert H. Trudeau, *Guatemalan Politics: The Popular Struggle for Democracy* (Boulder, Colo.: Lynne Rienner, 1993), 53-78. Also see Handy, *Gift of the Devil*, 149.

31. According to Jim Handy seventeen thousand people were arrested in the months following the coup and over one thousand politicians and labor leaders took asylum in foreign embassies. Handy, *Gift of the Devil,* 151.

32. Handy, *Gift of the Devil*, 156-67.

33. Handy, *Gift of the Devil*, 161-63.

34. See Phillip Berryman, *The Religious Roots of Rebellion: Christians in Central American Revolutions* (Maryknoll, N.Y.: Orbis Books, 1984), 174-80.

35. Blachman et al., *Confronting Revolution*, 37-40.

36. GAM was formed in 1984 primarily by women who had lost family members in the violence.

37. Protestant pastors fell victim to the violence as well. In 1980 alone, five Protestant pastors were killed.

38. Between January and November of 1980 alone, more than three thousand Guatemalans were abducted and killed by government security forces. Phillip Berryman, *Stubborn Hope: Religion, Politics, and Revolution in Central America* (Maryknoll, N.Y.: Orbis Books, 1994), 111-14.

39. See Sheldon H. Davis, "The Social Consequences of 'Development' Aid in Guatemala," *Cultural Survival Quarterly* 7 (Spring 1983): 34.

40. Sheldon H. Davis, "Guatemala: The Evangelical Holy War in El Quiché," *The Global Reporter* 1 (March, 1983): 8.

41. "Under the state of siege the military is empowered to arrest and hold suspects without charge, to take over private homes and offices at night, to force all former soldiers under the age of 30 to register at military bases, and to sentence suspected guerrillas to death before military courts." Davis, "Guatemala: The Evangelical Holy War in El Quiché," 34.

42. See Trudeau, *Guatemalan Politics,* 61.

43. See Edward L. Cleary, "Evangelicals and Competition in Guatemala," in *Conflict and Competition: The Latin American Church in a Changing Environment,* ed. Edward L. Cleary and Hannah Stewart-Gambino (Boulder, Colo.: Lynne Rienner, 1996), 167-95.

44. See Penny Lernoux, "The Fundamentalist Surge in Latin America," *The Christian Century* (January 30, 1988): 52; Mary Westropp, "Christian Counterinsurgency," *Cultural Survival Quarterly* 7 (Fall 1983): 28-31. Also see Deborah Huntington and Enrique Dominguez, "The Salvation Brokers: Conservative Evangelicals in Central America," *NACLA Report on the Americas* (January/February 1984): 2-37.

45. Burnett, *A History of Protestantism in Guatemala,* 217.

46. Huntington and Dominguez, "The Salvation Brokers," 26.

47. David Stoll, *Between Two Armies in the Ixil Towns of Guatemala* (New York: Columbia University Press, 1993), 186.

48. Stoll, *Between Two Armies in the Ixil Towns of Guatemala,* 156-64.

49. Berryman, *Stubborn Hope,* 121.

50. Stoll, *Between Two Armies in the Ixil Towns of Guatemala,* 169-77.

51. Ríos Montt alienated high-ranking members of the officer corps by giving preferences in promotions to those junior officers who helped bring him to power.

52. Blachman et al., *Confronting Revolution,* 41-43.

53. Trudeau, *Guatemalan Politics,* 70.

54. Berryman, *Stubborn Hope,* 142.

55. Anne M. Hallum, *Beyond Missionaries: Toward an Understanding of the Protestant Movement in Central America* (Lanham, Md.: Rowman and Littlefield Publishers, 1996), 108-9.

56. Susanne Jonas, "Electoral Problems and the Democratic Project in Guatemala," in *Elections and Democracy in Central America, Revisited: New and Enlarged Edition,* ed. Mitchel A. Seligson and John A. Booth (Chapel Hill: University of North Carolina Press, 1995), 25-44.

57. Less than 37 percent of registered voters took part in the election.

58. Berryman, *Stubborn Hope,* 127.

59. In particular, see "Para Construir la Paz" [To Build the Peace], pastoral letter of the Guatemalan bishops, 1984, and "El Clamor por la Tierra" [The Call for Land], pastoral letter of the Guatemalan bishops, 1988.

60. Hallum, *Beyond Missionaries,* 80.

61. See Berryman, *Stubborn Hope,* chap. 4, for documentation of acts of repression carried out against Protestants.

62. Berryman, *Stubborn Hope,* 137.

63. Hallum, *Beyond Missionaries,* 111.

64. David Stoll, *Is Latin America Turning Protestant? The Politics of Evangelical Growth* (Berkeley and Los Angeles: University of California Press, 1990). Also see Dennis Smith, "Coming of Age: A Reflection on Pentecostals, Politics, and Popular Religion in Guatemala," *Pneuma* (1991). Also see Marlo René López, "Evan-

gelicalismo y Neo-Pentecostalismo Independiente," in *Historia y misión del protestantismo hondureño* (San José, Costa Rica: Visión Mundial Internacional, Oficina Regional, 1993), 111-25.

65. Marlise Simons, "Latin America's New Gospel," *New York Times Magazine* (November 7, 1982).

66. Names and locations of churches were randomly chosen from specific sampling categories of different denominations provided by *Servicio Evangelizador para América Latina* (SEPAL) in Guatemala city. Since lists of members were unavailable for most churches, we asked permission to station interviewers outside of churches. Interviews were conducted with participants as they departed church services, or arrangements were made for a subsequent interview appointment. The random sample for religiously non-affiliated individuals was obtained through the use of screening questions on door-to-door interviews conducted in the same neighborhoods as other interviews.

67. See Smith, "Coming of Age." Also see Susan D. Rose and Steve Brouwer, "Guatemalan Upper Classes Join the Evangelicals," paper presented at the joint session meetings of the American Sociological Association and the Association for the Sociology of Religion, Atlanta, August 1988, 1-13. In our sample, more than 87 percent of the Neo-Pentecostals strongly agreed or agreed with the statement: "God gives health and wealth to those who do his will."

68. According to figures from the Central American Gallup affiliate (CID), approximately 10 percent of the Guatemalan population falls into the category of religiously non-affiliated. CID Gallup de Centroamerica, Opinión Pública, Guatemala #7 (agosto 1993): 31.

69. Since the sect members include Mormons, an aggressively evangelical and highly visible group, the perception of religious discrimination *may be* a correlate of the assertiveness of evangelical efforts.

70. These five items were subjected to factor analysis with all five loading at .60 or above on a single factor accounting for 65 percent of the common variance. Reliability tests yielded an alpha of .86.

71. See Smith, "Coming of Age," 5.

72. Each of these scores was significantly lower in Costa Rica.

73. The religiously non-affiliated also agree with this statement significantly more often than Catholics, suggesting that these individuals may be conflict-aversive as well.

74. That Neo-Pentecostals should have rated Ríos Montt highly is not surprising, given that he is a prominent member of the El Verbo congregation. High approval ratings for Ríos Montt among Historic Protestants are slightly more surprising. Apparently, Ríos Montt's popularity extends beyond Pentecostals to more traditional Protestants as well.

75. Jonas, *Electoral Problems and the Democratic Project in Guatemala*, 38.

76. Twice as many respondents reported frequent or very frequent discrimination in Guatemala as in a similar study conducted in Costa Rica.

77. Mitchell A. Seligson and Joel M. Jutkowitz, *Guatemalan Values and the Prospects for Democratic Development* (Pittsburgh: Development Associates, University of Pittsburgh/Asociación de Investigación y Estudios Sociales [ASIES], 1994), 91.

78. Hallum, *Beyond Missionaries*, 114.

10 NICARAGUA / ANDREW J. STEIN

1. E. Bradford Burns, *Patriarch and Folk: The Emergence of Nicaragua, 1798-1858* (Cambridge, Mass., 1991), 22-23; Jorge Eduardo Arellano, *Breve historia de la Iglesia en Nicaragua* (Managua, 1986), 51-58.

2. Burns, *Patriarch and Folk*, 68-69.

3. Ralph Lee Woodward Jr., "The Aftermath of Independence, 1821-c.1870," in *Central America since Independence*, ed. Leslie Bethell (New York, 1991), 30.

4. Arellano, *Breve historia*, 59; Burns, 69-70, reports that Guatemalan bishop Bernardo Pinol y Aycinena was appointed to follow de Viteri y Ungo in 1854, but due to the war, no bishop was in place until 1859.

5. For background literature on the Walker period see Ralph Lee Woodward Jr., "William Walker and the History of Nicaragua in the Nineteenth Century," *Latin American Research Review*, 1980 (15:1): 237-40; Alejandro Bolaños Geyer, *William Walker: The Gray-Eyed Man of Destiny*, 5 vols. (Lake St. Louis, Mo., 1988-91).

6. José Luis Velázquez, *La formación del estado en Nicaragua, 1860-1930* (Managua, 1992), 25-26, 35-43. Priests could seek court orders to require the peasants to pay these obligations.

7. Arellano, *Breve historia*, 60-61; Edgar Zúñiga, *Historia Eclesiástica de Nicaragua* (Managua, 1996).

8. Velázquez, *La formación del estado en Nicaragua*, 80-81.

9. They had been postponed by extreme regionalism and foreign intervention in Nicaragua.

10. J. Lloyd Mecham, *Church and State in Latin America* (Chapel Hill, 1934), 386-87; Velázquez, *La formación del estado en Nicaragua*, 97; Zúñiga, *Historia Elesiástica*. The limitation on entry of foreign clergy was a major blow to the church since many of its priests were not Nicaraguan nationals.

11. Velázquez, *La formación del estado en Nicaragua*, 82; Robert G. Williams, *States and Social Evolution: Coffee and the Formation of National States in Central America* (Chapel Hill, 1994), reports that more than two thousand peasants were executed or killed in combat in response to the usurpation of communal lands in Matagalpa province in 1881.

12. Arellano, *Breve historia*, 62-65.

13. Emilio Alvarez, *Las constituciones de Nicaragua* (Madrid, 1958); Knut Walter, *The Regime of Anastasio Somoza, 1936-1956* (Chapel Hill, 1993), 91-96, 171-76.

14. 1939, Article 6; 1948, Article 6; 1950, Article 8; 1974, Article 7. See Alvarez, *Las constituciones*; Organization of American States, *Constitution of the Republic of Nicaragua* (Washington, D.C., 1974).

15. Personal interview of bishop by author, Nicaragua, July 1994.

16. On this period see Philip J. Williams, "The Catholic Hierarchy in the Nicaraguan Revolution," *Journal of Latin American Studies* 17 (November 1985): 341-69, and idem, *The Catholic Church and Politics in Nicaragua and Costa Rica* (Pittsburgh, 1989); Arellano, *Breve historia*.

17. Conferencia Episcopal de Nicaragua, "Mensaje al pueblo nicaragüense," Managua, June 2, 1979; Williams, "The Catholic Hierarchy," 352-63.

18. Interview of bishop emeritus by author, Matagalpa, Nicaragua, July 1994.

19. For more on this, see Alvaro Argüello, S.J., "Participación del clero en el Consejo del Estado," in Consejo del Estado, *Boletín de Prensa* (Managua, July 1980); Junta

de Gobierno de Reconstrución Nacional, *Estatuto Fundamental y Ley de Derecho Ciudadano* (Managua, 1980).

20. República de Nicaragua, *Constitución de la República de Nicaragua* (Managua, 1987), 6.

21. Alvarez, *Las constituciones*, 907.

22. *Constitución Política de Nicaragua*, 1995 (Managua, 1996); for further discussion of the 1995 reforms and the church, see Andrew J. Stein, "The Church," in *Nicaragua Without Illusions: Regime Transition and Structural Adjustment in the 1990s*, ed. Thomas W. Walker (Wilmington, Del., 1997), 241.

23. See Conferencia Episcopal de Nicaragua, "Mensaje al Pueblo de Dios al iniciarse el año 1978," Managua, January 6, 1978, and "Mensaje ante el infausto deceso del Dr. Pedro Joaquín Chamorro," Managua, January 10, 1978, in "Iglesia Católica, crisis y democratización en Centro América," *Panorama Centroamericano* [Guatemala City] 26-27 (March-June 1990): 293-301.

24. Andrew J. Stein, "The Transformation of Nicaraguan Catholicism, 1950-1996: Generational Change, Pastoral Options, and Socio-Political Involvement," in *Religion and Change: The Experience of Contemporary Latin America*, ed. Margaret E. Crahan, forthcoming, discusses dozens of past works on the Church in the Sandinista period (1979-90) in terms of (a) the timing and nature of church support for sociopolitical change, and (b) the political orientation of the clergy; Williams, "The Catholic Hierarchy," 357-68.

25. Respectively, Fernando Cardenal, Ernesto Cardenal, Miguel D'Escoto, and Edgar Parrales. Conferencia Episcopal de Nicaragua, "La religión: sus postulados y sus manipulaciones: el FSLN y la Iglesia," Managua, October 1980; Williams, "The Catholic Hierarchy," 363-66; Margaret E. Crahan, "Religion and Politics in Revolutionary Nicaragua," in Mainwaring and Wilde, *The Progressive Church in Latin America*, ed. Scott Mainwaring and Alexander Wilde (Notre Dame, Ind., 1989), 52-57.

26. Conferencia Episcopal de Nicaragua, "Comunicados emitidos ante los recientes acontecimientos sufridos por la Iglesia Católica de Nicaragua," Managua, July 11, 1984, and "Carta del Episcopado Nicaragüense a las Conferencias Episcopales de Mundo," Managua, July 7, 1986; Michael Dodson and Laura O'Shaughnessy, *Nicaragua's Other Revolution: Religious Faith and Political Struggle* (Chapel Hill, 1990), 165-75; Domingo Urtasún, *Miguel Obando Bravo, Cardenal por la paz* (Managua, 1994).

27. Conferencia Episcopal de Nicaragua, "Aporte pastoral, la Constitución: garantía de libertad y soberanía ciudadana," Managua, June 9, 1986.

28. This assertion was based in part on the absence of any criticism by the official church of human rights abuses or murder of noncombatants by the Contras during the period 1981-88, in which the Contra War engulfed much of the northern and eastern parts of the country.

29. Interview of former priest by author, Managua, Nicaragua, July 1994.

30. Philip J. Williams, "The Limits of Religious Influence: The Progressive Church in Nicaragua," in *Competition and Conflict: The Latin American Church in a Changing Environment*, ed. Edward L. Cleary and Hannah Stewart-Gambino (Boulder, Colo., 1992), 140-41; Stein, "The Church," 240-44.

31. A 1995 national public opinion survey by the Instituto de Estudios Nicaragüenses (IEN) and the University of Pittsburgh showed that 84 percent considered church-state ties to be tolerant.

32. Stein, "The Church," 240-46.

33. CEN, *Segundo Concilio Provincial* (Managua, 1994), 68.

34. However, in one of the most crucial negotiations, the 1990 Protocols of Transition worked out between the FSLN and Chamorro government, both the church and the UNO coalition were excluded from having any role.

35. The electoral commission delayed nineteen days in releasing the final vote count, which the United States, the OAS, and the Catholic hierarchy immediately confirmed, despite lingering doubts and ambiguities. "Mensaje de Conferencia Episcopal a los fieles católicos y personas de buena voluntad," Managua, October 23, 1996, 1-2. The anti-FSLN posture is a sharp contrast with the more balanced "Carta Pastoral de los Obispos de Nicaragua con motivo del proceso electoral y de las elecciones del 20 de octubre de 1996," Managua, September 18, 1996. A survey found that 71.4 percent of the public thought that there were procedural irregularities, and 44.7 percent said that the elections were fraudulent. See Instituto de Estudios Nicaragüenses (IEN), "La gobernabilidad en Nicaragua: encuesta nacional realizada del 01 al 09 de abril de 1997," Managua, May 1997, 31.

36. Roberto Zub, "Rol de la Iglesia y religión en las elecciones 96 en Nicaragua," unpublished ms., Managua, 1996, 5-10.

37. IEN, "La gobernabilidad en Nicaragua," 8-25; "Seis meses del gobierno liberal: balance político y económico," *Confidencial* [Managua], July 13-19, 1997.

38. "Lo que dicen las encuestas," *Confidencial*, July 13-19, 1997, 11.

39. Data from 1995 indicate that the public trusts the church in Nicaragua along with the media and the electoral commission more than all other public institutions. Mitchell A. Seligson, *Los nicaragüenses hablan sobre la corrupción: una encuesta de opinión pública* (University of Pittsburgh/Casals and Associates, March 1997), 27-28; idem, "Democratic Values in Nicaragua, 1991-97," unpublished ms., Pittsburgh, Pa., October 1997, 4; United Nations Development Program, PNUD, *El desafío democrático: Reflexiones de las sociedades centroamericanas ante el resultado del Latinobarómetro 1996* (San José, 1997), 47.

40. Other less numerous historic denominations include the Nazarene Church and Mennonites. See Roberto Zub, *Protestantismo y elecciones en Nicaragua* (Managua, 1993), 20-21; Thelma Good, "125 años de la Obra Morava en Bluefields," *Revista de Historia del Protestantismo Nicaragüense* 2 (July 1992): 41-49.

41. Jorge Pixley, "Misión Extranjera e Iglesia Nacional: El caso Bautista," *Revista de Historia del Protestantismo Nicaragüense* 2 (July 1992): 51-59; Abelino Martínez, *Las sectas en Nicaragua: oferta y demanda de salvación* (San José, 1989), 27-34.

42. Wolfgang Bautz, Noel González, and Javier Orozco, *Política y religión, estudio de caso: los evangélicos en Nicaragua* (Managua, 1994), 33-35.

43. Zub has estimated the Protestant share of the national population to be slightly higher, in the range of 22-25 percent ("Rol de la Iglesia," 4).

44. Marvin Ortega, "La opinión política de los managuas," *Encuentro* 35 (September-December 1988); University of Pittsburgh Central American Public Opinion Project, 1991-96; Seligson, "Democratic Values."

45. See Jean Pierre Bastián, "Protestantismo popular y política en Guatemala y Nicaragua," *Revista Mexicana de Sociología* 48 (3) (July-September 1986): 189-90, 192-96; Martínez, *Las sectas*, 42-60; Dodson and O'Shaughnessy, *Nicaragua's Other Revolution*, 119, 200-2. The Nicaraguan bishops claim that the FSLN had a conscious policy to encourage Protestantism in order to weaken the Catholic Church. See *Segundo concilio provincial*, 84.

46. Margaret E. Crahan, "Religion, Revolution and Counterrevolution: The Role of the Religious Right in Central America," in *The Right and Democracy in Latin America*, ed. Douglas A. Chalmers et al. (New York, 1992), 175-76.

47. Bautz, González, and Orozco, *Política y religión*, 56-75, count more than 125 religious denominations or associations throughout Nicaragua. They conclude that most Protestants see the nation's problems rooted in sin, and exhibit a "tendency to reject direct participation in partisan life," though many do participate in politics in a low-profile way outside of party politics. See also Zub, *Protestantismo y elecciones*, 101-3, for a similar conclusion.

48. Zub, "Rol de la Iglesia," 3-4. Zub notes that the CCN was largely a Pentecostal movement, with little input from Moravians or Baptists.

49. Roberto Zub, *Oficio y modelos pastorales: análisis y reflexiones sociológicas sobre la identidad sociocultural y condiciones de la pastoral protestante en Nicaragua* (Managua, 1996), 105-9; Zub, "Rol de las Iglesias," 4-6.

50. Zub, *Protestantismo y elecciones*, 57-70; Bautz, González, and Orozco, *Política y religión*, 44-55.

51. Instituto Nicaragüense de Esta disticas y Censon (INEC), *Resumen censal: vii censo nacional de publacíon y III de vivienda* (Managua, 1996), 112.

52. CEN, *Segundo concilio provincial*, 146-147; Zub, *Oficio y modelos*; Secretariado Episcopal de América Central (SEDAC), "Nuestra salvación es Cristo: aporte de la Iglesia en la historia presente del hombre centroamericano" (San José, 1984), 17, 46-47.

53. For more on this, see Andrew J. Stein, "The Prophetic Mission, the Catholic Church and Politics: Nicaragua in the Context of Central America," Ph.D. diss., University of Pittsburgh, 1995, appendicies 2-4.

54. Ibid., 294-96. In 1997 there was a controversy in both El Salvador and Nicaragua with regard to the Catholic Church's opposition to governments extending religious freedom to the Unification Church of Rev. Moon. See Cardinal Obando's view of this, "Secta Moon ataca a los cristianos," *Iglesia* [Managua], July 1997, 12.

55. For a comparative discussion of Catholic responses to Protestants, see Brian H. Smith, *Pentecostalism and Catholicism in Contemporary Latin America* (Notre Dame, Ind., 1998).

56. "Mensaje de la Conferencia Episcopal de Nicaragua al Pueblo Nicaragüense," September 17, 1987; "Comunicado de la Conferencia Episcopal de Nicaragua," September 24, 1987; and "Clamor por la paz y el bien de Nicaragua," June 29, 1988.

57. See Stein, "The Church," 238-40, for a discussion of this period and the CEN's attitude toward the 1990 elections.

58. For Protestant relations with the FSLN government see Susan Hawley, "Protestantism and Indigenous Mobilization: The Moravian Church among the Miskitu Indians of Nicaragua," *Journal of Latin American Studies* 29 (1997):111-29.

59. The Bishops' Conference put most of the blame on Daniel Ortega and the FSLN, whom they considered to be acting in bad faith. See "La reconciliación," Managua, April 22, 1984; "Carta de la Conferencia Episcopal de Nicaragua al Presidente Daniel Ortega," December 6, 1985.

60. Stein, "The Church," 242-43.

61. See Richard Stahler-Sholk, "Structural Adjustment and Resistance," in *The Undermining of the Sandinista Revolution*, ed. Gary Prevost and Harry Vanden (New York, 1997).

62. Joel S. Migdal, "The State in Society: An Approach to Struggles for Domination," in *State Power and Social Forces: Domination and Transformation in the Third World*, ed. Joel S. Migdal, Atul Kohli, and Vivienne Shue (New York, 1994), 10, 20-24.

63. Migdal, "The State in Society," 29.

11 ARGENTINA / JOSÉ MÍGUEZ BONINO

1. On the *patronato real* in Latin America (royal patronage, henceforth *patronato*), also called *regalism,* see Marco Minghetti, *L'Etat et l'eglise* (Paris: Librairie Germer Bailliere, 1882); Faustino Legon, *Doctrina y ejercicio del Patronato Nacional* (Buenos Aires: J. Lajouane and Cia, 1920).

2. See Arnoldo Canclini, *La Libertad de cultos* (Buenos Aires: Artes Gráficas, 1986), 74. Nevertheless the Holy Office tried some dozens of cases, as the careful research of Boleslau Lewin has recorded. Boleslau Lewin, *La Inquisición en Hispanoamérica* (Buenos Aires: Proyección, 1972); also José T. Medina, *El Santo Oficio de la Inquisición en el Río de la Plata* (Buenos Aires: Huarpes, 1945). The British invasions of the La Plata River region in 1806-7 produced a brief parenthesis. In the short period of British control of Buenos Aires, the invader declared the right of the Catholic Church to continue its ministry. The bishop of Buenos Aires considered the struggle against the invasion as a sort of "religious war" and ordered the burning of some copies of the New Testament that had been distributed.

3. Eduardo Durnhoffer, *Mariano Moreno inédito* (Buenos Aires: Plusultra, 1972) 91, quoted by Canclini, *La Libertad*, 84.

4. See Canclini, *La Libertad*, 75.

5. *Estatutos, reglamentos y constituciones argentinas (1811-1898)* (Buenos Aires: Universidad de Buenos Aires, 1956), 73ff.

6. *Estatuto provisional para dirección y administración del estado, dado por la Junta de Observación* (Buenos Aires, 5 de mayo de 1815):

> Chapter II, Art. I, "The Roman Catholic Apostolic Church is the religion of the State"; Art. II: "All men shall observe the public religion and the Holy Religion of the State; any infraction of this article will be considered a violation of the fundamental laws of the Nation."

Provisional Statute given by the Junta de Observación and approved with changes by the Congress of Tucuman (*Estatuto provisional dado por la Junta de Observación y aprobado con modificaciones por el Congreso de Tucumán*), the Congress that declared Independence, on July 9, 1816.

Chapter 2: *On the Religion of the State* (Repeats without any modification the articles of the statute quoted above).

The Constitution of the United Provinces of South America (*Constitución de la Provincias Unidas en Sud-América*), 1819.

Section I. The Religion of the State:

> Art. I. "The Catholic Apostolic Church is the religion of the State. The government owes it its most powerful and effective protection; and the inhabitants of the territory their utmost respect, independently of their own private thoughts."
>
> II. "Any infraction of the previous article will be looked upon as a violation of the fundamental laws of the State."

Chapter III, "Powers of the Executive Branch," Art. LXXXVI: "Appoints archbishops and bishops proposed by the Senate."

Art. LXXXVII, "Presents to all offices, canonries, prebends, and offices of the churches, cathedrals, and collegiate and parochial churches, according to the laws." *The Constitution of the Republic of Argentina, approved by the general Constituent Congress on December 24, 1826* (Buenos Aires, December 24, 1826).
Section 1., "On the Nation and its religion"
Art. 1., Sec. 3: "Its religion [that of the Argentine nation] is Apostolic Roman Catholicism, to which it shall always grant the most effective and resolute protection, and its inhabitants the utmost support, independently of their religious beliefs."
Section 5a., "On Executive Powers"
Art. 70: "Before assuming office and in the presence of both houses of Congress, the president-elect shall swear the following oath to the president of the Senate: I (N...) swear by Our Father and the holy saints of the gospel to dutifully carry out the duties of the president as they are conferred on me: I shall protect the Catholic religion, preserve the integrity of and independence of the republic. . . . "

7. I am not including here the courageous work of Allen Gardiner in the Argentinian Patagonia, under the auspices of the Patagonia Missionary Society (later South American Missionary Society, SAMS), in 1850-52, among Ona Indians, which ended tragically with the death from hunger and scurvy of the missionaries, not because it is not significant but because it did not much affect the total situation. For general histories of Protestantism in Latin America, see Tomás Goslin, *Los evangélicos en América Latina* (Buenos Aires: La Aurora, 1956); Hans-Jürgen Prien, *Die Geschichte des Christentums in Lateinamerika* (Göttingen: Vandenhoeck und Ruprecht, 1978); Jean-Pierre Bastian, *Breve historia del protestantismo en América Latina* (México, D.F: Casa Unida de Publicaciones, 1986); Pablo A. Deiros, *Historia del cristianismo en América Latina* (Buenos Aires: Fraternidad Teológica Latinoamericana, 1992); Daniel P. Monti, *Los orígenes del protestantismo en el Río de la Plata* (Buenos Aires: La Aurora, n.d.).

8. On James (Diego) Thompson, see Deiros, *Historia del cristianismo*, 640-43.

9. For more detailed historical data, see the works on Latin American Church history and the study by Arnoldo Canclini indicated in previous notes.

10. For the discussions of the religious question in the Constitutional Assembly of 1853, see, among others, Canclini, *La Libertad*, 87-95; Emilio Ravignani, *Asambleas constituyentes argentinas*, vol. 4; and *Estatutos, reglamentos y constituciones argentinas*, 183-207.

11. The two key words here are *sostiene* (literally "supports") and *el culto* (literally "worship").

12. Later amendments did not introduce any changes in the articles concerning religion. See information on constitutional amendments between 1853 and 1898 in *Estatutos, reglamentos y constituciones de argentina;* and Carlos Ricardo Baeza, *Las Reformas de la Constitución Argentina* (Buenos Aires: A-Z Editora, 1989).

13. I have attempted to describe the theological and social features of the different streams of Latin American Protestantism in the book *Faces of Latin American Protestantism* (Grand Rapids, Mich.: Eerdmans, 1996).

14. See Haim Avni, *Argentina y la historia de la inmigración judía, 1810-1850* (Buenos Aires: AMIA, Editorial Universitaria Agnes, 1983).

15. Leonardo Senkman, *El antisemitismo en la Argentina* (Buenos Aires: Centro Editor de América Latina, 1989).

16. See a very informative discussion on this issue in María J. Lubertino Beltran, *Perón y la iglesia*, vols. 1 and 2 (Buenos Aires: Biblioteca Política Argentina, 1987).

17. For Catholicism and Protestantism after 1930, see the articles by Enrique Dussel and José Míguez Bonino, respectively, in *The Cambridge History of Latin America*, ed. Leslie Bethel, vol. 6, part 2, "1930 to Present" (Cambridge: Cambridge University Press, 1994), part 4, 547-604, and the corresponding bibliographical essays, 697-707.

18. Constitutional Assemblies were called and reforms introduced in 1860, 1866, 1898, 1949, 1957, and 1972. The last two were later annulled. There were no changes in the articles dealing with religious questions. However, at the end of the 1860 Assembly, Félix Frías tried without success to obtain a change in Article 2. The 1949 reform repealed Article 67, which stated as one responsibility of Congress "to promote their conversion [of indigenous populations] to Catholicism." But this constitution was annulled by the military government in 1955.

19. Emilio F. Mignone, *Witness to the Truth: The Complicity of Church and Dictatorship in Argentina, 1976-83* (Maryknoll, N.Y.: Orbis Books, 1988).

20. In view of the recent debate on the involvement of the nuncio, Pio Laghi, it is worth reading pages 89-91 of Mignone's book, which give an account of the ambivalent and changing character of his conduct, which corresponds also to my own experience. On pages 92ff. Mignone looks at the deeper institutional question that lies behind this almost unavoidable ambivalence.

21. Mignone, *Witness to the Truth*, 71.

22. *La iglesia católica y la reforma constitucional* (Buenos Aires: Conferencia Episcopal Argentina, Oficina del Libro, 1994).

23. See below.

24. The texts are taken from a recent formulation of the Constitution of the Province of Córdoba:

The Nation of Argentina, according to its cultural tradition, recognizes and grants to the Roman Catholic Apostolic Church the free and public exercise of its worship. Relations between it and the Federal State are based on the principles of autonomy and cooperation. It equally grants to other religions their free and public exercise, without any limitations, except those that morals, good customs and public order demand.

Freedom of conscience and religious freedom are inviolable. Their exercise is subject to the prescriptions of a good moral and public order. Nobody can be compelled to make public the religion he or she professes.

25. *Posición de las iglesias evangélicas frente a la reforma de la constitución*, by the ACIERA (*Alianza Cristiana de las Iglesias Evangélicas de la República Argentina*), CEP (*Confederación Evangélica Pentecostal*), and FAIE (*Federación Argentina de Iglesias Evangélicas*) (*De todos* 20 [Oct.-Dec., 1993], 13).

26. *Documento ecuménico sobre la Reforma Constitucional Argentina presentado a los señores miembros de la Asamblea Constituyente* (*Movimiento Ecuménico por los Derechos Humanos*, Paraná, 1998).

27. The presentation of this proposal by the writer of this article as a member of the Constitutional Assembly and the debate both in the commission and the plenary can be consulted in the acts and minutes of the Assembly, published by the Congress of Argentina.

28. The title is difficult to translate: *Fichero* literally means "file" or "index," and *cultos* would have to be translated in this context as "religious organizations," "religious bodies," or "religious communities," and includes all organized forms of religious life. Sometimes, instead of *fichero*, the word used is *Registro*, i.e. "registry" or

"record." These terms give the impression of a purely administrative question. However, the functions and authority accorded to the *Fichero* far exceed the objective "recording" function suggested by the title.

29. This process has been carefully researched and assessed by the Waldensian professor and jurist Alberto J. Soggin in his study *La liberta di culto nella Repubblica Argentina negli ultimi anni* (Milan: A. Giuffre Editore, 1963).

30. Ibid., 81.

31. Bishops Laguna, from Morón (Buenos Aires Province), Piña (from the Chaco), and Cassareto (San Isidro, Buenos Aires Province) have on several occasions spoken or written letters to their dioceses to this effect.

12 BRAZIL / KENNETH P. SERBIN

1. This phrase is suggested by Pamela Lowden, *Moral Opposition to Authoritarian Rule in Chile, 1973-90* (New York, 1996).

2. By and large, writes Peter McDonough, the members of the Brazilian elite "have not been acculturated to the cut-and-thrust of doctrinal debate; a lack of metaphysical certitude does not appear to bother them" (Peter McDonough, *Power and Ideology in Brazil* [Princeton, 1981], xxiii-xxiv).

3. Eduardo Hoornaert, "A evangelização do Brasil durante a primeira época colonial," in *História geral da Igreja na América Latina*, ed. Enrique Dussel, 11 vols., vol. 2, pt. 1, *História da Igreja no Brasil*. Primeira época (Petrópolis, 1983), 26-27.

4. José Oscar Beozzo, "Decadência e morte, restauração e multiplicação das ordens e congregações religiosas no Brasil," in *A vida religiosa no Brasil: enfoques históricos*, ed. Riolando Azzi (São Paulo, 1983), 96-97.

5. Hugo Fragoso, "O protestantismo no Brasil imperial," in *História geral da Igreja na América Latina*, ed. Dussel, vol. 2, pt. 2, *História da Igreja no Brasil*. Segunda época—século XIX, 237-48.

6. On Romanization, see Kenneth P. Serbin, "Priests, Celibacy, and Social Conflict: A History of Brazil's Clergy and Seminaries" (Ph.D. diss., Univ. of California, San Diego, 1993), chaps 2, 3; C. F. G. de Groot, *Brazilian Catholicism and the Ultramontane Reform, 1850-1930* (Amsterdam, 1996); Ralph Della Cava, *Milagre em Joaseiro*, 2d. ed., trans. Maria Yedda Linhares (Rio de Janeiro, 1977); idem, "Catholicism and Society in Twentieth-Century Brazil," *Latin American Research Review* 11:2 (1976): 11-12; idem, "Brazilian Messianism and National Institutions: A Reappraisal of Canudos and Joaseiro," *Hispanic American Historical Review* 48:3 (Aug. 1968): 402-20; Pedro A. Ribeiro de Oliveira, *Religião e dominação de classe: gênese, estrutura e função do catolicismo romanizado no Brasil* (Petrópolis, 1985); Martin N. Dreher, ed., *Imigrações e história da Igreja no Brasil* (Aparecida, 1993); Thomas C. Bruneau, *The Political Transformation of the Brazilian Catholic Church* (Cambridge, 1974), 11-51.

7. Beozzo, "Decadência e morte."

8. Sergio Miceli, *A elite eclesiástica brasileira* (Rio de Janeiro, 1988); de Groot, *Brazilian Catholicism and the Ultramontane Reform*, 93.

9. de Groot, *Brazilian Catholicism and the Ultramontane Reform*, chap. 5.

10. Robert M. Levine, *Vale of Tears: Revisiting the Canudos Massacre in Northeastern Brazil, 1893-1897* (Berkeley, 1992); also see Della Cava, "Brazilian Messianism"; on Europeanization, see George Reid Andrews, *Blacks and Whites in São Paulo, 1888-1988* (Madison, 1991); on millenarianism, also see Todd A. Diacon,

Millenarian Vision, Capitalist Reality: Brazil's Contestado Rebellion, 1912-1916 (Durham, 1991).

11. Paul Freston, "Protestantes e política no Brasil: da constituinte ao impeachment" (Ph.D. diss., Universidade Estadual de Campinas, 1993), 49. The history of Catholic-Protestant conflict in the twentieth century has yet to be researched in depth.

12. Scott Mainwaring, *The Catholic Church and Politics in Brazil, 1916-1985* (Stanford, 1986); Riolando Azzi, "O início da restauração católica no Brasil (1920-1930)," *Síntese* 10 (1977): 61-90; 11 (1977): 73-102.

13. Bruneau, *Political Transformation*, 37-39.

14. José Oscar Beozzo, "A Igreja entre a Revolução de 1930, o Estado Novo e a redemocratização," in *História geral da civilização brasileira*, ed. Boris Fausto, *III. O Brasil republicano. 4. Economia e cultura (1930-1964)* (São Paulo, 1960–), 334-41.

15. Simon Schwartzman, Helena Maria Bousquet Bomeny, and Vanda Maria Ribeiro Costa, *Tempos de Capanema* (Rio de Janeiro, 1984), 44-45, 56, 60-61; see also Alcir Lenharo, *Sacralização da política* (Campinas, 1986).

16. Alceu Amoroso Lima, *Indicações políticas* (Rio de Janeiro, 1936).

17. The National Basilica of Aparecida was built in 1954. I have developed the theme of state subsidization of the Church in several essays: see Kenneth Serbin, "Church-State Reciprocity in Contemporary Brazil: The Convening of the International Eucharistic Congress of 1955 in Rio de Janeiro," *Hispanic American Historical Review* 76:4 (Aug. 1996): 721-51; Kenneth Serbin, "Brazil: State Subsidization and the Church Since 1930," in *Organized Religion in the Political Transformation of Latin America*, ed. Satya Pattnayak (Lanham, 1995), 153-75; Kenneth Serbin, "State Subsidization of Catholic Institutions in Brazil, 1930-1964: A Contribution to the Economic and Political History of the Church," Helen Kellogg Institute for International Studies, Working Paper No. 181 (Notre Dame, Ind., 1992); Kenneth Serbin, "Igreja, estado, e a ajuda financeira pública no Brasil, 1930-1964: estudos de três casos chaves," *Textos CPDOC* (Rio de Janeiro, 1991). For the international context, see Ralph Della Cava, "Financing the Faith: The Case of Roman Catholicism," *Journal of Church and State* 35:1 (Winter 1993): 37-49; Ralph Della Cava, "Roman Catholic Philanthropy in Central and East Europe, 1947-1993: A Preliminary Inquiry into Religious Resources Networking" (unpublished paper, 1994); see also Brian H. Smith, *More than Altruism: The Politics of Private Foreign Aid* (Princeton, 1990).

18. On Aparecida, see Juliana Beatriz A. de Souza, "Mãe negra de um povo mestiço: a devoção a Nossa Senhora Aparecida e identidade nacional," *Estudos Afro-Asiáticos* 29 (March 1996): 85-102.

19. Beozzo, "A Igreja entre a Revolução," 334-41; see also Margaret Todaro Williams, "Church and State in Vargas' Brazil: The Politics of Cooperation," *Journal of Church and State* 18:3 (Autumn 1976): 443-62. This was an extraordinary achievement in comparison with such countries as Mexico, Chile, Cuba, and France, where the Church failed to reenter the public domain after being forced out. The Cristero War of the 1920s in Mexico provides the most interesting counterpoint to the Brazilian case. See, e.g., Roberto Blancarte, *Historia de la Iglesia católica en México* (Mexico City, 1992).

20. Freston, "Protestantes e política," 153-55.

21. 1. On base communities, see Marcello de Carvalho Azevedo, *Basic Ecclesial Communities in Brazil*, trans. John Drury (Washington, D.C., 1987); Faustino Luiz Couto Teixeira, *A gênese das ceb's no Brasil: elementos explicativos* (São Paulo, 1988); Leonardo Boff, *Ecclesiogenesis: The Base Communities Reinvent the Church,*

trans. Robert R. Barr (Maryknoll, N.Y., 1986); for an example of Freire's writings, see his *Pedagogy of the Oppressed* (New York, 1970); for an overview of the Catholic left, see Mainwaring, *Catholic Church and Politics*; on the Catholic University Youth, see Luiz Alberto Gómez de Souza, *A JUC: os estudantes católicos e a política* (Petrópolis, 1984); on *Ação Popular*, see Haroldo Lima and Aldo Arantes, *História da Ação Popular* (São Paulo, 1984); on the Basic Education Movement, see Luiz Eduardo Wanderley, *Educar para transformar* (Petrópolis, 1984).

22. For assessments of the Brazilian military regime, see Joseph Page, *The Brazilians* (Reading, Mass., 1995); Gláucio Ary Dillon Soares and Maria Celina D'Araujo, eds., *21 anos de regime militar* (Rio de Janeiro, 1994); Thomas E. Skidmore, *The Politics of Military Rule in Brazil, 1964-85* (New York, 1988); Ronald M. Schneider, *"Order and Progress": A Political History of Brazil* (Boulder, Colo., 1991); Maria Helena Moreira Alves, *Estado e oposição no Brasil (1964-1984)* (Petrópolis, 1985); Peter Flynn, *Brazil: A Political Analysis* (London, 1978); for figures on the dirty war, see Comissão de Familiares de Mortos e Desaparecidos Políticos et al., *Dossiê dos mortos e desaparecidos políticos a partir de 1964* (São Paulo, 1996), 9-18.

23. Clara Amanda Pope, "Human Rights and the Catholic Church in Brazil, 1970-1983: The Pontifical Justice and Peace Commission of the São Paulo Archdiocese," *Journal of Church and State* 27:3 (Autumn 1985): 429-52; Ralph Della Cava, "The 'People's Church,' the Vatican, and Abertura," in *Democratizing Brazil*, ed. Alfred Stepan (New York, 1989), 143-67.

24. On Herzog, see Paulo Markun, ed., *Vlado: retrato da morte de um homem e de uma época* (São Paulo, 1988); Hamilton Almeida Filho, *A sangue-quente: a morte do jornalista Vladimir Herzog* (São Paulo, 1978); Fernando Jordão, *Dossiê Herzog: prisão, tortura e morte no Brasil* (São Paulo, 1984); Trudi Landau, *Vlado Herzog: o que faltava contar* (Petrópolis, 1986); Ralph Della Cava, "Brazil: The Struggle for Human Rights," *Commonweal* 52, no. 20 (Dec. 19, 1975): 623-26; Jaime Wright, "D. Paulo e os direitos humanos—II," in *Paulo Evaristo Arns: cardeal da esperança e pastor da Igreja de São Paulo*, ed. Helcion Ribeiro (São Paulo, 1989), 72-73; for a reappraisal of the Herzog case, see Kenneth Serbin, "The Anatomy of a Death: Repression, Human Rights, and the Case of Alexandre Vannucchi Leme in Authoritarian Brazil," Helen Kellogg Institute for International Studies, Working Paper No. 248 (Notre Dame, Ind., Jan. 1998).

25. Archdiocese of São Paulo, *Brazil: Nunca Mais* (Petrópolis, 1985); for the English version, see *Torture in Brazil: A Report by the Archdiocese of São Paulo*, ed. Joan Dassin, trans. Jaime Wright (New York, 1986); on the research for the book, see Lawrence Weschler, *A Miracle, a Universe: Settling Accounts with Torturers* (New York, 1990); Wright, "D. Paulo e os direitos humanos—II," 70-71. The *Brasil: Nunca Mais* project was highly unusual, for in most other Latin American countries this kind of documentation has not been available. One exception is the extraordinary Centro de Documentación y Archivo para la Defensa de los Derechos Humanos, the so-called Archive of Terror of Paraguayan dictator Alfredo Stroessner's political police, discovered in Asunción 1992. On this archive, see Alfredo Boccia Paz, Myrian Angélica González, and Rosa Palau Aguilar, *Es mi informe—Los archivos secretos de la policía de Stroessner* (Asunción, 1994).

26. For a discussion of the development of the government truth commission, see Anthony W. Pereira, "Democracy and State Coercion: The Case of Brazil," paper presented to the 1997 Annual Meeting of the American Political Science Association, Panel 22-16, Washington, D.C., Aug. 30, 1997.

27. For a discussion of the concepts of the public and the prophetic, see José Casanova, *Public Religions in the Modern World* (Chicago, 1994), esp. chap. 5 on Brazil; on Catholic political change, see Bruneau, *Political Transformation*; Mainwaring, *Catholic Church and Politics*; Tânia Salem, ed., *A Igreja dos oprimidos* (São Paulo, 1981); Márcio Moreira Alves, *A Igreja e a política no Brasil* (São Paulo, 1979); Ralph Della Cava and Paula Montero. *E o verbo se faz imagem: Igreja católica e os meios de comunicação no Brasil, 1962-1989* (Petrópolis, 1991).

28. Mainwaring, *Catholic Church and Politics*, 74-75, 149, 181.

29. For a preliminary discussion of the Bipartite Commission, see Kenneth Serbin, "O diálogo secreto de bispos e generais nos anos da repressão," *Estado de São Paulo*, Caderno X (March 3, 1996); idem, "'Social Justice or Subversion?' The Secret Meetings of Brazil's Bishops and Military, 1970-1974," paper presented at the Latin American Studies Association XIX International Congress, Washington, D.C., Sept. 28-30, 1995; idem, "The Anatomy of a Death"; for a detailed study of the Bipartite Commission, see Kenneth Serbin, "Social Justice or Subversion? The Secret Dialogues of Brazil's Bishops and Generals," unpublished manuscript, 1998.

30. Mainwaring, *Catholic Church and Politics*; Thomas C. Bruneau and W. E. Hewitt, "Catholicism and Political Action in Brazil: Limitations and Prospects," in *Conflict and Competition: The Latin American Church in a Changing Environment*, ed. Edward L. Cleary and Hannah Stewart-Gambino (Boulder, Colo., 1992).

31. There is a variety of interpretations of the neo-conservative reaction; for a comprehensive overview, see José Oscar Beozzo, *A Igreja do Brasil* (Petrópolis, 1994), chap. 4; also see Carl Bernstein and Marco Politi, *His Holiness: John Paul II and the Hidden History of Our Time* (New York, 1996); José Comblin, *Cristãos rumo ao século XXI* (Petrópolis, 1996); Jean Daudelin and W. E. Hewitt, "Latin American Politics: Exit the Catholic Church?" in Pattnayak, *Organized Religion in the Political Transformation of Latin America*, 177-94; Serbin, "Priests, Celibacy, and Social Conflict," chap. 10; Kenneth Serbin, "Re-creating the Brazilian Church in the Post-Santo Domingo Era," paper presented at the Latin American Studies Association XVIIIth International Congress, Atlanta, Georgia, March 10-12, 1994; Ralph Della Cava, "Thinking about Current Vatican Policy in Central and East Europe and the Utility of the 'Brazilian Paradigm,'" *Journal of Latin American Studies* 25 (1993): 257-81; idem, "Vatican Policy, 1978-90: An Updated Overview," *Social Research* 59:1 (Spring 1992): 171-99; idem, "Política do Vaticano 1978-1990: uma visão geral," in *Catolicismo no Brasil atual*, ed. Pierre Sanchis, vol. 3, *Unidade religiosa e pluralismo cultural* (São Paulo, 1992), 231-58; idem, "The 'People's Church,' the Vatican, and Abertura"; Cleary and Stewart-Gambino, *Conflict and Competition*; Paula Montero, "Tradição e modernidade: João Paulo II e o problema da cultura," *Revista Brasileira de Ciências Sociais*, year 7, no. 20 (Oct. 1992): 90-112; José María Ghio, "The Latin American Church and the Papacy of Wojtyla," in *The Right and Democracy in Latin America*, ed. Douglas A. Chalmers, Maria do Carmo Campello de Souza, and Atilio A. Boron (New York, 1992); Pedro A. Ribeiro de Oliveira, "Estruturas da Igreja e conflitos religiosos," in *Catolicismo no Brasil atual*, ed. Pierre Sanchis, vol. 1, *Modernidade e tradição*, 41-66; Instituto de Estudos da Religião, "Estação de seca na Igreja," entire issue of *Comunicações do ISER*, year 9, no. 39 (1990); Penny Lernoux, *People of God: The Struggle for World Catholicism* (New York, 1989); Harvey Cox, *The Silencing of Leonardo Boff* (Bloomington, Ind., 1988); Mainwaring, *Catholic Church and Politics*, chap. 11; João Batista Libânio, *A volta à grande*

disciplina (São Paulo, 1983); for an example of a work targeted by Vatican criticism, see Leonardo Boff, *Church: Charism and Power*, trans. John Diercksmeier (New York, 1985).

32. Jorge G. Castañeda, *Utopia Unarmed: The Latin American Left after the Cold War* (New York, 1993).

33. John Burdick, *Looking for God in Brazil* (Berkeley, 1992); also see this work for a critical evaluation of the CEBs' attractiveness to the poor; also see the perceptive essay by this author, "The Progressive Catholic Church in Latin America: Giving Voice or Listening to Voices?" *Latin American Research Review* 29:1 (1994): 184-97; on CEB numbers, see the important statistical study by Rogério Valle and Marcelo Pitta, *Comunidades eclesiais católicas: resultados estatísticos no Brasil* (Petrópolis, 1994); for an appraisal of this research, see Pedro A. Ribeiro de Oliveira, "CEBs: o que são? Quantas são? O que fazem?" *Revista Eclesiástica Brasileira* 54 (Dec. 1994): 931-34; for skeptical views of previous large CEB estimates, see W. E. Hewitt, *Basic Christian Communities and Social Change in Brazil* (Lincoln, Neb., 1991), 7-10; Hewitt and Daudelin, "Latin American Politics: Exit the Church?" For a critical view of Burdick's work, see Manuel A. Vásquez, "Structural Obstacles to Grassroots Pastoral Practice: The Case of a Base Community in Urban Brazil," *Sociology of Religion* 58:1 (1997): 53-68.

34. Antônio Flávio de Oliveira Pierucci and Reginaldo Prandi, eds., *A realidade social das religiões no Brasil: religião, sociedade e política* (São Paulo, 1996).

35. The Church went through a similar process during the democratic-populist period from 1946 to 1964; see Serbin, "State Subsidization of Catholic Institutions in Brazil, 1930-1964."

36. CNBB, *Participação popular e cidadania: a Igreja no processo constituinte*, series "Estudos da CNBB," No. 60 (São Paulo, 1990).

37. Ivete Ribeiro and Ana Clara Torres Ribeiro, *Família e desafios na sociedade brasileira: valores como um ângulo de análise* (Rio de Janeiro, 1994).

38. Serbin, "Brazil: State Subsidization and the Church Since 1930;" also see Freston, "Protestantes e política." The Brazilian example paralleled the spectacular turn of events in Mexico, where Church and state renewed relations in 1992 after more than a century of estrangement and violent conflicts.

39. On Protestant growth, see Freston, "Protestantes e política," part 2; Antônio Gouvêa Mendonça and Prócoro Velasques, *Introdução ao protestantismo no Brasil* (São Paulo, 1990); on Umbanda, see Diana DeG. Brown, *Umbanda: Religion and Politics in Urban Brazil* (New York, 1994).

40. Gabriel Cipriani, "The Catholic Church and Religious Pluralism in Brazil," *Notícias CNBB* (International Edition) 6:16 (Jan.-March 1994): 1-4.

41. Statistics on the number of Protestants are precarious. This latest estimate is from Phillip Berryman, *Religion in the Megacity: Catholic and Protestant Portraits from Latin America* (Maryknoll, N.Y., 1996). On estimates for earlier years, see Freston "Protestantes e política," 27-35, 154, 157.

42. Rubem César Fernandes, *Censo Institucional Evangélico 1992: Primeiros Comentários* (Rio de Janeiro, 1992).

43. Burdick, *Looking for God in Brazil*; Comblin, "A Nova Evangelização," in Clodovis Boff et al., *Santo Domingo: ensaios teológico-pastorais* (Petrópolis, 1993), 215-16; "Demônios do fim do século (Análise da prática do exorcismo na Igreja Universal do Reino de Deus)," *Revista Eclesiástica Brasileira* 53 (Sept. 1993): 693-95.

44. Maria das Dores Machado, "Da teologia da prosperidade à participação no debate sobre a campanha de planejamento familiar—a Igreja Universal do Reino de Deus em perspectiva," unpublished paper, Rio de Janeiro, n.d.

45. It is important to keep in mind that traditional Catholicism was a largely passive phenomenon. Pentecostal growth should therefore not always be seen as a necessarily anti-Catholic phenomenon, but as part of an overall qualitative change in the nature of Brazilian religion that has included the appearance of the CEBs as well as the Catholic Charismatics, discussed below; see, for example, Cecilia Loreto Mariz, *Coping with Poverty: Pentecostals and Christian Base Communities in Brazil* (Philadelphia, Temple University Press, 1994).

46. Brown, *Umbanda*, 128, 162-64, 186-87; also see Ralph Della Cava, *A Igreja em flagrante: catolicismo e sociedade na imprensa brasileira, 1964-1980* (Rio de Janeiro, 1985), 168-69.

47. R. Andrew Chesnut, *Born Again in Brazil* (New Brunswick, N.J., 1997), 148-54.

48. Freston, "Protestantes e política," 167, 172, 218. As Freston points out, the history of Protestant-military relations has yet to be written.

49. Long out of vogue in Brazil as sociological and anthropological studies of religion dominated the field, studies of church-state relations are once again becoming necessary as the Pentecostals advance toward state power; see Freston, "Protestantes e política"; Antônio Flávio de Oliveira Pierucci, "Liberdade de cultos na sociedade de serviços: em defesa do consumidor religioso," *Novos Estudos CEBRAP* 44 (March): 3-11; Reginaldo Prandi, "Religião paga, conversão e serviço," *Novos Estudos CEBRAP* 45 (July 1996): 65-77; Emerson Giumbelli, "Da religião como problema social: secularização, retorno do sagrado, liberdade religiosa, espaço e comportamento religioso," unpublished paper. Likewise, the neglected financial angle of church-state relations is also coming into focus.

50. See, for example, Hugo Assmann, *A Igreja eletrônica e seu impacto na América Latina* (Petrópolis, 1986); Délcio Monteiro de Lima, *Os demônios descem do norte* (Rio de Janeiro, 1987).

51. Neo-Pentecostal churches in Latin America share a set of common characteristics. They are indigenously based and politically active, and they invest heavily in the media as a way of propagating their message. They also employ a "prosperity theology." However, their class base varies. In Brazil, for example, the Neo-Pentecostals primarily attract followers from the lower socioeconomic strata, whereas in Guatemala their membership is in the upper-middle class.

52. For an overview of the Universal Church, see Kenneth Serbin, "Brazilian Church Builds International Empire," *The Christian Century* (April 10, 1996): 398-403; Page, *The Brazilians*, chap. 15; also see numerous articles since the mid-1980s in such Brazilian dailies as *Folha de São Paulo, Jornal do Brasil*, and *O Estado de São Paulo*; also see Ronaldo Almeida, "A universalização do Reino de Deus," *Novos Estudos CEBRAP* 44 (March 1996): 12-23; Berryman, *Religion in the Megacity*; Mônica do Nascimento Barros, "A Batalha do Armagedon: uma análise do repertório mágico-religioso proposto pela Igreja Universal do Reino de Deus" (M.A. thesis, Universidade Federal de Minas Gerais, Belo Horizonte, 1995); Giumbelli, "Da religião como problema social"; also on the Universal Church and for an overview of Neo-Pentecostalism, see Ricardo Mariano, "Neopentecostalismo: os pentecostais estão mudando" (M.A. thesis, Universidade de São Paulo, São Paulo); on Brazilian reli-

gious expansionism, see Air Pedro Oro, "O 'expansionismo' religioso brasileiro para os países do Prata," *Revista Eclesiástica Brasileira* 54 (1994): 875-95.

53. Prandi, "Religião paga, conversão e serviço," 65-77.

54. Almeida, "A universalização do Reino de Deus."

55. Prandi, "Religião paga, conversão e serviço."

56. Prandi, "Religião paga, conversão e serviço"; Pierucci, "Liberdade de cultos."

57. Prandi, "Religião paga, conversão e serviço." In terms of religious and cultural transformation, some authors go so far as to speak of a "decatholicization" of Brazil. However, one should be cautious about jumping to such a conclusion. It is important to remember that the Catholic Church has served as the religious base for Christianity in Brazil for more than four centuries. There are a number of continuities between Catholicism and the new Pentecostal religions such as the Universal Church, discussed below; also see Serbin, "Brazilian Church Builds International Empire."

58. Freston, "Protestantes e política."

59. President João Café Filho (1954) was also Protestant. He was elected vice-president in 1951 and served out only part of the remainder of Vargas's term after the latter committed suicide in August 1954.

60. Freston, "Protestantes e política."

61. Roldão O. Arruda, "Acordo com Universal desagrada católicos," *O Estado de São Paulo* (Aug. 16, 1996); Carlos Eduardo Alves, "Serra tenta reduzir atrito com católicos," *Folha de São Paulo* (Aug. 20, 1996); Carlos Alvez, "Arns condena acordo com a Universal," *Folha de São Paulo* (Aug. 21, 1996). Interestingly, the Church's 1996 Fraternity Campaign theme focused on ethics in politics.

62. Serbin, "Brazilian Church builds international empire"; Pierucci, "Liberdade de cultos."

63. Pierucci, "Liberdade de cultos."

64. Kenneth Serbin, "Latin America's Catholic Church: Religious Rivalries and the North-South Divide," *North-South Issues* 2:1; Air Pedro Oro, *Avanço pentecostal e reação católica* (Petrópolis, 1996).

65. Rosinha Borges Dias, "Projeto pastoral 'Construir a Esperança,'" in *A presença da Igreja na cidade*, ed. Alberto Antoniazzi and Cleto Caliman (Petrópolis, 1994), 36-47.

66. Machado, *Carismáticos e pentecostais: adesão religiosa na esfera familiar* (Campinas, 1996).

67. Della Cava and Montero, *E o verbo se faz imagem.*

68. Oro, *Avanço pentecostal.*

69. On the new Catholic movements, see Oro, *Avanço pentecostal;* Machado, *Carismáticos e pentecostais;* Della Cava and Montero, *E o verbo se faz imagem,* 85-88; Lernoux, *People of God;* Ernesto Bernardes, "Na linha de frente da guerra," *Veja* (Sept. 20, 1995): 72-76; for a critical appraisal, see Luiz Eduardo Wanderley and Clodovis Boff, "Os novos movimentos eclesiais," *Revista Eclesiástica Brasileira* 52 (Sept. 1992): 702-6; on their relative lack of strength, see Comblin, "A nova evangelização," 219-22.

70. Roldao O. Arruda, "Carismáticos pensam diferente," *O Estado de São Paulo* (Aug. 16, 1996).

71. Oro, *Avanço pentecostal;* Conferência Nacional dos Bispos do Brasil, *Orientações pastorais sobre a Renovação Carismática Católica,* series "Documentos da CNBB," No. 53 (São Paulo, 1994).

72. Quotation of Presbyterian minister Caio Fábio d'Araujo and observation from Berryman, *Religion in the Megacity*, 3.
73. Pierucci, "Liberdade de cultos."
74. Freston, "Protestantes e política."

13 CHILE / MARTÍN POBLETE

1. See Brian Smith, *The Church and Politics in Chile* (Princeton, N.J.: Princeton University Press, 1982), 175-77. See also, Michael Fleet and Brian Smith, *The Catholic Church and Democracy in Chile and Peru* (Notre Dame, Ind.: University of Notre Dame Press, 1996); John Eagleson, ed., *Christians and Socialism* (Maryknoll, N.Y.: Orbis Books, 1975).

14 COLOMBIA / ELIZABETH E. BRUSCO

1. The news from Colombia during the last years of the twentieth century is full of accounts of the "cleansing" of "subversives"; the assassination of the leaders of an entire political party, the Unión Patriótica; the repression of labor unions; kidnappings by *narcotraficantes* (drug traffickers) and leftist guerrillas; the murders of judges, journalists, and legislators; and the scandalous activities of paramilitary death squads.
2. Some excellent scholarship details the origin and development of the two political parties in Colombia and the consequences of the conflict between them in shaping Colombian history. See, among others, Hartlyn 1988; David Bushnell "Politics and Violence in Nineteenth Century Colombia," in *Colombia: The Contemporary Crisis in Historical Perspective*, ed. Charles Bergquist et al. 1992, 11-30.
3. Hartlyn summarizes the differences between the parties during the nineteenth century as follows:

In general, the Conservatives were wedded to a view that approximated the previous colonial order, emphasizing close cooperation between the church and the state, a strong, central administration and protectionism. The Liberals, more influenced by the industrial, liberal-democratic powers of the nineteenth century, generally argued for federalism, separation of church and state, and free-trade economic policies (Hartlyn 1988, 19).

4. Hubert Schwan and Antonio Ugalde, "Orientations of the Bishops of Colombia toward Social Development, 1930-1970," *Journal of Church and State* 16, no. 3 (1974): 480. The authors analyzed data from a range of sources on Roman Catholic bishops who held office in Colombia between 1930 and 1970. They found that 65 percent of the bishops were born in Conservative municipalities, while only 11 percent came from Liberal municipalities. The actual percentage of Conservative bishops is probably higher, because 14 percent of the bishops were born in Bogotá, and hence their party affiliation is unknown.
5. A few Colombian evangelical historians have produced works describing the growth of the movement. See Burford de Buchanan 1995; and Díaz Escandón 1994. Other works on Colombian evangelicalism include Brusco 1995.
6. Jorge Pablo Osterling 1989, 239, dates the establishment of the first Catholic diocese to January 9, 1533, in Santa Marta on the Caribbean coast. The first seminary—Colegio Seminario del Señor San Bartolomé—was founded in Bogotá in 1582.
7. Earlier visits by Protestant missionaries are recorded, including that of James Thompson of the British and Foreign Bible Society in 1824 (Burford de Buchanan

1995, 37). However, the first actual Colombian evangelical congregation grew out of the efforts of Barrington Pratt.

8. A census conducted by the Conferederación Evangélica de Colombia (CEDEC) during the worst period of persecution against Evangelicals reported a 51 percent increase in Protestant Church membership between 1948 and 1953. During this same time, "27% of the Protestant Churches of Colombia and 38% of their preaching points were closed by the action of National Police and fanatical Roman Catholics" (10-1). The CEDEC Census committee reported that over 50,000 Colombians and 750 foreigners attended Protestant services weekly, and that a conservative estimate of the total number of Protestants in Colombia at the time was over 100,000 people.

9. The April 30, 1952, bulletin lists the CEDEC members as follows: Assemblies of God, Calvary Holiness Church, Christian and Missionary Alliance, Colombian Evangelical Crusade Church, Colombian Gospel Missionary Union, Conference of Mennonite Brethren, Cumberland Presbyterian Mission, Evangelical Union of South America, Foursquare Gospel Church, Independent Evangelical Church of Villarrica, Independent Gospel Tabernacle of Casanare, Interamerican Association of Evangelical Churches, Mennonite Mission in Colombia, South American Indian Mission in Colombia, Synod of the Presbyterian Church in Colombia, United Evangelical Tabernacle of Colombia, and Wesleyan Methodist Church.

10. One set of copies of the bulletins is housed in the Presbyterian Historical Society archives in Philadelphia.

11. Daniel Levine writes: "It is difficult to imagine a more effective mechanism of ostracism, or a more telling example of the fusion of civil and religious powers than these arrangements" (Levine 1981, 71).

12. During fieldwork in Colombia during the 1980s, I traveled with the Colombian Bible Society representative as he toured evangelical churches in the Magdalena Valley. He recounted many instances of individuals being detained, stoned, or otherwise harassed because they owned a Bible. Bible-owning has become one of the key distinguishing features of contemporary Colombian *evangélicos*, even for those who are illiterate or semi-literate.

13. In just one example of many, CEDEC reports an incident on February 5, 1952, in Galicia, Bugalagrande, Valle. Protestants holding a prayer meeting in a convert's home were attacked by six men, including the inspector of police and a police sergeant. They beat the assembled Protestants with the flat side of a machete and the butt of a gun. Bibles and prayer books were destroyed or confiscated. The account ends by saying that a lawyer was consulted about instituting criminal proceedings against the attackers: "The lawyer's reply gives a good indication of the state of law and order in rural Colombia today. He said that if one of the victims were to denounce the attackers before a criminal judge, he would be shot, either by the policeman denounced, or by friends of theirs. He added that in a country region such as Galicia there is absolutely no relief or redress available for the abuse of public power" (1-16-21).

14. In an echo of this language, in 1992 Pope John Paul called Protestants who are stealing Latin Americans from the Roman Catholic flock "rapacious wolves."

15. The Summer Institute of Linguistics occupies a unique position in the spectrum of evangelical denominations in Colombia. It is not a member of CEDEC, and Colombian evangelical leaders routinely take care to dissociate themselves in all ways from SIL activities. Stoll's 1982 book provides fine detail on how SIL became entrenched in Colombia (165-97). This involves the persistence of SIL founder, Cameron

Townsend, and an odd alliance with one of the fathers of Colombian anthropology, Gregorio Hernandez de Alba, who was seeking international assistance for founding of a Division of Indian Affairs. Hernandez de Alba saw the SIL as a means of disengaging Indian communities from the sway of the Catholic clergy, and also as a method of acquiring, free or with little cost, linguists to study the approximately fifty Indian languages, training for Colombians to carry out that task in the future, and flight service into remote regions (167).

16. Protestant ministers were sometimes accused of serving as chaplains for the bandits who proliferated during this time.

17. Wilde 1988, 114. For a study of the tension between the hierarchy's emphasis on control and the activism of grassroots groups, see Daniel Levine, "Religion, the Poor, and Politics in Latin America Today," in Levine 1986, 187-217.

18. The list of under-represented or unrepresented groups that finally found voice in the constitutional assembly included, in addition to Protestants, indigenous peoples of Colombia, and leftist political parties

19. The following articles of the 1991 Constitution have implications for religious freedom: Article 13 says that "all individuals are born free and equal before the law, will receive equal protection and treatment from the authorities, and will enjoy the same rights, freedoms, and opportunities without any discrimination on account of gender, race, national or family origin, language, religion, political opinion, or philosophy." Article 18 says that "freedom of conscience is guaranteed. No one will be importuned on account of his/her convictions or beliefs or compelled to reveal them or obliged to act against his/her conscience." Article 19 says that "freedom of religion is guaranteed. Every individual has the right to freely profess his/her religion and to disseminate it individually or collectively. All religious faiths and churches are equally free before law." Article 42 says that "religious marriages will have civil effects within the limits established by law. . . . Also having civil effects are decrees of annulment of religious marriages issued by the authorities of the respective faiths within the limits of established law." Article 68 says that "parents have the right to select the type of education for their minor children. In state institutions, no individual may be obliged to receive religious instruction."

15 PERU / JEFFREY KLAIBER, S.J.

1. The classic work on this topic is Pierre Duviols, *La destrucción de las religiones Andinas* (Duviols 1977).

2. Iris Gareis, "Extirpación de idolatrías e inquisición en el virreinato del Perú," *Boletín del Instituto Riva-Agüero* 16 (1989): 69.

3. Mary M. McGlone, "The King's Surprise: The Mission Methodology of Toribio de Mogrovejo," *The Americas* 50, no. 1 (July 1993): 75.

4. Gabriela Ramos, "Política eclesiástica y extirpación de idolatrías: discursos y silencios en torno al Taqui Onqoy," in Ramos and Urbano 1993, 143.

5. Jeffrey Klaiber, "Religión y justicia y Túpac Amaru," *Allpanchis* 19, vol. 16 (1982): 173-86.

6. Antonine Tibesar, *The Americas* 11 (January 1955): 229-83; Margaret E. Crahan, "Civil-Ecclesiastical Relations in Hapsburg Peru," *Journal of Church and State* 20, no. 1 (Winter 1978): 93-111.

7. Teodoro Hampe-Martínez, "Recent Works on the Inquisition and Peruvian Colonial Society, 1570-1820," *Latin American Research Review* 31, no. 2 (1966): 44.

8. Ibid., 46. See also Noé Zevallos, *Toribio Rodríguez de Mendoza* (Lima: Editorial Bruño, n.d.).

9. Jeffrey Klaiber, *Independencia, iglesia y clases populares* (Lima: Universidad del Pacífico, 1980): 43-44. See also Manuel Jesús Aparicio Vega, *El Clero patriota en la Revolución de 1814* (Cuzco, 1974), 236-46.

10. See Antonine Tibesar, "The Peruvian Church at the Time of Independence in the Light of Vatican II," *The Americas* 26 (April 1970): 349-75; Jeffrey Klaiber, *The Catholic Church in Peru* (Washington, D.C.: The Catholic University of America Press, 1992), 45-47.

11. Klaiber, *The Catholic Church in Peru*, 98.

12. Ibid., 77-78.

13. Ibid., 100.

14. José Pareja Paz-Soldán, *Las Constituciones del Perú* (Lima, 1954), 793-94, 796.

15. Víctor Andrés Belaunde, *Trayectoria y Destino: Memorias Completas* (Lima, 1976), 2:791-92.

16. Klaiber, *The Catholic Church in Peru*, 353.

17. *Relaciones Institucionales Vigentes entre la Iglesia Católica y la República del Perú* (Lima, July 1980), Articles 6, 7.

18. Ibid., Article 10.

19. Ibid., 15-16.

20. Enrique Chirinos Soto and Francisco Chirinos Soto, *Constitución de 1993: Lecturas y Comentario* (Lima, 1994), 92.

21. Samuel Escobar, ed., *Precursores Evangelicos: Cartas de Diego Thompson: Memorias de Francisco Penzotti* (Lima, 1984), 40.

22. Klaiber, *The Catholic Church in Peru*, 93-94.

23. Wenceslao Oscar Bahamonde, *The Establishment of Evangelical Christianity in Peru (1822-1900)* (doctoral thesis, Hartford, Conn., 1952), 118.

24. Juan B. A. Kessler, *Historia de la Evangelizacion en el Peru* (Lima, 1993), 236.

25. Bahamonde, *The Establishment of Evangelical Christianity*, 176.

26. John M. MacPherson, *At the Roots of a Nation: The Story of San Andrés School in Lima, Peru* (Edinburgh, 1993), 174-76.

27. Klaiber, *The Catholic Church in Peru*, 354.

28. Jeffrey Klaiber, "The Church in Peru: Between Terrorism and Conservative Restraints," in Cleary and Stewart-Gambino 1992, 100.

29. *Latinamerica Press* (October 25, 1990), 7.

30. This author was one of the invited guests at the special seminar organized by CONEP held at Villa la Paz retreat house, outside of Lima, December 11 to 13, 1989.

31. Bishop Luis Bambarén Gastelumendi, *Sectas y política* (Chimbote, 1990), 5.

32. *Diario La República* [Lima] (June 2, 1990), 5.

33. *Página Libre* [Lima] (June 3, 1990), B5.

34. *Contexto* [Lima] (July 8, 1994), 1.

35. *Normas Legales* (September 1995), 28.

36. *Latinamerica Press* (September 21, 1995), 1.

37. *Diario La República* (December 29, 1996), 12-13.

16 Venezuela / David A. Smilde

1. Given the excellent literature existing on Church-state relations in nineteenth-century Venezuela, in this chapter I will focus on the twentieth century. In addition to

Watters 1933 and Mecham 1966, see a recent treatment by Rafael Ortega Lima Ruiz, *Visión de las Relaciones Iglesia-Estado Durante la Epoca de Guzmán Blanco en Venezuela* (Caracas, 1997).

2. On the Venezuelan Church in the twentieth century, especially the recent decades, see Levine 1981; Levine 1992; and Bryan Froehle, "The Catholic Church and Politics in Venezuela: Resource Limitations, Religious Competition, and Democracy," in Cleary and Stewart-Gambino 1992.

3. Congreso Nacional, "Ley Aprobatoria del Convenio Celebrado entre la República de Venezuela y la Santa Sede Apostólica," *Gaceta Oficial de la República de Venezuela*, no. 27, 478, June 30, 1964.

4. "Subsidio a la Iglesia no ha sido recortado," *El Nacional*, January 14, 1998.

5. Polls show that it is one of the most trusted and respected institutions in Venezuela. See "El Presupuesto de Dios" [editorial by Janet Kelly], *El Nacional*, January 15, 1998.

6. A study of Caracas (Froehle, "The Catholic Church and Politics in Venezuela") found that more than two-thirds of all parish priests were foreign born.

7. In January 1998, less than a week after the Venezuelan Episcopal Conference (CEV) published a highly critical assessment of the "progressive impoverishment of the majority" during the government of Rafael Caldera, the Executive announced that it would be cutting the ecclesiastical allocations for 1998 by almost $30 million (see "Ejecutivo redujo en 75% subsidio a la Iglesia Católica," *El Nacional*, January 11, 1998). However, the dominant parties in the Congress said they would not approve the cut. Ten days later, the archbishop of Maracaibo, Ramón Pérez Morales, announced the removal of Monsignor Gustavo Ocando Yanarte as the executive president of *Corporación Niños Cantores* (CNC). Ocando had personally built up the CNC, including a highly popular television station that has been consistently critical of the Caldera administration. Local priests were outraged by the archbishop's decision and sent letters to the Nunciature in Caracas and the Vatican arguing that Ocando's removal was a political concession to the Caldera government's discontent with the Church ("Arzobispo Pérez Morales: 'La Santa Sede me consolida como la Iglesia de Maracaibo,'" and "Monsignor Gustavo Ocando Yanarte: 'Miraflores presionó para mi destitución,'" *El Nacional*, January 27, 1998).

8. There is no easy solution to the terminological problems regarding non-Catholic religions in Latin America. In Venezuela, Catholics refer to all of these religions as Evangelicals. Pentecostals and Baptists refer to themselves as Evangelicals, to denote their prioritization of the Gospel (*el Evangelio*). Here I will use "Evangelical" only to refer to these Pentecostals and Baptists. I will use "New Religious Movements" (NRMs) to refer to all the new religions, including those who refer to themselves as Evangelical.

9. Asdrúbal Rios Troconis, *De los Pequeños Principios a las Grandes Realizaciones* (Maracaibo, 1976), 126-46.

10. Document 30 in Fray Cesáreo de Armellada, *Fuero Indígena Venezolano* (Caracas, 1977), 56-57. De Armellada's book is a compilation of 229 historical documents on the state's indigenous policy.

11. Ibid., 8-9.

12. "Extensión de la Ley de Patronato a los cultos no católicos. Decreto de 24 de octubre de 1911," in Hermann González Oropeza, S.J., *Iglesia y Estado en Venezuela* (Caracas, 1997), 397.

13. De Armellada, *Fuero Indigena Venezolano,* documents 138, 146-48.

14. Ibid., document 173; see also documents 193 and 195.

15. Ibid., documents 192, 206.

16. Apart from the writings of de Armellada, these arguments are made in an analysis written by Padre Hermann González at the request of the Ministry of the Interior when the Indigenous Commission was being reorganized in 1976 (Hermann González Oropeza, "Secuencia Ideológica en Relación al Indigenismo en la Legislación," 1976).

17. Fray Cesáreo de Armellada, personal letter to the archbishop of Caracas, Rafael Arias Blanco, 1959. In a similar spirit is Hermann González Oropeza, S.J., "Informe del Señor Arzobispo de Caracas Sobre Asuntos Misionales," draft for letter to the president (later corrected) from Monsignor Rafael Arias Blanco, 1962.

18. In several historical documents the possibility of a non-missionary indigenous policy is quite specifically left open. In the 1841 Law on Reduction and Civilization of Indians, for example, the first article states: "The Executive branch is authorized to promote, by all the means available to it, the reduction and civilization of the Indians in the Territory of the Republic, making them gather in settlements under the direction of the officials it believes it convenient to establish" (de Armellada, *Fuero Indigena Venezolano*, document 47 [p. 79]). The same language is used in numerous other historical documents (ibid., documents 1, 21, 25, 77, 82, 108, 111, 114, 133). No statements can be found that the missions supported by the state must be Catholic religious orders, a fact pointed out by Padre González in his analysis (González Oropeza, "Secuencia Ideológica"). Furthermore, despite de Armellada's interpretation (see above), the 1911 law clearly extended all provisions of the Law of Patronage to non-Catholic churches, not just those under the state's supervision. Through the 1950s there was indeed consistent support for the exclusivity of the concessions of territories to religious orders (see de Armellada, *Fuero Indigena Venezolano*, documents 146, 147, 148, 173, 193, 195). However, in later agreements (1956 and 1967) this exclusivity was specifically restricted to those areas within the territory that had an active mission center (ibid., document 203, 3d clause; document 217, 20th clause).

19. "Combatimos el Colonialism a Nivel Mundial pero a Escala Nacional lo Practicamos Contra Las Comunidades Indígenas; Denuncia el Doctor Esteban al Emilio Monsoyi, Antropologo de la UCV," *El Nacional*, July 15, 1976.

20. Movimiento por la Identidad Nacional, "Resoluciones de las Jornadas El Indígena y la Identidad Nacional," unpublished pamphlet, 1979.

21. Comisión Especial para Investigar las Actividades de las Misiones Religosas entre la Población Indígena Venezolana, Cámara de Diputados, Congreso Nacional de la República de Venezuela, June 2, 1980. *Informe Final a la Cámara de Diputados*. Presentado por Alexis Ortiz.

22. "Renunció Alexis Ortiz a la comisión que Investiga las 'Nuevas Tribus,'" *El Nacional*, July 15, 1980.

23. Hermann González Oropeza, "Memorandum Sobre El Indigenismo en el II Seminario Internacional para el Desarrollo de la Comunidad," August 25, 1980, circulated to the Nunciature, the Ministry of Foreign Relations, and Ministry of the Interior.

24. Comisión General No. 3. II Seminario Internacional para el Desarrollo de la Comunidad, August 22, 1980.

25. The issue resurfaced in 1982 as a result of complaints made by Monsignor Mariano Gutierez and pushed by *El Nacional,* one of the two leading daily newspa-

pers in Venezuela. This led to a series of criticisms and replies with the same actors and arguments as those of 1979-80.

26. Fray Cesáreo de Armellada was one of the most consistent advocates of the exclusive right of religious orders to evangelize indigenous groups; yet he was also an early voice defending the NTM (Cesáreo de Armellada, "Ataques a los misioneros no católicos," *La Religion*, December 21, 1978).

27. "Misioneros católicos rechazan trabajo realizado por 'Nuevas Tribus,'" *Ultimas Noticias*, June 21, 1980.

28. Jamie Bou, *Informe de las Actividades Realizadas por la Misión Nuevas Tribus de Venezuela Durante el Año de 1973 en el Estado Bolívar y el Terriotrio Federal Amazonas,* anexo 4 (Puerto Ayacucho, T. F. Amazonas, May 1974).

29. Jaime Bou, "La Misión Evangélico 'Nuevas Tribus' a la Opinión Pública Venezolana," paid advertisement in *El Nacional*, February 7, 1988.

30. Consejo Evangélico de Venezuela, "El Consejo Evangélico de Venezuela a la Opinión Pública Nacional: Manifiesto del Primer Congreso Nacional Evangélico de Misiones Indigenistas," paid advertisement in *El Universal*, May 27, 1980.

31. Interview with Daniel Oquendo, assistant director of the *Dirección de Justicia y Cultos*, January 14, 1998.

32. Ibid.

33. Cámara de Diputados, República de Venezuela, "Exposición de Motivos y Proyecto de 'Ley de Comunidades, Pueblos y Culturas Indígenas,'" November 1995.

34. "Misión 'Nuevas Tribus' viola leyes venezolanas," *El Nacional,* November 30, 1996.

35. Interview with Néstor Luis Alvarez, director of the *Dirección de Justicia y Cultos* [DJC], January 15, 1998.

36. Personal communication from DJC, October 1997.

37. During the controversy, figures of one thousand and four thousand applications were widely cited. However, when the minister of justice approved all those that were delayed, the number was actually 676.

38. Letter from *Dirección de Justicia y Cultos* to Unicristiana, Consejo Evangélico de Venezuela, Confederación Pentecostal de Venezuela, Godofredo Marín, Partido ORA, December 19, 1996.

39. Interview with Godofredo Marín, December 4, 1997.

40. "Piden interpelar a Min-Justicia por negar legalización de iglesias," *El Nacional,* October 9, 1998.

41. "Gobierno autorizó 676 cultos," *El Universal,* November 6, 1997.

42. "Supervisar los cultos es función de seguridad de Estado," *El Universal,* November 20, 1997. In Venezuelan Evangelical vernacular, the term *pastor* is indeed given to those who have reached a point in their faith that they feel comfortable preaching in public.

43. Interview with Daniel Oquendo, January 14, 1998.

44. Interview with Jacobo García, president of the Evangelical Council of Venezuela (CEV), January 15, 1998.

45. Interview with Robert Gómez, president of the Pentecostal Evangelical Confederation of Venezuela (CEPV), January 14, 1998.

46. Interview with Daniel Oquendo.

47. "El país reclama la aprobación de Ley General de Cultos," *El Nacional,* November 30, 1996.

48. Interview with Robert Gómez.

49. Interview with Jacobo García.

50. *Dirección de Justicia y Cultos*, "Proyecto de *Ley Orgánica de Cultos*" (1997).

51. Letter from Hernán Sánchez Porras, Secretario General de la Conferencia Episcopal de Venezuela, to Ramón Guillermo Aveledo, Presidente de la Cámara de Diputados, June 27, 1997.

52. "Un calderista acude al confesor," *El Universal*, November 20, 1997.

53. "Supervisar los cultos es función de seguridad de Estado," *El Universal*, November 20, 1997; "Misión 'Nuevas Tribus' viola leyes venezolanas," *El Nacional*, November 30, 1996.

54. Interview with Néstor Luis Alvarez.

55. "Supervisar los cultos es función de seguridad de Estado," *El Universal*, November 20, 1997.

56. "Gobiernos extrajeros financian invasión de sectas en Venezuela." *El Nacional*, September 16, 1997.

57. "Editorial: Sectas inaceptadas," *El Nacional*, September 16, 1997.

58. Interview with Néstor Luis Alvarez.

59. *Constitución de la República de Venezuela* 1961.

60. República de Venezuela, Gobierno del Distrito Federal, Despacho del Gobernador, Asdrúbal Aguiar Aranguren, *Decreto 0400*, September 1, 1995.

61. Frente Coalición Cristiana, "Conoce y Defiende tu Derecho," October 6, 1995.

62. It is worth pointing out that in recent years municipal authorities have clashed not only with plaza preachers, but also with street vendors and others whose activities in the downtown area are seen as "disorderly."

63. Interview with Pedro Prado, September 30, 1997.

64. "Gobierno autorizó 676 cultos," *El Universal*, November 6, 1997.

65. See Benedict Anderson, *Imagined Communities: Reflections on the Origin and Spread of Nationalism* (London, 1983).

66. See Maritza Montero, *Ideología, Alienación e Identidad Nacional: una Aproximación Psicosocial al Ser Venezolano* (Caracas, 1984).

67. Susanne Hoeber Rudolph and James Piscatori, eds., *Transnational Religion and Fading States* (Boulder, Colo., 1997).

68. Max Weber, "The Sociology of Law," *Economy and Society* (Berkeley 1978).

BIBLIOGRAPHY

Acerbi, Antonio. *Chiesa e democrazia: Da Leone XIII al Vaticano II*. Milan: Vota e Pensiero, 1991.

Acton, Lord John E. *Essays on Church and State*. New York: Thomas Y. Crowell, 1968.

Adame, Jorge. *El Pensamiento Político y Social de los Católicos Mexicanos 1867-1914*. México: UNAM, 1981.

Alberigo, Guiseppe, et al. *The Reception of Vatican II*. Washington, D.C.: Catholic University of America Press, 1987.

Almquist, A. M. *Burgess of Guatemala*. Langley, B.C.: Cedar Books, 1985.

Alves, Rubén. *Protestantism and Repression: A Brazilian Case Study*. Maryknoll, N.Y.: Orbis Books, 1985.

Aubert, Roger. *Tolérance et Communauté humaine: Chrétiens dans un monde divisé*. Paris: Casterman, 1952.

Aubrey, Roger. *La misión siguiendo a Jesús por los caminos de América Latina*. Buenos Aires: Editorial Guadalupe, 1990.

Avni, Cr. Haim. *Argentina y la historia de la inmigración judía, 1810-1850*. Buenos Aires: AMIA, Editorial Universitaria Agnes, 1983.

Baez Camargo, G. *Protestantes enjuiciados por la Inquisición en Iberoamérica*. 4 vols. Mexico: Casa Unida de Publicaciones, 1960.

Bantjes, Adrian A. "Idolatry and Iconoclasm in Revolutionary Mexico: The De-Christianization Campaigns, 1929-1940," *Mexican Studies* 13, 1 (1997): 87-120.

Barranco Villafan, Bernando, and Raquel Pastor Escobar. *Jerarquía Católica y Modernización Política en México*. Mexico City: Palabra Ediciones, Centro Antonio de Montesinos, 1989.

Barret, David B., ed. *World Christian Encyclopedia*. Nairobi: Oxford University Press, 1982.

Bastian, Jean-Pierre. *Breve historia del protestantismo en América Latina*. México, D.F: Casa Unida de Publicaciones, 1986.

———. *Historia del Protestantismo en América Latina*. Mexico: Casa Unida de Publicaciones, 1990.

———, ed. *Protestantes, Liberales y Francmasones, Sociedades de Ideas y Modernidad en América Latina*. México: Siglo XIX, FCE-LEHILA, 1990.

Bergquist, Charles, et al., eds. *Colombia: The Contemporary Crisis in Historical Perspective*. Wilmington, Del.: Scholarly Resources, 1992.

Bernstein, Carl, and Marco Politi. *His Holiness: John Paul II and the Hidden History of Our Time*. New York: Penguin, 1996.

Berryman, Phillip. *The Religious Roots of Rebellion: Christians in Central American Revolutions*. Maryknoll, N.Y.: Orbis Books, 1984.

———. *Stubborn Hope: Religion, Politics, and Revolution in Central America*. Maryknoll, N.Y.: Orbis Books, 1994.

————. *Religion in the Megacity: Catholic and Protestant Portraits from Latin America.* Maryknoll, N.Y.: Orbis Books, 1996.

Blachman, Morris J., William M. LeoGrand, and Kenneth E. Sharp, eds. *Confronting Revolution: Security through Diplomacy in Central America.* New York: Pantheon, 1986.

Blancarte, Roberto. "Church-State Relations: From Debate to Disarray." In *Rebuilding the State: Mexico after Salinas,* edited by Mónica Serrano and Victor Bulmer-Thomas. London: Institute of Latin American Studies, University of London, 1996.

Boff, Leonardo. *Ecclesiogenesis: The Base Communities Reinvent the Church.* Translated by Robert R. Barr. Maryknoll, N.Y.: Orbis Books, 1986.

Bolivia. Subsecretariado de Culto. *El fenómeno religioso no católico en Bolivia: Una primera aproximación.* La Paz: Ministerio de Relaciones Exteriores y Culto, 1996.

Bowen, Kurt. *Evangelism and Apostasy: The Evolution and Impact of Evangelicals in Modern Mexico.* Montreal: McGill-Queen's University Press, 1996.

Boyle, Kevin, and Juliet Sheen, eds. *Freedom of Religion and Belief: A World Report.* New York: Routledge, 1997.

Brockman, James R. *Romero: A Life.* Maryknoll, N.Y.: Orbis Books, 1989.

Brooke, James. "Religious Issue Roils Colombia," *New York Times* (June 19, 1994).

Bruneau, Thomas C. *The Political Transformation of the Brazilian Catholic Church.* Cambridge, 1974.

————. *The Church in Brazil: The Politics of Religion.* Austin, Tex.: University of Texas Press, 1982.

Bruno, Cayetano S.D.G. *El Derecho Público de la Iglesia en Indias.* Salamanca, Consejo Superior de Investigaciones Científicas, Instituto San Raimundo de Peñafort, 1967.

Brusco, Elizabeth E. *The Reformation of Machismo: Evangelical Conversion and Gender in Colombia.* Austin, Tex.: University of Texas Press, 1995.

Burdick, John. *Looking for God in Brazil: The Progressive Catholic Church in Urban Brazil's Religious Arena.* Berkeley and Los Angeles: University of California Press, 1993.

————. "The Progressive Catholic Church in Latin America: Giving Voice or Listening to Voices?" *Latin American Research Review* 29:1 (1994): 184-97.

Burford de Buchanan, Jeanne. *La Iglesia en Colombia: Una Historia.* Santa Fé de Bogotá: Asociación Pro-Cruzada Mundial, 1995.

Bushnell, David. "Politics and Violence in Nineteenth Century Colombia." In Bergquist et al., *Colombia: The Contemporary Crisis in Historical Perspective,* 11-30.

Canclini, Arnoldo. *La Libertad de cultos.* Buenos Aires: Artes Gráficas, 1986.

Cañete, Perdo Vicente. *Syntagma de las Resoluciones Prácticas Cotidianas del Derecho Real Patronazgo de las Indias.* Buenos Aires: Talleres Gráficos, Mundial, 1973.

Casanova, José. *Public Religions in the Modern World.* Chicago: University of Chicago Press, 1994.

Castañeda, Jorge G. *Utopia Unarmed: The Latin American Left after the Cold War.* New York: Vintage, 1993.

Castro Arenas, Mario. *La Rebelión de Juan Santos.* Lima: Milla Batres, 1973.

Catholic Church, Diocese of Tijuana. *Plan Pastoral, 1989-1994, hacia una Iglesia Nueva.* Tijuana: La Diocese, 1989.

Cavalcanti, A. B. "Unrealistic Expectations: Contesting the Usefulness of Weber's Protestant Ethic for the Study of Latin American Protestantism," *The Journal of Church and State* 37, 2 (1995): 289-308.

Ceballos Ramírez, Manuel. *El Catolicismo Social: un Tercero en Discordia, Rerum Novarum, "la cuestión social" y la movilización de los católicos mexicanos (1891-1911)*. México: El Colegio de México, 1991.

Chalmers, Douglas A., Maria do Carmo Campello de Souza, and Atilio A. Boron, eds. *The Right and Democracy in Latin America*. New York: Greenwood, 1992.

Chaves, Mark, "On the Rational Choice Approach to Religion," *Journal for the Scientific Study of Religion* 34, 1 (1995): 98-104.

Chesnut, R. Andrew. *Born Again in Brazil*. New Brunswick, N.J.: Rutgers University Press, 1997.

Chong, Dennis. *Collective Action and the Civil Rights Movement*. Chicago: University of Chicago Press, 1991.

Cleary, Edward L. *Crisis and Change: The Church in Latin America*. Maryknoll, N.Y.: Orbis Books, 1985.

———. *The Struggle for Human Rights in Latin America*. Westport, Conn.: Praeger, 1997.

Cleary, Edward L., and Hannah Stewart-Gambino, eds. *Conflict and Competition: The Latin American Church in a Changing Environment*. Boulder, Colo.: Lynne Rienner Publishers, 1992.

———. *Power, Politics, and Pentecostals in Latin America*. Boulder, Colo.: Westview, 1997.

Colby, Gerard, and Charlotte Dennett. *Thy Will Be Done: The Conquest of the Amazon-Nelson Rockefeller and Evangelism in the Age of Oil*. New York: Harper Collins, 1995.

Coleman, John A. *The Evolution of Dutch Catholicism, 1958-1974*. Berkeley and Los Angeles: University of California Press, 1978.

Coleman, William J. *Latin American Catholicism: A Self-criticism*. Maryknoll, N.Y.: Maryknoll Publications, 1958.

Comisión Episcopal para el Apostolado de los Laicos. *¿Qué piensan los laicos mexicanos del sínodo '87?* Mexico City: CEM, 1986.

Conferência Nacional dos Bispos do Brasil. *Rumo ao Novo Milênio: Projeto de Evangelização da Igreja no Brasil em Preparação ao Grande Jubileu do Ano 2000*. São Paulo: Editorial Salesiana Don Bosco, 1996.

Correa, Eduardo J. *El Partido Católico Nacional y sus Directores: Explicación de su Fracaso y Deslinde de Responsabilidades*. 2d ed. México: Fondo de Cultura Económica, 1991.

Cox, Harvey. *The Silencing of Leonardo Boff*. Bloomington, Ind., 1988.

Dassin, Joan, ed. *Torture in Brazil: A Report by the Archdiocese of São Paulo*. Translated by Jaime Wright. New York: Vintage, 1986.

Daudelin, Jean, and W. E. Hewitt. "Latin American Politics: Exit the Catholic Church?" In *Organized Religion in the Political Transformation of Latin America*, edited by Satya R. Pattnayak, 177-94. New York: University of America Press, 1995.

Decke, Gerd, ed. *The Encounter of the Church with Movements of Social Change in Various Cultural Contexts*. Part 2. Geneva: Department of Studies, Lutheran World Federation, 1977.

Deiros, Pablo A. *Historia del cristianismo en América Latina*. Buenos Aires: Fraternidad Teológica Latinoamericana, 1992.

Dekker, James C. "North American Protestant Theology: Impact on Central America," *The Mennonite Quarterly Review* 58 (August Supplement 1984): 378-93.

de la Hera, Alberto. *Iglesia y Corona de la América Española*. Madrid: Ed. Maptre, 1992.

De la Rosa, Martín, and Charles A. Reilly, eds. *Religión y política en México*. Mexico City: Siglo XXI, 1985.

de Las Casas, Bartolomé. *In Defense of the Indians*. Translated by Stafford Poole. DeKalb: Northern Illinois University Press, 1992.

Della Cava, Ralph. "Brazilian Messianism and National Institutions: A Reappraisal of Canudos and Joaseiro," *Hispanic American Historical Review* 48, 3 (August 1968): 402-20.

——. "Brazil: The Struggle for Human Rights," *Commonweal* 52, no. 20 (December 19, 1975): 623-26.

——. "Catholicism and Society in Twentieth-Century Brazil," *Latin American Research Review* 11, 2 (1976): 11-12.

——. "The 'People's Church,' the Vatican, and Abertura." In *Democratizing Brazil*, edited by Alfred Stepan, 143-67. New York: Oxford University Press, 1989.

——. "Vatican Policy, 1978-90: An Updated Overview," *Social Research* 59, 1 (Spring 1992): 171-99.

——. "Financing the Faith: The Case of Roman Catholicism," *Journal of Church and State* 35, 1 (Winter 1993); 37-49.

——. "Thinking about Current Vatican Policy in Central and East Europe and the Utility of the 'Brazilian Paradigm,'" *Journal of Latin American Studies* 25 (1993): 257-81.

Delpar, Helen. "Colombian Liberalism and the Roman Catholic Church," *Journal of Church and State* 22, 2 (1980): 271-93.

de Souza, Juliana Beatriz. "Mãe negra de um povo mestiço: a devoção a Nossa Senhora Aparecida e identidade nacional," *Estudos Afro-Asiáticos* 29 (March 1996): 85-102.

Diacon, Todd A. *Millenarian Vision, Capitalist Reality: Brazil's Contestado Rebellion, 1912-1916*. Durham, N.C.: Duke University Press, 1991.

Díaz Escandón, Samuel. *La Libertad Religiosa en Colombia: Leyes y Sentencias Complementarias*. Santa Fé de Bogotá: Buena Semilla, 1994.

Documento ecuménico sobre la Reforma Constitucional Argentina presentado a los señores miembros de la Asamblea Constituyente. Paraná: Movimiento Ecuménico por los Derechos Humanos, 1998.

Dodson, Michael, and Laura O'Shaughnessy. *Nicaragua's Other Revolution: Religious Faith and Political Struggle*. Chapel Hill, N.C.: University of North Carolina Press, 1990.

D'Onorio, Joel-Benoît, ed. *Le Saint Siege dans les relations internationales*. Paris: Cerf-Cujas, 1989.

Dussel, Enrique, ed. *The Church in Latin America 1492-1992*. Maryknoll, N.Y.: Orbis Books, 1992.

Duviols, Pierre. *La Destrucción de las Religiones Andinas*. Mexico, D.F.: Universidad Nacional Autómona de México, 1977.

Dyck, Arthur, ed. *Human Rights and Global Mission of the Church*. Cambridge, Mass.: Boston Theological Institute, 1985.

Eagleson, John, ed. *Christians and Socialism*. Maryknoll, N.Y.: Orbis Books, 1975.

Ekelund, Robert B., Jr., Robert F. Hebert, and Robert D. Tallison. "An Economic Model of the Medieval Church," *Journal of Law, Economics, and Organization* 5, 2 (1989): 305-31.

Estatutos, reglamentos y constituciones argentinas (1811-1898). Buenos Aires: Universidad de Buenos Aires, 1956.

Fleet, Michael, and Brian Smith. *The Catholic Church and Democracy in Chile and Peru*. Notre Dame, Ind.: University of Notre Dame Press, 1996.

Freire, Paulo. *Pedagogy of the Oppressed*. New York: Continuum, 1970.

García Gutiérrez, Jesús. *Apuntes para la Historia del Origen y Desenvolvimiento del Regio Patronato Indiano hasta 1857*. México: Ed. Jus-ELD, 1941.

Garrard-Burnett, Virginia, and David Stoll, eds. *Rethinking Protestantism in Latin America*. Philadelphia: Temple University Press, 1993.

Gastalver, Matilde, and Lino F. Salas. *Las comunidades eclesiales de base y el movimiento popular en México*. Mexico City: Ibero-American University, 1983.

Gill, Anthony. *Rendering unto Caesar: The Catholic Church and State in Latin America*. Chicago: University of Chicago Press, 1998.

Gill, Anthony, and Keshavarzian. "State Building and Religious Resources," *Politics and Society*. Forthcoming.

Gleijeses, Piero. *Shattered Hope: The Guatemalan Revolution and the United States, 1944-1954*. Princeton, N.J.: Princeton University Press, 1991.

Goff, James. "The Persecution of Protestant Christians in Colombia," *Sondeas*, no. 23. Cuernavaca: CIDOC, 1968.

Goldin, Liliana, and Brent Metz. "An Expression of Cultural Change: Invisible Converts to Protestantism among Highland Guatemala Mayas," *Ethnology* 30, no. 4: 325-38.

Gómez Ciraza, Roberto. *México ante la Diplomacia Vaticana: El período triangular 1821-36*. México: Fondo de Cultura Economica, 1977.

González López, Jesús, ed. *Relaciones Iglesia-Estado: Análisis Teológico-Jurídico desde América Latina*. Bogotá: Consejo Episcopal Latinoamericano, n.d.

Goslin, Tomás. *Los evangélicos en América Latina*: Siglo XIX los comienzos. Buenos Aires: La Aurora, 1956.

Grayson, George. *The Church in Contemporary Mexico*. Washington: Center for Strategic and International Studies, 1992.

———, ed. *Prospects for Mexico*. Washington: Center for the Study of Foreign Affairs, 1988.

Greeley, Andrew M. *The Catholic Myth: The Behavior and Beliefs of American Catholics*. New York: Collier Books, 1990.

Griffith, Nicholas. *The Cross and the Serpent: Religious Repression and Resurgence in Colonial Peru*. Norman, Okla.: University of Oklahoma Press, 1996.

Hageman, Alice L., and Philip E. Wheaton, eds. *Religion in Cuba Today: A New Church in a New Society*. New York: Association Press, 1971.

Hallum, Anne M. *Beyond Missionaries: Toward an Understanding of the Protestant Movement in Central America*. London: Rowman and Littlefield Publishers, 1996.

Handy, Jim. *Gift of the Devil: A History of Guatemala*. Boston: South End Press, 1984.

Hartlyn, Jonathan. *The Politics of Coalition Rule in Colombia*. Cambridge: Cambridge University Press, 1988.

Hawley, Susan. "Protestantism and Indigenous Mobilization: The Moravian Church among the Miskito Indians of Nicaragua," *Journal of Latin American Studies* 29 (1997):111-29.

Hennelly, Alfred T., ed. *Santo Domingo and Beyond*. Maryknoll, N.Y.: Orbis Books, 1993.

Hewitt, W. E. *Base Communities and Social Change in Brazil.* Lincoln, Neb.: University of Nebraska Press, 1991.

Hocken, Peter. "Dialogue Extraordinary," *One in Christ* 24, 3 (1988): 202-13.

Hoeber Rudolph, Susanne and James Piscatori, eds. *Transnational Religion and Weak States.* Boulder, Colo.: Westview, 1997.

Houtart, François, and André Rousseau. *The Church and Revolution.* Maryknoll, N.Y.: Orbis Books, 1971.

Huntington, Samuel P. *The Third Wave: Democratization in the Late Twentieth Century.* Tulsa, Okla.: University of Oklahoma Press, 1991.

Hurtado, Alberto, S.J. *¿Es Chile un Pais Catolico?* Santiago: Editorial Los Andes, 1941.

Iannaccone, Laurence. "Religious Practice: A Human Capital Approach," *Journal for the Scientific Study of Religion* 29, 3 (1990): 297-314.

———. "The Consequences of Religious Market Structure," *Rationality and Society* 3, 2 (1991): 156-77.

———. "Voodoo Economics? Reviewing the Rational Choice Approach to Religion," *Journal for the Scientific Study of Religion* 34 (1995): 76-88.

La iglesia católica y la reforma constitucional. Buenos Aires: Conferencia Episcopal Argentina, Oficina del Libro, 1994.

Instituto de Estudos da Religião. "Estação de seca na Igreja," *Comunicações do ISER,* year 9, no. 39 (1990).

Ireland, Rowan. *Kingdoms Come: Religion and Politics in Brazil.* Pittsburgh: University of Pittsburgh Press, 1991.

Jiménez Urresti, Teodoro. *La libertad religiosa: Declaración del Concilio Ecuménico Vaticano II.* Edición bilingue latino-castellana. Madrid: Colección de Pastoral Aplicada, 1965.

Klaiber, Jeffrey. "La Utopía andina y cristiana." In *Cristianismo y mundo colonial: Tres estudios acerca de la evangelización de Hispanoamérica,* edited by Johannes Meier, 37-62. Münster, Germany: Aschendorff, 1995.

Landsberger, Henry, ed. *The Church and Social Change in Latin America.* Notre Dame, Ind.: University of Notre Dame Press, 1970.

Lannon, Frances. *Privilege, Persecution, and Prophecy.* Oxford: Clarendon Press, 1987.

Latourette, Kenneth Scott. *Christianity in a Revolutionary Age: The Nineteenth Century outside Europe.* New York: Harper and Brothers, 1961.

Legon, Faustino. *Doctrina y ejercicio del Patronato Nacional.* Buenos Aires: J. Lajouane and Cia, 1920.

Lehmann, David. *Democracy and Development in Latin America: Economics, Politics, and Religion in the Postwar Period.* Philadelphia: Temple University Press, 1990.

Lenski, Gerhard. *The Religious Factor: A Sociological Study of Religion's Impact on Politics and Family Life.* Garden City, N.Y.: Doubleday, 1963.

Lernoux, Penny. *Cry of the People: The Struggle for Human Rights in Latin America— The Catholic Church in Conflict with U.S. Policy.* New York: Penguin, 1982.

———. *People of God: The Struggle for World Catholicism.* New York: Penguin, 1989.

Levine, Daniel H. *Religion and Politics in Latin America: The Catholic Church in Venezuela and Colombia.* Princeton, N.J.: Princeton University Press. 1981.

———. *Popular Voices in Latin American Catholicism.* Princeton, N.J.: Princeton University Press, 1992.

———, ed. *Religion and Political Conflict in Latin America.* Chapel Hill, N.C.: University of North Carolina Press, 1986.

Levine, Robert M. *Vale of Tears: Revisiting the Canudos Massacre in Northeastern Brazil, 1893-1897.* Berkeley and Los Angeles: University of California Press, 1992.

Lewin, Boleslau. *La Inquisición en Hispanoamérica.* Buenos Aires: Proyección, 1972.

Lipset, Seymour Martin, ed. *Elites in Latin America.* New York: Oxford University Press, 1968.

López, Marlo René. "Evangelicalismo y Neo-Pentecostalismo Independiente." In *Historia y misión del protestantismo hondureño,* 111-25. San José, Costa Rica: Visión Mundial Internacional, Oficina Regional, 1993.

López Beltrán, Lauro. *Diócesis y obispos de Cuernavaca, 1875-1978.* Mexico, 1978.

Lowden, Pamela. *Moral Opposition to Authoritarian Rule in Chile, 1973-90.* New York: Macmillan, 1996.

Lubertino Beltran, María J. *Perón y la iglesia.* 2 vols. Buenos Aires: Biblioteca Política Argentina, 1987.

Lynch, John. *The Spanish American Revolutions 1808-1826.* 2d ed. New York: Norton, 1986.

Mackay, J. A. *Ecumenics: The Science of the Church Universal.* Englewood Cliffs, N.J.: Prentice-Hall, 1964.

Mainwaring, Scott. *The Catholic Church and Politics in Brazil, 1916-1985.* Stanford, Calif.: Stanford University Press, 1986.

Mainwaring, Scott, and Alexander Wilde, eds. *The Progressive Church in Latin America.* Notre Dame, Ind.: University of Notre Dame Press, 1989.

Margadant, Guillermo F. *La Iglesia ante el Derecho Mexicano: Esbozo Histórico-jurídico.* México: Miguel Angel Porrúa, Librero-Editor, 1991.

Mariz, Cecilia Loreto. *Coping with Poverty: Pentecostals and Christian Base Communities in Brazil.* Philadelphia: Temple University Press, 1994.

Marshall, Paul. *Their Blood Cries Out: The Worldwide Tragedy of Modern Christians Who Are Dying for Their Faith.* Dallas, Tex.: Word Publishing, 1977.

Martin, David. *Tongues of Fire: The Explosion of Protestantism in Latin America.* Oxford: Blackwell Publishers, 1990.

Martínez Assad, Carlos, ed. *Religiosidad y política en México.* Mexico City: Ibero-American University, 1992.

Martínez Martínez, Bishop Jorge. *Memorias y Reflexiones de un Obispo.* Mexico: Editorial Villicafia, 1986.

Martz, J. D. *Colombia: A Contemporary Political Survey.* Chapel Hill, N.C.: University of North Carolina Press, 1962.

Mecham, J. Lloyd. *Church and State in Latin America.* 2d ed. Chapel Hill, N.C.: University of North Carolina Press, 1966.

Medina, José T. *El Santo Oficio de la Inquisición en el Río de la Plata.* Buenos Aires: Huarpes, 1945.

Metz, Allan. "Protestantism in Mexico: Contemporary Contextual Developments," *Journal of Church and State* 36, no. 1 (Winter 1994): 65-66.

Meyer, Jean. *La Cristiada.* 3 vols. México: Siglo XXI, 1972.

———. *Historia de los Cristianos en América Latina, siglos XIX y XX.* México: Vuelta, 1989.

Migdal, Joel, Atul Kohli, and Vivienne Shue, eds. *State Power and Social Forces: Domination and Transformation in the Third World.* New York: Cambridge University Press, 1994.

Mignone, Emilio F. *Witness to the Truth: The Complicity of Church and Dictatorship in Argentina, 1976-83.* Maryknoll, N.Y.: Orbis Books, 1988.

Míguez Bonino, José. *Faces of Latin American Protestantism.* Grand Rapids, Mich.: Eerdmans, 1996.

Miller, Daniel R., ed. *Coming of Age: Protestantism in Contemporary Latin America.* New York: University Press of America, 1994.

Minghetti, Marco. *L'Etat et l'eglise.* Paris: Librairie Germer Bailliere, 1882.

Montero, Paula. "Tradição e modernidade: João Paulo II e o problema da cultura," *Revista Brasileira de Ciências Sociais,* year 7, no. 20 (October 1992): 90-112.

Monti, Daniel P. *Los orígenes del protestantismo en el Río de la Plata.* Buenos Aires: La Aurora, n.d.

Moreno, Pedro, ed. *Handbook of Religious Liberty.* Charlottesville, Va.: The Rutherford Institute, 1996.

Moreno, Pedro, and John W. Whitehead. *Iglesia y Estado en Las Américas.* La Paz, Bolivia, 1994.

Morgan, Martha L., and Monica Alzate Buitrago. "Constitution-making in a Time of Choices," *Yale Journal of Law and Feminism* 4, 2 (1992).

Murray, John Courtney. "La déclaration sur la liberté religieuse," *Nouvelle Revue Theologique* 88, 1 (January 1966): 41-67.

———, ed. *Religious Liberty: An End and a Beginning: The Declaration on Religious Freedom: An Ecumenical Discussion.* New York: Macmillan, 1966.

NISBCO (National Interreligious Service Board for Conscientious Objectors). *Post.* May 2, 1997.

North, Douglass. *Structure and Change in Economic History.* New York: Norton and Company, 1981.

Nuñez, Emilio A., and William Taylor. *Crisis in Latin America: An Evangelical Perspective.* Chicago: Moody Press, 1989.

Osterling, Jorge Pablo. *Violence, Conflict, and Politics in Colombia.* New York: Academic Press, 1989.

Pike, Frederick B. "The Catholic Church in Central America," *Review of Politics* 21, 1 (January 1959): 86-91.

———. *The Conflict between Church and State in Latin America.* New York: Alfred A. Knopf, 1964.

Pius, Augustin. *Religious Freedom in Church and State: A Study in Doctrinal Development.* Baltimore: Helicon, 1966.

Poblete, Renato. *Crisis Sacerdotal.* Santiago: Editorial del Pacifico, 1965.

Poblete, Renato, and Carmen Galilea. *Movimiento Pentecostal e Iglesia Católica en medios populares.* Santiago, Chile: Centro Bellarmino, 1984.

Pope, Clara Amanda. "Human Rights and the Catholic Church in Brazil, 1970-1983: The Pontifical Justice and Peace Commission of the São Paulo Archdiocese," *Journal of Church and State* 27, 3 (Autumn 1985): 429-52.

Prien, Hans-Jürgen. *Die Geschichte des Christentums in Lateinamerika.* Göttingen: Vandenhoeck und Ruprecht, 1978.

Ramos, Gabriela, and Henrique Urbano, eds. *Catolicismo y extirpación de idolatrías, siglos XVI-XVIII.* Cuzco: Centro de Estudios Regionales Andinos Bartolomé de Las Casas, 1993.

Reid Andrews, George. *Blacks and Whites in São Paulo, 1888-1988.* Madison, Wis.: University of Wisconsin Press, 1991.

Rembao, A. *Discurso a la Nación Evangélica.* Buenos Aires, Casa Publicadora "La Aurora," 1949.

Retamal Fuentes, Fernando. "La libertad de conciencia y la libertad de las religiones en los grandes sistemas contemporáneos—América Latina," *Teología y Vida* 37 (1996): 307-39.

Robeck, Cecil. "Evangelization or Proselytism of Hispanics? A Pentecostal Perspective," *Journal of Hispanic and Latino Theology* 4, 4 (1997): 42-43.

Roberts, W. Dayton. *Strachan of Costa Rica.* Grand Rapids, Mich.: Eerdmans, 1971.

Rodano, John A. "Pentecostal-Roman Catholic International Dialogue," *Mid-Stream* 31, 1 (January 1992): 26-31.

Romero, Oscar. *Voice of the Voiceless.* Maryknoll, N.Y.: Orbis Books, 1985.

Sánchez Bella, Ismael. *Iglesia y Estado en la América Española.* Pamplona: Ediciones Universidad de Navarra, 1990.

Sandidge, Jerry L. *Roman Catholic/Pentecostal Dialogue (1977-82): A Study in Developing Ecumenism.* 2 vols. Frankfurt und Main: Verlag Peter Lang, 1987.

Schlesinger, Steven, and Steven Kinzer. *Bitter Fruit: The Untold Story of the American Coup in Guatemala.* New York: Anchor Press/Doubleday, 1983.

Sedano Olivera, Alicia. *Aspectos del Conflicto Religioso de 1926 a 1929: Sus Antecedentes y Consecuencias.* México: INAH, 1966.

Seligson, Mitchell A., and Joel M. Jutkowitz. *Guatemalan Values and the Prospects for Democratic Development.* Pittsburgh: Development Associates, University of Pittsburgh/Asociación de Investigación y Estudios Sociales (ASIES), 1994.

Sepúlveda, Juan. "El nacimiento y desarrollo de las Iglesias evangelicas." In *Historia del Pueblo de Dios en Chile,* edited by M. Salinas. Santiago: Ediciones Rehue, 1987.

Serbin, Kenneth. "Igreja, estado, e a ajuda financeira pública no Brasil, 1930-1964: estudos de três casos chaves," *Textos CPDOC.* Rio de Janeiro, 1991.

——. "State Subsidization of Catholic Institutions in Brazil, 1930-1964: A Contribution to the Economic and Political History of the Church," Helen Kellogg Institute for International Studies Working Paper No. 181 (Notre Dame, Ind.: University of Notre Dame, 1992).

——. "Re-creating the Brazilian Church in the Post-Santo Domingo Era," paper presented at the Latin American Studies Association Eighteenth International Congress, Atlanta, Georgia, March 10-12, 1994.

——. "Church-State Reciprocity in Contemporary Brazil: The Convening of the International Eucharistic Congress of 1955 in Rio de Janeiro," *Hispanic American Historical Review* 76:4 (August 1996): 721-51.

——. "The Anatomy of a Death: Repression, Human Rights, and the Case of Alexandre Vannucchi Leme in Authoritarian Brazil," Helen Kellogg Institute for International Studies Working Paper No. 248 (Notre Dame, Ind.: University of Notre Dame, 1998).

Shiels, W. Eugen, S.J. *King and Church: The Rise and Fall of the Patronato Real.* Chicago: Loyola University Press, 1961.

Smith, Brian. *The Church and Politics in Chile.* Princeton, N.J.: Princeton University Press, 1982.

——. *More than Altruism: The Politics of Private Foreign Aid.* Princeton, N.J.: Princeton University Press, 1990.

————. *Religious Politics in Latin America: Pentecostal vs. Catholic.* Notre Dame, Ind.: University of Notre Dame Press, 1998.

Smith, Brian, and Michael Fleet. *The Catholic Church and Democracy in Chile and Peru.* Notre Dame, Ind.: University of Notre Dame Press, 1997.

Smith, Christian, and Liesl Ann Haas. "Revolutionary Evangelicals in Nicaragua: Political Opportunity, Class Interests, and Religious Identity," *Journal for Scientific Study of Religion* 36, 3 (1997): 440-54.

Smith, Peter, ed. *Latin America in Comparative Perspective: New Approaches to Methods and Analysis.* Boulder, Colo.: Westview, 1995.

Sobrino, Jon. *Companions of Jesus: The Jesuit Martyrs of El Salvador.* Maryknoll, N.Y.: Orbis Books, 1990.

Soggin, Alberto J. *La liberta di culto nella Repubblica Argentina negli ultimi anni.* Milan: A. Giuffre editore, 1963.

Stam, J. "La Mision Latinoamericana y el imperialismo Americano: 1926-1928." In *Contribuciones para una historia del Protestantismo en America Latina.* Mexico: Comunidad Teológica, 1981.

Stark, Rodney. "Do Catholic Societies Really Exist?" *Rationality and Society* 4, 3 (1992): 261-71.

Stark, Rodney, and William Sims Bainbridge. *The Future of Religion: Secularization, Revival and Cult Formation.* Berkeley and Los Angeles: University of California Press, 1985.

Stein, Andrew J. "The Transformation of Nicaraguan Catholicism, 1950-1996: Generational Change, Pastoral Options, and Socio-Political Involvement." In *Religion and Change: The Experience of Contemporary Latin America,* edited by Margaret E. Crahan. Forthcoming.

Steingenga, Timothy, and Kenneth Coleman, "Protestant Political Orientations and the Structure of Political Opportunity: Chile, 1972-1991," *Polity* 27, 3 (1995): 465-82.

Stoll, David. *Fishers of Men or Founders of Empire?: The Wycliffe Bible Translators in Latin America.* London: Zed Press, 1982.

————. *Is Latin America Turning Protestant?* Berkeley and Los Angeles: University of California Press, 1990.

————. *Between Two Armies in the Ixil Towns of Guatemala.* New York: Columbia University Press, 1993.

Sullivan, John L., et al. *Political Tolerance and American Democracy.* Chicago: University of Chicago Press, 1982.

Tangeman, Michael. *Mexico at the Crossroads: Politics, the Church, and the Poor.* Maryknoll, N.Y.: Orbis Books, 1994.

Tibesar, Antonine. "The Suppression of the Religious Orders in Peru, 1826-1830, or the King versus the Peruvian Friars: The King Won," *The Americas* 39 (October 1982): 205-39.

Todaro Williams, Margaret. "Church and State in Vargas' Brazil: The Politics of Cooperation," *Journal of Church and State* 18, 3 (Autumn 1976): 443-62.

Trudeau, Robert H. *Guatemalan Politics: The Popular Struggle for Democracy.* Boulder, Colo.: Lynne Rienner Publishers, 1993.

United Nations, Truth Commission Report. "De la locura a la esperanza, la guerra de doce años en El Salvador: Informe de la Comisión de la Verdad," *ECA* 533 (March 1993): 269-75.

United States Catholic Conference. *Sects and New Religious Movements: An Anthology of Texts from the Catholic Church, 1986-1994.* Washington, D.C.: U.S. Catholic Conference, 1995.

Van Oss, Adrian C. *Catholic Colonialism: A Parish History of Guatemala: 1524-1821.* New York: Cambridge University Press, 1986.

Vásquez, Manuel A. "Structural Obstacles to Grassroots Pastoral Practice: The Case of a Base Community in Urban Brazil," *Sociology of Religion* 58, 1 (1997): 53-68.

Villapando, W. et al., eds. *Protestantismo y Inmigracion en la Argentina.* Buenos Aires: Casa Pubicadora "La Aurora," 1970.

Wanderley, Luiz Eduardo, and Clodovis Boff. "Os novos movimentos eclesiais," *Revista Eclesiástica Brasileira* 52 (September 1992): 702-6.

Warner, R. Stephen. "A New Paradigm for the Sociological Study of Religion in the United States," *American Journal of Sociology* 98, 5 (1993): 1044-93.

Watters, Mary. *A History of the Church in Venezuela: 1810-1930.* Chapel Hill, N.C.: University of North Carolina Press, 1933.

Weschler, Lawrence. *A Miracle, a Universe: Settling Accounts with Torturers.* Chicago: University of Chicago Press, 1998.

White, John Henry. *Catholics in Western Democracies.* New York: St. Martin's Press, 1981.

Whitfield, Teresa. *Paying the Price: Ignacio Ellacuría and the Murdered Jesuits of El Salvador.* Philadelphia: Temple University Press, 1994.

Wilde, Alexander. "Creating Neo-Christendom in Latin America." In *Democracy in Latin America: Colombia and Venezuela*, edited by Donald Herman. New York: Praeger, 1988.

Williams, Philip J. "The Catholic Hierarchy in the Nicaraguan Revolution," *Journal of Latin American Studies* 17 (November 1985): 341-69.

Williams, Philip J., and Knut Walter. *Militarization and Demilitarization in El Salvador's Transition to Democracy.* Pittsburgh: University of Pittsburgh Press, 1997.

Williams, Robert G. *States and Social Evolution: Coffee and the Rise of National Governments in Central America.* Chapel Hill, N.C.: University of North Carolina Press, 1994.

Wirpsa, Leslie. "Economics Fuels Return of *La Violencia*," *National Catholic Reporter* (October 24, 1997), 11-15.

CONTRIBUTORS

Elizabeth E. Brusco is associate professor of anthropology at Pacific Lutheran University in Tacoma, Washington. She has carried out fieldwork on the impact of evangelical conversion on gender roles in Colombia (1982-83), on the experience of Colombian evangelicals during *La Violencia* (1989), and on the political involvement of Colombian evangelicals surrounding Colombian constitutional changes of 1991 (1994). She is the author of *The Reformation of Machismo: Evangelical Conversion and Gender in Colombia* (University of Texas Press, 1995), and co-editor (with Laura Klein) of "The Message in the Missionary: Local Interpretations of Religious Ideology and Missionary Personality," *Studies in Third World Societies* 50 (January 1994).

Roderic Ai Camp teaches at Harvey Mudd College. He has served as visiting professor at the Colegio de México and the Foreign Service Institute and has taught at the University of Arizona and Tulane. His most recent publications on Mexico include *Politics in Mexico* (1993), *Generals in the Palacio: The Military in Modern Mexico* (1992), *Entrepeneurs and Politics in Twentieth Century Mexico* (1989), *Memoirs of a Mexican Politician* (1988) and *Crossing Swords* (1997).

Edward L. Cleary, O.P., is professor of political science and director of Latin American Studies at Providence College. He is author and editor of seven books on Latin America, including *The Struggle for Human Rights in Latin America* (1997) and *Power, Politics, and Pentecostals in Latin America* (1997).

Margaret E. Crahan received her doctorate from Columbia University (1967) and is currently Dorothy Epstein Professor of Latin American History at Hunter College and the Graduate School and University Center of the City University of New York. From 1982 to 1994 she was the Henry R. Luce Professor of Religion, Power, and Political Process at Occidental College. Dr. Crahan has done fieldwork in Argentina, Brazil, Chile, Colombia, Costa Rica, Cuba, El Salvador, Guatemala, Honduras, Mexico, Nicaragua, Panama, Paraguay, Peru, Spain, Switzerland, and Uruguay on topics spanning the sixteenth through the twentieth centuries in Latin America. She has published over sixty articles and books, including *Africa and the Caribbean: Legacies of a Link* (co-edited with Franklin W. Knight, 1979) and *Human Rights and Basic Needs in the Americas* (1982).

Anthony Gill received the Ph.D. from UCLA and is currently an assistant professor at the University of Washington. He specializes in political economy and South American politics. Gill is author of *Rendering unto Caesar: The Catholic Church and the State in Latin America* (1998) as well as articles in the *American Journal of Political Science* and the *International Journal of Social Economics*. He is currently researching the regulation of religious markets in Latin America.

Jeffrey Klaiber, S.J., received the Ph.D. from the Catholic University of America and is now a full professor of history at the Catholic University of Peru in Lima. He is currently head of the humanities department. He is a specialist in Peruvian political history and Latin American church history. He held the Jesuit Chair at Georgetown University in 1990-91. He is the author of *The Catholic Church in Peru, 1821-1985* (1992), *Religion and Revolution in Peru, 1824-1976* (1977), and *Iglesia, Dictaduras, y Democracia en América Latina* (1997).

José Míguez Bonino is professor emeritus of systematic theology and ethics of the Facultad Evangélica, ISEDET, in Buenos Aires, Argentina. Among his numerous books are *Doing Theology in a Revolutionary Situation* and *Toward a Christian Political Ethics*.

Pedro C. Moreno is a Bolivian lawyer trained at San Andrés University. He received a master's degree in law and diplomacy from The Fletcher School of Law and Diplomacy, Tufts University. He also completed the specialization in negotiation and conflict resolution at Harvard University. He currently works as international coordinator with The Rutherford Institute, a civil-liberties organization. Moreno has given lectures on religious-liberty issues and met with government officials and religious leaders in close to forty countries in Asia, the Middle East, Latin America, North Africa, Europe, North America, and Oceania to discuss religious-liberty concerns. He is the editor of the *Handbook on Religious Liberty around the World* and has co-authored (with John W. Whitehead, founder and president of The Rutherford Institute) a book in Spanish entitled *Iglesia y Estado en Las Américas (Church and State in the Americas)*. He has also authored numerous editorial articles (including one on Latin American Pentecostals published by the *Wall Street Journal*) in English and Spanish that have been published in more than twenty countries.

Martín Poblete, a native Chilean, is chairman of the Columbia University Seminar on Latin America, lecturer at Rutgers University, and permanent advisor on Latin America at the Northeast Bishops' Hispanic Catholic Center in New York.

Kenneth P. Serbin is assistant professor of history at the University of San Diego. He received the Ph.D. from the University of California, San Diego, in 1993. His research focuses on the Catholic church and social and reproductive issues in Brazil and the relationship between religion and democracy. He is currently working on several projects, including a book on church-military relations in the 1970s, another on sexuality and social conflict in seminary training, and a study of the practice and politics of abortion in contemporary Brazil. He is a former fellow of the Helen Kellogg Institute for International Studies at the University of Notre Dame and a former research associate of the North-South Center at the University of Miami. At the University of San Diego he directs the TransBorder Institute and the Internationalization of the Curriculum Committee and offers classes in the history of Latin America.

Paul E. Sigmund is professor of politics and former director of the Latin American Studies Program at Princeton University. He is the author or editor of seventeen books and more than two hundred articles on political theory and Latin American politics, including *St. Thomas Aquinas, On Politics and Ethics* (1988); *Liberation Theology at the Crossroads: Democracy or Revolution?* (1990); *The*

United States and Democracy in Chile (1993); and "Religious Human Rights in Latin America," in *Religious Human Rights in Global Perspective: Legal Perspectives,* edited by Johan van de Vyver and John Witte (1996).

John H. Sinclair, retired Presbyterian missionary and mission board executive, has specialized in the history of denominational mission work in Latin America and bibliography of Protestantism in Latin America. Sinclair served as a missionary in Venezuela and Chile (1948-61) and is the author of two bibliographical volumes, numerous articles, and two missionary biographies. He served as chair of the Latin America Department of the National Council of Churches, U.S.A.; consultant to the World Council of Churches and the Global Mission Unit of his denomination; visiting professor of missions; and has been a frequent lecturer at ecumenical conferences. Among his publications are articles in *Historia General de la Iglesia en America Latina; Enciclopedia de la Iglesia Cristiana; Protestantismo y Cultura en America Latina; Protestantism in Latin America: A bibliographical guide;* and *Juan A. Mackay: Un escoces con alma latin.* Sinclair holds a B.A. from Baker University and a B.D. and master's degree in theology from Princeton Theological Seminary.

David A. Smilde is a doctoral candidate in sociology at the University of Chicago and research associate at the Centro de Estudios de Desarrollo of the Universidad Central de Venezuela. His research on evangelical Protestantism in Venezuela has been supported by the Social Science Research Council and a Fulbright-Hays Dissertation Abroad Fellowship. His publications include "Letting God Govern: Supernatural Agency in the Social Practice of Latin American Evangelicals," *Sociology of Religion* 59 (3); and "El Clamor Por Venezuela: Latin American Evangelicalism as a Collective Action Frame," in *Latin American Religion in Motion: Tracking Innovation, Unexpected Change, and Complexity,* edited by Christian Smith and Joshua Prokopy (forthcoming).

José Luis Soberanes Fernández is currently teaching at the Institute of Juridical Research of the National Autonomous University of Mexico (UNAM) in Mexico City. He is the author of numerous articles on church-state relations in Mexico.

Timothy J. Steigenga holds the Ph.D. from the University of North Carolina and is currently serving as an assistant professor at Colby College, Waterville, Maine. From 1995 to 1997 he served as the Title VI Visiting Professor of Latin American Studies at the University of Massachusetts and the University of Connecticut. He has published articles on religion and politics in Latin America in the *Latin American Research Review, Polity,* and the *Review of Religious Research.* He has also published in numerous edited volumes, including *Rethinking Protestantism in Latin America,* edited by Virginia Garrard-Burnett and David Stoll, *Coming of Age: Protestantism in Contemporary Latin America,* edited by Daniel R. Miller (1994), and *Let my People Live: Faith and Struggle in Central America,* coordinated by Gordon Spykman (1988).

Andrew Stein is assistant professor of political science at Tennessee Technological University in Cookeville. He received his degrees from Kenyon College (B.A.), New York University (M.A.), and the University of Pittsburgh (M.A., Ph.D.). His areas of specialization include religion and politics, public opinion, and elections in Central America.

INDEX

Trumbull, David, 31-32
Twenty-sixth of July Movement, 90

Ubico, Jorge, 154
Umbanda, 213, 214
United Fruit Company (UFCO), 155
United States: embargo on Cuba, 98, 108, 111; and Guatemalan coup, 155
Universal Church, 214, 215, 216, 331.57n

Valdivieso, Archbishop Rafael Valentín, 220, 221
Vargas, Getúlio, 208
Vargas Llosa, Mario, 264-65, 266
Vatican, the: dialogue with Protestants, 39-40; in Mexico, 140; and Pente-

costalists, 22; relations with Castro, 7; and Romanization of Peru, 258
Vatican II. *See* Vatican, the
Venezuela: Catholic identity in, 277-79; challenges of new religious movements in, 281-83; evangelization of indigenous in, 271-75; registering of religious bodies in, 275-76
Vicariate for Solidarity, 229-30, 231, 233
Virgin of Aparecida, 56, 216, 218
Von Helder, Sergio, 56

Walker, William, 176
Wood, Thomas, 262

Ydígoras Fuentes, Miguel, 157